Volume 11: Chinese Religions Going Global

Annual Review of the Sociology of Religion

Editors

Enzo Pace, Luigi Berzano and Giuseppe Giordan

Editorial Board

Peter Beyer (*University of Ottawa*)
Anthony Blasi (*Tennessee State University*)
Olga Breskaya (*University of Padova*)
Roberto Cipriani (*Universita di Roma Tre*)
Xavier Costa (*Universidad de Valencia*)
Franco Garelli (*Universita di Torino*)
Gustavo Guizzardi (*Universita di Padova*)
Dick Houtman (*Erasmus University, Rotterdam*)
Solange Lefebvre (*Universite de Montreal*)
Patrick Michel (*CNRS, Paris*)
Ari Pedro Oro (*Universidade Federal do Rio Grande do Sul*)
Adam Possamai (*University of Western Sydney*)
Ole Riis (*Agder University*)
Susumu Shimazono (*University of Tokyo*)
William H. Swatos, Jr. (*Augustana College*)
Jean-Paul Willaime (*EPHE, Sorbonne*)
Monika Wohlrab-Sahr (*University of Leipzig*)
Linda Woodhead (*Lancaster University*)
Fenggang Yang (*Purdue University*)
Sinisa Zrinscak (*University of Zagreb*)

VOLUME 11

The titles published in this series are listed at *brill.com/arsr*

Volume 11: Chinese Religions Going Global

Edited by

Nanlai Cao, Giuseppe Giordan and Fenggang Yang

BRILL

LEIDEN | BOSTON

Library of Congress Cataloging-in-Publication Data

Names: Cao, Nanlai, editor. | Giordan, Giuseppe, editor. | Yang, Fenggang, editor.
Title: Chinese religions going global / edited by Nanlai Cao, Giuseppe Giordan and Fenggang Yang.
Description: Leiden ; Boston : Brill, [2021] | Series: Annual review of the sociology of religion, 1877-5233 ; volume 11 | Includes bibliographical references and index.
Identifiers: LCCN 2020050097 (print) | LCCN 2020050098 (ebook) |
  ISBN 9789004443167 (hardback) | ISBN 9789004443327 (ebook)
Subjects: LCSH: China–Religion. | Chinese diaspora–Religious aspects. | Globalization–Religious aspects.
Classification: LCC BL1803 .C449 2021 (print) | LCC BL1803 (ebook) |
  DDC 200.951–dc23
LC record available at https://lccn.loc.gov/2020050097
LC ebook record available at https://lccn.loc.gov/2020050098

Typeface for the Latin, Greek, and Cyrillic scripts: "Brill". See and download: brill.com/brill-typeface.

ISSN 1877-5233
ISBN 978-90-04-44316-7 (hardback)
ISBN 978-90-04-44332-7 (e-book)

Copyright 2021 by Nanlai Cao, Giuseppe Giordan and Fenggang Yang. Published by Koninklijke Brill NV, Leiden, The Netherlands.
Koninklijke Brill NV incorporates the imprints Brill, Brill Hes & De Graaf, Brill Nijhoff, Brill Rodopi, Brill Sense, Hotei Publishing, mentis Verlag, Verlag Ferdinand Schöningh and Wilhelm Fink Verlag.
Koninklijke Brill NV reserves the right to protect this publication against unauthorized use. Requests for re-use and/or translations must be addressed to Koninklijke Brill NV via brill.com or copyright.com.

This book is printed on acid-free paper and produced in a sustainable manner.

Contents

Preface VII
Acknowledgements XII
Notes on Contributors XIII

1   Bargaining with God in the Name of Family
    Chinese Christian Entrepreneurs in Italian Coffee Bars   1
        Ting Deng

2   From China with Faith
    Sinicizing Christianity in Europe   20
        Nanlai Cao

3   A Bridge between the Spiritual and the Worldly
    The Puhuasi Buddhist Temple in Prato (Italy)   37
        Fabio Berti and Valentina Pedone

4   Exploring Chinese Catholicism in the Italian Peninsula
    A Sociological Study of the Chinese Catholic Community in Italy   58
        Marco Guglielmi

5   Encounter, Initiation, and Commitment
    Christian Conversion among New Chinese Migrants in Britain   77
        Xinan Li, Line Nyhagen, and Thoralf Klein

6   Chinese Christian Community in Germany
    Home-Making and Chineseness   97
        Jie Kang

7   Going Global and Back Again
    The Transformation of Chinese Christian Networks between Southeast Asia and China since the 1980s   115
        Chris White and Jifeng Liu

8   The Ironies of Bringing Christ to the Motherland
    The Interaction Ritual Chains of Chinese-Canadian Evangelicals over Short-Term Missions to China   138
        Jonathan Tam

9   Between Cultural Reproduction and Cultural Translation
    A Case Study of Yiguandao in London and Manchester   157
       Hung-Jen Yang

10 Global Dao
    The Making of Transnational Yiguandao   174
       Nikolas Broy

11 Tension between the Chinese Government and Transnational Qigong Groups
    Management by the State and Their Dissemination Overseas   194
       Utiraruto Otehode and Benjamin Penny

12 To Be or Not to Be a Confucian
    Explicit and Implicit Religious Identities in the Global Twenty-First Century   210
       Anna Sun

13 Diverse Religious Experiences among Overseas Chinese in the United Arab Emirates   236
       Yuting Wang

14 Chinese Muslim Diaspora Communities and the Role of International Islamic Education Networks
    A Case Study of Dubai   255
       Jacqueline Armijo and Shaojin Chai

    Index   279

Preface

Nanlai Cao, Giuseppe Giordan, Fenggang Yang

Four decades of economic reform and opening up in China has brought about dramatic social and cultural changes associated with globalization. As China is being increasingly integrated into global economy, more and more Chinese live transnational lives and practice religion globally. So far the scholarship of the interrelationship between religion and globalization in the Chinese religious field has primarily been set in the historical context of the encounter between Western Christian missionaries and local Chinese agents, and little is known about a global Chinese religious field that is in the making. By now the relationship has become substantially diversified, with an increasing number of Chinese people going abroad for various religious as well as non-religious reasons, including planting new temples and churches to reach local people as well as serving the Chinese diaspora. A reverse trend in the globalization of Chinese religions has also occurred as more and more diasporic Chinese religious groups seek to build or rebuild their ties to the motherland for religious, economic or cultural reasons.

At the present stage of China's globalization, there is an intellectual urgency of going beyond the China/West dichotomy in the common narrative of globalization that assumes western concepts and forces transform the lives of local Chinese people. This volume seeks to challenge the dichotomous ordering of the western global and the Chinese local, and to add a new perspective for understanding religious modernity globally. Our contributors come from diverse social science disciplines and from four different continents. Together we aim at applying a social scientific approach to systematically researching the globalization of Chinese religions.

A distinctive feature of this volume is its geographic focus on Europe with 8 of the 14 chapters examining various cases of Chinese religion and Chinese religious communities in Italy, France, Britain, Germany and Austria. Much of the literature on immigrant Chinese religions has tended to be based on research conducted in North America, which contributes to a dominant paradigm for the sociological study of religion worldwide. As Europe is becoming the new centre of global migration from other countries, it provides a new and different social context for conceptualizing religion and globalization with reference to these new migrants who lack long histories of settlement overseas.

While we have sought to diversify our cases based on religion, half of the 14 chapters focus on Christian religion, especially Protestantism. This overrepresentation, we believe, may well speak to the mobility and transcendent nature of congregational Christianity, giving Chinese Christians a unique institutional advantage in setting up diasporic communities globally. In contrast, chapters focusing on indigenous Chinese religions like Yiguandao and Chinese Qigong mainly invoke the story of the westernization of Chinese religious traditions as an alternative form of spirituality in a shifting global field.

Ting Deng's opening chapter provides an in-depth ethnographic picture of a group of Chinese Christians who operate Italian coffee bars in Bologna, a major hub of Wenzhou Christian coffee bar business. This study shows vividly how religion, business and the family interact in the life of Chinese immigrant Christians in Italy, especially how traditional family values help to solve the moral dilemmas faced by these migrant entrepreneurs when they find their conservative Christian morality in conflict with secular entrepreneurial values. The picture of Chinese Christian bar owners with a dual identity navigating morally ambiguous daily life provides a timely counterpoint against the view of Chinese migrants in Europe as purely economic agents. This seems to be a common ground reached by both Deng's chapter and other chapters on Chinese religion in Europe in this volume.

In Chapter 2 Nanlai Cao explores the rise of Protestant Christianity in the Chinese diaspora in Italy and France as both a case of the sinicization of Christianity and a product of China's reform-era globalization. This ethnographic account shows that in the current context of China's aggressive business outreach and mass emigration Christianity has become a vital social force and moral resource in binding Chinese merchants and traders in diaspora. Drawing on multisited fieldwork, the analysis captures the rise of a sinicized Christianity in secular Europe with an emphasis on ethnic congregational dynamics, migrant lay leadership and a self-envisioned Chinese-led global mission movement.

In Chapter 3 Fabio Berti and Valentina Pedone document the development and social functions of a major Buddhist temple in Prato, the largest Chinese migrant business center in Italy. The picture of Puhuasi Temple and wealthy Chinese lay Buddhists who publicly engage with Italian society by making donations nationwide seems to contrast sharply with their Christian counterparts who tend to form large exclusive ethnic congregations. It is a minority religion positive about outreach, interaction with and assimilation to the host society, reflecting complex intertwined dynamics between religion and ethnicity.

In Chapter 4 Marco Guglielmi provides a timely case study of Chinese Catholics in the West. In contrast to the significant and growing literature on Chinese Protestantism in North America and Europe, we have little in-depth knowledge about their Catholic counterparts. This study examines both the historical development and the current situation of the Chinese Catholic community in Italy, a far smaller minority compared to the Chinese Protestant counterpart. The self-enclosed nature of the Chinese Catholic community and its parallel ritual life separate from that of the Italian parishes echoes the situation of Chinese Protestant congregations in Europe, and the Chinese Catholics seem to be less transnational than the Protestant group.

Chapter 5 by Xinan Li, Line Nyhagen, and Thoralf Klein documents the recent Chinese Christian presence in Britain. While Christianity is supposedly the dominant religion among British Chinese, a large number of Chinese Christians in Britain are new converts. This differs from their counterparts in other European nations, especially those Wenzhou Christians who have brought with them their indigenous faith tradition from China. The uniqueness of this British Chinese Christian group lies in its members being mostly students and professionals recently coming from the PRC. This current wave of Chinese migrants are considered having stronger personal and political connections to the motherland than the previous ones, thus reshaping the socio-religious dynamics of Chinese Christian communities in contemporary Britain.

Chapter 6 by Jie Kang captures the dynamic rise and active operation of a Germany-centred transnational and independent Chinese Christian network sustained by ethnic Chinese ministries from Hong Kong, Taiwan, Singapore, Malaysia and North America. Interestingly, backed by this transnational church network, Chinese Christian fellowships in Germany mainly target Chinese students from the mainland as potential converts, and do not interact with German churches or church organizations. There are much internal cultural, linguistic, political diversity within the Chinese congregants, and they need to constantly negotiate different identities, religious and otherwise and carve out a transnational Chinese Christian space not directly linked to the PRC.

In Chapter 7 Chris White and Jifeng Liu explore transnational Chinese Christian networks linking south Fujian and southeast Asia with a focus on the role of overseas Chinese Christians in southeast Asia. Previous literature has focused on the role of popular religion in connecting south China with Southeast Asia, this study shows how the overlooked Christian networks operate between China and southeast Asia, mainly by funding church building projects in the city of Xiamen and making investment in theological training for Chinese Christians from both the Xiamen region and other parts of China.

In Chapter 8 Jonathan Tam draws on a case study on Chinese Canadian evangelicals' short-term missions (STM) to China to point out serious contradictions and ironies in the STM experience and explores the meaning making process associated with STM. Ethnographic interviews with some Chinese Canadian evangelical youths before and after STM trips provide rich data on how they negotiate their ethnic, national and religious identities. There has been little research on STM from the ethnic Chinese in the West. This study might fill a gap in our knowledge.

In the following two chapters both Hung-Jen Yang and Nikolas Broy focus on the global spread and engagement of Yiguandao, an indigenous syncretic Chinese religion. They both draw on multisited ethnographic fieldwork and contribute to our understanding of perhaps the most transnational indigenous Chinese religion today that claims 30 million members worldwide.

In Chapter 9 Hung-Jen Yang explores the globalization of Yiguandao with special reference to Yiguandao missionaries and followers in Britain. It highlights two distinctive approaches or strategies of adaption taken by the Yiguandao missionaries to spread the Chinese religion in the West. Using the diasporic Chinese community (the Vietnamese Chinese enclave) and the Yiguandao branch temple attended by mainly westerners in London and Manchester as two contrasting cases, Yang shows a vivid and convincing picture of how an indigenous Chinese religion has been able to adapt to the condition of global modernity.

In Chapter 10 Broy provides an overview of the origin, evolution and innovation of the movement and a solid specific case study of a Yiguandao branch in Vienna, suggesting the connection between Taiwanese business migration and Yiguandao proselytization. Unlike most transnational Chinese religious movements that operate mainly among ethnic Chinese, this study shows the missionary outreach efforts of Yiguandao as a unique form of Asian spirituality appealing to non-Chinese practitioners.

In Chapter 11 Utiraruto Otehode and Benjamin Penny detail the rise of transnational qigong networks, a new phenomenon emerged since the ban of Falungong and other qigong groups in the PRC in the late 1990s. By emphasizing the role of state regulations, it adds to the growing literature on transnational Chinese religious networks that has conventionally focused on the mobility of immigrant religion. The main contribution of this study thus lies in its analysis of the connection between the Chinese state management of qigong and the flourishing of several qigong groups overseas such as Falunggong, Putigong and Tian Gong that have reacted differently to state categorization and pressures.

In Chapter 12 Anna Sun examines transnational Confucianism as a religious identity in the twenty-first century by mainly using the case of a small community of ethnically Chinese Indonesians who identify themselves as Confucians. While lack of clear religious identification has traditionally characterized the presence of Confucianism in East Asia and parts of Southeast Asia, contemporary Confucianism offers a case of the increasing transformation of implicit religious identity into explicit religious identity in the development of transnational and global religious life.

The last two chapters examine the faith and life of Chinese migrants with a geographic focus on Dubai, UAE. Yuting Wang gives a careful portrait of several Chinese religious groups in Dubai with an emphasis on diverse individual experiences of soul-searching among overseas Chinese. The chapter by Jacqueline Armijo and Shaojin Chai draws on historical analysis of China's Islamic education and recent fieldwork conducted in Dubai. It explores the role of religious and language training in the formation and expansion of the Chinese Muslim diasporic community of Dubai, which has become both a centre of international trade and an Islamic education hub for Chinese Muslims.

The 14 case studies collected in this volume all deal with an increasingly globalized and mutable Chinese religious field, a phenomenon that is still unfolding and to a large extent has been shaped by the unique cultural and linguistic experience of the mobile religious subjects in response to the secular and religious culture of the host society. They demonstrate that Chinese religions will continue to adapt to the condition of global modernity, in which process multiple forms of global interconnectedness lead to multiple sinicizations. What would be the effects of economic and geopolitical power shifts, new immigration regime, changing state-religion relations, the coming of age of the second generation and the world's growing anxieties about China's powerful rise on Chinese religions on a global stage? While providing locally grounded explorations and explanations to the mechanisms and modes of cross-border religious and cultural exchanges, our contributors have raised important and meaningful issues that help identify new trends and theoretically fruitful areas for future exploration.

Acknowledgements

This volume is a product of international collaboration with colleagues based in five different continents. The initial idea of this volume took shape as part of a larger institutional collaboration between Renmin University of China and the University of Padova. Nanlai Cao and Giuseppe Giordan held numerous discussions and meetings in China, Italy and via WeChat and Skype. Fenggang Yang joined the project at a later stage to contribute his expertise. The approach taken in the volume and themes developed in each chapter were the result of mutual engagement and collaboration among all the editors and contributors. We would like to thank our contributors for their commitment, their collegial support and their willingness to meet deadlines, without which this volume would not be possible.

Notes on Contributors

Jacqueline Armijo
(Harvard University, Ph.D.), a scholar of Islam in China, has taught at Cornell University and Stanford University, as well as overseas at Zayed University (UAE), Qatar University, and the Asian University for Women (Bangladesh). Armijo lived in the UAE from 2003–2010, where she documented the rapidly developing relations between China and the GCC, focusing on educational and cultural relations, and the growing role of the Chinese Muslim diaspora community there.

Fabio Berti
is Full Professor of Sociology at the Department of Social, Political and Cognitive Sciences of the University of Siena. For over twenty years, using both quantitative and qualitative methods, he has been conducting research on migratory processes and on the dynamics of social integration; in recent years he has been dealing with social inequalities, food poverty, degrowth theory and rural welfare. Currently he is the Director of the Laboratory of inequalities at the University of Siena.

Nikolas Broy
is assistant professor at the Institute for the Study of Religion at Leipzig University. Nikolas' research focuses on the social history of religion in Chinese societies, and he is particularly interested in Chinese Buddhism, popular religious sects, and vegetarianism, but also in globalization of religion and in sociology of religion. He has received his doctorate from Leipzig University and he has worked and studied at universities in Leipzig, Göttingen, Beijing, Kyoto, Taipei, and Hefei.

Nanlai Cao
is professor in the school of philosophy and Institute of Buddhism and religious theory at Renmin University of China. He received a PhD in anthropology from The Australian National University and is author of *Constructing China's Jerusalem: Christians, Power, and Place in Contemporary Wenzhou* (Stanford University Press 2010) and co-editor of *Religion and Mobility in a Globalizing Asia: New Ethnographic Explorations* (Routledge 2014). He currently serves on the editorial board of *Sociology of Religion: A Quarterly Review*.

Shaojin Chai

trained as a political scientist at University of Notre Dame, Indiana, and has broad research interests in the role of religion in international affairs and grassroots movements. His current research focuses on China's ideological and cultural strategies overseas and China-MENA relations. He has taught at universities in the UAE and been invited to lecture on the above topics in China and elsewhere. He also advises on intellectual, cultural and charitable activities for many Chinese institutions and communities.

Ting Deng

is currently a Postdoctoral Research Associate at Brown University's Population Studies and Training Center. She received her Ph.D. in anthropology from The Chinese University of Hong Kong in December 2018. Her current book project, based on her Ph.D. dissertation, is concerned with the emerging phenomenon of coffee bars in Italy being taken over by Chinese migrants. Her research interests more broadly include transnational migration, Chinese diaspora, intercultural dynamics, ethnic interactions, social inclusion/exclusion, urban anthropology, and contemporary Italy.

Giuseppe Giordan

is Professor of Sociology at the University of Padova (Italy). He is Coordinator of the International Joint PhD programme on *Human Rights, Society and Multi-level Governance,* and Co-editor of the *Annual Review of the Sociology of Religion* (Brill). His sociological research focuses on the interaction between religion and spirituality, religious and cultural pluralism, religions and human rights.

Marco Guglielmi

obtained an international joint Ph.D. from the University of Padova in 2019. From the same year, he is a research fellow at the Center for Religious Studies of Bruno Kessler Foundation in Trento. His main research interests include religion and migration, religion and human rights, Orthodox Christianity, and Christian minorities in Italy. His last publication is 'Orthodox Christianity in a Western Catholic Country: The Glocalization of Orthodox Diasporas in Italy', in *Global Eastern Orthodoxy: Religion, Politics and Human Rights*, Springer 2020.

Jie Kang

is a research fellow at MPI's Department of Religious Diversity. She was awarded a PhD degree in 2014 in Sinology from the University of Leipzig and is the author of "House Church Christianity in China: From Rural Preachers to City

Pastors" published by Palgrave in 2016. Her general interest is in transnational religious networks in China and among the Chinese diaspora abroad, missionary movement, state-church relations, religion and nationalism, including national identity.

Thoralf Klein
is Senior Lecturer in History at Loughborough University. His main interest lies in exploring the transformation of modern China, and especially of its relation to the wider world, in the last 200 years. Within this broader framework, he has published several works on the history of Christian missions in China.

Xinan Li
gained his doctorate by researching Chinese Christian communities in the UK at Loughborough University. He is trained as a sociologist of religion with research interest in religion in Chinese society and Chinese diaspora.

Jifeng Liu
is Assistant Professor in the Center for Southeast Asian Studies and the Belt and Road Research Institute at Xiamen University. He received his PhD in sociology and religious studies from Leiden University and was a research fellow at the Max Planck Institute for the Study of Religious and Ethnic Diversity. His research interests include religion in Chinese societies, Southeast Asian Chinese, transnational networks, as well as ethnicity and religion in Southeast Asia.

Line Nyhagen
is Reader in Sociology at Loughborough University. She is an expert in the sociology of religion and the sociology of gender and has published widely on gender, feminism, citizenship and migration in relation to Islam and Christianity.

Utiraruto Otehode
is a PhD candidate at the Australian National University. His research interest includes religion, Qigong and folk medicine in the state system and social practice. He obtained a doctorate in social science at Hitotsubashi University in Japan in 2009. Before moving to the Australia, he was a lecturer at Toin University of Yokohama. His current research project focuses on Buddhist Culture Tourism.

Valentina Pedone
is Associate Professor of Languages and Literatures of China and South East Asia at the *Department of* Education, Languages, Intercultures, Literatures and

Psychology of the University of Florence. Her research focuses on Chinese migration to Italy with a special attention on cultural issues in a broad sense (language, religion, gender, ethnicity, artistic expression, media). In 2013 she published the volume *A Journey to the West: Observations on the Chinese Migration to Italy* (Firenze University Press).

Benjamin Penny

is a historian of religions in China who has worked on medieval China, the nineteenth century and contemporary times. His most recent books are *The Religion of Falun Gong* (Chicago: University of Chicago Press, 2012) and *Religion in Taiwan and China: Locality and Transmission* (Edited with Hsun Chang, Taipei: Academia Sinica, Institute of Ethnology, 2017). He is currently working on a set of manuscript diaries from mid-nineteenth century Hong Kong.

Anna Sun

(PhD in sociology, Princeton University, 2008) is Associate Professor in the Department of Religious Studies at Duke University. Her research focuses on contemporary Confucianism and conceptual and methodological issues in the study of Chinese religions. Her first book is *Confucianism as a World Religion: Contested Histories and Contemporary Realities* (Princeton: Princeton University Press, 2013). An edited volume on the sociology of spirituality, *Eminently Social Spirituality: Context, Practice, Power* (co-edited with Brian Steensland and Jaime Kucinskas), is forthcoming for Oxford University Press. She is currently completing a book manuscript on the social life of prayer in contemporary urban China and beyond.

Jonathan Tam

is a faculty member of the Canadian Chinese School of Theology at Tyndale University. His research applies a microsociological lens to transnationalism, ethnicity, and religion. Outside of academia, his YouTube channel "Dr. Jon Tam" helps people build soft skills and gain career clarity. He holds a doctorate in sociology from the University of Oxford.

Yuting Wang

is Associate Professor of Sociology at the American University of Sharjah. She is the author of *Between Islam and the American Dream: An Immigrant Muslim Community in Post-9/11 America* (Routledge, 2014). Her current research examines the increasing influence of China in the Arabian Gulf. Her writings reflect on the implications of BRI on ethnic and religious minorities, especially the Chinese Muslims. Her new book *Chinese in Dubai: Money, Pride, and Soul-Searching* is forthcoming from Brill in September 2020.

Chris White

is the Assistant Director of the Center on Religion and the Global East at Purdue University. He received his PhD (Xiamen University) in Modern Chinese History and was a research fellow with the Max Planck Institute for the Study of Religious and Ethnic Diversity. His publications include the monograph *Sacred Webs: The Social Lives and Networks of Minnan Protestants, 1840s-1920s* (Brill, 2017) and the edited volume *Protestantism in Xiamen, Then and Now* (Palgrave, 2019).

Fenggang Yang

is Professor of Sociology and Director of Center on Religion and the Global East, Purdue University. He is the author of *Chinese Christians in America: Conversion, Assimilation, and Adhesive Identities* (1999), *Religion in China: Survival and Revival under Communist Rule* (2012); and *Atlas of Religion in China: Social and Geographical Contexts* (2018). He has served as the President of the Society for the Scientific Study of Religion, and the East Asian Society for the Scientific Study of Religion.

Hung-Jen Yang

is Associate Professor at Institute of Sociology, Academia Sinica, Taiwan. One of his research projects is the three-year research project, "Cultural Border Crossing in Yiguandao: the Discourses and Practices of Yiguandao Cultivators in English-Speaking Countries." His works in progress include "The Social Construction of the 'Five Religions, One Origin' Discourse: From Redemptive Societies to Contemporary Yiguandao" and "The Transnational Transmission of Yiguandao from Taiwan, Malaysia to the UK: A Sociological Analysis of Religion" (in Chinese).

CHAPTER 1

Bargaining with God in the Name of Family
Chinese Christian Entrepreneurs in Italian Coffee Bars

Ting Deng

Coming from a devout Protestant family, Yang was expected to join the Sunday afternoon services at the Chinese immigrant church every week. However, she had been unable to do so since her parents bought a neighborhood bar in the previous year. "There's no way out [*mei banfa*]," she said. "The business has to be taken care of by someone and, in my family, it turns out that that's me. If we all went to church, we would have to close the business for half a day, and then we'd probably lose some regular clients because they need a place where they can go every day." She pondered the situation for a while and then added, "But I do read the Bible in our coffee bar when things aren't busy." Yang and her family thus compromised their religious ethics for their family's economic prosperity. The statement, "no way out" (*mei banfa*) was used to justify their actions of compromise that were discouraged by or contradictory to their professed religiosity. These actions thus imply that the ways of practicing Christianity are quite negotiable in everyday life.

Since the economic downturn of the late 2000s, coffee bars in Northern and Central Italy have been increasingly purchased by Chinese immigrant families striving to achieve economic prosperity through self-employed entrepreneurship. Among the varieties of coffee bars, however, self-employed Chinese immigrant families have found a niche in catering to typically male-dominated community clientele, especially for marginalized social groups including retired working-class men and migrant workers of all types. Many of these Chinese families, commonly from the Greater Wenzhou area[1] have been

---

1   In this chapter, I use Wenzhou as a cultural term, rather than an administrative concept. It includes both the administrative region of Wenzhou and the county of Qingtian, which is 60 kilometres from Wenzhou City. Geographically, the county of Qingtian shares borders with Yongjia, Wencheng, and Ruian, which are three counties of Wenzhou. It became a part of Lishui, rather than Wenzhou, only after an administration redistribution in 1963. Among the Chinese coffee bar owners that I met in Bologna, some hail from Qingtian, others from Ruian, Wencheng, or peripheral areas of Wenzhou City. While I do not wish to deny their self-sustained differences of the sub-regional identities, for the purposes of this chapter I do not make a distinction between Wenzhou and Qingtian, as their entrepreneurship and cultural

Protestant Christians for generations before emigration. Yet as shown in the case of Yang's family, the Christian doctrines that the Chinese immigrant families espouse often clash with their entrepreneurial ethics.

This chapter examines the deeply intertwined relations between entrepreneurial aspirations, religious experiences, and family values among Chinese immigrants practicing Christianity in Italy. All three of those aspects, which represent the three major social domains of business, religion, and family for Chinese Christians in Italy, were involved in Yang's moral dilemma described above. The questions asked by this chapter are: How do migrant Chinese Christians deal with conflicting ethical issues in their lives? How do they make decisions and negotiate ethical practices when their religious principles and commitments contradict their entrepreneurial aspirations, and how do they justify their behaviors? Taking Chinese coffee bar owners in Italy as an example, the chapter investigates the moral practices of Chinese Christian migrant entrepreneurs under the seemingly contradictory "double bind" (Bateson 1972) of being both a successful entrepreneur and a good Christian. It explores how these religious practitioners deal with conflicts between religious ethics and economic practices, while simultaneously seeking legitimate moral guidance for the mundane dilemmas that they confront in their everyday lives. It also sheds light on how family ethics are strategically deployed to justify, interpret, and legitimize those business practices that are not morally compatible with their religious ethics.

The existing literature on the Chinese religious diaspora has highlighted the role of religiosity in Chinese immigrant lives overseas. In line with the Weberian tradition, scholars have shown that religiosity can, among other social functions, serve as a determinant factor in economic development and migrant capitalism as well as provide effective networking resources and social capital (Guest 2003, Kalir 2009, Tong 2013), and reconstruct diasporic identity (Cao 2013, Han 2011, Nyíri 2003, Tan 2013). Instead of adopting a functionalist interpretation of Chinese immigrants' religious networks or taking their religious identities as a static concept, this chapter chooses to view religion as "an important ethical domain" (Robbins 2016: 770). Located "at the heart of ethics," religion provides "a sort of archive, tradition, or primary resource for ethical thought and understanding" that regulates religious subjects' moral lives (Lambek 2012: 364). Religious ethics are thus examined as a form of "ordinary ethics" (Das 2012) in migrants' everyday lives that interacts with other ethical

---

identity of out-migration do not contain serious differences on my particular analytical level. For instance, intermarriage is not uncommon and many of them attend the same Chinese Christian churches, maintaining frequent interactions with each other.

domains, such as business and family. As pointed out by Oxfeld (2010), moral ambivalence exists in all moral systems and the ways in which Chinese Christian migrant entrepreneurs negotiate as moral subjects in their everyday practices when ethical principles of varying social domains clash and contradict each other represent the major subject of this chapter's inquiry. For the purposes of this chapter, no particular distinction is made between the two terms of "ethics" and "morality" regardless of the terminological debates involving them (see Fassin 2015 and Laidlaw 2018). Instead, Zigon's (2008) approach is deployed to examine the interpersonal level of religious morality in which an individual's routine moral life focusing on religiosity is challenged and must be negotiated and reconstructed by self-conscious ethical work.

The data for the present study were collected during fourteen months of ethnographic fieldwork conducted primarily in Bologna, a city in northern Italy, and its surrounding areas between 2014 and 2015, as well as short revisits in 2016, 2018, and 2019. Bologna is the seventh most populous city and the capital of one of the most prosperous regions in Italy. It is in many ways a city of migrants, as its labor market has recruited numerous cheap migrant laborers from both Italy and abroad, including Chinese immigrants, for its industrial districts and service sector economy. Bologna witnessed the early spread of neighborhood bars in its emerging suburban neighborhoods and residential areas serving new migrants from rural areas and Southern Italy in the postwar economic boom of the 1950s. Now it can be considered a typical Northern city experiencing the displacement of ownership from aging Italian proprietors, many of whom used to be migrant entrepreneurs themselves, to the new transnational migrants, among which a large proportion is ethnically Chinese immigrants, regardless of their religious confession. Participant observation and informal interviews were the major research methods used during the fieldwork in Bologna. Six neighborhood bars managed by Chinese Christian families were visited over periods of three months or longer, and all of the families, or at least some of their family members, actively practiced the Christian religion. Regular visits were made to the Chinese Church of Bologna, which most of the Chinese interlocutors were involved in, and their religious events were attended throughout the fieldwork period. All of the names used in this chapter are pseudonyms.

This chapter begins by illustrating the Chinese moral subjects' two major social roles as migrant entrepreneurs and Christians. It then examines the moral dilemmas that they face in the management of their neighborhood bars, followed by their moral practices in dealing with those dilemmas, including how they cope with ethical issues in terms of clientele management and time management during their everyday business practices. After that, the role of family values as a bridging form of ethics is discussed. In doing so, the chapter aims to achieve an understanding of the complex moralities of three social domains of business, religion, and family in Chinese Christian entrepreneurs' migrant lives, with the broader purpose of contributing to the debate on the relationship between economics and religion from the perspective of everyday moral practices in the context of Chinese religious diaspora.

1   As Immigrant Entrepreneurs

Virtually all Chinese coffee bar owners encountered in this research, both Christian and otherwise, hailed originally from rural or peripheral areas of the greater Wenzhou region, located in southern Zhejiang Province. They were mostly migrant families composed of parents (first-generation immigrants to Italy) and their unmarried children or young married couples (second-generation immigrants). The first-generation immigrants had usually started their family-managed coffee bar businesses around ten to fifteen years after emigrating to Italy. Their children, who were often involved in the management of their businesses, were usually born in China before being reunited with their parents in Italy during their teenage years.

In spite of their diverse religious identities, Chinese immigrants in Italy often share several common features as economic migrants who joined the mass migration to Europe "to get rich quickly" (Li 1999) in the post-Mao era. Coming from typically impoverished areas with low educational backgrounds, they often started off as surplus rural laborers involved in artisanship, commerce, and other nonagricultural activities to make a better living for themselves prior to their transnational migration. Many of them were involved in internal migration from the rural to urban areas of southern Zhejiang Province or to other Chinese cities for self-employed small entrepreneurship. Their migration to Europe was often due to a "sense of relative deprivation" and a "chain effect" (Li 1999) of better business opportunities and economic returns, rather than pure economic survival. Furthermore, their previous experience in small entrepreneurship often provided them with more motivation to start up their own businesses once the opportunity arose compared with other Chinese immigrant workers. It is thus safe to say that immigrant entrepreneurship is a fundamental part of the first-generation Chinese interlocutors' complex identity associated with migration and the mercantile culture in the Greater Wenzhou area (Gates 1996, Zhang 2002, Xiang 2005).

Such immigrant entrepreneurship is a process of striving toward economic aspirations. While economic prosperity can be clearly perceived as the goal of transnational migration, how one achieves such a goal is diverse and historically contingent. For instance, it is quite common to find a Chinese coffee bar owner who had previously worked in several different business sectors as a wage worker, business owner, or both. The pursuit of economic achievement for Chinese transnational migrants who had moved from southern Zhejiang Province to Italy is thus a process of upward social mobility that involves decades of migration trajectories, commonly moving from undocumented migrant labor to legalized small business ownership. The classic trajectory is composed of three steps: 1) settling down by working for co-ethnic businesses ranging from subcontracting workshops that contribute to the world-renowned "made in Italy" sectors (particularly the fast fashion industry) (Ceccagno 2017, Krause 2018) to catering and trading businesses found through their social networks; 2) legalizing their residence while accumulating economic, social, and cultural capital for eventual business opportunities; and 3) starting up their own self-employed business in imitation of their co-ethnic fellows' successful examples.

Furthermore, family often plays a crucial role in Chinese immigrant entrepreneurship in Italy. Family businesses engaged in by Chinese immigrants are usually low-skilled and labor-intensive small enterprises that rely on self-employment and the exploitation of unpaid family labor. This often requires the Chinese immigrants to follow a family-based plan across generations in order to achieve social and economic upward mobility. Some people migrated upon getting married and having their first child. Some men emigrated first and then, after they had legalized their migrant identity, were reunited with their wives and children. Still other couples emigrated simultaneously, leaving behind their children with grandparents until they could bring them later via official means. While the parents actively participated in capital accumulation, their children were often sent to local schools and grew up to become effective laborers and contributors to the family business, having been effectively equipped with a greater degree of local knowledge and cultural capital.

Since the turn of the millennium, coffee bars in Italy have gradually become a new and, in many cases, ideal business opportunity for many Chinese immigrant families who have already accumulated a certain amount of economic capital, language competence, local knowledge, and other necessary business skills. Such bars became a positive business niche in which the families could maximize their income and survive economic restructuring, even though some of them were not even consumers of coffee. Their action of taking over a coffee bar, like any other business, was simply a means of achieving economic prosperity and a better life. It was based on careful business calculations of the types of capital and resources necessary for business management and what benefits the business could bring to them. In short, Chinese management of coffee bars in Italy represents a form of embedded migrant entrepreneurship that is situated at the intersection of the Chinese owners' persistent pursuit of economic return maximization and the existing opportunity structure enabled by Italy's shifting economic environment and changing class and ethnic composition (see Deng 2020).

2   As Christians

The Greater Wenzhou area, where most Chinese immigrant entrepreneurs in Italy originate, is China's largest Christian center and known as "China's Jerusalem" (See Cao 2011). The Chinese coffee bar owners encountered in this research mostly came from Christian families that had converted to the religion generations ago. Their particular version of Christianity is an indigenized way of life and a cultural fact that is rooted in everyday cultural values and practices (Cao 2008). Those values and practices were brought from China by these migrant subjects to eventually form a new version of diasporic religion that regulates and contributes to their migrant lives in a secularized European context, as shown in Cao's (2013) study about the Wenzhou Christian entrepreneurs' migration trajectories to Paris.

The Chinese Christian migrants encountered in this research were mainly affiliated with the Chinese immigrant churches in their respective cities of residence. In Bologna, this was usually the Chinese Church of Bologna (*Bologna Huaren Jiaohui* or CCB as used in the rest of this chapter), which is the largest of the three Chinese Protestant Christian churches run by Chinese immigrants in the city. According to the person in charge at the CCB, nearly 70 Chinese immigrant households were attending the CCB as of 2015. This number is in line with my observations conducted during the present research, with attendance of Sunday worship service averaging around 200 each week – a number that doubled for the Christmas celebration show.[2]

---

[2] When I went back to Bologna in December 2019, I was informed by the person in charge at the CCB and other active participants that more than 100 Chinese households were attending the CCB, accounting for more than 300 regular participants, and the number doubled again for the Christmas show. Their own theory about the rapid increase in attendance was that more Chinese Christians moved to Bologna for small businesses, given the city's position as a commercial hub, in addition to more second-generation Chinese immigrants having gotten married or giving birth in the past years. However, it is almost impossible to provide a precise number of the Chinese Christian population in Bologna as many do not regularly attend Church activities while others are from neighboring cities without Chinese Christian churches.

The operation of the CCB is mainly dependent on volunteer work by the congregation, and there are no religious professionals working for the church. All church staff members, including preachers, are volunteers. For example, Uncle Li is the person in charge of the CCB and is also a coffee bar owner. The preachers for Sunday worship, who take turns giving sermons at various Chinese immigrant churches in Italy, are primarily immigrant entrepreneurs as well, while professional preachers from the Wenzhou area or other Chinese regions are occasionally invited as guest speakers.

The CCB organizes various religious activities that require the congregation members, both first-generation Chinese immigrants and their children, to devote a considerable amount of time in service of the church. Apart from weekly religious activities, such as Sunday worship and Bible studies targeting different age groups, there are also other special events such as the Christmas celebration and Easter shows. A number of events specifically aimed at the younger generation, such as spirituality classes, seminars, and summer camps, are regularly organized together with other Chinese immigrant churches across Italy. Children can also attend musical instrument classes and Mandarin Chinese lessons offered by the church, in many cases free of charge. Furthermore, free meals cooked by volunteer workers are commonly provided when events are held in the evening.

These activities are more than enough to fill up the rather limited leisure time enjoyed by Chinese Christian immigrants. Similar to their counterparts in Paris, they spent most of their leisure time in service of the Chinese immigrant church with which they are affiliated (see Cao 2013). The case of Enlai, a vendor at a local market and coffee bar owner, offers a typical example of the everyday lives of Chinese Christian entrepreneurs in Bologna who consider themselves pious Christians and who actively join in church activities. The lives of Enlai, his wife, and their three children are structured around family, business, and the church. Enlai was a member of the adult worship instrument team, which performs worship music once a month, but also gathered together to practice every week. He and his wife were volunteer workers who provided logistical support for various activities by, for example, cooking dinners biweekly for the church's youth fellowship gatherings. Enlai's three children were all members of the youth choir and the Sunday worship team, and all of them had learned to play multiple musical instruments in the CCB and regularly attended music lessons every Saturday. The three siblings were also among the main performers in the Christmas show and other events. Two of the children, who were fluent in both Chinese and Italian, also served as interpreters at certain events when necessary. The three siblings also attended summer camps and spirituality classes held in other Italian cities on a rotating basis.

The church served as almost the only legitimate social space for Chinese Christian immigrants. By regulating the congregants' leisure time, the Chinese immigrant religious institutions had drawn social boundaries between the church members and the world beyond their religious community. Uncle Li, the CCB leader and bar owner, explained his perception of the differences between Chinese Christians and other, non-Christian immigrants, saying:

> We all do business. This is the same, and we do have contact with each other, but we can't have intimate and close relationships. In the end, we have different lifestyles. We're walking on two different paths. They enjoy themselves with feasting and other kinds of entertainment. Some people have very messy private lives. But, we people of the church [*jiaohui de ren*] are different from them. We don't go out drinking or gambling. We spend most of our time serving the church and glorifying God. Our belief isn't just empty words; it's about our lifestyle.

Uncle Li's words implied a strong sense of moral superiority over the non-Christian Chinese immigrants, who were perceived as less morally "good" and trustworthy in comparison with the "people of the church." Accordingly, he felt that only the latter were legitimate individuals to socialize with, since they shared not only the same religious faith, but also a way of life.

3   Moral Dilemmas in the Neighborhood Bar Business

Being a Christian and an entrepreneur does not necessarily pose a moral contradiction, as the two identities belong to two different social domains of morality. For example, Christianity often serves positive social functions and contributes to Chinese Christians' pursuit of entrepreneurial aspirations in their overseas experiences. The diasporic churches, as crucial ethnic religious communities, are a "safe harbor" (Guest 2003) where Chinese immigrants can find various social supports and resources for their immigrant lives and business ambitions. Christianity has also provided for Wenzhou Christians in Paris a non-market moral discourse that challenges the secular state production of illegality in terms of immigration control and management and so legitimizes their household economy and morally ambiguous business practices, such as tax evasion and employment of undocumented workers in the context of market modernity (see Cao 2013). This moral discourse is also very popular among Chinese Christians in Italy. Christianity further moralizes church fellows' business practices through religious rituals. For instance, the key figures of the CCB always visit new business sites managed by their fellow church members and hold a small ceremony of prayers and blessings. They call this a family visit (*jiafang*). In this way, the business is seen as being blessed by God, who is in turn glorified by their business prosperity.

Nevertheless, the mutual support and reinforcement of the two domains is not always consistent. Chinese Christian immigrants who manage coffee bars have encountered particular moral dilemmas and ambivalence between their entrepreneurial aspirations and religious morality. In spite of the presence of a variety of coffee bars in Italy, the most common type that Chinese immigrants manage is the neighborhood bar, which serves as a male-dominated local community center. These neighborhood bars, commonly a hybrid of café, bar, grocer, and game room, are one of the few social spaces accessible to socially marginalized individuals, including retired working-class men, internal and transnational migrant workers, as well as slot machine addicts. These people, usually men, who regularly spend their leisure time in a particular neighborhood bar, are the main clients that the baristas socialize with on daily basis. The baristas, who are often business owners as well, also serve as an integral part of the coffee bar community that they manage.

The low profitability of the coffee bar business often requires that the owners extend the opening hours by exploiting unpaid and flexible family labor. A neighborhood bar usually opens early in the morning and closes in the early evening. However, some of the Chinese-managed coffee bars stay open until midnight or even later if there are clients present. It is also not unusual to see a neighborhood bar open for business on Sundays, such as Yang's establishment mentioned in the opening episode of this chapter. The self-employed Chinese families usually have to rely on all of their available family laborers to invest their time in the business in order to maximize their economic profits while saving the labor cost of hiring employees. Family laborers are thus usually mobilized to the maximum extent, and each one has to work more than ten hours a day on a regular basis, and in some cases more than twelve hours. It is also common to see an owners' family live in the same neighborhood, often upstairs in the same building, where their coffee bar is located.

The nature of the neighborhood bar business made it a somewhat reluctant choice for Chinese Christians, at least in the early days when it was first becoming popular among Chinese immigrants. Several Chinese Christians confessed to me their hesitance and reluctance to step into the business, as they thought neighborhood bars were not a decent and moral business that would be compatible with their religious ethics. Their concerns were mainly related to the following two aspects.

First, as "good" Christians, they felt that one must live a moral life in which excessive drinking and gambling, are perceived as sins and are thus absolutely forbidden. Those who engage in such morally unacceptable behaviors are considered to be "bad" people from whom they must keep a safe distance. However, alcoholic drinks and slot machines often comprise a considerable portion or even the majority of profits for a neighborhood bar business. In some cases, slot machines were the only reason for Chinese immigrants to engage in the coffee bar business, since slot machines could make considerable profits without expending any additional labor, so long as the coffee bar was open for business. Those regular customers who drink and gamble a great deal, in other words, the alcoholics and slot machine addicts who were "bad" people according to their moral criteria, were often those with whom they would have to socialize on a daily basis. Thus they are no longer able to keep themselves isolated solely in their religious community when renegotiating locality in an exclusionary European society (Cao 2013). This kind of social interaction was considered a significant challenge in their moral and religious lives.

Second, in their understanding of being a "good" Christian, one must devote oneself to God and actively engage in church activities. However, a neighborhood bar business may not allow them to spend as much time as they would normally be able to in pursuit of religious activities. The locations of neighborhood bar businesses are not concentrated in ethnic enclaves like so many other Chinese ethnic businesses, but rather are distributed throughout various local neighborhoods, sometimes in peripheral areas that can be quite remote. Due to long working hours and the need to better exploit flexible family labor, many Chinese owners move their homes so that they can live geographically closer to their businesses. Furthermore, many neighborhood bars are open every day of the week without holidays, including Sundays and church holidays, in order to maintain a regular clientele. Therefore, this kind of intensive business schedule can represent another significant challenge in these Chinese Christians' lifestyles.

The two concerns outlined above represent their worries and anxieties about detachment from their religious communities and loss of their diasporic Christian identity that is perceived as crucial for their immigrant lives and entrepreneurship. Neighborhood bars are one of the few businesses in which Chinese immigrants engage with local society in their everyday lives. Managing such a bar means that their Christianity is challenged in terms of both their way of life and their sense of moral superiority. They can no longer maintain their relative self-isolation and conduct their social lives primarily within their ethnic religious community. On the contrary, they need to socialize with non-Christians and non-Chinese, who are commonly perceived as morally inferior in order to maintain their social boundaries with the outside world.

4 Negotiating Religious Morality

In spite of their moral ambivalence toward the neighborhood bar business, Chinese Christians have not rejected this new entrepreneurial opportunity. Despite some initial hesitance, more and more Chinese Christians, just like their non-Christians counterparts, have stepped wholeheartedly into this business niche and accept it as just one of the few sectors to which they can gain access. Chinese Christians actively negotiate business practices and religious prescriptions in their everyday management of neighborhood bars. These negotiations, both discursive and active, have particularly addressed issues of clientele management and time management in order to maintain their diasporic Christian identity and close attachment to their ethnic religious community. In the process of negotiation, they strive to moralize the space that they manage, reconstruct their moral discourses of Christianity, and negotiate social boundaries in their everyday practice of attempting to be a "good" Christian.

4.1 *Clientele Management*

For Chinese Christian entrepreneurs, one of the most controversial aspects of the neighborhood bar business is the composition of its clientele, many of whom are perceived as morally "bad," since they can be involved in excessive drinking, gambling, and sometimes lecherous behaviors. In this new social context, Chinese Christian entrepreneurs often emphasize their conscientiousness and efforts in constructing the neighborhood bars that they manage into moral spaces.

Shan, an active volunteer worker at the CCB, had managed a neighborhood bar together with her husband and their elder son for over two years. She often proudly told me how their coffee bar was different from other places. On one occasion, she said:

> In fact, coffee bars are not all the same. Good people go to good ones and bad people go to bad ones. For example, bad guys don't come to our place. We don't offer good service to bad people, and so after one or two times they don't come back again. Our clients all know that we are doing regular [*zhenggui*] business; we are serious people and our coffee bar is a serious place, so they know that they have to behave in a respectful

way here. Once, a client brought two friends here. Then, one friend started saying something dirty. Our client stopped them right away and told them it was inappropriate to make such jokes here ...

Shan's words, especially the qualitative adjectives, such as "good," "regular," "serious," "respectful," "dirty," and "inappropriate," demonstrate her self-perception of moral superiority as a Christian. Through the dichotomous differentiation between "good" and "bad" coffee bars, as well as "good" and "bad" clients, she moralized her family-managed business through their active practices of selecting appropriate clients and regulating behaviors for the construction of a morally "good" space. My participant observation in Shan's establishment also confirmed her words that clients were received with different attitudes. She and her family would smile at the clients whom they considered to be "good," while acting indifferently toward those whom they considered to be "bad."

Nevertheless, their criteria concerning "good" or "bad" clients were not simply about engagement in non-ethical practices such as excessive drinking or gambling. Instead, they were also based on whether or not they were beneficial to their businesses. The alcoholics and slot machine addicts, who were perceived as morally "bad" people, were not necessarily the "bad" clients that they attempted to exclude from their business, so long as they made no trouble, paid their tabs on time, and behaved "in a respectful way" that would not "affect other good clients' impression of our coffee bar," as Shan put it. These criteria, rather than being related to the practices of religious ethics or spirituality, seemed instead to be in line with the overarching discourse of *suzhi* (quality) that embraces self-worth and self-development and justifies social hierarchies in pursuit of modernity in post-Mao China (Kipnis 2006, Yan 2008). As Cao (2009) has pointed out, in a period of rapid marketization, the religiosity of contemporary Chinese Protestant Christians has also been "shaped by desires and practices of self-making among neoliberal individuals" (54).

In terms of justifying the gambling business in neighborhood bars, Uncle Li's words can be viewed as representative:

> Now, Italy is facing a serious economic crisis. More and more desperate people are playing slot machines with a few coins just to try their luck. Few of them are real gamblers. It's just a game. Yet, frankly speaking, we know that slot machines are not good things. But what else can we do? We are people of the church. The bottom line is that we ourselves do not touch them.

Uncle Li's words demonstrate that, on the one hand, slot machines are admittedly unacceptable in light of their moral and religious ethics; on the other hand, such rules are negotiable in practice, so long as they themselves follow the rules and maintain social boundaries between them and the gambling and gamblers, who are not included in the notion of "us."

4.2   Time Management

The other main challenge in neighborhood bar management involves time conflicts between business practices and religious duties. The exploitation of flexible and unpaid family labor is a major strategy used to solve this dilemma. While some family members attend religious activities, the other members then need to replace them and take over their work shifts.

The most significant time clash takes place on Sundays. The CCB holds its Sunday worship services in the afternoon. However, only a few Chinese Christians regularly closed their coffee bars for half a day to attend Sunday worship. Dong, whose coffee bar was located 15 minutes away from the CCB by car, told me of her family's concerns and strategies:

> It's not good to be absent at every Sunday gathering, so we take turns going to church. This week my husband and I will go, and next week my three kids will go together. When I can't go, I'll listen to the sermon on my smartphone. We have an online worship group. It's also acceptable to worship in this way. The only problem is that, on Sundays when my husband and I go to church, my eldest daughter has to work really long hours. She usually works the morning shift from 5 AM to 3 PM, but in those cases she has to work until 6 PM when I have come back from church and finished cooking the dinner for the family. However, this is the only solution we have.

Dong's words demonstrate how her family's religious morality is maintained at the cost of significant exploitation of flexible and unpaid family labor. This exploitation becomes even more intense when other unexpected matters occur. For example, once when Uncle Li and his wife brought a group of newly converted Christians to Milan for baptisms, their son had to take care of the business for the entire two days, working from 6 AM to 11 PM each day. Their son complained to me, saying, "I was tired to death! But what else could I do? It's our family business. Someone has to take care of it." In the cases of both Dong and Uncle Li, the Chinese religious subjects deployed family values in order to overcome the dilemmas between business interests and religious ethics.

It is worth noting that those who regularly closed their coffee bars to attend Sunday worship were not necessarily more religious than those not doing so. Instead, such decisions turned out to be a result of rational and careful business calculations of opportunity cost. Choosing to take a Sunday afternoon break or not depends more on business needs than how much a family adheres to Christianity. Enlai and his family, who were mentioned earlier, actively served as volunteer workers at the CCB, and were among the few Chinese who kept their businesses closed on Sunday afternoons. Although often emphasizing that it was an unconditional duty for a Christian, Enlai once offered another version of the story. He claimed that it was because a large portion of his clientele consisted of employees working in nearby offices, and that the Sunday afternoon break did not really affect much of his business profits. Uncle Li's family even conducted an experiment on Sunday afternoons to see if they would encounter a significant economic loss due of a half-day closure. After a couple of weeks, his family decided to continue taking the half-day break, since "there was no sense," in staying open in the afternoon, as Uncle Li's son told me. Since their business was usually good in the evenings, his son would re-open the business immediately after the Sunday service.

5 Family Values as Bridging Ethics

In spite of Chinese Christians' active engagement in moralizing their coffee bar enterprises through clientele management and time management, the business is still considered to be a morally ambiguous one among these religious subjects. The feeling of embarrassment resulting from this paradox, which Michael Herzfeld (2005) would call the "cultural intimacy" between religious ethics and entrepreneurial practices, was most likely the reason that they often felt it necessary to further justify the moral legitimacy of their businesses.

Family values were frequently mentioned in their justifications and often outweighed religious ethics. Shan told me about her family's moral struggles before they decided to step into the neighborhood bar business, saying:

> At the beginning, we refused to do this business. We are people of the church. We thought it would not be good to do the coffee bar business because only bad people are always there. In fact, we missed out on several profitable coffee bars. We also missed the best time for managing such a bar. But now the economy is becoming worse and worse. We have no other choice. We have to maintain our livelihood. We have to raise two kids.

Shan's "no other choice" statement echoes Yang's words of "no way out" (*mei banfa*). This discourse was used to justify the Chinese Christian subjects' controversial and, to them, embarrassing business practices by highlighting their powerlessness in the face of an adverse economic structure. Shan's words described the business choice as the only survival strategy available to them in order to exercise their parental duties to their children. Family values were a taken-for-granted and unchallengeable argument repeatedly used to justify not only the exploitation of unpaid family labor, but also actions that were incompatible with other moral principles, including religious prescriptions. Family values were also a topic that came up frequently when Chinese Christians talked about their entrepreneurial aspirations and immigrant lives.

Although belonging to another ethical domain, family values are intertwined with both business ethics and religious morality for Chinese Christian immigrants in Italy. Furthermore, familism is an integral part of their dual identities as both entrepreneurs and Christians. On the one hand, family solidarity is fundamental for Chinese immigrant entrepreneurs to achieve economic prosperity. As discussed earlier, the immigrant family is their most basic economic unit. Their transnational migration is a family plan, their business is a family business that relies on self-employment of unpaid family labor, and their children are often fundamental laborers in an effort to achieve upward social and economic mobility. This form of self-employed family business has high requirements for the maintenance of family integrity and solidarity, which are also the fundamental family ethics highlighted in their everyday lives.

Meanwhile, Christianity provides Chinese Christian immigrants an ethical framework that legitimizes and reinforces their family ethics, which are at the core of their version of Christianity. Maintaining family integrity is described as God's order, and the devotion to one's own family is a way of glorifying God. The CCB, as a religious institution, paid more attention to families than to single religious individuals. As mentioned earlier, the way in which the CCB counted its congregation was based on family units, and "family visits" were made when a family started a new business. Even though the coffee bar business was perceived as morally ambiguous, they believed that this business could receive God's blessing, as it was a way of achieving good for the family.

The CCB also attached a considerable degree of importance to the cultivation of family values among believers. Family values were one of the major topics throughout all of the sermons attended during research at the CCB. For instance, in one of the Sunday worship services, the preacher, who was also an immigrant entrepreneur, gave a sermon entitled "The Whole Family's Happiness" (*Quan Jia Fu*). During the talk, the preacher repeatedly emphasized that mass migration from Wenzhou to Europe with entrepreneurial achievement was a result of strong family values and, of course, God's grace. While praising the work ethics of Chinese Christians in Italy, he exhorted them to maintain good family traditions. He also emphasized the importance of co-ethnic solidarity, which he described as a large family of Chinese immigrants, for the collective benefit of Chinese in Italy.

Family values are a paramount type of morality that can also function as a bridging form of ethics that mediates the moral conflicts between Chinese immigrants' entrepreneurial aspirations and religious practices. While Christianity is something that can be negotiated in everyday religious practices, family ethics, including conjugal stability and patriarchal authority, are seen as something that cannot be compromised. For example, divorce is extremely stigmatized in this Chinese community, even though it has become somewhat commonplace in urban China and, while discouraged, is not explicitly prohibited by most denominations of Protestantism. When business practices are perceived to be harmful to family integrity, economic benefits can also be compromised. For instance, criticism came from several Chinese Christians about some Chinese immigrants' abuse of gendered strategies in the neighborhood bar business. Shan stated:

> It is true that female baristas are often more desirable, since most of our clients are men, but we cannot sacrifice everything just for money. We are people of the church and we have our bottom lines. I know in some families the husband works the daytime shift while the wife works in the evening, wearing revealing clothes and staying aside with some men who play slot machines until very late. The couple can hardly meet each other. Yes, they can make more money, but the family could be broken. What's the sense of that in the end?

Whether what she described about those families is true or not, her words show a strong opinion that entrepreneurship is family focused and family ethics are more fundamental than economic interests, and that Christian morality is deployed to support and reinforce family ethics.

6 Conclusion

The relationship between religious ethics and economic actions has been widely studied since Weber (2013 [1905]), who argued for a causal relationship between Protestant religious ethics and capitalist economic development. This chapter, meanwhile, showcases an empirical case in which religious ethics posed something of a moral dilemma against the pursuit of economic ends. It sheds light on a more complex and intertwining relationship between religious morality and entrepreneurial values in the context of transnational migration. As dual-identity moral subjects, Chinese Christian immigrant entrepreneurs in Italy have to face the moral dilemmas and contradictions implicitly embedded in the interplay between religion and the businesses they engage in. However, they are not simply regulated and disciplined by religious prescriptions in order to live a moral life; instead, these religious subjects actively negotiate ways of being ethical Christians in their everyday moral practices, while still maintaining their entrepreneurial aspirations.

The ethnographic analysis of this research ultimately shows that family values are a form bridging ethics that mediate Chinese coffee bar owners' moral conflicts between their entrepreneurial aspirations and religious morality. Family is at the core of both Chinese immigrant entrepreneurship and their religious ethics and, as the basic economic and social unit, is fundamental for self-employed Chinese immigrants to achieve upward social and economic mobility. Christianity and family values thus reinforce each other through everyday religious practices, and the latter provides an ethical framework for the religious subjects to negotiate moral ambivalence. When economic actions contradict religious morality, family values can be used to legitimize these economic actions as understandable, negotiable, and reluctantly acceptable. Taking the ethical domain of family values into consideration, this ethnographic study also shows that Chinese immigrant entrepreneurs do not merely prioritize economic interest over religious ethics in their business activities. Instead, their religious practices must be understood within the context of the complex and intertwining moralities of the various social domains that regulate their economic, social, and cultural lives.

Acknowledgements

I am grateful to all my interlocutors in Italy who shared their lives and stories with me and especially to the Chinese Church of Bologna for their support. I thank Professor Nanlai Cao, Professor Giuseppe Giordan, and Professor Fenggang Yang for comments and suggestions that have helped with the improvement of this chapter. I also thank James Wang for suggestions and editing.

References

Bateson, Gregory. 1972. *Steps to an Ecology of Mind*, Chicago, University of Chicago Press.
Cao, Nanlai. 2008. "Boss Christians: The Business of Religion in the "Wenzhou Model" of Christian Revival." *The China Journal* 59: 63–87.

Cao, Nanlai. 2009. "Raising the Quality of Belief: *Suzhi* and the Production of an Elite Protestanism." *China Perspectives* 2009/4: 54–65.

Cao, Nanlai. 2011. Constructing China's Jerusalem: Christians, Power, and Place in Contemporary Wenzhou. Stanford, CA: Stanford University Press.

Cao, Nanlai. 2013. "Renegotiating Locality and Morality in a Chinese Religious Diaspora: Wenzhou Christian Merchants in Paris, France." *The Asia Pacific Journal of Anthropology* 14(1): 85–101.

Ceccagno, Antonella. 2017. *City Making and Global Labor Regimes: Chinese Immigrants and Italy's Fast Fashion Industry*, Hampshire: Palgrave Macmillan.

Das, Veena. 2012. "Ordinary Ethics." Pp. 133–149 in *A Companion to Moral Anthropology*, edited by Didier Fassin. Oxford: Wiley-Blackwell.

Deng, Ting. 2020. "Chinese Immigrant Entrepreneurship in Italy's Coffee Bars: Demographic Transformation and Historical Contingency." *International Migration* 58(3). doi: 10.1111/imig.12655.

Fassin, Didier. 2015. "Troubled Waters: At the Confluence of Ethics and Politics." Pp. 175–210 in *Four Lectures on Ethics: Anthropological Perspectives*, edited by Michael Lambek et al. Chicago: HAU Books.

Gates, Hill. 1996. China's Motor: A Thousand Years of Petty Capitalism. Ithaca, NY: Cornell University Press.

Guest, Kenneth J. 2003. God in Chinatown: Religion and Survival in New York's Evolving Immigrant Community. New York and London: New York University Press.

Han, Huamei. 2011. " 'Love Your China' and Evangelise: Religion, Nationalism, Racism and Immigrant Settlement in Canada." *Ethnography and Education* 6(1): 61–79.

Herzfeld, Michael. 2005. *Cultural Intimacy: Social Poetics in the Nation-State*, 2nd Ed. New York: Routledge.

Kalir, Barak. 2009. "Finding Jesus in the Holy Land and Taking Him to China: Chinese Temporary Migrant Workers in Israel Converting to Evangelical Christianity." Sociology of Religion 70(2): 130–156.

Kipnis, Andrew. 2006. "*Suzhi*: A Keyword Approach." *The China Quarterly* 186: 295–313.

Krause, Elizabeth L. 2018. *Tight Knit: Global Families and the Social Life of Fast Fashion*. Chicago: Chicago University Press.

Laidlaw James 2018. "Fault Lines in the Anthropology of Ethics." Pp.174–96 in *Moral Engines: Exploring the Ethical Drives in Human Life*, edited by Cheryl Mattingly et al. Oxford: Berghahn.

Lambek, Michael. 2012. "Religion and Morality." Pp. 341–358 in *A Companion to Moral Anthropology*, edited by Didier Fassin. Oxford: Wiley-Blackwell.

Li, Minghuan. 1999. " 'To Get Rich Quickly in Europe!': Reflections on Migration Motivation in Europe." Pp. 181–198 in *Internal and International Migration: Chinese Perspectives*, edited by Frank N. Pieke, and Hein Mallee. Richmond: Curzon.

Nyíri, Pál. 2003. "Moving Targets: Chinese Christian Proselytising among Transnational Migrants from the People's Republic of China." *European Journal of East Asian Studies* 2(2): 263–301.

Oxfeld, Ellen. 2010. *Drink Water, but Remember the Source: Moral Discourse in a Chinese Village.* Berkeley: University of California Press.

Robbins, Joel. 2016. "What is the Matter with Transcendence? On the Place of Religion in the New Anthropology of Ethics." *Journal of the Royal Anthropological Institute (N.S.)* 22: 767–808.

Tan, Chee-Beng. 2013. "Tianhou and the Chinese in Diaspora." Pp. 417–429 in *Routledge Handbook of the Chinese Diaspora*, edited by Tan Chee-Beng. London: Routledge.

Tong, Joy Kooi-Chin. 2013. *Overseas Chinese Christian Entrepreneurs in Modern China: A Case Study of the Influence of Christian Ethics on Business Life.* London: Anthem Press.

Weber, Max. 2013 [1905]. *The Protestant Ethic and the Spirit of Capitalism.* London: Routledge.

Xiang, Biao. 2005. *Transcending Boundaries: Zhejiangcun: The Story of a Migrant Village in Beijing.* Leiden & Boston: Brill.

Yan, Hairong. 2008. *New Masters, New Servants: Migration, Development, and Women Workers in China.* Durham, NC: Duke University Press.

Zhang, Li. 2002. *Strangers in the City: Reconfigurations of Space, Power, and Social Networks within China's Floating Population.* Stanford: Stanford University Press.

Zigon, Jarrett. 2008. *Morality: An Anthropological Perspective.* Oxford: Berg.

CHAPTER 2

From China with Faith

Sinicizing Christianity in Europe

Nanlai Cao

Christianity has figured prominently in the history of China–West encounters.[1] While stories and studies of western missionaries to China are plentiful and common, the neglected other side of the coin is the western opposition of Chinese immigrants based on perceived non-Christian compatibility. In U.S. history there was a long period of time from 1882 to 1965 when Chinese immigration was strictly restricted by the federal Chinese Exclusion Act of 1882 and the national quota system (1943–1965). Although economic competition in the American west appeared to be the major motivation behind Chinese exclusion, lack of Christian values and allegiances on the part of the Chinese was a paramount concern among American policy-makers and factored strongly in the moral argument against Chinese immigration, especially the immigration of Chinese women because of "the widely held view that all Chinese women were prostitutes" (Chan 1991: 95). Much of the stereotypical knowledge about the Chinese being immoral "pagans" and "heathens" was partly derived from early western Christian missionary encounters in China, and partly a byproduct of racial distinction and white supremacy. Due to the exclusion-era law prohibiting the immigration of the wives or families of Chinese, there was an extremely skewed sex ratio among the Chinese in the U.S. during the first half of the twentieth century, and white missionary-led churches in the bachelor society of Chinatown served as important "rescue homes" for women facing the serious problems of concubinage and prostitution (Cayton and Lively 1955). Both in China and the Chinese diaspora early Western missionaries conceived of their work to evangelize "heathens" in the "aggregated paganism", thus distancing themselves from the indigenous elements of the Chinese world.

---

1 The work was supported by the fund for building world-class universities (religious studies) of Renmin University of China (Project No. KYGJD2020003). This chapter is a revision and adaption of an article of mine that appeared in the journal *Religions* in 2019 entitled "A Sinicized World Religion?: Chinese Christianity at the Contemporary Moment of Globalization."

Soon after the establishment of the People's Republic of China in 1949, foreign missionaries were expelled by the new Communist regime. Christianity has been thoroughly indigenized through close contact with immediate local Chinese realities. The influence upon Chinese Christianity directly brought by western missionaries has faded away but a lot comes from immigrant Chinese Christian churches overseas instead, exhibiting a mode of mutual penetration between the Chinese churches in China and those based in diaspora. Since the turn of the new century Europe has become increasingly the center of global migrations from other parts of the world. Chinese immigrants, such as those from Chinatowns in Paris and Rome, have formed transnational church networks that originate in China, and whose operations largely rely on ethnic trading communities and networks. Therefore, this is a story of multidirectional religious transmission under globalization, rather than an overwhelmingly unidirectional movement from the global center to the passive margin or the cultural penetration and reconstruction of Chinese society by the West that characterizes the early modern phase of globalization (see Casanova 2018). The following analysis is based on multisited ethnographic fieldwork conducted among the Chinese diasporic communities in Paris and Rome spanning a decade.

1 The Rise of a Household-Based Chinese Christianity in Diaspora

So far, little scholarly attention has been paid to the globalization of Chinese Christianity or the story of Chinese Christianity on a global stage. Research on Chinese Christianity in diaspora has mainly focused on Chinese conversion to Christianity which is the majority religion in the Western context (see, e.g., Cao 2005, Yang 1999). However, we know little about how Chinese migrants brought with them their own homegrown Christian faith to the West and other parts of the world from China and created their religious diaspora and mission stations.[2] The mass participation of Chinese merchants and traders in migrant churches in Europe contrasts sharply with the mass conversion of Chinese professionals (scholars and students) to Christianity in the United States (see Yang and Tamney 2006). The latter group has been well documented, while increasingly secularized Europe provides a new context for researching Chinese Christianity that cannot be seen simply in terms of a unidirectional mode of assimilation to a Western religious culture, but rather the antidote to cultural assimilation.

---

2 See Cao (2013) and Cao et al. (2018) for two notable exceptions.

Unlike in the United States, where religion in general and Christianity in particular enjoys privileged status in society, in highly secularized Europe, state regulatory framework generally discourages the active presence of immigrant religion in social life, and churchgoing is not considered a virtue by the public.[3] However, as this study shows, a highly indigenized Chinese Christianity has taken roots in post-Christian Europe almost in total isolation from local European Christians and churches. In recent decades, a large number of Chinese Christians, originated from the coastal Chinese city of Wenzhou, have migrated to Europe especially France and Italy without proper travel documents and with a sole purpose to make money.[4] Many of them were previously rural migrant entrepreneurs and itinerant traders within China before emigration (Li 1999). According to various estimates by immigrant church insiders, there are hundreds of Chinese churches across Europe. Italy is home to around 70 Chinese churches and nearly 30,000 Chinese believers, constituting the largest presence of Chinese Christianity in Europe. In Rome alone, according to the estimation of some Chinese church leaders, currently 10% of 30,000 Chinese in the city are Christians. France has the second largest Chinese church community in Europe, with around 40 Chinese churches and 10,000 church members, mostly concentrated in the urban districts of Paris. One important feature that distinguishes these Chinese Christians in Europe from those in North America is that they are mostly not new converts but had become Christians in China before emigration.

Since the turn of the new century, the large group of Chinese migrant traders and merchants from the Wenzhou region has acquired great visibility and begun to dominate the Chinese churches in Europe. There are also Wenzhou Christian merchants in North America, but they do not form their own place-based business enclave or congregations, partly due to their small population and their spatial dispersion. Chinese immigrants from Fujian and Guangdong (Canton) have traditionally dominated Chinatowns and Chinese Christian churches in North America whereas Wenzhou immigrants are latecomers. One Wenzhou preacher in Italy speaks of the divergent migration trajectories of these three different Chinese groups,

---

3   See Berger et al. (2008) for a contrast between the religiosity of the United States and the secularity of Europe.
4   The issue of migrant illegality is generally downplayed in the church setting. When asked, they often invoke the notion of God's grace to provide moral legitimacy for their theoretically illegal migration and business practices.

> Not many Wenzhou people went to America, though. As America and China are separated by sea, it's difficult for people to be illegally smuggled into America. In Europe, it's much easier. Back then some European countries such as Romania and Yugoslavia were both communist countries, who offered free entries to Chinese nationals. Chinese people could enter these countries and cross their border into Italy or France without much difficulty. There are a lot of Cantonese and Fujianese people who came to Italy much earlier (than Wenzhou Chinese). Their journeys were more treacherous as they had to forge fake passports and took ferries to cross the sea.

The Chinese communities in Europe are heterogeneous in terms of their geographic origins, their migratory patterns and the multiplicity of the waves of their migration. However, it seems that only these Wenzhou people have been able to build their ethnic, place-specific congregations and evangelistic networks to such a grand scale and with such high visibility across Europe, thanks to the practical logic of Christian entrepreneurs and the dynamic, locally developed business model of Wenzhou church development (Cao 2008).

They are known as China's global go-getters, spreading Chinese commerce across the globe. In particular, they operate small businesses such as garment factories and trade light industrial products between China and Europe and across Europe. Gateway cities like Paris and Rome have become the business centers of Chinese wholesale products in Europe, flourishing with businesspeople coming from all parts of Europe to purchase the products imported from China. Nowadays, increasingly businesspeople from different parts of Europe can fly to China and import products directly from there. As a result, Wenzhou people have recently moved into the service industry that includes restaurants, cafes, bars, grocery stores, supermarkets and hotels. Lay leaders in the migrant Wenzhou church are mostly "rich folks" who have made a fortune in this new place. They have brought an indigenous Chinese Christianity to Europe along with their household-based economy. Popularly known as "China's Jerusalem", the coastal Chinese city of Wenzhou is home to thousands of self-started home-grown Protestant churches and a million Protestants (around 20% of the local population), and has become a regional center of global capitalism since the 1990s (Cao 2010).

Most Chinese churches in Europe are not officially registered as religious organizations but as nonprofit organizations due to various legal restrictions in the host society. Specifically, in France Chinese churches tend to be registered as "Association" in accordance with the French association law of 1901, and in Italy as "Organizzazione Non Lucrativa di Utilità Sociale" (ONLUS). Some do not register at all for the purpose of avoiding official scrutiny or just for convenience. Furthermore, most of them have actively avoided contact with non-Chinese local churches or congregations in Europe. The formation and expansion of this diasporic religious community relies heavily on these Wenzhou traders' newfound wealth from transnational business and the informal household-based model of church development. This can be seen as a natural extension of the extensive house church networks operating in legal gray areas in mainland China. Wenzhou churches in Europe are usually controlled and managed by a small number of nondenominational male lay leaders or "boss Christians" who financially contributed the most to purchasing or acquiring the church properties (cf. Cao 2011 chap. 4) The churches also serve as a nexus of social power for them. Not unlike rural house churches in China, the household economy constitutes the backbone of church development in the Chinese diaspora, and accordingly migrant churches always refer to the number of households (hu) as the basic unit rather than the number of baptized individuals when calculating membership size. Chinese migrant church leaders encourage the practice of endogamy among church members both as a way to achieve, and as a byproduct of, congregational stability, and the ethnic community, the congregation, and individual households form many concentric circles with God being at the center. This tight-knit community and family atmosphere is especially salient among Wenzhou Chinese immigrants in France. Wenzhou Christians in France enjoy a relatively long history with some geographic advantage in conducting business and religious activities, which tend to develop around Paris – the international trade metropolis.

One Paris-based Wenzhou preacher and garment trader says that if his business fails, he can still rely on the 180 households in his church, and the brothers and sisters would not let him starve. Migrant church leaders are not only socioeconomically connected to their congregations within France but also maintain transnational ties with those who lead migrant Wenzhou churches in other European nations and whom they had prior contact back in the Wenzhou church in China before their emigration. This has resulted in transnationally coordinated efforts to fund new Chinese church building projects both in China and in Europe and to launch high-profile joint petitions against the recent Chinese state-led cross-removal campaign that removed hundreds of rooftop crosses in Wenzhou and the surrounding regions in Zhejiang Province.[5] Church workers and lay leaders often further expand their networks throughout the European Union as their family businesses move from one

---

5 For details of the church cross-removal campaign, see Cao 2017.

country to another, seeking new opportunities and taking advantage of the visa-free regime in the Schengen zone. Accordingly, there is a preacher rotation system (paigong) following the Wenzhou model of church development, through which preachers regularly rotate among migrant churches within the host country and sometimes even across different Schengen countries. Both in conducting church work and doing business, they take Europe as a whole.

Wenzhou Chinese churches in France might be a unique case. Against the backdrop of China's current globalization, however, their strategy of adaptation is not uncommon. The growth of Chinese Christianity in Italy proceeds in a similar fashion but in an institutionally distinct way as in France. Comparing to the tight-knit ethnic religious enclave centering in Paris, Chinese migrant churches in Italy spread all over its long, narrow, strip-shaped territory in geographically dispersed settings and are mainly organized into three distinct but interconnected parishes (muqu), namely the northern parish, the middle parish and the southern parish. This parish system is clearly borrowed from the Wenzhou model of church development in China. Unlike in Wenzhou where each parish is responsible for dispatching preachers to different churches to conduct services, in Italy it is the national central board of deacons that is in charge of the entire preacher-dispatch system among the immigrant Chinese Christian community and coordinates church work between different parishes. In France, Chinese churches tend to concentrate in Paris and there is thus no need to adopt this parish system.

All of the three Chinese Christian parishes in Italy operate under the national central board of deacons (zonghui zhishihui). In both countries, Chinese merchant families play an essential supportive role behind the expansion of immigrant Chinese Christian church. In particular, Wenzhou Chinese merchants, traditionally with a strong cultural emphasis on familialism, dominate the leadership structure of the immigrant churches. Developing in two different countries in parallel, Chinese migrant Christian communities share the same family model of operation, characterized by congregational independence, an autonomous space, and a conservative patriarchal morality, while adapting to different local contexts.

2   Migrant Entrepreneurship and Lay Leadership

Among countries in the European Union, Italy's lax immigration control and less developed commercial economy are external factors behind why Italy-based Chinese Christians tend to have higher mobility and develop even stronger internal religious bonding. Many of them obtained residence permits in

Italy in the 1990s thanks to the amnesty law that was exercised every few years in the country. After the economic crisis in the Euro-zone, Italian industries suffered from heavy damages. Many enterprises and businesses went bankrupt and were closed down. The crisis has led to many Chinese Christian businesspeople migrating out of the surrounding parishes that they used to live. It is also not uncommon for them to relocate during seasonal downtime. The spatial dispersion of more than fifty major Chinese immigrant churches throughout the Italian territory allows these mobile traders and merchants to find their new churches or meeting points nearby relatively easily wherever they travel.[6] This unique religious spatial arrangement, together with a centralized nationwide preacher rotation and dispatch system, also encourages mobile religious agents such as lay leaders and preachers to move from one place to another without losing their social and religious capital within the larger ethnic religious system. Their credentials and leadership positions are recognized not only throughout the national system of Chinese church coworkers in Italy, but also in neighboring Greece and Malta, where there are newly planted Chinese migrant churches.

Unlike their counterparts in Italy who scatter around the country and are governed by a centralized national pastoral system, most Chinese immigrants in France have chosen to live in Paris due to the availability of vast business opportunities there. Furthermore, many Chinese Christians in Paris I have come to know have arrived in France from Italy, seeking business opportunities. For them, Italy is more suitable as a transfer station while France is the true final destination. Due to the dominance of socioeconomically advantaged elite and elderly overseas Chinese immigrants, the immigrant Chinese churches in Paris have developed in a highly competitive context with each protecting its relative organizational independence and guarding against the act of "stealing sheep" by other churches. The oldest Parisian Wenzhou Chinese church that claims more than a thousand registered members has recently split into several smaller churches because of unresolved internal conflicts among elderly lay leaders.

Chinese immigrant churches in Europe are, after all, not elite Chinese organizations overseas like the chamber of commerce, but constitute a large, openly participatory domain and a popular grassroots movement of new immigrants. The nationwide system of Chinese Christian parishes which spread

---

6   In Italy, besides a major unified evangelical Chinese Church system that consists of more than fifty churches and more than two hundred centrally appointed preachers across the nation, there is a much smaller, separately organized Pentecostal and charismatic-oriented Chinese church system called the Chinese revival church (huaren fuxing jiaohui).

all over Italy acts as a good example. It has not only met the need of mass social participation by nonelite immigrants who are often on the move for new business opportunities and who are relatively socioeconomically homogenous, but made it possible to mobilize material and pastoral resources readily across regions for the launch of new church programs and the staging of major evangelistic events.

In Europe, owing to various institutional and legal restrictions these boss Christians can hardly purchase properties and build churches in the same way as they do back in China. In one case their plan to purchase a multi-million-euros' worth of Catholic Church property in Rome was vetoed by the Vatican after receiving approval from the municipal government. Nevertheless, these merchants have financially contributed to the expansion of translocal Wenzhou church space that accrues enormous moral prestige to Wenzhou Christians worldwide (Cao 2013). Wenzhou immigrants have dominated the Chinese churches in Europe, especially in such major gateway cities as Paris and Rome. They are able to build large ethnic congregations and evangelistic networks across the European continent. One Chinese-speaking South Korean missionary, who was invited to temporally minster a Chinese fellowship in Rome, once described to me half-jokingly what he saw in the ethnic church community there making him feel like being in the "Republic of Wenzhou" (Wenzhou gongheguo).

Under this centralized pastoral system, more than two-hundred lay preachers have been chosen to affiliate with the national board of coworkers (zonghui tonggong), and each Sunday they are dispatched to different Chinese churches across Italy to deliver sermons. This number is still growing as more Chinese churches are being planted in Italy and need immediate pastoral resources and service. One young preacher belonging to this national system of co-workers told me that all of the preachers within this system work as part-time volunteers and do not receive remuneration or reimbursement of travel expenses in any form because they consider their work as an act of self-sacrifice and spiritually meaningful. This means they have to use personal funds to cover their substantial travel expenses. As a result, only well-to-do merchants or traders can afford to take this mobile job.

When immigrant Chinese merchants, consciously or unconsciously, bring and integrate a relatively successful business model and pragmatic business logic into their church organizations, the operation of the latter would resemble that of an immigrant business enterprise. Wenzhou merchants' family businesses and their immigrant churches are isomorphic in operational logic and organizational structure. In particular, immigrant church leadership tends to lie in the hands of close relatives as in the case of immigrant family firms.

There is strong mutual support between the members of the church community both religiously and commercially. This institutional isomorphism is further reflected in their practices of investment, endogamy, and the construction of family relationship, all of which is conducted in a similar fashion with achieving family solidarity and fulfilling communal commitment as the ultimate goal and fundamental value.

The immigrant family and the family-style church provide the perfect emotionally supportive context for the transmission of the religion cross generationally. Chinese youth spend much time socializing with one another in various church settings such as youth fellowship meetings, bible study groups, youth group outings, summer and winter camps, Christmas performance, and evangelization-related activities, and consequently they tend to meet their potential mates in a highly controlled Chinese context. Sometimes the training of the younger generation of preachers and church leaders also starts from the immigrant family-style church. Young would-be preachers are usually arranged to first practice preaching in front of an audience that includes their parents and grandparents or in front of their home churches attended by relatives before being formally considered and appointed by the national board of deacons of the immigrant Chinese church.

This institutional isomorphism can also find expression in the use of church space. One direct example is the story of a Wenzhou church lay leader and garment businessman in Paris who uses the site of the local church as his business office. When he was asked about why his office address on his business card is the same as that of the church, he frankly responded "when activities are held in the church, this is the office for the church, otherwise it is the office for my business." The line between the church and the secular business world is rather casual and ambiguous, which to some extent reflects the pragmatic business logic of immigrant lay leaders.

The church's nonregistered status also allows lay leaders to merge business with religion without legal hurdles. This partly explains why many of the Chinese immigrant churches are not formally registered as religious sites. Without an overarching central interpretive authority structure in managing religious practices and symbols, immigrant churches are prone to becoming a multifunctional community center that caters to the socioeconomic needs of the immigrants who, instead of taking cultural assimilation for granted, value social, material, and spiritual connections with the Chinese homeland. This highly mobile household-based Chinese Christianity, with its emphasis on transnational religious connections and institutional and spatial autonomy in diaspora, provides an important counterpoint against the popular views on

Christian conversion and cultural assimilation that characterize the research paradigm of US-based immigrant religions (see Warner 1993).

3 Repaying China's "Gospel Debts" to Europe

In recent years, backed by China's intensified commercial engagement with Europe, there has been a shift of direction in today's Chinese mission movement, from a Western mission-founded into-China movement focusing on work among Chinese minorities to an ethnic Chinese-led global mission movement. This has much to do with the worldly engagements of diasporic Chinese Christians in Europe who are spearheading this movement and who seek to integrate their evangelical work with the Chinese state-led "one belt, one road" initiative for global development. These Chinese Christian lay leaders have intentionally developed connections with hegemonic state discourse on cultural nationalism as embodied in the Chinese dream of national rejuvenation. In so doing, they flexibly position themselves as a contributing force in the current Chinese project of nation building and global reordering rather than a force of global western cultural imperialism. It is noteworthy that unlike what Western missionaries in China did a century ago, today's Chinese Christians in Europe are not evangelizing local Europeans, but forming exclusive congregations, although there is a popular discourse in the church highlighting the role of the diaspora Chinese in a self-envisioned "reverse mission" to Europe. There are tight national and ethnic boundaries undergirding this Chinese "mission" which mainly targets fellow Chinese immigrants at the current stage.

This ethnic focus may seem to contradict the idea of reverse mission. However, the tension becomes resolved when the ethnic Chinese churches engage in charitable activities in the larger society as an evangelizing strategy. For example, during the COVID-19 global pandemic, many Chinese churches in Italy organized "face mask gospel" (kouzhao fuyin) outreach activities on the street, handing out desperately needed surgical face masks with gospel tracts to local Italians for free. In one short video that went viral on the internet a young Chinese female church worker cheerfully shouted to the Italians who accepted the masks with the gospel, "Forza Cina, forza Italia, Gesa ti ama" (go China, go Italy, Jesus loves you). This story illustrates the ethnic dimension of reverse mission, the burden of which seems to mainly rest on the shoulders of the second-generation bilingual immigrants. This expectation for the second generation is further confirmed by a fulltime Chinese preacher who has lived in Rome for almost thirty years. As he states:

> We are the first generation of Chinese emigrating to Italy, a little late compared to other countries in Europe where generations of Chinese have settled before us. Our problem is that we cannot preach the Gospel to Italians because we cannot speak Italian well. Surely, we can deal with spoken Italian in daily life, but when it comes to professional preaching, we are far from being qualified. My son is 24 years old this year, studying Italian in a university in Rome. If one day he receives God's calling, he will make a good preacher to Italians, as he understands Italy as well as China.

In recent months since the outbreak of the COVID-19 pandemic, some Chinese lay preachers in Italy have in their livestreamed online sermons resolutely linked the current public health crisis in Europe to Europe's "spiritual crisis" and the increasing "lack of testimony" among Europeans. Europe needs spiritual revival (lingming fuxing), and Chinese churches can work together to bring God's blessings to Europe. This is a recurring theme repeatedly popped up in the sermons and church-run seminary training courses in migrant Chinese churches. The regular and frequent face-to-face gathering of mobile migrant Chinese church leaders from different parts of Europe, facilitated by the visa-free scheme of the Schengen region, further strengthens such a Chinese-centered vision among the first generation of immigrants. While they acknowledge a debt to Europeans for bring Christianity China a century ago, they now assume the responsibility of global evangelization. In contrast to France where French republicanism stresses cultural assimilation and where laïcité has been a dominant ideological principle of secularism in society, Italy is far more tolerant to the public presence of immigrant religions, and a lot of immigrant Chinese Christian evangelistic projects and outreach activities have taken place in Italy.

Sponsored by the "one belt, one road" gospel network, the first Sino-Europe evangelism symposium (hua'ou xuanjiao yantao dahui) was held in Rome in September 2017 with the theme "Challenges and Mission of the Chinese Church in Europe in the 21st Century". Topics discussed include the Islamization of Europe, refugee crisis, homosexual marriage, youth problems, and the Chinese evangelical mission in Europe. In October 2018, a pan-Europe pastoral ministry and leadership symposium (quanou jiaomu ji jiaohui lingxiu yantaohui) with the theme "calling and mission" (huzhao yu shiming) was held in Rome and attended by nearly 200 people. Church leaders from 12 European nations were invited to share information about the Chinese churches in their respective nations and consolidate the Chinese evangelistic vision.

Facilitated by the discourse on globalizing Chinese Christianity, some high-profile evangelical events have taken place in Italy. Under the larger context of religious and cultural pluralism in Italy, Chinese immigrant churches have successfully staged several public special gatherings (tehui) that brought together young Chinese from different parts of Europe. At such occasions, Christian-filtered Chinese cultural values are celebrated and inscribed in European public space, where issues of cohabitation, homosexuality, and abortion are increasingly tolerated. Evangelical Christianity offers these Chinese migrants a new lens in which to interpret their migrant experience and identity as well as articulate a spiritual defense against cultural assimilation into European secularity and social liberalism.

The most spectacular and memorable church activity I participated in during my field trip to Europe was "Love in Rome Century Music Festival" (ai zai luoma) on June 30th, 2018. The Chinese evangelical music event in the heart of the Eternal City was the first major European public event for evangelical Chinese Christians with the aim to celebrate the Apostles Peter and Paul 1950 years after their martyrdom. Officials from the municipal government of Rome were invited to attend to lend legitimacy to this Chinese cultural event. The choice of the location – the Circus Maximus – where Christians were said to be persecuted by the emperor Nero in ancient Rome, burn alive or eaten by wild beasts, was a deliberate attempt to symbolically mark the change in the spatial structure of global Christianity and highlight the spiritual role of the Chinese. The event featuring several Chinese Christian pop music stars drew several thousand young evangelical and Pentecostal Chinese Christians not only from Rome and from all over Italy, but also from other European countries who arrived on coaches. According to my count at the scene, there were approximately 3000 to 4000 attendees at this event. Some evangelistic Chinese church leaders put the event attendance number at 20,000, which is a gross exaggeration apparently out of a desire to put them at the central of a great revival. According to the main organizer, the resources and funds for producing this public event mostly came from the Wenzhou church in mainland China. The total cost for this three-hour concert was six million yuan (about 800,000 US dollars). Although there are strict financial regulations in Europe, money can easily flow between China and Europe in both directions through informal channels. Sometimes, Chinese immigrants can even complete their business transactions in Europe by simply mobilizing and transferring funds between their bank accounts within China.

Preachers from Wenzhou, China were invited to give sermons and prayers in Rome in Mandarin Chinese and to help convert new Chinese immigrants. The concert opened with a short documentary introducing the history of Chinese migration from Wenzhou to Europe, putting the evangelical Christian event in the reform-era context of China's economic globalization. This shift in the direction of the new mission movement is not only reflected in the spatial movement of pastors and lay preachers but also seen in the movement of religious objects. Bibles, hymn books, and even choir robes used in the Chinese churches in Europe are almost all imported from China.

The main idea that has emerged from my close encounters and interactions with these migrant Chinese Christians and enables me to think Chinese Christianity differently is that the usual nation-state centered framework of church-state relations might not be adequate in capturing the dynamism and vitality of Chinese Christianity at this contemporary global moment. As China's official restrictions on religion increasingly motivate the Chinese house church to channel its resources to a "reverse mission" overseas, a group of transnational Chinese Christians have actively engaged in producing religious activities and events that link China and Europe and in attaching evangelistic meanings and symbolic markings to Europe's urban space. For instance, the Mission Center (xuanjiao zhongxin) of the Chinese Christian Church in Italy used to be mainly responsible for organizing and supporting short-term mission trips each summer to the interior, western regions of China, often in collaboration with the Wenzhou church in China. It has shifted its priority in operation since the Chinese government stepped up measures against Christian missionary activities and their mission stations in ethnic southwestern China, to which they had regularly conducted evangelization from Europe, were closed down. Targeting the unreached potential converts in Europe, especially the Chinese immigrant youth and second-generation youth at the current stage, these well connected and globally positioned lay leaders and preachers quickly redirected their resources and energies back to Europe.

Given the fact that there are few new immigrants directly coming from China, the Chinese church in Europe is facing stagnant development. While Chinese immigrants are on the decline, the number of Chinese tourists traveling to Europe and Chinese students studying in Europe is on the rise. Seizing this new opportunity, the Chinese church community in Rome has printed many travel guide brochures that contain gospel tracts and distribute them at tourist attractions, introducing the faith to Chinese tourists and students. As one church worker describes this new evangelistic strategy, characteristically,

> Just like plants dispersing seeds, we don't expect them (the tourists and students) to stay here and germinate now, but we hope they get enlightened and go back to China and take action there. Maybe some of them only stay in Europe for three or five years and go back to China, but that's okay. They can go back to their posts and play their parts (in promoting Christianity).

In the same line of using Europe as a base for Chinese evangelism, a Chinese Christian preacher couple who attend the same migrant church has set up a tourist company that caters to the need of Chinese Christian customers from both Europe and China who come to Rome to visit the footsteps of the apostles in the Bible in order to deepen their spirituality. The Christian wife acts as tour guide and Italian–Chinese interpreter. They are proud of their ability to tease out and narrate the spiritual significance of the European city based on solid biblical knowledge in guided tours. Besides operating regular tours for tourists from China, the Christian tour company has been most frequently used by members of Europe-based Chinese churches and visiting Chinese pastors and preachers from other parts of the world. Sometimes they offer discounted service to those who can bring along potential Chinese converts, thus creating an ethnic religious and commercial node within the larger structure of the enclave economy. They also organize frequent group pilgrimage trips to Jerusalem for Chinese guests in Europe and those directly from China. Near China's public holidays such as the golden week for the National Day, their online advertisement would urge Chinese Christians in Europe to invite their relatives back in China to visit Europe's historical Christian sites, by making euro payments in Europe for the tour services.

The strong emphasis on the central role of the Chinese race in the evangelistic vision of bringing Christian blessings to Europe seems unequivocally ethnocentric. It nevertheless speaks to the reality of China's rising soft power on the global stage associated with its economic rise that has culturally empowered Chinese migrant traders and merchants in general. It comes no surprise that Chinese Christian groups choose to emphasize ethnic or subethnic identity as a deliberate evangelistic strategy in a historically and traditionally Christian cultural context (cf. Nyíri 2003). This also seems to be a common pattern among Asian American Christians (Yang and Ebaugh 2001).

However, the main difference between Chinese Christians in Europe and their counterparts in America is the former's strong cultural entwinement with the Chinese state and its being a salient marker of communal identity. This echoes what I have depicted in a previous study on the phenomenon of "spiritual nationalism" in the reform-era Chinese Christian context. I use the term to capture the multilayered process in which advantaged urban Chinese Christians internalize nation state norms, fashion themselves as modern religious subjects compatible with the nation-building project, and adapt and contribute to the rise of nationalism from below (Cao 2012). Some Chinese Christian groups have formulated what they call "God's China vision" (zhongguo yixiang), meaning that China will rise not only in the economic sphere but also in the spiritual realm. As one Wenzhou Christian businessman put it, characteristically, "The international community is paying great attention to China. To look at the GDP, China is now the second largest economy. In the spiritual field China may take the last baton in the global evangelical movement."

The competing and even militant global religious vision can be found in the Chinese-led "Back to Jerusalem Movement". The ultimate goal of the China vision is for the Chinese to evangelize the Muslim nations in the Middle East and eventually bring the Gospel back to Jerusalem. Although the "Back to Jerusalem Movement" has incurred criticism from some Western-based China ministries for being a scam, today, in the Chinese immigrant church circle, many believe that the Gospel came from Jerusalem and it must be brought back to Jerusalem eventually. In their narratives, this is like running a relay race in which different countries and peoples in different periods play different roles in this great mission of evangelizing the globe. It is not exaggerating to say that a transnational geography of Chinese Christianity has emerged with the Chinese diaspora in Europe being the center of God's mission. However, the discourse about Chinese as the main vehicle for bringing the gospel to Europe is kept very general and almost always with reference to the expected role of second-generation Chinese immigrants in reaching out to potential (non-Chinese) European converts. This attests to the fact that there is currently a general lack of inter-ethnic exchanges and trust among the first generation in the Chinese churches in Europe.

In secularized Europe, evangelical Christianity can provide a normative and morally superior context for migrant Chinese to imagine their native place and a shared future of their cultural positioning in an increasingly exclusionary context (Cao 2013). In France, more than in Italy, Chinese immigrant churches have developed in the direction of high tension with the secular culture of the host society, creating a parallel society and an enclave of identities, faith, and businesses. To fend off unwelcome secular cultural influence from the mainstream society, some indigenous Chinese preachers have used a conservative religious language associated with moral absolutism to train young church members and church workers. In so doing, these immigrant churches are able to effectively pass on their evangelical faith to the younger generation in a spiritual and moral enclave.

This Sinocentric project of global evangelization involves a redemptive process in which the entrepreneurial class of Chinese Christians seek to overcome victimization and suffering inflicted by secular state modernity through repaying China's "gospel debts" (fuyin zhai) to missionary-sending Western nations a century ago. Their prophetic vision is that China will eventually rule the world not only in economic terms, but also in the spiritual realm, and China will transform from a traditional missionary receiving nation to a glorious missionary sending nation.

4 Conclusion

Christian missionaries have traditionally travelled in a north-to-south direction. Early western missionaries in China were instrumental in sinicizing Christianity by integrating the interpretation of religious dogma with traditional Chinese classics and by negotiating the faith tradition in relation to local cultural customs. A century ago when British Methodist missionary and leading sinologist W. E. Soothhill – who spent twenty five years conducting missionary work in Wenzhou – engaged in the sinicization of Christianity by translating hymns and parts of the Holy Bible into romanized Wenzhou dialect (Sang Iah Sing Shi), he would have not imagined this contemporary moment at which an ethnic Chinese-led global mission movement has gradually come into being in Europe drawing on pre-existing diasporic Wenzhou business networks. Indeed, the sinicization of Christianity has taken disparate paths in a globalized world, leading to incorporation into an imagined universal Christianity (Madsen 2017).

In the earlier phase of globalization, lack of Christianity constituted part of a moral argument to justify the exclusion of Chinese labor immigrants and strict border control in late 19th century North America. However, today's diasporic Chinese church networks have spread horizontally across the Schengen region and created diaspora preaching stations in the global north. The increasingly coordinated development of a sinicized Christianity in Europe has spiritualized and moralized private Chinese business and familial interests, and Europe is even presented as an important battleground of the global evangelization of the gospel by the Chinese.

References

Berger, Peter, Grace Davie and Effie Fokas. 2008. *Religious America, Secular Europe?: A Theme and Variations.* London and New York: Routledge.

Cao, Nanlai. 2005. "The Church as a Surrogate Family for Working Class Immigrant Chinese Youth: An Ethnography of Segmented Assimilation." *Sociology of Religion* 66: 183–200.

Cao, Nanlai. 2008. "Boss Christians: The Business of Religion in the 'Wenzhou Model' of Christian Revival". *The China Journal* 59: 63–87

Cao, Nanlai. 2010. *Constructing China's Jerusalem: Christians, Power, and Place in Contemporary Wenzhou.* Stanford: Stanford University Press.

Cao, Nanlai. 2012. "Elite Christianity and Spiritual Nationalism." *Chinese Sociological Review* 9: 27–47.

Cao, Nanlai. 2013. "Renegotiating Locality and Morality in a Chinese Religious Diaspora: Wenzhou Christian Merchants in Paris, France." *The Asia Pacific Journal of Anthropology* 14: 85–101.

Cao, Nanlai. 2017. "Spatial Modernity, Party Building, and Local Governance: Putting the Christian Cross-Removal Campaign in Context." *China Review* 17: 29–52.

Cao, Nanlai, Giuseppe Giordan, and Enzo Pace, eds. 2018. "Chinese Religions in China and Italy." *Religioni e Società* 91.

Casanova, Jose. 2018. "Locating Religion and Secularity in East Asia Through Global Processes: Early Modern Jesuit Religious Encounters." *Religions* 9: 349.

Cayton, Horace R. and Anne O. Lively. 1955. *The Chinese in the United States and the Chinese Christian Church*. New York: Bureau of Research and Survey, National Council of the Churches of Christ in the United States.

Chan, Sucheng. 1991. "The Exclusion of Chinese Women, 1870–1943." Pp. 94–146 in *Entry Denied: Exclusion and (the Chinese Community in America 1882) the Chinese Community in America, 1882–1943*, edited by Sucheng Chan. Philadelphia: Temple University Press.

Li, Minghuan. 1999. "'To Get Rich Quickly in Europe!': Reflections on Migration Motivation in Europe." Pp. 181–198 in *Internal and International Migration: Chinese Perspectives*, edited by Frank N. Pieke, and Hein Mallee. Richmond: Curzon.

Madsen, Richard. 2017. "Multiple Sinicizations of Multiple Christianities." Pp. 319–326 in *Sinicizing Christianity*, edited by Zheng Yangwen. Leiden, Netherlands and Boston, MA, USA: Brill.

Nagata, Judith. 2005. "Christianity Among Transnational Chinese: Religious Versus (Sub)ethnic Affiliation." *International Migration* 43: 99–130.

Nyíri, Pál. 2003. "Moving Targets: Chinese Christian Proselytising among Transnational Migrants from the People's Republic of China." *European Journal of East Asian Studies* 2(2): 263–301.

Soothill, William E. 1907. *A Mission in China*. Edinburgh: Oliphant, Anderson & Ferrier.

Warner, R. Stephen. 1993. "Work in Progress toward a New Paradigm for the Sociological Study of Religion in the United States." *American Journal of Sociology* 98: 1044–93.

Yang, Fenggang. 1999. *Chinese Christians in America: Conversion, Assimilation, and Adhesive Identities*. University Park: Penn State University Press.

Yang, Fenggang, and Joseph Tamney. 2006. "Exploring Mass Conversion to Christianity among the Chinese: An Introduction." *Sociology of Religion: A Quarterly Review* 67: 125–29.

Yang, Fenggang and Helen Rose Ebaugh. 2001. "Religion and Ethnicity among New Immigrants: The Impact of Majority/Minority Status in Home and Host Countries." *Journal for the Scientific Study of Religion* 40(3): 367–378.

CHAPTER 3

A Bridge between the Spiritual and the Worldly
The Puhuasi Buddhist Temple in Prato (Italy)

Fabio Berti and Valentina Pedone

1   Introduction

In less than thirty years Prato, an Italian city close to Florence, has become the European city with the highest percentage of people of Chinese origin among the resident population as well as of Chinese-run enterprises. In big European metropolises, such as London and Paris, the number of Chinese immigrants is larger than Prato's; however, in no other middle-level European city (Prato has over 190,000 inhabitants), do the Chinese who reside legally represent over 11% of the total population and are involved in as concentrated a manner in business activities (Italian Ministry of work 2017). As we will see shortly, a number of conditions have led to this record, some connected to the origin of this migratory phenomenon (the southeastern part of Zhejiang Chinese province), others related to the specificities of the Italian Prato itself. Although this migration has been changing constantly in line with local and global changes, nonetheless the flow has been nonstop for over three decades, and shows no signs of ceasing.

A social process of this dimension could not but attract the attention of the host society: the city of Prato has been involved for many years now in a heated debate between those who see the Chinese presence as a curse for the city and those who focus on the opportunities offered by immigration.

Chinese immigration to Prato has some peculiarities that distinguish it from other local immigration flows, in particular the occupational rate of Chinese immigrants (much higher than average), as well as their business acumen and, more in general, their high rate of economic success.[1] These peculiarities have often been used publicly to accuse Chinese immigrants of excessive materialism and a complete lack of interest in integrating into the local social and cultural context.

---

1 For a detailed account on the changing landscape caused by the combination of global and local economic dynamics in Prato, and the role in such process played by Chinese migration, refer to Ceccagno (2017).

Nonetheless, contrary to the more stereotyped representations that have circulated over time, Prato's Chinese immigrants are not just tireless workers that have made self-exploitation their lifestyle; in the many years of their settlement in the city, they have also expressed values that are different from economic ones, such as the need for many to practice their religion. There are many different religious organizations in Prato formed entirely by Chinese immigrants, reflecting the numerous cultural subdivisions within the Chinese community. Although academic literature has broadly treated the topic, most existing scholarship on the Chinese community in Prato has focussed solely on entrepreneurship, to the exclusion of other such social and cultural activities. By touching on some of these other aspects, the present paper attempts to partially fill that void.

Among the many Chinese religious organizations in Prato, the Puhuasi Buddhist temple (henceforth Puhuasi) is one of the most organized and active. It is worth trying to understand what the Puhuasi represents and what social "function" it fulfills, within both the city and the Chinese community. The paper first provides a brief description of the main characteristics of the Chinese immigration to Prato, referring the reader to the vast literature on the subject for further analysis; then it retraces the path that led to the inauguration of the Puhuasi in 2009, highlighting how it has been integrated in the urban context; lastly, it addresses the roles played by the Puhuasi in the lives of its Chinese congregation. This last part will be primarily based on in-depth interviews with 15 casually selected Chinese frequenters of the temple in the summer of 2015.[2]

2   Chinese Population in Prato

Right after World War II, the city of Prato received numerous influxes of immigration that contributed to developing its so-called "industrial district" (Becattini, 2000): at first these were local migrations, coinciding with the breakdown of Tuscany's sharecropping system, then they were migrations from Southern Italy, especially Campania, Apulia and Sicily, and lastly, beginning in the 1980s they were foreign migrations (Bracci, 2016; Cardini, 2004). In 1951, Prato was a city of 77,000 inhabitants, while today (end of 2017) it has over 193,000

---

2 These were semi-structured interviews conducted in Chinese with a sample of 15 Chinese followers of the Temple within the framework of the state-funded research project (Prin) *Migrazioni, legami familiari e appartenenze religiose: interrelazioni, negoziazioni e confini* (scientific coordinator: Cristina Papa, University of Perugia).

inhabitants, of which 38,199 (20%) are foreigners, thus becoming the Italian city with the highest proportion of foreign residents.[3]

The very peculiarity of the Prato experience is nonetheless that over half of the foreigners are Chinese, who, at the end of 2017, numbered 20,695, that is about 11% of the population.[4] Not only does present-day Chinese immigration into Europe present characteristics and dynamics that differ from those of other groups of immigrants (Ma Mung, 2004), but the ways in which Chinese migrants settle in different areas can also differ, as is the case of several Italian cities with an established Chinese population (Barberis, 2011). The Chinese in Prato were attracted by a local context in which certain productive infrastructures already existed, as well as logistics and an industrial culture, all capable of satisfying their migratory project, which was entirely oriented to entrepreneurship (Ceccagno, 2017).

Most of Prato's Chinese immigrants come from the city of Wenzhou and its outskirts, along the southeast coast of Zhejiang Province, following the policy of reform and opening promoted by Deng Xiaoping from the end of the 1970s. It has been from the start mainly an economic migration facilitated by the strikingly similar traits between the productive contexts of the sending and the receiving areas. The so-called "Wenzhou model" presents analogies with the local Italian model that characterizes Prato,[5] since both systems feature small family-run businesses specialized in a single stage or component of the final product typical of the local industry.[6] By taking advantage of informal personal loans granted by friends and relatives, many "enterprise-families" of Wenzhou migrated not only across China, but also to Europe and North America, where they were able to rapidly build a high number of specialized markets, just as they did in Prato, where the system of informal loans made it possible to develop all the sectors of the so-called "pronto-moda" or fast-fashion model (Ceccagno, 2017; Krauze, 2018).

---

3   For a focus on data on migrants in Prato, please refer to Prato's office of statistics (http://statistica.comune.prato.it).
4   Although we do not have reliable updated data, to have an image of the actual Chinese presence in Prato, one should add to the regular residents the many naturalized citizens and the irregulars. An estimate by Irpet, presented at a conference in 2013 (Irpet 2013), stated a maximum of 8,700 irregular Chinese citizens, while, to confirm the conflictual climate that pollutes public discourse in Prato, Pieraccini (2010) spoke of as many as about 30,000 "clandestine migrants".
5   We refer to the industrial district model that grew up in Italy during the '60s–'70s and '80s and that in the following years, while maintaining some similarities with the past, underwent profound transformation (Dei Ottati 2014; 2018).
6   On these aspects please refer to: Shi (2004); Wei, Li, Wang (2007).

From the second half of the 1990s there was a gradual differentiation within the Chinese migration flow: new migrants started to arrive from the province of Fujian and the Dongbei area. Both of these new flows were mostly a consequence of the profound changes that have occurred in the last decades in these areas, notably in the decommissioning of the swamp government-run industries of the Dongbei area, which started in the 1990s, and the relative deprivation of the rural areas of Fujian. These new groups have constituted a sort of "reserve army" (Berti, Valzania, 2017), useful for the needs of the Wenzhou entrepreneurs around Europe (Pieke, Nyiri, Thuno, Ceccagno, 2004).

The process of assimilation of the Chinese migrants into the Prato district economy can be interpreted as a sort of "local delocalization", which, at the beginning, allowed Italian contractors to avoid moving production abroad while also filling in the gap left by the generational turnover inside those same enterprises (Ceccagno, 2003; 2014). When the first Chinese migrants arrived in Prato in the 1990s, the industrial district was in the midst of a crisis due to a series of structural contingencies (namely, increasing international competition with limited resources for internationalizing; the depreciation of the US dollar; scarce investments in research and innovation; the crisis of the family-based productive system; and the spread of new cultural models) that the Chinese presence managed to attenuate, thus postponing the worst effects of the crisis over the years to come. Chinese entrepreneurship gained an increasingly important role in the district economy, both for its size and for the aspects of originality and diversification that can be found within it. Some Chinese migrants managed to get to the top of the entire production chain, moving from the role of contractor for Italian companies to that of final entrepreneur in the fast-fashion apparel industry. At the same time, many of them (including former textile entrepreneurs) started processes of diversification of their own businesses, especially moving towards other third-sector activities, commercial activities or new forms of food catering: in many cases the choice to abandon the pronto moda sector to open a store has been caused by increased economic stability and free time available to migrants, in other words, by a better quality of life. In this sense, it has been said that a new "middle class" has grown up within the Chinese community of Prato (Berti, Pedone, Valzania, 2013).

These few observations are necessary to understand that the Chinese in Prato play an important social and economic role in the city (Irpet, 2013), in close connection with its other social components. By considering the social functions fulfilled by the Puhuasi within Prato's Chinese community, we intend to characterize the experience of this group of immigrants in aspects that hitherto have not been directly treated. The Puhuasi is not at all the only place of worship frequented by Prato's Chinese immigrants, and, more broadly, in

Tuscany there are several other important places of worship connected, directly or indirectly, to migrant communities. As far as the Chinese group is concerned, there are rather influential Catholic and Evangelic Christian churches attended exclusively by Prato's Chinese citizenry (Vicziany, Fladrich, Di Castro, 2015),[7] while, for what concerns other migrant groups, the mosque in Colle Val d'Elsa is a place of worship that has received important media coverage (Berti, 2007).With this in mind, the next paragraphs will outline some of the specificities of the Puhuasi in relation to the local Chinese and non-Chinese population.

3   Chinese Flexible Religiosity and the Forms It Has Taken in Prato

The religiosity of the Chinese is a topic that has always been as interesting as it is controversial, especially after the Maoist experience. Taoism and Buddhism, as China's most important religions up to modern times (Yang Fenggang, 2011), along with Confucianism, represent, in their various forms and influences, the Chinese "common base", which has remained surprisingly constant beneath all the violent changes of history (Granet, 1922). At the end of the 16th century, thanks to the role of the Jesuit Matteo Ricci, Christianity too made its timid appearance in China, but it was only with the European and North American colonial occupation, which took place after the Opium Wars (1839–1860), that it started to attract a substantial number of followers. The establishment of the People's Republic of China under the leadership of the Chinese Communist Party and, especially the Cultural Revolution that shook China from 1966 to 1976, placed a ban on religions, which in some occasions became real persecution (Overmyer, 2009)

Even though there are authoritative opinions contrary to such clear settings (Johnson, 2017), today China is considered the country with the highest percentage of atheist citizens in the world: for example an international Gallup poll of 2012, reported in the Washington Post, stated that 47% of Chinese considered themselves truly atheist (Fisher, Dewey, 2013). It is necessary to specify that those who practice the so-called "Chinese folk religion" hardly consider themselves as belonging to a religion: many Chinese consider the status of "religious" to refer only to those who belong to an established religious institution, especially a Christian one, and simple affiliation to a Buddhist, Taoist

---

7   According to Vicziany, Fladrich and Di Castro (2015), in 2011, Chinese Buddhists in Prato were about one hundred, that is one third of Chinese Christians (both Catholic and Evangelic Christians) in Prato at the same time.

or Confucian temple is not always considered equivalent to "having a religion" (MacInnis, 1994; Yang, 2006;).

The historical basis for this situation of ostensible atheism lies in Article 5 of the Common Program adopted by the First Political Advisory Conference of the Chinese People (1949), and later on by the various subsequent editions of the Constitution allowing religious freedom for the Chinese people: Communist China developed the conviction that religion was a temporary phenomenon, destined to dwindle away spontaneously with the passing of the pre-revolutionary social contradictions. This initial indifference of the Communist government to religion gradually changed toward the end of the 1950s,[8] and later the Cultural Revolution categorically discouraged any form of religious freedom, forbidding religious people to wear monastic garb (Bianchi, 2015). A new historical phase started in China in the 1980s, when Document 19 of the Communist Party found the Cultural Revolution's repressive measures against religion counterproductive and so opened the way to tolerance, as long as the official religious institutions (Buddhism, Daoism, Islam, Catholicism and Protestantism) remained under State control.

From this point on there was a blossoming of attention towards religions that led to a new jump in the number of believers, although the topic is still very controversial. A survey carried out in some Chinese urban contexts between 1995 and 2005 (Yao, 2007) stated that only 5.5% of those interviewed considered themselves religious, while 51.8% considered themselves "not religious". At the same time, though, 23.1% of those interviewed stated that they regularly "prayed or worshipped" Buddha; 23.8% that they periodically made offerings to their ancestors, 27-1% that they adhered to *feng shui* principles; and 38.5% that they used divination to pinpoint auspicious dates. Overall, among many Chinese, the line between religious belief and superstition, as is also clear in the interviews done in Prato, seems quite fine. In 2010 the Beijing Academy of Social Science published new results of a similar survey revealing that today only 15% of the Chinese population consider themselves not religious, while 85% state that they practice some sort of religion (Qiu, Jin, 2010), definitely confuting the government's claim of total atheism in China.

The religious affiliation of the Chinese immigrants cannot but reflect, at least partially, the dynamics that characterize mainland China. Although there are no available data on the religious practices of the Chinese in Prato, a survey carried out on a sample in Turin seems to confirm behaviors only apparently in

---

8 Between the 1950s and the 1970s Buddhist and Taoist places of worship decreased considerably, from 60,000 to about 8,000 (Bianchi 2015).

contradiction, fluctuating between forms of pure indifference toward religion to approaches that are more ambiguous. It suffices that among the respondents who did not identify with any religion, 29% stated that they practice some form of divination. In any case, according to this study, Buddhism appears to be the major religion among Chinese immigrants (59% of those interviewed in Turin stated that they do not belong to any religion, while 31.6% stated they were Buddhists) (Zoccatelli, 2009).

Prato seems to be a special case because, compared to the rest of China, these immigrants from Wenzhou are dominantly Protestant and stand out among international Chinese migration on this specific count, which distinguishes them from other Chinese immigrants (Hunter, Chan, 1993; Cao, 2010). In fact, in Prato, as in many other Italian cities where there is a numerous population from southeast Zhejiang, there is an Evangelic Chinese Church that has been active for years. The religiosity of the Prato Chinese seems to echo the religious revival in China, as demonstrated by the high number of Chinese religious organizations, other than the Puhuasi, located in the city, such as: the Protestant Church 基督教堂 *Jidu jiaotang*; the Overseas Chinese Catholic Church 华人天主堂 *Huaren tianzhu tang*; the True Jesus Church 真耶稣会 *Zhen Yesu hui*; the Christadelphians 弟兄会 *Xiongdi hui*; the Charismatic Church 灵恩派 *Ling'en pai*; the Seventh-day Adventists 安息日会 *Anxiri hui*; the Life Church 生命堂 *Shengming tang*; the Jehovah's Witnesses 耶和华见证会 *Yehehua jianzheng hui* and the Falun Gong 法轮功.[9] Among these, the Puhuasi, being the only Chinese place of worship open also to non Chinese followers, it is also the one that Prato non Chinese inhabitants are most familiar with. The Puhuasi is also the Chinese place of worship that is considered by outsiders as the most typically "Chinese", since Buddhism is mostly perceived as a non-European, specifically Asian religion. This Temple, in addition to its followers and active practitioners, also has the aim of representing an entire "community", real or presumed, in the same way that mosques do for the Islamic religion, which in the eye of public opinion represents all immigration from North Africa.

4 The "Social" Function of the Puhuasi

Run by the Buddhist Association of the Chinese community,[10] the Puhuasi Temple of Prato was inaugurated in 2009 after two years under construction, and in

---

9   We thank Prof. Zhou Yongming (University of Wisconsin-Madison) for this list of Chinese religious institutions in Prato that he provided to Valentina Pedone in 2015.

10 This association was already active in Prato in 2000, when it was founded also to distinguish its members from those of another association, the Association of the Friendship

November 2017 it underwent an important self funded renovation that enlarged it from 700 to 1,400 square meters, thus enabling it to host several thousand followers from outlying areas. Externally, the architecture of the Temple does not look like a typical Chinese Buddhist Temple, but the interior is rather complex and refined, made up of a series of spaces, some of which are dedicated to "association" activities, while others are directly connected to the Buddhist cult: as Daniele Parbuono (2013: 34) writes: " the social space in question has the form of a temple that is not only a temple, but a series of temples; a series of temples that are not only a series of temples, but that rather aim at becoming a monastery".

In the first years of operation, the Temple could only count on the presence of a single part time monk, shared with a monastery in China, so that the followers mostly self-organized the cult's functioning, since no official "religious guide" was available to lead them. Only on particular occasions could the followers count on having monks sent directly from China[11]; with the renovations, in order to fill the need to have permanent on-site guidance, lodgings for the monks have also been added. The day of the inauguration, 80 monks who had come straight from China were invited, thus showing how determined the congregation was to transform the Temple into a monastery.[12]

According to a report issued on November 24th 2017 by Ansa (the most important information agency in Italy), the Chinese religious community of Prato has invested 2 million euros from 2009 to date on renovating the Temple, confirming the strength of their communal network, stronger than other immigrant networks, locally but also nationwide. Contrary to other religious organizations formed by Chinese immigrants or by immigrants of other ethnicities, the organization that manages the Puhuasi has proved over the years its ability to reach people willing to fund a project that seeks visibility not only within the community itself, but also outside it.

The commitment and, in some respects, the strength of the Buddhist Association of the Chinese community emerge from the massive voluntary activity it carries on, an activity symptomatic of the Temple's desire to be an active agent for integrating Chinese residents in the Prato society, its attempt

---

of the Chinese of Prato, (Associazione d'Amicizia dei cinesi di Prato), started up in 1998, with the primary goal of teaching Chinese to immigrant children.

11 On the disputes among different Buddhist schools, lineages and affiliations that in some cases have come into conflict in Prato in the past years, on the types of ceremonies that are held at the temple and, more in general, on the evolution of the religious activities, please refer to Bianchi (2020).

12 To date, the temple has nor institutional or economical help from the PRC government. For an account on the fluctuating relation between the Puhuasi and the Chinese institutions, please refer to Bianchi (2020).

to provide a different image from the most negative stereotypes that tend to represent them as forming closed communities uninterested in relating to Italian society. Since its constitution, the Association has focused on cooperating with many local and nationwide endeavors to help people suffering hardships. For instance, after an earthquake in central Italy[13] they donated 35,000 euros to the Red Cross for purchasing pediatric medical devices. They also paid for an emergency mobile kitchen and donated 25,000 euros more to the Maternity and Infancy Association of Prato. In 2012, 450 wool sweaters produced at Chinese pronto moda factories were donated to the inmates of the local prison. Aid was also provided for the victims of a boat disaster that occurred in Italy in 2012[14] and for another earthquake in central Italy in 2012.[15] Even more symbolic are the donations that from 2015 the Buddhist Association of Prato has been making to the Solidarity Emporium,[16] during the Buddha festivity. In 2017 over 800 liters of olive oil and 350 kilos of rice were collected among the followers of the Temple and destined to the approximately 1000 families in economic straits (of which only 10 that had access to the Emporium were Chinese).

Even the place chosen for the Puhuasi is indicative of the clear desire of the Chinese Buddhists in Prato to gain visibility and recognition by the whole city and not to be relegated within the Chinese community. The Temple is not located within Prato's so-called Chinatown, a neighborhood where the Chinese represent over half of the population and thus is very recognizable by the whole city population. The Puhuasi is located outside this neighborhood, near the city's historic center, in Piazza del Mercato Nuovo, a square where an open market is periodically held. According to Parbuono (2016: 185) "the site for the Temple was a strategic political choice: near the Chinese but not inside, near the Italians, but not inside". In this sense it is even more interesting to reconstruct the path followed over the years by the Chinese New Year's celebration: the first few years that this occasion was publicly celebrated, the dragon dance and parade was not organized by Chinatown and the industrial area. Sometimes another event would be organized in a different area outside the city where recently some especially wealthy Chinese families have moved. Then, beginning with the 2015 event, coinciding with the shift in power from a

---

13 The earthquake that hit the city of L'Aquila in 2009.
14 The Costa Concordia disaster.
15 The earthquake that hit the Emilia Romagna region in 2012.
16 Emporio della solidarietà (the Solidarity Emporium) in Prato is a place for the free distribution of basic staples, especially food, to families that are in economic difficulty and are flagged by the municipality social services and by volunteer associations that deal with poverty.

right-wing party administration that did everything in its power to contain the Chinese presence, to a left-wing party administration, the dragons and lions were able to do their dance in front of the City Hall.[17] Hence, thanks to the Puhuasi and the activities of its Association, not only Buddhists, but the entire Chinese community managed to gain space in the public sphere, so that the Temple today has become a sort of exclusive domain, where the Sino-Pratese stakeholders display their idea of a possible coexistence (Parbuono 2016). There is no such engagement with the non-Chinese inhabitants of Prato on behalf of any of the many other Chinese religious entities active in the city.

While the Puhuasi seems to actively work for a deeper acceptance of the local Chinese, on the contrary, the promotion of the Buddhist religion among the Italian inhabitants does not seem to be an important objective. While there is an actual involvement by Italians in some of the practices offered by the Temple, most of the activities that are organized for them at the temple (lectures on Chinese Buddhism and meditation, cooking classes, calligraphy and painting exhibitions, conferences on tea ceremony, and so on) seem rather addressed to the general promotion and integration of the local Chinese community. From a survey done by Bianchi (2019), what clearly emerges is that these activities are not aimed at proposing a new faith to the non-Chinese, but to display the values and cultural aspects of Chinese civilization that are considered too obscure or underappreciated in Italy. The target public of the Puhuasi for religious matters remains the Chinese population that has settled in Italy.

5   Who Attends the Puhuasi and Why

Most of the followers of the Puhuasi are women. This trend resembles a more general predominance of women over men in attending places of worship (Palmisano, Giorgi, 2016), also reflected in the Italian Catholic context, where churches are mainly attended by women.[18]

We interviewed a sample of 15 followers (13 women and 2 men) throughout July and August 2015. The interviews were conducted in Chinese inside various service rooms of the temple, after gaining permission from the director of the Puhuasi. These conditions were purposely sought for, so that the interviewees

---

17 Nevertheless, in "right wing" party opinion, Chinese citizens are always conceptualized as a whole; they are considered as the scapegoat of the local crisis and victims of the fantasy (which never existed) of a "Paradise Lost" of the city of Prato, with its mythical and nostalgic memories (Bracci, 2013).

18 On this topic please refer to the data of Istat's 2011 census.

could feel protected and had complete linguistic control over their answers. The respondents linked the aforementioned lack of gender balance to a combination of gender stereotypes and workplace dynamics.

> At the temple there are more women. Because women go to pray, while men haven't understood this aspect yet. Women do housework, womanly things: *famiglia, lavare, bambini* (tr. family, washing, children) … men mostly work and make money. Italy is the same, it's very common. So there are more women studying Buddhism, going to ceremonies, going to pray, while men go to make money.
> man, 40 years old

> Women today are better people. Look, here it's all women. In China as well, men play cards, drink, go to clubs.
> woman, 50 years old

The scarce male presence at the temple is also attributed to a different way for men and women to practice their religiosity: in the words of the people interviewed, the men are more skeptical, rational, practical, and for this reason they practice their religiosity in a manner that does not interfere with their ambitions and pragmatism.

> In my opinion there are more women believing in Buddhism, there are also more women attending the temple. Maybe because they are more prone to probe their own sense of emptiness, they have more spiritual needs. Males are busy, maybe they do not need these things. Yet I believe that in the deep knowledge of the Buddhist doctrine there are more male intellectuals, experts with higher education. Women, usually, those of advanced age, go to the temple instead. For instance they burn incense and ask for peace, tranquility and health.
> woman, 30 years old

> Males' and females' faith should be sought in their hearts,[19] it does not show outside. Many women are more active, many men prefer to stay home. Active in the sense that they come to the temple to pray. Males only believe in their hearts, do not love to come to the temple.
> woman, 45 years old

---

19   In Chinese thought, heart 心 *xin* is a concept that has a rather complex meaning. Since it does not only refer to the emotional sphere, it is often translated in English as heart-mind.

In the words of the female interviewees, attending a Buddhist temple is often considered in Chinese general public opinion as something typical of superstitious, uneducated and humble people. One can infer a largely shared narrative (although contested by the same female interviewees) that links these characteristics to a feminine outlook. Nonetheless, there is also a positive discourse, as we will see, that depicts women as more caring and responsible, an inclination that demonstrated by their commitment to pray for the family. Thus women, even though they do not feel entirely supported in this effort, accept the task of attending the Temple for the sake of benefitting their entire family.

> Women have patience to come here to pray. For instance, my husband is a believer as well, but in the family only one person can afford to go out to pray. However, if that person is me, I am sure that my husband will be in good health since I will do my prayers for him, that's it.
> woman, 55 years old

It appears that there is a contrast between men who are drained by their jobs and women who take on the responsibility for the spiritual well-being of their families by physically going to pray for them, as if it were a schematic division of duties. However, some of the female interviewees feel unhappy about this state of affairs, and suggest that the lack of male attendance at the Temple could be related to masculine superficiality or even fragility.

> It's about reputation (laughs). It's the patriarchal mentality. They are afraid to be laughed at. There was a time in China, that religions ... Maoist Communism destroyed these beliefs at the time [...] Whoever was born in the last 50 years actually never learned what Buddhism was. This is why in recent times people think that praying is something to be very ashamed of. My female acquaintances don't care at all about this reputation.
> woman, 50 years old

The visible male absence at the Temple seems to be perceived by some of the followers as an escape from family duties. As we will argue, the Wenzhou family enterprise officializes this absence by transferring the responsibility for prayers to some of its members, who become especially invested with this task, i.e. women and older people.

The age difference between the Temple attendants is as evident as the gender one, with a majority of older followers, as is also the case for other faiths. This is related by the respondents to a greater availability of spare time, an argument not evoked for the gender difference, since most Wenzhou migrant women in Italy work as much as the men.

> Usually there are more older people, they have more time. Young people work, for the most part they work a lot, they do not have time.
> woman, 45 years old

The wish to escape solitude is also considered a factor encouraging older people to attend the Temple. The Puhuasi can thus serve as a place of socialization for older Chinese immigrants.

> Why are there all these older people at the temple? Because they are all about 70 years old, they are already in their retirement age. They have children here, back home there is nobody looking after them, maybe they lost their wives, they have been left alone [...] if a person in their 70s or 80s has all relatives who go to work, then they feel sad and lonely. There are many elderly people here.
> man, 48 years old

On this topic, it should be remembered that many older people who recently arrived in Italy from China have done so to rejoin their families, and that the reason for such a life change in old age is that the migrant family neither wants nor is able to go back to China (Berti, Pedone, Valzania, 2013). These elderly people can struggle to find a role in their family residing abroad, or better yet, in the diasporic Wenzhou enterprise-family. Their main responsibility in such a structure is to take care of the children when they are not at school and their parents are at work, but even attending the Temple can be a way to contribute to family harmony. As we have already observed for gender difference, it is easy to detect a contrast between male adults, completely lost in the mission of economic emancipation, and the elderly and women, who go to the Temple to burn incense and ask for peace, tranquility, health and even money for the entire family.

> As far as age is concerned, what can I say, those who are at a more advanced age have more spare time. Young people, even when they enter in contact with Buddhism ... are busy, they have their jobs, make money, hence they have little time. There are very young people that after they have finished studying and enter society, they must earn money, there is nothing to do, they have no time anymore.
> woman, about 50 years old

> There are many more old people than young ones, the elderly come here every day to ask for money for their children.
>
> woman, 45 years old

In Italy there is no such thing as a closeknit Chinese community ready to provide mutual help (Ceccagno, Rastrelli, 2008; Berti, Pedone, Valzania, 2013). Rather the competition between families is fierce and individuals end up defending themselves mostly from their fellow countrymen and from solitude. As suggested in the accounts of the respondents, the Wenzhou migration towards Italy implies a rigid organization of the family unit, aimed at rapid economic emancipation, with a strong purpose shared by each family member. According to their competences, possibilities and inclinations, each component of the family contributes to the success of the migratory adventure, and even attending a temple can be a part of this function.

6 Between Faith, Cultural Identity and Material Needs

The Puhuasi covers an important social and identity function because in Prato, as in other places of worship attended by immigrants (Garnett, Hausner, 2015), the religious experience and the sharing of rituals and festivities represent an important point of conjunction between the migrants, their family and their culture of origin. The Temple is perceived as a "controlled space in which the migrant manages to keep together the 'here' and 'there', the 'inside' and the 'outside', the 'self' and the complex context that surrounds them" (Parbuono, 2016: 182); it represents a 'piece' of China in the foreign land, a place of recognition capable of providing safety in a context that at times can even be hostile. Actually, this supposedly genuine Chinese space is in fact transnational, since the fact that it is on Italian soil and that it serves the abovementioned specific purposes connected to the migratory project makes the Temple a place where these migrants may project or preserve a sense of living in China, deriving from context-based conditions. After all, the first advantage of the religious affiliation in immigration has often been that of creating a protected community where immigrants and their families could feel safe from risks (Hirschman, 2004). Different respondents have in fact stressed how they feel unsafe in Prato and how they live in constant fear of being victims of violence or criminality.

> The situation of safety in Prato is terrible, there are many bag snatching episodes, also many robberies, even at home, there are often burglars. It

seems that it is other foreigners, other immigrants who live in Italy. There are also some Chinese, I see many who have been mugged or robbed, there is no safety. This is why many people have changed cities and moved to places that are more peaceful.
    woman, 30 years old

The Temple, from this point of view, can represent a safe space, protected and capable of providing some serenity to those who live in difficult situations, for instance because they are busy with stressful, time-consuming jobs, and so on, or because they live in constant fear of becoming victims of crime.

Some respondents declared they got interested in Buddhism only after their experiences as migrants, which is rather common. After all, as Warner (2000) affirms, migration does not weaken the religious sentiment but, on the contrary, it stresses the need for an ultimate meaning and pushes one to rethink the contents that define his or her self-identity. From this point of view, the re-elaboration of religion, in its personal and collective dimension, represents a real laboratory of change and adaptation.

Before, I was an atheist. There is a saying that goes: if you are born in the New China, you grow up under a red flag (laughs). I graduated from high school in 1986, then I taught in middle school for a few years, while I was teaching I attended college, I studied three years of Chinese literature at the University of Hangzhou. I used to study at home, by myself. I have passed 13 exams, I studied *Chinese literature*, then also pedagogy and psychology. Only in 2007 did I encounter Buddhist thought, I was reading the sutra of the diamond, and after reading that Buddhist classic, I started to believe in Buddhism. I read it on the internet. After that I started believing in Buddhism. Later, I met a master here. Only after I met him did I understand that in Buddhism, the important thing is to attain to *wisdom*. After that, through theory and study, I changed my way of thinking.
    man, about 40 years old

Before, I did not have any faith, I did not believe in anything, I thought that all of it was just superstition. Later on, in the last two years, I've started to get interested, because I got sick.
    woman, 30 years old

Others stressed that after attending the Puhuasi their way of being Buddhist changed. Previously they had practiced their faith in a more "popular" way by considering Buddhism as a kind of a superstition, while now they experience their religion in a deeper way. Actually, the Temple is also a place for studying and analyzing Buddhist doctrine.

> There are many ways of being a Buddhist, before it was like a superstition, only now that I am a Buddhist I understand that. When I got close, it was because I was looking for riches, peace in the family, to make more money, for these reasons I got closer. Because of these silly things. Then, here, they taught me to study Buddhism.
> woman, 45 years old

For some respondents, believing seems almost a strategy; Buddhism for some appears as the perfect faith for an entrepreneurial migratory project such as what is typical of the Wenzhou migration. Various respondents allude several times to the fact that Buddhism is successful, especially in Prato, because it is somehow directly connected to a chance to "become rich". Although Buddhism professes detachment from material desires, in some interviews it is referred to as a source of wealth, because it is seen as professed by wealthy people. Even though most respondents accuse this outlook of being a form of superstition, they also claim that it is a widespread habit to ask for wealth in prayers (for this reason, as already seen, the elderly are sent to pray, so that they contribute to the economic success of the family, according to an idea of family as a team united for a shared goal). Moreover, in this perspective on Buddhism, great importance is given to the concept of "retribution in the same life", according to which, if one does good deeds, s/he will receive good luck in return (this could also play a role in the importance of charity and commitment to civic activities, such as the Emporium of solidarity mentioned before), which seems to be for the interviewees an effective investment also on the spiritual level, to gain better profits. This practical, almost strategic, view on religious practice becomes distinctive of the Wenzhou diasporic group also because it explains how prayer can be directed toward obtaining greater safety against crime and seeking some sort of comfort in a life of constant risks related to business and commercial activities.

> Some people have success and they are Buddhists, so then I got curious and started getting interested in Buddhism. Then, in Buddhism there is an idea of cause and effect with which I agree a lot.
> woman, 30 years old

> I think that those who believe in Buddhism can be a bit wealthier, because it is a matter of retribution, because if they often go to the temple

and do good deeds, if they do good, their virtue grows and so they obtain big a compensation, such as wealth and health.

woman, 50 years old

Sakiamuni Buddha pronounced the words prayers and pain, those who have the more pain want to be free of their pain. For this reason there are people of all social classes here, rich, middle class and poor. But the poor, when the family has more pain inside the heart, then they make a bigger effort to be free of the pain and then they believe and practice with more effort. But the rich are the biggest believers, theirs is a different kind of thought, it is not practice to reach illumination, to awake, to become wise. They want to make more money and so they pray, they pray.

woman, 35 years old

7   Some Conclusions

In a city like Prato, where Chinese immigration has an important role in every sphere, from the economic to the demographic, and for urbanistic and social issues, at ten years since its inauguration, the Temple has consolidated its presence and visibility, playing important roles both in "external" relations and in "internal" relations for the Chinese collectivity of Prato. Among the most important rituals and gatherings carried out by the Puhuasi, shared lunches are especially common: the main such lunches are held on occasion of religious celebrations for "pure land" Buddhism, including spring festival and lanterns festival. Besides lunches, parades, Chinese language courses for children and lectures on sacred texts are also commonly held at the Puhuasi (Parbuono, 2018). Externally, the Puhuasi seems to provide for the lack of other forms of political representation and social recognition of the numerous Chinese in Prato, and internally, it fulfills the same social function as the Catholic Church did for Italian immigrants in the USA, where it represented not only a place of worship, but also a center for socialization, providing an opportunity to assume roles of leadership and civic participation that would not be accessible outside the pale (Ambrosini, 2007). It must be borne in mind that, although numerous Chinese in Prato belong to other religious organizations, especially to a very organized and developed transnational network of Chinese protestant churches, the Puhuasi seems to be the only such association that seeks interaction and visibility outside the Chinese group, and, to some extent, in the name of the Chinese group.

Buddhist worship in the case of Prato, contrary to other "immigrant" religions, ends up facilitating relations with the native population of Prato. It is one thing to see the Chinese only as business-minded people, intent exclusively on enriching themselves at all costs, with little or no respect for migrant and safety regulations (as they have often been depicted in the local news media (Zhang, 2019)), and it is another thing is to see Chinese immigrants as Buddhists, since Buddhism is a religion that has always been perceived in Italy as professing peace and reciprocal respect. As concerns public opinion, Buddhism is not perceived in the same potentially menacing way as Islam is, and hence the Temple is not comparable to a Mosque (Cesari, 2005). In this sense, the Temple, with its activities and festivals, its opening towards the institutions and the local population, enhances the likelihood of social recognition and integration for all the local Chinese, even the non-Buddhists, since it works purposefully as an instrument of cultural promotion of Chinese culture to non-Chinese.

On the "inside", on the other hand, the non-strictly spiritual functions of the Temple are perfectly integrated with the migration projects of many Chinese who live in Prato. Even though many Chinese immigrants in past years have given up on the idea of getting rich at all costs, which was the initial motivation for their migration adventure, and preferred to look for a better quality of life in Prato (Berti, Pedone, Valzania, 2013), the Buddhist faith is still often used to evoke those material benefits that are important for the Chinese migration project. Besides this kind of utilitarian consumption, the Temple also provides occasions for Chinese immigrants to organize their activities, and to be able to express their diasporic cultural identity, just as the Catholic immigrants did inside the churches in the USA at the beginning of the 20th century (Hirschman, 2004).

References

Ambrosini M. (2007), *Gli immigrati e la religione: fattore d'integrazione o alterità irriducibile?*, in "Studi Emigrazione/Migration Studies", XLIC, 165.

Baldassar L., Johanson G., McAuliffe N. and Bressan M. (eds) (20159), *Chinese Migration to Europe: Prato, Italy and Beyond*, Palgrave Mcmillan, London.

Barberis E. (2011), *Imprenditori cinesi in Italia. Fra kinship networks e legami territoriali*, in "Mondi Migranti", 2.

Becattini G. (2000), *Il bruco e la farfalla. Prato nel mondo che cambia (1954–1993)*, Le Monnier, Firenze.

Berti F. (2007), *Paura, ignoranza, razzismo: quando il dialogo diventa un confronto tra sordi. Considerazioni a partire dal caso della "moschea" di Colle di Val d'Elsa*, in R. De Vita, F. Berti, L. Nasi (a cura di), *Ugualmente diversi. Culture, religioni, diritti*, FrancoAngeli, Milano.

Berti F., Pedone V., Valzania A. (a cura di)(2013), *Vendere e comprare: Processi di mobilità sociale dei cinesi di Prato*, Pacini Editore, Pisa.

Berti F., Valzania A. (2017), *Marx, Weber e i cinesi di Prato. Note sui processi di integrazione in un contest locale*, in "Sociologia", 3.

Bianchi E. (2014), *Alcune riflessione sugli immigrati cinesi e il loro rapporto con il Buddismo*, in C. Barbarella (a cura di), *Identità e pluralità nel dialogo interreligioso*, AliseiCoop Pubblicazioni, Perugia.

Bianchi E. (2015), *La Cina che crede, un revival dall'alto*, in www.cinaforum.it.

Bianchi E. (2020), *The Puhuasi 普華寺: Longing for Trustworthiness and Recognition. Recent Transformations in the Religious Identity and Institutional Affiliation of the Chinese Buddhist Temple in Prato*, in "Journal of Chinese Buddhist Studies", 33.

Bracci F. (2013), *The 'Chinese Deviant': Building the Perfect Enemy in a Local Arena*, in L. Baldassar, G. Johanson, N. McAuliffe, M. Bressan (eds), *Chinese Migration to Europe: Prato, Italy and Beyond*, Palgrave Macmillan, London.

Bracci F. (2016), *Oltre il distretto. Prato e l'immigrazione cinese*, Aracne, Roma.

Cao N. (2010), *Constructing China's Jerusalem: Christians, Power and Place in the City of Wenzhou*, Stanford University Press, Stanford.

Cardini F. (2004), *Breve storia di Prato*, Pacini Editore, Pisa.

Ceccagno A. (2003), *New Chinese Migrants in Italy*, in "International Migration", 41.

Ceccagno A. (2012), *The hidden crisis: the Prato industrial district and the once thriving Chinese garment industry*, in "Revue europenne des migrations internationals", 24.

Ceccagno A. (2014), *The Mobile Emplacement: Chinese Migrants in Italian industrial Districts*, in "Journal of Ethnic and Migration Studies", 1.

Ceccagno A. (2017), *City Making and Global Labor Regimes: Chinese Immigrants and Italy's Fast Fashion Industry*, Palgrave Mcmillan, London.

Ceccagno A., Rastrelli R. (a cura di)(2008), *Ombre cinesi? Dinamiche migratorie della diaspora cinese in Italia*, FrancoAngeli, Milano.

Cesari J. (2005), *Mosque conflicts in European cities. Introduction*, in "Journal of Ethnic and Migration Studies", 31, 6.

Dei Ottati G. (2014), *A transnational fast fashion industrial district: an analysis of the Chinese businesses in Prato*, in "Cambridge Journal of Economics", 38, 5.

Dei Ottati G. (2018), *Marshallian Industrial Districts in Italy: the end of a model or adaptation to the global economy?*, in "Cambridge Journal of Economics", 42, 2.

Fisher M., Dewey C. (2013), *A surprising map of where the world's atheists live*, in "The Wishngton Post", 23 maggio.

Garnett J., Hausner S.L., (eds)(2015), *Religion in Diaspora Cultures of Citizenship*, Palgrave Mcmillan, London.

Granet M. (1922), *La religion des Chinois*, Albin Michel, Paris.

Hirschman C. (2004), *The role of religion in the origin and adaptation of immigrant groups in the United States*, in "International Migration Review", 38, 3.

Hunter A., Kwong Chan K. (1993), *Protestantism in Contemporary China*, Cambridge University Press, Cambridge.

Irpet (2013), *Prato: il ruolo economico della comunità cinese*, Irpet, Firenze.

Istat (2015), *Appartenenza e pratica religiosa tra i cittadini stranieri*, Statistiche report Istat, Roma.

Johnson I. (2017), *The Soul of China. The return of religion after Mao*, Pantheon, New York.

Krause E. (2018), *Tight Knit: Global Families and the Social Life of Fast Fashion*, University of Chicago Press, Chicago.

Lombardi S. (2009), *The Wenzhou Model of Development through the Lenses of Industrial Districts*, in G. Johanson, R. Smith and R. French (eds), *Living Outside the Wall. The Chinese in Prato*, Cambridge Scholars Publishing, Cambridge.

Ma Mung E. (2004), Dispersal as a Resource, in "Diaspora: A Journal of Transnational Studies", 13, 2..

MacInnis D.E. (1994), *Religion in China Today. Policy and Practice*, Orbis Books, Maryknoll (New York).

Ministero del Lavoro (2017), *La comunità cinese in Italia. Rapporto annuale sulla presenza dei migrant*, in https://www.lavoro.gov.it/documenti-e-norme/studi-e-statistiche/Documents/Rapporti%20annuali%20sulle%20comunit%C3%A0%20migranti%20in%20Italia%20-%20anno%202017/Cina-Report-2017.pdf.

Overmyer D.L. (2009), *Local Religion in North China in the Twentieth Century the Structure and Organization of Community Rituals and Beliefs*, Brill, Leiden, Boston.

Palmisano S., Giorgi A. (2016), *D come Donne, D come Dio*, Mimesis, Milano.

Parbuono D. (2013), *L'Umbria guarda "ancora" la Cina. Tangible e intangible: rapporti universitari e prospettive di ricerca*, in E. Bianchi, D. Parbuono (eds), *L'Umbria guarda la Cina*, Morlacchi, Perugia.

Parbuono D. (2015), *Da Prato a Wenzhou: i pellegrinaggi dei migranti cinesi*, in F. Giacalone (a cura di), *Pellegrinaggi e itinerari turistico-religiosi in Europa. Identità locali e dinamiche transnazionali*, Morlacchi, Perugia,.

Parbuono D. (2016), *Il centro del centro. Il Tempio buddhista e il capodanno cinese nello spazio urbano di Prato*, in "Anuac", 5, 1.

Parbuono D. (2018), *Chinese Migrations and Pilgrimages around Prato (Italy) and Wenzhou (China)*, in F. Giacalone, K. Griffin (eds), *Local identities and Transnational Cults within Europe*, Cabi, Oxfordshire/Boston.

Pieke F., Nyiri P., Thuno M., Ceccagno A. (2004), *Transnational Chinese. Fujianese Migrants in Europe*, University Press, Stanford.

Pieraccini (2010), *L'assedio cinese: il distretto senza regole degli abiti low cost di Prato*, 2a ed. aggiornata, Gruppo 24 ore, Milano.

Qiu Y., Jin Z. (2010), *Annual Report on Chinese Religions* (series: *Blue Book of Religions*), Social Sciences Academic Press, Beijing.

Shi J. (2004), *Analysis of Historical System of the Wenzhou Model*, in "The Chinese Economy", 37.

Vicziany M., Fladrich A.M., Di Castro A.A. (2015), *Religion and the Lives of the Overseas Chinese: What Explains the "Great Silence" of Prato?*, in L. Baldassar, G. Johanson, N. McAuliffe, M. Bressan (eds), *Chinese Migration to Europe: Prato, Italy and Beyond*, Palgrave Macmillan, London.

Warner R.S. (2000), *Religion and New (Post-1965) Immigrants: Some Principles Drawn from Field Research*, in "American Studies", 41, 2/3.

Wei Y., Li W., Wang C. (2007), *Restructuring Industrial Districts, Scaling up Regional Development: A study of Wenzhou Model – China*, in "Economic Geography", 83.

Yang Fenggang (2011), *Religion in China*, Oxford University Press, Oxford.

Yang Fenggang (2006), *The red, black, and grey markets of religion in China*, in "Sociological Quarterly" 47.

Yao Xinzhong (2007), *Religious Belief and Practice in Urban China 1995–2005*, in "Journal of Contemporary Religion", 22, 2.

Zhang Gaoheng (2019), *Migration and the Media: Debating Chinese Migration to Italy, 1992-2012*, Toronto University Press, Toronto.

Zoccatelli P.L. (2009), *Religione e spiritualità tra gli immigrati cinesi a Torino*, paper presented at "The 2009 Cesnur Conference", Salt Lake City, Utah, June 11–13, 2009 (http://www.cesnur.org/2009/slc_zoccatelli_ita.htm).

CHAPTER 4

Exploring Chinese Catholicism in the Italian Peninsula

A Sociological Study of the Chinese Catholic Community in Italy

Marco Guglielmi

1   Introduction

Over the last two decades important changes have occurred in the sociocultural fabric of the Italian peninsula. Although the country remains characterised by the cultural and religious hegemony of the Catholic Church, recent trends and phenomena shaped the Italian religious landscape (Garelli, Guizzardi, Pace 2003; Pace 2011, 2013). Foremost, these changes have been stimulated by the flow of immigrants, especially from the 1990s onwards and in the more recent phases of European integration. They have promoted religious diversification and a pluralisation of Christianity in the Italian peninsula (with regard to the Veneto region, Guglielmi 2020), which would appear to reflect also some of the transnational trajectories of Catholicism at the global level (Pasura, Erdal 2016).

The Chinese Catholic communities studied in this article became established in the period coinciding with these transformations in the Italian religious landscape and in the Catholic world. The 'Chinese Catholic Community in Italy' has in fact developed over the last few decades thanks to the consistent growth of the Chinese diaspora in western countries and at the same time on account of the expansion of Christianity in various territories in the Chinese homeland. It is an unexplored topic of study, and is currently subject only to initial sociological researches (Guglielmi 2018). It would appear that the basis of such a lack of research may be identified in social-scientific literature on the Chinese Catholic diasporas in western countries. Although there is no lack of sociological literature on Chinese Christianity forming part of the Protestant world in North America (among the most important studies, Yang 1999; Yang, Tamney 2006; Cao 2005), it would appear that in fact little attention has been paid to Chinese Catholicism in the United States and in general to the entire experience of Chinese Christianity in the Old Continent. With respect to the case of Italy the scant attention dedicated to the religious life of a national group of immigrants so widespread in Italy denotes quite an unusual situation

(Zoccatelli 2010; Vicziany, Fladrich, Di Castro 2015; Palombaro 2017; Cao, Giordan, Pace 2018).

This study forms part of the more general path of research that explores the topic of Chinese Catholicism. Social scientists have extensively investigated the Catholic Church in China (from the historical point of view, Bays 2011; Chu 2012; and from a sociological perspective, Madsen 1998; Chan 2012), emphasizing the main nuances of this religious tradition in the 'Middle Kingdom', and the specificities of its establishment within Chinese society. On the other hand, at the beginning of the twenty-first century, we may state that the Christian faith has become a fully indigenous religion in China through a 'sinicisation' of Christianity (Cao 2019). Considering this backdrop, our study forms part of the research that examines the diasporas of Chinese Catholicism in western countries.

The first section of this work presents a 'mapping' of the Chinese Catholic communities scattered throughout the Italian peninsula, and reconstructs from the historical point of view their recent development in Italy. The purpose of the second section is to offer an overview of some basic traits of the Chinese Catholic clerics, religious brethren, and faithful in Italy. Furthermore, we seek to offer some indications of the religious activity occurring within these communities of immigrants (such as the liturgies, sacraments, and conversions). In the third section, we deal with the main patterns of settlement of the Chinese Catholic communities in the Italian context, attempting to define their hybridisation with the host society. Finally, in the last section (4) we dwell on the impact that the transnational character of migration flows and transnational religious ties may have on the rooting of Chinese Catholic communities in Italy. In particular, we examine the 'World Day of Prayer for the Church in China' established by the Vatican as a transnational religious event.

The data and estimates presented in the research were collected through a collaboration with the Pastoral Migrant Office of the Catholic Church of northeastern Italy, and with some religious leaders of the 'Chinese Catholic Community in Italy'. Moreover, qualitative data was collected through in-depth interviews (5 with Chinese Catholic priests serving in Italy and 5 with Italian priests engaged in the pastoral care of Chinese immigrants) and ethnographic observations within a Chinese Catholic community in the Veneto Region in the period 2017–2019.

2   The Spread of Chinese Catholic Communities in the Italian Peninsula

Chinese migrations to Italy began in the early decades of the twentieth century, and for the most part originated in the Zhejiang region in the south-east area of the country. A profound understanding of these migrations would require an analysis of the variation of historical and political conditions that have influenced their main dynamics over time (Benton, Pieke 1998; Ceccagno, Rastrelli 2008). We would not be able to examine such variations in this study, but we would like to point out that they have influenced the progressive changes in Chinese migratory flows towards the various Italian regions in both quantitative and qualitative terms in the twentieth century.

The first immigration of Chinese citizens to Italy dates back to the First World War. However, the constitution of what may be considered as a real first community occurred in Milan in the 1930s, following the arrival of Chinese migrants who had come to the city from other European countries such as France and Belgium. Subsequently, with the establishment of the People's Republic in 1949, China closed its borders and curbed the international mobility of its citizens, restricting the development of migratory flows abroad. The Chinese migration phenomenon did not resume in a vigorous manner until the period of economic reforms implemented in China in the late 1970s. These reforms also led to a re-establishment of relations with the Chinese communities that had remained abroad.

In this respect, scholars believe that the death of Mao Zedong (1893–1976) may be identified as the main turning point between the initial phase of migration that was actually rather contained and opposed by the Chinese State and a second phase of migration which, on the contrary, was quantitatively sustained and encouraged by the Chinese State. In particular, this second phase began as Deng Xiaoping (1904–1997) became the leader of the Chinese government in 1978.[1] In this new scenario, Europe soon became one of the main destinations for Chinese migrants and in the second half of the 1980s Italy also began to record a significant growth in the number of immigrants arriving from China.

In 1996 the Chinese community in Italy counted a total of 29,000 citizens (excluding minors), while in 2003 the figure rose to 100,000 persons, to which must be added the irregular immigrants estimated at approximately 25–30% of the Chinese population present in the Italian territory (data from Samarini, De Giorgi 2011: 150–155). In a short time, the Chinese population in Italy established itself in various areas of economic activity and in the world of family

---

1   Giordan, Ling and Valzania (2018) propose a more articulated illustration (divided into five 'phases') of the growth of Chinese immigration in Italy. Our study is restricted to a general overview of this subject as Chinese Catholicism has only recently become established in Italy, unlike the Chinese Protestant churches that were studied in the aforementioned article.

business, developing an 'ethnic economy' focused on the catering and textile sectors. Over the last two decades, however, it appears that an increasing professional and entrepreneurial differentiation has occurred within the Chinese immigrant population, and a greater distribution of the same outside the big Italian cities and the principal manufacturing districts (with respect to the Veneto region, Rasera, Sacchetto 2018).

According to the latest data provided by the Italian National Institute of Statistics (ISTAT), 290,681 Chinese citizens were resident in Italy in January 2018, corresponding to 5.7% of the foreign population in the country. This figure has grown considerably over the last six years, given that in 2012 the Chinese population in the Italian peninsula, again according to the ISTAT, amounted to 197,064 persons. As mentioned above, irregular immigration must also be counted in the estimate. To understand this situation, which influences the migratory flows and transnational ties of the Chinese Catholics, we have to consider the Chinese networks that facilitate illegal immigration and the phenomenon of Chinese labour trafficking. In fact, over the last ten years criminal organisations have teamed up with traditional family networks that would usually facilitate the migration of family members and acquaintances (Ceccagno, Rastrelli 2008: 39–65).

In this exploration of the Chinese Catholic presence in Italy, the broad growth and development of Catholic communities of immigrants in the peninsula has to be considered within the institutional conformation of Catholic pastoral centres for immigrants. Owing to the great increase in migratory flows that has occurred since the 1990s, over the last twenty years within the Catholic Church particular structures have been created with the aim of ensuring religious assistance to Catholic immigrants residing in Italy. They are generically referred to as pastoral centres for Catholic immigrants and are coordinated by the Migrantes Foundation, the Episcopal Commission for Migration, and the Pontifical Council for the Pastoral Care of Migrants and Itinerant People. These centres may be formal and, that is, established canonically, or informal, and they may present a variety of organisational typologies more or less specifically structured, depending on the size of the immigrant community. They are entrusted with the mission to unite the foreign faithful in their respective national groups so as to offer liturgies and sacraments in the language of the immigrants' country of origin through the so-called 'ethnic chaplains'. Moreover, they set up certain services suitable for meeting needs related to the condition of being a migrant (Chilese, Russo 2013).

The 'Chinese Catholic Community in Italy' was founded in 2006 and developed within the institutional and ecclesiastical structure mentioned above.

TABLE 4.1 Distribution of Chinese Catholic Communities in the Italian Territory (2018)

Bologna	Padua
Brescia	Palermo
Civitavecchia	Perugia
Cosenza	Prato
Empoli	Reggio Emilia
Florence	Rimini
Fucecchio (FI)	Rome
Macerata	Turin
Milan	Treviso
Naples	Venice

After an initial period of growth, the local communities reached a total figure that appears to have substantially remained unchanged in recent years. The current national coordinator of these communities is Don Xian Ming 'Paolo' Kong, who serves in the Chinese Catholic community in Naples. Table 4.1 and map 4.1 show the distribution of the Chinese Catholic communities in the Italian peninsula.

The 20 Chinese Catholic communities are located mostly in northern and central Italy, while there are 2 communities in the Lazio region, and only 3 in the southern regions (Campania, Calabria and Sicily). The settlement of the communities would thus appear to follow the trend of settlement of the Chinese immigrants present in the national territory. It is more deeply rooted in the regions of northern Italy and in central areas of the country around the economic and industrial centres in which there seems to be a better socio-economic fabric and a more advantageous labour market.

In a long interview with the national coordinator of the communities Don 'Paolo' Kong in April 2017, we were informed that the total number of faithful at the national level is estimated at around 1,000 persons. Moreover, the most numerous communities appear to be those located in the central and northern regions: Prato (200–250 faithful), Milan (200–250 faithful), Rome (100–150 faithful), Rimini (100–150 faithful), and Naples (80–100 faithful). These Catholics faithful seem to originate from three large areas of China in particular: about 70% appear to come from the eastern coastal province of Zhejiang, about 15% from the southernmost province of Fujian, and approximately 10% appear to be from the municipalities or provinces of Shanghai, Hebei and Dongbei.

MAP 4.1   The Chinese Catholic Community in Italy (2018)

3   A Sociological Overview of the Chinese Catholic Community in Italy

The settlement of these Chinese Catholic communities occurs in an Italian society shaped by secularisation, whereby there is a growing tendency – as is widespread among most Italians – to claim a religious affiliation while living a 'nonreligious' day-to-day life (Garelli 2011, 2016). In this regard, groups of immigrants who follow the Catholic faith generally seem to develop an opposite tendency, considering both the societal role that religion still plays in their countries of origin and the major level of their religious practice compared to that one of Italians. The pastoral activity towards immigrants of the Catholic Church operates in the presence of such transformations within Italian society. In this sense, Chinese Catholicism develops in the midst of these religious variations, which occasionally appear to put in contrast the world of Catholic immigrations with that of the Italian faithful.

According to the data collected in the research, in 2018 nine 'ethnic chaplains' from China with an average age ranging from 40 to 50 years were incardinated within the sphere of the Pastoral Care of Migrants and Itinerant People of the Catholic Church. Generally, the latter have been educated and trained in Catholic seminaries and institutions in China and after, during diverse steps of their religious career, sent to Italy as missionaries for Chinese migrants (in some cases, also to achieve Pontifical academic qualifications). Furthermore, two other Chinese priests were incardinated in Macerata at the Li Madou Study Centre, the cultural association named after the missionary Father Matteo Ricci. This centre was founded on the occasion of the 4th centenary of the death of the famous Jesuit missionary with the aim of promoting intercultural exchanges between Europe and China, and fostering inter-religious dialogue and the study of Catholicism.[2] Finally, in 2018, about forty Chinese priests were studying at the pontifical academic institutions in Rome, and in the same city five young Chinese men were attending the seminary in preparation for the priesthood.

An equally recent trend is the growing number of Chinese consecrated men in Catholic religious orders in Italy, especially in the Franciscan male and female orders. According to our estimates, in 2018 in the Order of Friars Minor Conventual (O.F.M.Conv.) there were ten Chinese friars serving in convents in various Italian regions, together with three other Chinese novices in training and five Chinese friars who serve in a Franciscan community recently established in China. Moreover, there were a few Chinese friars undergoing training in Rome, also in the Order of Friars Minor (O.F.M.). Since September 2015, this religious order has administered the parish in which the Chinese Catholic community of Prato is established with the aim of developing missionary activities focusing on Asian immigrants and the process of integration between the Italian and Chinese communities. In particular, this mission is pursued in accordance with the mandate of two Chinese friars, who are supported by two other Italian friars and three Chinese Franciscan nuns.[3]

Finally, another subject of interest concerns the recent attempt to develop a Chinese monastic presence in Italy. Three Chinese monks reside at the

---

2 The website of the Li Madou Study centre can be visited at URL: http://www.limadou.org (Accessed: 4 February 2019).
3 However, there appear to be no Chinese novices and friars in the order of the Friars Minor Capuchin (O.F.M.Cap.) in Italy.

Monastery of Camaldoli in the province of Arezzo, the headquartered of the Camaldolese monastic order of St. Benedict (O.S.B.). Father Yuese 'Joseph' Huang Wong has been living in this monastery since 2005, and over a period of ten years he has tried to introduce at least five other Chinese novices to the monastic life. As he told us in a long interview in July 2017, his religious vocation in Italy appears not to be affected by a cultural distance between Italy and China. Indeed, he found important similarities between the experience of Chinese Buddhist monasticism and the Italian Catholic monastic reality: "The monastic life that I lead here is certainly not a new dimension in my homeland, given the long tradition of Buddhist monasticism in China. There are many similarities between Buddhist and Benedictine monasticism, and these are mainly related to such practices as fasting, meditation, vigils, silence and community life. The most evident differences, however, are those that occur at the doctrinal level" (for a theological perspective on this point, Barnhart, Wong 2001). From Father Joseph's optimistic point of view, in the future these common bases may facilitate the emergence of a real Chinese Catholic monastic community in Italy and in the motherland.

With regard to the life of the Chinese Catholic communities that have spread throughout the peninsula, the liturgies are usually celebrated once a week in the principal groups and once a month in the minor communities. According to the data acquired in the research, an average of five baptisms of Chinese adult faithful are celebrated in the most numerous communities every year. This number of conversions maintains at a stable level the total number of the faithful, which, for economic and professional reasons, is decreased by the departure of entire families that go to join the Chinese diasporas in other European countries.

Again, according to the estimates considered, the number of weddings and funeral celebrations is very low. From a sociological point of view, these two sacraments may be interpreted as 'rites of passage' in the life of a faithful. The number of celebrations of such rituals in the liturgical activity of a religious community of immigrants suggests the breadth of the depth and stability of its establishment in a host territory. This indication seems to suggest the close relationship that these Chinese faithful maintain with their country of origin during the time they spend abroad and the sort of 'precariousness' that still appears to distinguish these religious communities in Italy. In this respect, due to mixed marriages the number of Italian faithful present in these parishes is also very low. This indication presents further evidence regarding the depth of the settlement of a religious community of immigrants in the socio-cultural fabric of a new country.

Following a qualitative vision elaborated through in-depth interviews conducted during the research, we have tried to define the main socio-religious profiles of Chinese Catholic faithful in Italy. First of all, it would appear that a part of the Chinese Catholic community in Italy is composed of followers of the Catholic faith who were already baptised in China, while another part seems to include faithful of the majority religions of their homeland (such as the traditional Chinese folk religion, Taoism, and Buddhism) who have converted to Catholicism in Italy. Other Chinese faithful, instead, derive from the experience of Chinese Protestantism, and after their arrival in Italy turned to Catholicism. On the other hand, in some cases the opposite may occur, and Catholics who have come to in Italy may convert to Protestantism. With regard to the latter situation, factors that should be taken into consideration are the growth of Protestant congregations in China (Yang 2016: 9–11) and the widespread phenomenon of 'house churches' (Kang 2016), besides the recent development of Chinese evangelical churches in Italy (Giordan, Ling, Valzania 2018). Finally, a part of the Chinese Catholic community seems to be composed of immigrants who have arrived in Italy without any fundamental religious bonds due to the atheistic education that they received in China. In such cases, adopting an approach that may be defined as almost 'missionary', Chinese Catholic priests attempt to introduce them gradually towards a relationship with the 'sacred' and a knowledge of the Christian faith.

According to Don Jing Xiao 'Giuseppe' Xia, a Chinese priest who arrived in Italy in 2006 and is currently in charge of Chinese pastoral care in the Veneto region, a high-priority requirement is the organisation of communities capable of bringing together Chinese families of lifelong Catholics and recently converted ones scattered across the various territories, allowing them to enter into contact with each other (interview in April 2017). Instead, Don Bo 'Giuseppe' Feng, a Chinese priest who has been in Italy for 8 years, emphasises the importance of working on common aspects between Chinese and Christian culture: "In China there is an ancient system, a centuries-old culture which presents many of the virtues that distinguish the Christian religion, such as filial piety, compassion and love for one's neighbours. It would be advisable to examine these common aspects in order to facilitate a significant encounter between Chinese culture and Catholicism and the evangelisation of our Chinese brothers in the homeland and abroad" (interview in March 2019). In short, as we shall see in the next section, from the sociological points of view the challenge of developing patterns and practices relating to encounters between these two socio-cultural realities would appear to offer ample space for experimentation.

4 Patterns of Settlement of Chinese Catholic Communities in Italy

The life and the activity of these religious communities are quite diversified and change mainly in relation to their size and the number of the faithful. However, it is possible to identify some aspects and issues that are common to the various communities. First of all, focusing on the linguistic aspect, we may state that the language used in the liturgy and in religious activity in general is Mandarin or Wenzhou dialect, according to the main habits of each community. The use or avoidance of the language of the host country in the liturgical sphere (considering the various possibilities and degrees of use of this language) is an indication of the solidity of the rooting of a religious immigrant community within the socio-cultural fabric of a new country. In our case study, it appears that the Chinese communities find it difficult to interact with the Italian societal environment and develop a religious activity that may promote a contamination between the two national realities through the vernacular dimension.

However, the data collected during the research appears to suggest that the communities presenting the highest numbers of faithful have developed social activities and pastoral practices that favour an interaction with the host context and an engagement with the institutions present in the Italian territories. For example, some Chinese communities have organised after-school activities for children, summer oratories for students (referred to in the Italian Catholic Church as 'Summer Groups' or the 'GREST' summer breaks), trips and pilgrimages, and Italian and Chinese language courses. In some provinces pastoral care has also been organised in hospitals and prisons for the Chinese sick and prisoners. Therefore, it seems that some of the larger Chinese communities have thus been able to 'incorporate' some pastoral practices consolidated in Italian parishes.

Furthermore, a particular practice organised by these communities is the national pilgrimage that the Chinese Catholic faithful carry out in one of their communities on 24 May each year to pray for their church in the motherland (in 2008 and 2012 in Rome, in 2009, 2017 and 2019 in Naples, in 2010 in Macerata, in 2011 in Rimini, in 2013 in Prato, in 2014 in Turin, and in 2018 at Assisi). This pilgrimage started in 2008 following the guidelines and the decision of Pope Benedict XVI to establish on this date the 'World Day of Prayer for the Church in China'. On this occasion, the Chinese Catholic communities in Italy, and also the structures of the Italian Catholic Church designated to provide pastoral care for migrants, become involved in the organisation of this national event.

To sum up, in this case study, which focuses on the relationship between religion and immigration, there do not seem to be significant paths of contamination among the 'Chinese Catholic community in Italy', the host society, and the Italian Catholic Church. In fact, in this religious community of immigrants there seems to be no hybridisation of a large impact related to the new environment (and *vice versa*) (Robertson 1992). According to this view, the Chinese Catholic communities appear to experience difficulties in developing the nuances of true cultural hybrids that blend religious universalism with forms of local particularism (Beyer 2007; Roudometof 2016).

Remarks made by the national coordinator Don 'Paolo' Kong indicate some of the difficulties encountered by the Chinese faithful in relation to the host context: "There is a great difference between the Italian language and that spoken by the Chinese, and this makes it difficult for the faithful to learn the language of the host country. Nor is the Italian culture very similar to that of the Chinese people, starting from the simplest things, such as food" (interview in April 2017). These linguistic and socio-cultural differences certainly do not facilitate the development of cultural hybrids, and this is probably the main barrier in relations between Italians and the Chinese. In this regard, in an interview in May 2017 an Italian Catholic priest engaged in the pastoral care of Chinese faithful ironically noted that "the true Chinese wall in Italy" is precisely the great difficulty experienced and the considerable efforts Asian immigrants have to make when they attempt to learn European languages.

However, as previously mentioned, some adaptations on the part of the larger communities may be identified, especially in pastoral practices aimed at young people. The experience of the Chinese Catholic parish in the city of Prato appears to corroborate this view. The vast presence of Chinese immigrants in the city and its hegemony in the local economic fabric, which has made Prato a case study that has attracted attention at the international level (for instance, Baldassar *et al.* 2015), has stimulated the local Catholic diocese to dedicate special attention to this community of immigrants over the last two decades. Data provided by the ISTAT reveal that 20,643 Chinese immigrants were present in the Province of Prato in 2018, accounting for 54% of the entire immigrant population. According to this situation, a Chinese priest has been serving Catholic compatriots resident in the city since the year 2000. Since 2015, the Italian parish hosting the Chinese Catholic community has been supervised by the Order of Friars Minor (O.F.M.), who have supported the settlement of Chinese male and female clerics and have promoted events that have facilitated the encounter between the Italian and Chinese communities.[4]

---

4 In the Italian national and local press many articles have been published on the Chinese Catholic community of Prato. For instance, a recent article describes an event at which groups of Italian and Chinese young faithful and Italian and Chinese clerics gather for prayer

It is quite likely that the growth of the 'Chinese Catholic Community in Italy' and especially the development of its major communities in other Italian cities (such as Bologna, Milan, and Rome) may favour the emergence of further experiences of encounters and powerful paths of hybridisation.

5 Examining Religious Transnationalism within Chinese Catholicism in Italy

Having reference to situations and events described by the Chinese Catholic priests in the in-depth interviews collected in the research, an analysis of the transnational ties of these communities of immigrants seems to indicate a heterogeneous and discontinuous situation. In fact, the Chinese Catholic faithful do not usually have Italian citizenship and live in Italy with a residence permit. They return to their homeland generally once a year, when they can take a break from their work. However, visits to their homeland do not occur frequently and undertaking such a journey is not something that would interest the entire population of immigrants. It depends on several variables, such as the legal status of the immigrants, their professional situation, their financial resources, their state of health (possibly a significant factor, considering the length of the journey), the type of documents required for repatriation, and their personal situation in the motherland. In summary, Chinese migratory flows within Catholic communities do not seem to be distinguished by a significant transnational character and by the development of cross-border phenomena, unlike other immigrant communities in Italy such as that of the Romanians (Cingolani 2009).

In such a scenario it is difficult to hypothesise that the 'Chinese Catholic Community in Italy' and the Catholic Church in China have developed the traits of a transnational religion (Levitt 2007). The concept refers to solutions to newfound situations that people face as a result of migration and presents distinct blends of religious universalism and local particularism. Although a connection does exist between the Catholic world in China and the Catholic institutions in Italy, institutional forms of transnationalism between the Catholic Church in China and the Chinese Catholic communities in Italy do not appear to be relevant. Moreover, nor do transnational forms of religious practice among Chinese Catholics in Italy appear to have developed, as the

---

in a textile factory building owned by a Chinese entrepreneur. The ritual referred to was performed at the first 'Preghiera Giovani' (Prayer for Youth) meeting promoted by the Catholic diocese of Prato and which is to be held monthly at different churches (Il Tirreno 2017).

transnational trajectories of this immigrant community do not appear to significantly involve their religious sphere.

Examining transnationalism, Levitt coined the term 'social remittance' to describe the content of its flows, and illustrated the dynamic referring to "the ideas, behaviours and social capital that flow from receiving to sending communities" which become "tools with which ordinary individuals create global culture at the local level" (Levitt 2001: 11; also Levitt, Lamba-Nieves 2010). Consequently, in some situations transnational processes can lead to changes in the religious landscapes, and immigrants may stimulate forms of cultural diffusion at the local level both in the host country and in the country of origin. Within these trajectories, which, as stated are not particularly relevant in the specific case of the Chinese Catholics in Italy, transnational religious ties may foster the strengthening of religious communities and affect power dynamics occurring among state institutions and civil societies.

> We argue that transnational religious connections create organisational and cultural change in local houses of worship and alter the global power dynamics within international religious communities. Transnational religious connections also modify the way followers of a faith interact with public institutions and those who adhere to other faiths. Sometimes this results in positive interactions that allow religious values to strengthen civil society; sometimes it increases conflict between groups. What is clear is that transnational religious connections have a significant power to create social and religious change.
> OFFUTT, MILLER 2016: 527

According to this perspective, the 'World Day of Prayer for the Church in China' held on 24 May appears to have acquired the status of a transnational religious event. As anticipated in the previous section, in 2007 Pope Benedict XVI issued a *Letter to the Catholics of China* (2007a, 2007b), in which he speaks of his own closeness and that of the 'Universal Church' to the Chinese Catholic Church, and refers to some aspects of the ecclesiastic stance regarding the complicated situation of the Catholic Church in China. Furthermore, he proclaimed the creation of a day of prayer dedicated to Catholics in China: "On that same day, the Catholics of the whole world – in particular those who are of Chinese origin – will demonstrate their fraternal solidarity and solicitude for you" (Benenetto XVI 2007a). The following year he composed a prayer addressed to the Chinese Marian cult of the Madonna of Sheshan (Benedict XVI, 2008), who thus became the Patron of China and is venerated on 24 May, the day that has been dedicated to the Holy Virgin Mary by the Catholic Church since 1815.

On that particular occasion, a transnational religious event appears to 'unite' the Chinese Catholics who have emigrated to various continents with those living in China. In some countries the Chinese faithful no longer living in their homeland participate in national pilgrimages or liturgies organised by the dioceses where they reside. The Catholic faithful in China participate in liturgies organised by the local dioceses and a few of them participate in a pilgrimage to the Sheshan Basilica and Marian shrine in Shanghai. From a sociological perspective, it appears possible to identify some institutional forms of religious transnationalism in this event, particularly in the trajectories linked to its organisation. It seems more difficult to identify on this occasion forms of transnational religious practice among the Chinese Catholic faithful (and this might become a specific subject of study). However, adopting an anthropological perspective focused on the modes of conceptualizing religious presence, we may argue that in this event the religious experience of the faithful abroad is mediated and addressed by the 'sacred' towards or with an emphasis on their 'brothers' in the homeland.[5]

Finally, this event appears to have an impact on the power dynamics of international relations, and has direct effects on the relations between China and the Vatican. It seems to aim the promotion of both a strengthening of Chinese Catholic communities present in the homeland and around the world, and also at directing a religious pressure marked by a transnational character on the government and state institutions in China. On the one hand the event seems to promote the establishment and public presence of the Chinese Catholic Church at the global level, and on the other hand to reaffirm the question of the exercise of religious freedom in China.

6 Conclusions

Considering the number of communities and the total number of adherents to the 'Chinese Catholic Community in Italy' we may conclude that its presence in the Italian religious landscape is marginal. However, the number of Chinese priests in Italy who have come to this country for reasons relating to studies and the recent growth of Chinese who have been consecrated in religious orders are significant indications, suggesting a scenario that is open to possible forms of evolution.

---

5 Regarding this anthropological view, we refer for example to the concept of 'diaspora spirituality' related to the theories of transcendence and notions of mediation (for instance, Beliso-De Jesús 2014).

The Chinese Catholic communities in Italy do not seem to have developed in-depth paths of hybridisation with Italian society and Catholicism. Above all, great differences at the linguistic and cultural levels do not seem to have favoured a rooting in the socio-cultural reality of the host country. Moreover, this situation also appears to have been promoted by the fragile stability of this national community in the Italian context, in particular due to the trajectories of its migratory flows and its 'ethnic economy'. Yet it seems that some major communities have developed different patterns of settlement, and have 'incorporated' some of the pastoral practices of the Italian Catholic Church. The Chinese Catholic community in Prato appears to be an evident example of this process, oriented towards forms of contamination and an encounter between the Chinese and Italian faithful.

The issue appears to form part of the more general question (and also the challenge) of integrating the Catholic communities of immigrant into the normal life of the Italian parishes. They are in fact currently hosted by the local communities, but they do not participate in their community life and activities. Their liturgies and services are normally parallel to and yet separate from the life of the Italian parishes, and only rarely are the immigrants included in the diocesan and local pastoral councils (Ambrosini 2016). In our view, a condition such as this may promote multiple processes of blending and negotiation within the religious and socio-cultural dimensions of the Chinese Catholic immigrants on the part of both the faithful and the communities (for instance, a reference can be made to the case of the Chinese conversion to Christianity in the United States (Yang 1998)).

The transnational religious ties of the Chinese Catholic communities in Italy seem to leave room for possible future changes. In particular, the Provisional Agreement between the Holy See and the People's Republic of China signed by Pope Francis in September 2018 appears to represent a development in the delicate 'Chinese question' within the Catholic Church. The latter agreement may favour above all an increase in transnational institutional ties between Chinese Catholicism and the Catholic world in western countries. This would occur in a context which, as we have seen in our consideration of the 'World Day of Prayer for the Church in China' as a transnational religious event, there still seems to be a limited experience of forms of transnational religious practices. On the other hand, fresh trends related to the religious transnationalism in the recent global growth and spread of Chinese Pentecostal and Charismatic Christianity (Yang, Tong, Anderson 2017) may also have an incremental effect on these practices.

To conclude, qualitative research focusing on the faithful at the micro level might be a useful further step in the sociological exploration of this religious community in Italy. A first area of research might be the reality of Chinese Catholic entrepreneurs in Italy. In fact, considerable attention has been paid to the analysis of the relationship between faith and economic development in Chinese Protestant Christianity in the motherland and abroad (Cao 2010; Tong 2012), while the Catholic world has drawn a low level of attention (Gao, Yang 2015). An investigation of the intersections between Catholic doctrine, economic activity, and the social capital of the Chinese population abroad might emphasise the bonds that link Chinese Catholicism to the situation of diaspora in western countries.

Finally, a second area of research might focus on the everyday life of these religious communities in the Italian territory, which have risen from the status of a religious minority in the country of origin to one of a religious majority in the host country. As some research has shown (Yang, Ebaugh 2001; Kislev 2014), the change in the majority/minority status in a religious community in the diaspora influences the dynamics of its settlement and the definition of its identity. This perspective would allow us to identify some less evident stances and attitudes of the Chinese Catholic faithful in Italy. Since they have passed from the condition of a religious minority in a country belonging to the eastern world, to the condition of diaspora in one of the more Catholic countries in the western world.

References

Ambrosini, Maurizio. 2016. "Protected but Separate. International Immigrants in the Italian Catholic Church." Pp. 317–335 in *Migration, Transnationalism and Catholicism: Global Perspectives*, edited by Dominic Pasura and Erdal Marta Bivand. London: Palgrave Macmillan.

Baldassar, Loretta, Johanson, Graeme, McAuliffe, Narelle, and Massimo Bressan, eds. 2015. *Chinese Migration to Europe: Prato, Italy, and Beyond*. London: Palgrave Macmillan.

Barnhart, Bruno, and Joseph H. Wong, eds. 2001. *Purity of Heart and Contemplation: A Monastic Dialogue Between Christian and Asian Traditions*. New York: Continuum.

Bays, Daniel H. 2011. *A New History of Christianity in China*. West Sussex, UK: Wiley-Blackwell.

Beliso-De Jesús, Aisha. 2014. "Santería Copresence and the Making of African Diaspora Bodies." *Cultural Anthropology* 29: 503–526.

Benedetto XVI (Ratzinger, Joseph Aloisius). 2007a. "Letter of the Holy Father Pope Benedict XVI to the Bishops, Priests, Consecrated Persons and Lay Faithful of the Catholic Church in the People's Republic of China." Rome, Saint Peter's, May 27. Available at URL: https://w2.vatican.va/content/benedict-xvi/en/letters/2007/documents/hf_ben-xvi_let_20070527_china.html (Accessed: February 6, 2019).

Benedetto XVI (Ratzinger, Joseph Aloisius). 2007b. "Explanatory Note: Letter of His Holiness Pope Benedict XVI to Chinese Catholics." Rome, Saint Peter's, May 27. Available at URL: http://w2.vatican.va/content/benedict-xvi/en/letters/2007/documents/hf_ben-xvi_let_20070527_china-note.html (Accessed: February 6, 2019).

Benedetto XVI (Ratzinger, Joseph Aloisius). 2008. "Prayer of His Holiness Benedict XVI to Our Lady of Sheshan: On the Occasion of the World Day of Prayer for the Church in China." Rome, Saint Peter's, May 24. Available at URL: https://w2.vatican.va/content/benedict-xvi/it/prayers/documents/hf_ben-xvi_20080515_prayer-sheshan.html (Accessed: February 6, 2019).

Benton, Gregor, and Frank Pieke. 1998. *The Chinese in Europe*. New York: St. Martin's Press.

Beyer, Peter. 2007. "Globalization and Glocalization." Pp. 98–117 in *The SAGE Handbook of the Sociology of Religion*, edited by James A. Beckford and N.J. Demerath III. Los Angeles: Sage.

Cao, Nanlai. 2005. "The Church as a Surrogate Family for Working Class Immigrant Chinese youth: An Ethnography of Segmented Assimilation." *Sociology of Religion* 66: 183–200.

Cao, Nanlai. 2010. *Constructing China's Jerusalem: Christians, Power, and Place in Contemporary Wenzhou*. Stanford: Stanford University Press.

Cao, Nanlai. 2019. "A Sinicized World Religion?: Chinese Christianity at the Contemporary Moment of Globalization." *Religions* 10: 1–12.

Cao, Nanlai, Giordan, Giuseppe, and Enzo Pace, eds. 2018. "Special Issue: Chinese Religions in China and Italy." *Religioni e Società* 91: 15–74.

Ceccagno, Antonella, and Renzo Rastrelli. 2008. *Ombre cinesi? Dinamiche Migratorie della Diaspora Cinese in Italia*, con la collaborazione di Salvati Alessandra. Roma: Carocci.

Chan, Shun-hing. 2012. "Civil Society and the Role of the Catholic Church in Contemporary China." Pp. 123–137 in *Christianity in Contemporary China: Socio-Cultural Perspectives*, edited by Francis Lim. London: Routledge.

Chilese, Monica, and Giovanna Russo. 2013. "Cattolici dal mondo in Italia." Pp. 215–234 in *Le Religioni nell'Italia che Cambia: Mappe e Bussole*, edited by Enzo Pace. Roma: Carocci.

Chu, Cindy Yik-yi. 2012. *The Catholic Church in China*. New York: Palgrave Macmillan.

Cingolani, Pietro. 2009. *Romeni d'Italia: Migrazioni, Vita Quotidiana e Legami Transnazionali*. Bologna: Il Mulino.

Gao, Shining, and Fenggang Yang. 2015. "Religious Faith and the Market Economy: A Survey of Faith and Trust of Catholic Entrepreneurs in China." *The Ecumenical Review* 67: 120–140.

Garelli, Franco. 2011. *Religione all'Italiana: L'Anima del Paese Messa a Nudo*. Bologna: Il Mulino.

Garelli, Franco. 2016. *Piccoli Atei Crescono: Davvero una Generazione Senza Dio?* Bologna: Il Mulino.

Garelli, Franco, Guizzardi, Gustavo, and Enzo Pace, eds. 2003. *Un Singolare Pluralismo: Indagine sul Pluralismo Morale e Religioso degli Italiani*. Bologna: Il Mulino.

Giordan, Giuseppe, Ling, Han, and Andrea Valzania. 2018. "La Chiesa Cristiana Cinese in Italia." *Religioni e Società* 91: 45–55.

Guglielmi, Marco. 2018. "La Comunità Cattolica Cinese in Italia." *Religioni e Società* 91: 66–74.

Guglielmi, Marco. 2020. "L'impatto dell'immigrazione sulle congregazioni cristiane: la pluralizzazione del Cristianesimo nella regione Veneto." *Mondi Migranti*: 75–96.

Kang, Jie. 2016. *House Church Christianity in China: From Rural Preachers to City Pastors*. London: Palgrave Macmillan.

Il Tirreno. 2017. "Veglia di Preghiera Italo-Cinese nella Fabbrica di Chinatown." *Il Tirreno*, October 10. Available at URL: http://iltirreno.gelocal.it/prato/cronaca/2017/10/10/news/veglia-di-preghiera-italo-cinese-nella-fabbrica-di-chinatown-1.15970049 (Accessed: November 8, 2018).

Kislev, Elyakim. 2014. "The Effect of Minority/Majority Origins on Immigrants' Integration." *Social Forces* 15: 1–30.

Levitt, Peggy. 2001. *The Transnational Villagers*. Oakland: University of California Press.

Levitt, Peggy. 2007. *God Needs No Passport: Immigrants and the Changing American Religious Landscape*. New York: The New Press.

Levitt, Peggy, and Deepak Lamba-Nieves. 2010. "Social Remittances Revisited." *Journal of Ethnic and Migration Studies* 37: 1–22.

Madsen, Richard. 1998. *China's Catholics: Tragedy and Hope in an Emerging Civil Society*. Cambridge, MA: Harvard University Press.

Offutt, Stephen, and Grant Miller. 2016. "Transnationalism." Pp. 525–545 in *Handbook of Religion and Society*, edited by David Yamane. New York: Springer.

Pace, Enzo. 2011. *Vecchi e Nuovi Dei: La Geografia Religiosa dell'Italia che Cambia*. Milano: Paoline.

Pace, Enzo, ed. 2013. *Le Religioni nell'Italia Che Cambia: Mappe e Bussole*. Roma: Carocci.

Palombaro, Ottavio. 2017. "The Protestant Ethic and the Spirit of Wenzhou Entrepreneurs in Milan and in Their Homeland." *Review of Religion and Chinese Society* 4: 87–107.

Pasura, Dominic, and Erdal Marta Bivand, eds. 2016. *Migration, Transnationalism and Catholicism: Global Perspectives*. London: Palgrave Macmillan.

Rasera, Maurizio, and Devi Sacchetto. 2018. *Cinesi tra le Maglie del Lavoro*. Milano: Franco Angeli.

Robertson, Roland. 1992. *Globalization: Social Theory and Global Culture*. London: Sage.

Roudometof, Victor. 2016. "Globalization." Pp. 505–524 in *Handbook of Religion and Society*, edited by David Yamane. New York: Springer.

Samarini, Guido, and Laura De Giorgi. 2011. *Lontane, Vicine: Le Relazioni fra Cina e Italia nel Novecento*. Roma: Carocci.

Tong, Joy K.C. 2012. *Overseas Chinese Christian Entrepreneurs in Modern China: A Case Study of the Influence of Christian Ethics on Business*. London: Anthem Press.

Vicziany, Marika, Fladrich, Anja Michaela, and Andrea A. Di Castro. 2015. "Religion and the Lives of the Overseas Chinese: What Explains the 'Great Silence' of Prato?" Pp. 215–231 in *Chinese Migration to Europe: Prato, Italy, and Beyond*, edited by Loretta Baldassar, Graeme Johanson, Narelle McAuliffe, and Massimo Bressan. London: Palgrave Macmillan.

Yang, Fenggang. 1998. "Chinese Conversion to Evangelical Christianity: The Importance of Social and Cultural Contexts." *Sociology of Religion* 59: 237–257.

Yang, Fenggang. 1999. *Chinese Christians in America: Conversion, Assimilation, and Adhesive Identities*. University Park (PA): Penn State University Press.

Yang, Fenggang. 2016. "Exceptionalism or Chinamerica: Measuring Religious Change in the Globalizing World Today." *Journal for the Scientific Study of Religion* 55: 7–22.

Yang, Fenggang, and Helen Rose Ebaugh. 2001. "Religion and Ethnicity among New Immigrants: The impact of Majority/Minority Status in Home and Host Countries." *Journal for the Scientific Study of Religion* 40: 367–78.

Yang, Fenggang, and Joseph Tamney, eds. 2006. "Special Issue: Conversion to Christianity among the Chinese." *Sociology of Religion* 67: 123–204.

Yang, Fenggang, Tong, Joy K.C., and Allan H. Anderson, eds. 2017. *Global Chinese Pentecostal and Charismatic Christianity*. Leida: Brill.

Zoccatelli, PierLuigi. 2010. "Religione e Religiosità fra i Cinesi a Torino: «Religione Cinese», Identità Secolare e Presenze di Origine Cristiana." Pp. 203–254 in *Cinesi a Torino: La Crescita di un Arcipelago*, edited by Luigi Berzano, Carlo Genova, Massimo Introvigne, Roberta Ricucci, and PierLuigi Zoccatelli. Bologna: Il Mulino.

CHAPTER 5

Encounter, Initiation, and Commitment

Christian Conversion among New Chinese Migrants in Britain

Xinan Li, Line Nyhagen, and Thoralf Klein

1 Introduction: The Chinese Christians in Britain

In the 2011 UK Census (ONS 2015), which included the category of religion by self-identification, the British Chinese are recorded as the least religious compared with other ethnic minority groups.[1] Among the nearly 400,000 British Chinese in England and Wales, over half (56%) do not identify with any religious tradition. This figure surpasses that of ten years earlier by 3% (cf. Weller 2008). This must be seen in the context of the rapid growth of the Chinese population in Britain by 73% since 2001, when the previous Census took place (ibid.). The 2011 Census data also shows that two religions, Christianity and Buddhism, are predominant among the religious British Chinese, and that Christians almost double the proportion of Buddhists.

The Chinese in Britain – a term encompassing individuals who self-identify as Chinese in political, ethnic, or cultural senses, either with or without British citizenship – tend to organise themselves into social groups and communities on the basis of economic activity, trade, clan/familial relation, birthplace, and religion (Jones 1987; Benton and Gomez 2008), as do Chinese diasporas elsewhere in the world. Since the late 1970s, a multitude of Chinese schools, media, churches and temples, and community centres, have been built to provide social services for and to organise the Chinese in Britain (Benton and Gomez 2008). However, in comparison with the durability of faith-based Chinese communities, communities organised around non-religious principles often fail to sustain over a longer period of time (Jones 1987; Benton and Gomez 2008). Some structural attributes of the Chinese diaspora in Britain, such as its dispersal across Britain, and the intra-ethnic competition among business

---

1 In the UK Census, 'British Chinese' include individuals of Chinese origin who are full citizens of the UK. The given categories of religion in the UK Census do not include Daoism and Chinese folk religion. Folk religious beliefs and practices remain popular in contemporary China and among the Chinese in diaspora (cf. Madsen and Siegler 2011). In China, the religiosity of the Chinese is diffused rather than expressed in institutionalised religions (cf. Yang 1961).

individuals and between groups from different geographical origins, have been identified as causes for the lack of stable social and communal organisations and institutions among the Chinese in Britain (Benton and Gomez 2008). Despite the challenges caused by such structural issues, shared religious identities and commitment have the potential to positively influence the stability and longevity of Chinese community-based organising. In our own research, we have observed that Christianity can be a powerful counter-point to the general lack of institutional affiliation commonly seen among the Chinese in diaspora.

By focusing on the *new* Chinese migrants, we acknowledge that there have been some generational changes[2] in the Chinese population in contemporary Britain. Although the definition of Chinese-ness remains a contested issue, and there is insufficient statistical analysis of the demographical structure of the Chinese population in Britain, based on existing literature and our own research experience we contend that two large generational groups can be differentiated with some general characteristics for identification. The previous generation of Chinese migrants in Britain can be characterised as the Chinese who migrated before the 1980s, are largely Cantonese/Fuzhounese-speaking with limited English proficiency, and work mainly in labour-intensive businesses such as restaurants, groceries, laundry, housekeeping etc. In contrast, the new generation migrated to Britain after the 1980s, are more capable of speaking Mandarin-Chinese, have better English proficiency, and mainly work as business/financial professionals, academics, entrepreneurs and self-employed creative workers. The generational changes in the Chinese population in Britain have also impacted on the organisational and ministerial structures of Chinese Christian communities in Britain.

In terms of theological orientation, the mainline Christian tradition adhered to by Chinese in Britain is that of Protestant Evangelicalism[3] (cf. Bebbington 1989). Communities of Chinese Christians in Britain have been built since the early 1950s. In 1951, the first Chinese Church in London (CCIL) was founded by Reverend Stephen Y.T. Wang (CCIL 2000). It has now become the largest Chinese church in Britain with seven congregations in London, operating and supporting many (Chinese) Christian ministries.[4] In 1961, Chinese

---

2 The notion of generation in this chapter draws from Mannheim's (1998) sociological understanding of generation. It is not predicated on biological heredity and kinship relationship. Rather, it refers to a stratifying consciousness formed when individuals relate to one another due to certain shared experiences of historical events and other social locations.
3 In our usage, the terms Christian and Christianity refer to Protestant Evangelicals Christians and Protestant Evangelicalism, unless otherwise specified.
4 For information on CCIL, see: https://ccil.org.uk/en/about-us/our-church/ [accessed 21 September 2020].

Overseas Christian Mission (COCM, initially affiliated with CCIL and later branching off as an independent operation) was established. It has grown to become the largest transnational Chinese Christian mission organisation in Europe, with boards also in the United States, Hong Kong, Singapore, and Malaysia (COCM 2010). For seven decades, COCM has been responsible for planting and supporting 128 Chinese churches and fellowships operating in seventy-one British cities and towns.[5] A range of Chinese Christian ministries and organisations with a primary focus on Christian evangelism and providing social services such as family support, counselling, rehabilitation of gambling addicts, resource coordination, and Christian publishing, have also emerged over the years.[6]

As stated previously, the generational changes in the Chinese population in Britain have brought organisational and ministerial changes to British Chinese Christian communities. The most noticeable change is the re-orientation of evangelical ministry toward the proselytisation of new Chinese migrants and large numbers of Chinese students (as well as visiting scholars from mainland China) studying in British colleges and universities. Many independent Chinese churches have thus launched their Mandarin-Chinese-speaking ministries since the 2000s, some of which have led to the emergence of Mandarin-Chinese-speaking congregations. As for the missionary organisations, taking COCM as an example, since 2012 it has shifted its missionary focus from the evangelisation of already existing Chinese immigrant communities to the development of student and second-generation British Chinese evangelical ministries and the support of campus-based Chinese student ministries.

The academic literature on religious dimensions of the lives of Chinese migrants in Britain is scant, but a few extant studies have documented the presence of Christianity within the Chinese diaspora in Britain (Liu 1992; Li 2012; Dickson 2013; Huang and Hsiao 2015; Huang 2017) and more broadly in Europe (Nyíri 2003; Cao 2005; Rao 2017). These studies have covered a wide range of topics such as community organisation, identity construction, moral and ethical conduct, value change through initial contact with Christianity, religion and gender, Christian evangelism, religious proselytisation and conversion. These studies resonate with the burgeoning research on religion, and

---

[5] For COCM's list of Chinese churches and fellowships in Britain, see: https://docs.wixstatic.com/ugd/76492a_4734f84da65949fd962fd96142cceoc7.pdf [accessed 21 September 2020].

[6] For COCM's list of Chinese Christian ministries and organisations in Britain, see: https://docs.wixstatic.com/ugd/76492a_19c8495ad45449a4812260bf063977fe.pdf [accessed 21 September 2020].

particularly Christianity, among the Chinese diaspora in North America since the late 1990s (e.g., Yang 1999; Guest 2003; Wang 2004; Wang and Yang 2006; Abel 2008) and contribute to a broader understanding of Christianity in the Chinese diaspora in the West.

The focus of the present study emerged from the observation that a large number of members of the Chinese Christian communities in Britain, including those who have inherited a nominal Christian identity from their families, are converts to Christianity. We contend that a qualitative analysis of the process of religious conversion can provide an in-depth understanding of not only the phenomenon of conversion, but also the socio-religious dynamics of Chinese Christian communities in contemporary Britain.

In the following sections, we first provide a brief introduction to the theoretical model of religious conversion applied in our empirical study, before outlining the methodological rationale. Further, we draw on the empirical data to discuss the three stages of Christian conversion we have identified, namely, *encounter, initiation, and commitment*, which typically feature in the conversion trajectories of Chinese migrant Christians in Britain. Finally, we conclude the chapter by drawing connections between conversion and community-building, where the importance of commitment-centred conversion is key to understanding the continuous growth of Chinese Christian communities in Britain.

2   Religious Conversion: A Processual Model

Religious conversion is one of the most discussed issues in the existing literature on global Chinese Christianity (e.g., Yang 1999; Wang 2004; Hall 2006; Wang and Yang 2006; Wong 2006; Yang and Tamney 2006; Abel 2008; Fiedler 2010; Klein 2011). The term denotes 'changes in a person's religious belief that can happen suddenly and gradually', which are 'accompanied by an alternate view of reality and of self, and in general also entails a reconstruction of biography' (Jindra 2014: 10). Conversion can also take different directions, such as 'changes from one religion to a new one, a shift from no religious commitment to religious faith, and renewal of one's religious faith within one religious group' (ibid.).

We view religious conversion, and particularly Christian conversion, as a processual phenomenon and use a three-stage sequential model (see Figure 5.1) to demonstrate the prominent processual pattern that emerged in the analysis of trajectories of Christian conversion among Chinese migrants in

FIGURE 5.1   Three sequential stages in religious conversion processes

Britain. The model was derived from a critical synthesis of theoretical perspectives, drawing especially on Rambo (1993) and Gooren (2010). The idea of *stages* of personal development in conversion draws on developmental psychology and the psychology of religion (cf. Fowler 1981; Streib 2005; Fowler and Dell 2006; Jindra 2008).

For a person to convert to a religion, the person needs to firstly *encounter* religious objects or persons to gain knowledge as well as initial impressions of the religion. However, for the person to develop commitment to the religion, they need to go through a liminal stage, that of *initiation*, whereby the person gains further information and experience about the religion with regard to beliefs, practices, and communities by being exposed to specific religious cultures. Later in this chapter, we note that the individual's agency, i.e., the person's decision to convert, expressed verbally, marks the successful initiation. Lastly, once the religiously initiated person is ready to declare their faith and the newly gained religious identity in public and is willing to practice the religion in terms of devotions and ethics, the person reaches the "culmination of conversion", which is the stage of commitment (Rambo 1993: 168).

In this study, we characterise the new Chinese migrant Christians' commitment in terms of belonging along two different dimensions, namely, the sense of belonging to the faith tradition and the sense of belonging to specific faith communities. After a brief presentation of the research methodology in the next section, the subsequent three sections are dedicated to an empirically informed discussion of the three stages of Christian conversion of new Chinese migrants in Britain.

3   Methodology

This chapter provides a sociological account of how new Chinese migrants convert to Christianity, which anticipates explaining, at least partially, the continuous growth of Chinese Christian communities in Britain. The study takes a qualitative approach, using ethnographic methods that enable the analysis of 'religion as practiced and experienced by ordinary people in the contexts of their lived everyday lives' (McGuire 2008: 96).

The main investigative tools of this study are semi-structured interviews and participant observation. Through purposive[7] and snowball sampling, thirty Chinese[8] Christians who have lived in Britain for at least five years were recruited[9] for in-depth interviews. All of them are committed Christians, who have been baptised and participated in one or multiple Christian communities for at least five years. Two white British lay Christians with experience in Christian evangelism among Chinese students and migrants were also interviewed. Compared with conventional congregational ethnographies of Christianity, due to the scarcity of literature documenting Chinese Christians' experiences in a British context, one of the researchers, Xinan Li, practiced *short-term* and *multi-sited* participant observation (cf. Marcus 1995) within institutionalised Christian gatherings such as church congregations, Christian fellowships, Bible study groups, Christian camps and conferences, in nine cities and towns in England. The field work began in January 2016 and lasted for over one year, enabling the researchers to situate individual cases in their respective local contexts. This multi-sited ethnographic work is also a 'bottom-up approach in mapping out the ever-unfolding mobility and connections' in Chinese migrant Christian communities in Britain (Xiang 2013: 283).

The subsequent three sections draw on original empirical data to illustrate and discuss the three stages of Chinese migrants' Christian conversion, which also sheds light on the socio-religious contexts in both contemporary Britain and China.

4   Encounter: The Initial Contact with Christianity

The experience of encounter with religion is a window through which the person can get in touch with religious content (beliefs and practices) and

---

7   The sample was purposefully intended to reflect the internal diversity of the Chinese population in Britain.
8   Due to the internal diversity in the Chinese diaspora, the study operationally takes the participants' self-identification of Chinese-ness for granted. In terms of place of origin and ancestral roots, the interviewed participants encompass *Chinese* people from mainland China, Hong Kong, Macau, Taiwan, Malaysia and Singapore. Most speak Mandarin Chinese and English; some also speak Cantonese. Both Mandarin Chinese and English were used in the interviews.
9   This practical criterion was used due to advice from experienced Chinese Christian ministers in Britain. According to British immigration laws, those who have legally worked in Britain for five years can apply for permanent residency and British citizenship. This does not mean, however, that all participants had obtained British citizenship at the time of the interview. Some Chinese migrants choose to not apply for British citizenship for practical reasons.

communities. Methodologically, the researcher can only indirectly access the experience of encounter as recounted by the converts as part of their *biographical reconstructions*, which reflect the religious frame of reference adopted through their conversion (cf. Snow and Machalek 1984). The analysis of the participants' experiences of encountering Christianity can show where and how conversion begins, and can also help us understand the influence of contextual factors in conversion.

Political restrictions, even suppression of religion, can take many forms ranging from the central government's ideological exclusion and local government's policy making and implementation. Christianity, although present in China for several hundred years, has never been considered part of the socio-cultural orthodoxy in contemporary China. Moreover, it has largely been construed as a Western religion or ideology in the public discourse. Nevertheless, despite various political constraints, Christianity has been continuously growing in contemporary China, with its religious content and representations accessible, in one way or another, to the public's lived experience, as evidenced in these interview excerpts:

> I knew there were quite a few churches in my city before I became a Christian [...] They are probably what you would call "three-self" [*sanzi*, "三自", our note] churches[10] [...] when I graduated in 2011 and started working for a local newspaper, a colleague of mine invited me to a meeting and to talk with a nun [...] she's a Catholic, quite devout.
> Male participant from Kunming, aged 33

> I was very down at that time [because of the divorce, our note] and a friend of mine came to visit me a lot to comfort me [...] and sometimes brought me some booklets about Christianity [...] She invited me to a church and said that my broken heart could be healed. I refused a couple of times, because I'm a university teacher [...] as a scientist, I didn't believe the God stuff [...] I went only for the sake of politeness, because she's been very kind [...] After I became a Christian, I got to know that the church we went to was the largest Christian church in China [...] It is probably the first church built by Hudson Taylor.
> Female participant from Zhejiang, aged 56

---

10   The officially sanctioned Protestant Churches in China following along the principles of self-governance, self-support, and self-propagation.

My grandma is a Christian [...] She didn't read much, but she's got a Bible [...] I remember, when I was just a little girl, she used to tell me some stories from the Bible about the first man Adam and first woman Eve, the Great Flood [...] Of course, I heard about the name Jesus long before coming to the UK in the 80s when those English Christians tried to 'lure' me to their homes for Bible studies.

Male participant from Hubei, aged 49

My first contact with Christianity was through the English teacher in the university [in China, our note]. I'm still not sure whether she's a Christian or not [...] She didn't "preach" to us, but used some passages from the English Bible to teach us [...] I must say, before that, I'm no stranger to Christianity at all. I saw some wedding ceremonies in beautiful gothic churches on the TV and in films [...] solemn but romantic [...] I often fantasised that I would have my wedding in a church.

Female participant from He'nan, aged 33

The four interview excerpts above present just a few examples of how today's Chinese could have encountered Christianity through objects (e.g., church buildings), individuals (e.g., family members, colleagues, friends, foreign English teachers), and cultural representations (e.g., books, TV dramas, films, music) of the religion. In our research, a majority of the interview participants have had some initial contacts with Christianity before their migration to Britain. Four of the thirty participants said that they have 'become Christians' before their migration; three of whom did not receive baptism until their arrival in Britain. This was due to their concerns over possible social prejudice, political repression, and familial conflict[11] that could potentially occur as a result of their baptism being interpreted as a public declaration of Christian faith in China.

Contrasting with the socially and politically restrictive sphere for Christianity in China, the historical and cultural Christian heritage in Britain provides an important source for the Chinese migrants' *imagination* of Britain as a "Christian nation". Our interviews have documented a number of narratives in which the new Chinese migrants, on their initial arrival in Britain, had expressed appreciation of the beauty of old English country parish churches and cathedrals dispersed across towns and cities in Britain. Such impressions of initial contact

---

11   During field work, Xinan Li, one of the researchers, observed that there are different patterns of responses to Christian conversion from the converts' families, varying from indifferent and resistant to cooperative and supportive.

with Christianity in Britain can have consolidated the view of Christianity as a Western religion, which is widely held among the Chinese. It may have led to some Chinese Christian converts' sentiment of bemoaning the decline of established Christian institutions in contemporary Britain (cf. Woodhead 2016) after their Christian conversion (see also Huang and Hsiao 2015).

Nevertheless, despite notable encounters with British Christian cultural heritage, we contend that encounters on a personal basis, i.e., encountering Christianity through personal contact with campus-based student Christian groups and various Christian evangelical and social-support ministries affiliated to local white English, international, and Chinese churches, plays a more important role contributing to the Christian conversion of new Chinese migrants (see also Li 2012; Dickson 2013).

Previous studies have documented that for many Chinese immigrants who convert to Christianity in the United States, proselytisation-oriented Christian hospitality that constitutes an important part of the "religious organisational ecology" in the host society (Yang and Wang 2006:180) contributes greatly to Christian conversion (see also Abel 2008). This is also true for the new Chinese migrants in Britain, as illustrated in the quote below:

> I received leaflets about their [local English Christians, our note] free café and went simply because it was free and I can practice my English [...] I didn't care too much whether they were Christians or not in the first place [...] They sometimes talked about God or Jesus and the Bible, which I didn't have that much interest in either [...] It seemed that our conversations [with local English Christians, our note] always remained at a very shallow level. But that was enough for me as a new-comer [...] I just thought religion is not a bad thing, it is supposed to teach people to do good things [...] I read the Bible [...] I thought it's a good thing for me to learn more about the Western culture [...]
> Female participant from Shanghai, aged 38

The interview excerpt above is a participant's account of how she was attracted to Christianity in Britain. She is a student-turned immigrant and now a full-time Christian missionary in Britain, ministering primarily to Chinese students and visiting scholars. Her experience of encountering Christianity in Britain is very typical among large numbers of Chinese student-turned immigrant Christians whom we have met during our research. Although some of them were indifferent, reluctant, or even resistant to get involved in religion in the first place, many have remained open to hospitable invitations to Christian-affiliated social events and groups, including those issued by local

English-dominated churches. Getting involved in events and groups such as a free international café or home-based Christian fellowships, often with meals provided, offers migrants opportunities to learn about English language and culture, and to gain insight into local English communities and British society more broadly. In this respect, local Chinese Christian communities may seem less attractive to some new Chinese migrants, as they do not provide the same opportunity to learn English. However, as quoted above, some new Chinese migrants face cultural, linguistic and religious barriers in communicating with English Christians, and choose instead to affiliate with local Chinese Christian communities in Britain. With their unique ethnic-cultural identity, Chinese Christian communities generate a strong sense of belonging for new migrants. The issues of identity and belonging will be discussed further below.

To further unpack the above-quoted female participant's experience from a personal encounter with Christianity (with an attitude of indifference) in Britain to becoming a Christian missionary eight years after her first arrival in Britain in 2004, we need to understand her experience of *becoming* a Christian before her vocational commitment as a Christian missionary. This developmental process of *becoming* a Christian, which in this study is termed *initiation*, is examined in the next section.

5   Initiation: The Introduction to Christianity through Culture

Initiation is an anthropological concept capturing a liminal process in a person's life in which the person is (often formally) introduced *into* a social group (cf. van Gennep 1960). For those who have encountered Christianity in various circumstances, before committing themselves to the faith, a further exposure to a Christian *culture*[12] facilitates their decision of conversion. In this study, we identify a particular Chinese Evangelical Christian culture (the CEC culture) in which the majority of our research participants are situated. Through the CEC culture, Christian beliefs, practices, and forms of communal life are introduced and communicated to the potential converts – those who have encountered Christianity and remained open to further exposure to the culture of the religion. The analysis of our empirical data allows us to characterise the CEC culture in three aspects: 1) the assumption and articulation of a unified

---

[12]   The term "culture" denotes a dynamic social process in which multiple dispositions are formed and particular identities are constructed, articulated, and maintained through individuals and institutions' endeavours to seek and provide coherent narratives (cf. Bielo 2009: 10–12).

Chinese identity (often overlooking intra-ethnic differences), 2) the propagation of Evangelical Christianity as mainstream (often overlooking a broader Christian theological spectrum), and 3) the emphasis on Christian evangelism and religious proselytisation.

Our finding of the first characteristic of the CEC culture, that of a unified Chinese identity, resonates with previous studies (e.g., Yang 1998; Guest 2003; Nyíri 2003; Huang and Hsiao 2015). It can be argued that some intra-ethnic differences in sub-ethnicity, pre-migration place of origin, and dialect play a role in the everyday lives of the British Chinese, and they may also be the source for different ministerial trajectories within Chinese Christian institutions (churches and para-church organisations). However, being recognised as a large ethnic minority category in Britain is notably important for our participants. When relating to or interacting with non-Chinese individuals and communities, Chinese Christians often assume and articulate a unified Chinese identity. An example can be found in the ethnography of a Chinese Christian fellowship in M town (MCCF) in the Midlands region in England. Below is a summary of the ethnographic account of an event of dispute between the leaders of MCCF and a white British lay Christian evangelist over the choice of baptismal venue for a new Chinese student convert.

> At the time of the ethnographic field work (2015), MCCF was a newly established Chinese Christian fellowship that met weekly for Bible study in a room borrowed from a local Anglican church (St. John's – a pseudonym). The core membership of MCCF comprised five Chinese mainlanders. Around ten people regularly attended the weekly meetings (twenty attendees at most). The majority of the MCCF members were Mandarin-speaking Chinese mainlanders. At times, attendees from Hong Kong, Taiwan, and Singapore were also present. MCCF was based in a local Anglican church (St. John's) with four of its core members attending the church. At the same time, some of the MCCF attendees also frequented an international café based in St. John's which was a joint and cross-denominational lay Christian international ministry organised by local white British Christians (not necessarily members of the St. John's). The dispute occurred when a Chinese student who, after attending a Bible study group led by a local white British Christian couple (organisers of the international café at the St. John's), decided to convert to Christianity by baptism. The local white British Christian couple, who identify as Pentecostal Charismatic Christians, contended that the baptism needed to be taken at a small local Pentecostal church of which they were members. Their proposal was made on the basis of questioning the theological and

spiritual validity of baptism at an established and "secularised" Anglican church such as St John's. However, the leaders of MCCF argued that it was better for the baptism service to be conducted at St. John's. This was because they considered the Anglican church, despite its institutional decline throughout England, a "mainstream" (and therefore more acceptable) church, representing an important part of what they construed as white British culture. The baptism of a Chinese person in an Anglican church could be viewed as a sign of the Christian God's "universal love for all people" including the Chinese. Moreover, by going ahead with the baptism in an Anglican church, the Chinese would demonstrate their expectation and intent to integrate into the local British community.

In the ethnography of MCCF, we observed that although more than half of its members were Mandarin-speaking Chinese mainlanders, sub-groups were created to accommodate non-Mandarin-speaking Chinese attendees. In the event of the above described dispute, all members of MCCF, some of whom also attended the white British couple's Bible study group, regardless of the intra-ethnic difference, supported the proposal of MCCF leaders. The Chinese student convert was eventually baptised at St. John's in February 2015.

Our research also observed that many new Chinese migrants, with their relatively better English proficiency than the previous generation and an eagerness to learn about Western culture, tend to be drawn to international evangelical Christian ministries operated by white British Christians in an effort to integrate into the local British society. However, the effective push for their Christian conversion often comes from the Chinese Christian communities. This phenomenon is pithily captured, in the words of an experienced Chinese Christian leader in Britain as, "a British hook but with a Chinese cook", which is also a strategy widely applied by many Chinese Christian institutions in Britain, particularly in the student ministries.

What the "Chinese cook" analogy means is, on the one hand, referring to the food culture particular to Chinese people. Our research, as well as previous studies, have documented that group meals with Chinese dishes in church halls, restaurants, or individual homes, especially during Chinese festive seasons, have been crucial in strengthening the communal bonding among Christian members of particular Chinese Christian communities and in evangelising the invited non-Christian friends. In an ethnography of a regular group meal organised by a voluntarily organised Chinese Christian fellowship in a Chinese restaurant, where both Christians and non-Christians were present, we noted the important role of a Christian ritual, that of "prayer of grace before meal", which contributed to the display and performance of the organisers' Christian identity. The practice in effect introduced one of the key Christian devotional practices, that of prayer, to the participants. It also facilitated subsequent conversations on religious affairs, which is not a common everyday topic for Chinese individuals during mealtimes. While the Christians took it as an opportunity for Christian evangelism, the non-Christians at the meal were exposed to a Christian culture articulated in Chinese terms and within a familiar Chinese social context.

On the other hand, the analogy of "a Chinese cook" indicates the effectiveness of introducing Christianity in Chinese linguistic and cultural contexts. For the new Chinese migrants who have encountered Christianity after their arrival in Britain through English-speaking British Christians, the religious language and theist worldviews would initially be alienating. This sense of alienation could be extended even if they later got in touch with and participated in Chinese Christian communities. This phenomenon is captured in the interviews where some of our participants have reported to be "unable" to or "uncomfortable" with praying in their mother tongues (Mandarin Chinese or other Chinese dialects) due to the lack of religious vocabularies when transiting from the British English-speaking Christian contexts to the Chinese Christian settings. This emotional and linguistic detachment from Christianity can be compensated once tenets of Christian beliefs and practices, as well as a larger ethnic Chinese Christian community in Britain, are introduced to them. This may be through individual communication or via participation in large Chinese Christian events, such as the evangelical events and Christian camps organised by different local Chinese Christian churches and fellowships and by the aforementioned missionary agencies, such as COCM.

So far, we have discussed the question left at the end of the last section concerning the possible ways through which the new Chinese migrants can become Christians, at least in part. Our discussion focuses on the role of a particular Chinese Evangelical Christian culture in Britain in the introduction and communication of tenets of Christian beliefs, practices, and the communal life in ordinary everyday social settings such as group meals. The next section will proceed to discuss the influence of the CEC culture on the individuals who can be regarded as potential converts to Christianity. Our analysis will focus on the development of religious commitment.

6   Commitment: The Cultivation of Religious and Communal Belonging

For researchers, an operational marker to identify a Christian convert is the reception of baptism (cf. Yang 1999). For many Chinese Christians we have interviewed, baptism remains an important marker of conversion as a theological and ecclesial necessity. Another crucial marker of conversion, however, is the "repentance of sins" and "the confession and reception of Jesus as the personal Lord and Saviour", in Christian parlance. A common practice of this confession of faith in Chinese Christian communities in Britain is to have the converted person verbally utter a prayer of decision, A.K.A., *juezhi* prayer (决志祷告). Sociologically, this practice indicates that the *agency* of the individual as verbally expressed through the prayer is of great importance to mark the person as Christian convert. We contend that this practice also marks the successful *initiation* of a potential convert. Furthermore, the reception of baptism, which individuals may take a long time to decide upon, is as a marker for a "full" convert. It shows the person's readiness for a public declaration of their faith and newly gained Christian identity, and their willingness to keep exploring and practicing the faith. This readiness and willingness of the new converts is characterised as *commitment* in this study.

Sociologically, the term commitment can be understood as a person's investment of finance, time, emotion and so forth in communities and collective activities, which needs to be developed and cultivated over time (c.f. Becker 1960). According to our observation and preceding literature (see also Coleman 2003; Gooren 2010), the religiously initiated Chinese Christian converts, at least for a period of time, tend to acquire additional theological knowledge for the development of further understanding of tenets of the faith. At the same time, with the increase in devotional practices of the faith (e.g., church-going, scripture-reading, praying) their emotional attachment to the faith tends to increase, as they seek to rely, sometimes overly, on the frame of reference provided by Christianity to interpret social and personal events and experiences. Lastly and most desirably (from the Christian institutions' point of view), the converts are expected to become active members participating and serving in a specific local Christian community, and sometimes carrying out the Christian evangelical mission beyond their own locality.

We capture the new Chinese migrant Christians' commitment in terms of belonging, that is, the religious persons' self-identification or identification by others in a "stable, contested or transient way", through which they orient themselves in accordance with religious teachings and ethical norms (Yuval-Davis 2006: 199). Belonging can be observed along two dimensions: the sense of belonging to the religious faith (religious belonging), and the sense of belonging to a specific faith community (communal belonging).

To cultivate religious belonging, the converts often actively seek to deepen their intellectual understanding of spiritual, religious, and theological knowledge. This is achieved by increasing their devotional practices (both public and private) such as attending church and Christian events, praying, and reading religious materials. By doing so, the converts are likely to consolidate their intellectual and emotional attachment to the religious language and interpretive framework that they have acquired through their practices. An example of how the sense of religious belonging for Chinese Christian converts is developed is provided here:

> The idea of God was OK for me [...] We Chinese have always believed in *tian* [天, translated as Sky, which religiously can be rendered as Heaven, suggesting a transcendent realm beyond the human and material world, our note]. I just find the idea of sin [*zui*罪, in Chinese can also be transliterated as crime, our note] quite puzzling. I'm not a bad person, at least not a criminal. That's why I always refused to admit that I'm a sinner and confess my sins [...] His [the preacher's, our note] sermon that night helped me a lot. I remembered he asked us to write down whatever we have done wrongly in the past and make a wish to try to correct them in the future and nail it on the cross. [...] I think it's a very good idea [...] Now I have read the Bible, and found that many things that we might consider OK are not allowed in God's eyes [...] I'm not perfect, and I can't promise to correct all my bad habits instantly, but at least I now have the motivation to try [...] I think you just have to look around and see what a mess we [the human beings, our note] have made in the world, the wars, plagues, death [...] I do wish that more people can admit their sins, come to Jesus, and do the right things [...]
> (Female participant from Hubei, aged 45)

This rather long interview excerpt exhibits the process of a female participant's acceptance of the Christian doctrine of sin, upon which she based her change of attitude and her development of Christian commitment. As Smith (2007: 172) has pointed out, the Christian belief of sin can sound 'negative and gloomy', even 'intellectually far-fetched' for non-Christians, which is one of the many intellectual stumbling blocks for Christian conversion. However, as a result of religious encounters and faith initiation, the "belief content of the Christian faith gives rise to certain practices and experiences – particularly emotional ones – that many people find highly engaging, compelling, persuasive, and convincing" (Smith, 2007:167). The conversion of this particular female participant occurred during her attendance at a COCM organised gospel camp in 2016, at which one of us (Xinan Li) was also present as a participant observer. The preacher's sermon mentioned by the female participant and which facilitated her acceptance of the belief, drew a linkage between the Christian notion of sin and the Chinese legal-moral concept of *zui* by relocating the abstract theological idea in people's everyday experience. Having accepted the belief on the ground of its experiential relevance, she not only shifted her negative emotion attached to the belief of sin to the interpretive attribution of her real-world experience to the Christian view of human nature as intrinsically evil and therefore in need of religious redemption, but also developed a "missionary attitude" (Gooren, 2010: 49) as part of her commitment to Christian evangelism, as she "wished more people to come to Jesus".

The cultivation of religious belonging contributes to the cultivation of communal belonging and *vice versa*. While the Christian belief system includes interpretations of metaphysical realities, it also emphasises the importance of community life and provides moral and ethical instructions. Our research identifies three faith-informed ethics, namely, love, care, and voluntary communal service (see also Nyhagen and Halsaa 2016). New Chinese Christians can learn and practice Christian ethics by voluntarily serving in different roles in communities ranging from cooks, drivers, facility managers, and event coordinators, to Bible and Sunday-school teachers, pastoral supporters and counsellors, worship leaders, and lay preachers. Their service can, in turn, contribute to their own belonging to the community and also to the broader CEC culture in which newcomers can encounter and potentially be initiated to Christianity. Some Chinese migrant Christians in Britain commit not only to Chinese-specific communities but also to local British and wider international Christian ministries and communities. Having developed a religious belonging that is based on and rooted in a strong ethnic Chinese identity, such migrants are also able to orient themselves toward a universal and cosmopolitan Christian community[13] (cf. Huang and Hsiao 2015).

7   Conclusion: Conversion and Community

This chapter has examined different stages of conversion to Christianity among the new Chinese migrants in Britain. Applying a three-stage processual model, including *encounter, initiation* and *commitment*, it suggests a dynamic sociological connection between Christian conversion and the building and growth of contemporary Chinese Christian communities in Britain. Starting from encountering Christianity in various circumstances in China and/or Britain, to going through the process of faith initiation in a particular Chinese Evangelical

---

13   An example is the current COCM's mission statement, entitled "Reaching the Chinese to Reach Europe".

Christian culture, the new Chinese migrants can develop their commitment to the Christian faith and to communities in which they are situated. Our findings also suggest that some new Chinese migrant Christians, especially the young and well-educated, have developed an international and cosmopolitan orientation in their Christian commitment. We conclude that the commitment-centred conversion, upheld by mainline Chinese Christian institutions and practiced by individual Chinese Christians, contributes to and is likely to sustain the continuous growth of the Chinese Christian communities in Britain.

References

Abel, Andrew Stuart. 2008. " 'It's the People Here': A Study of Ritual, Conversion, and Congregational Life Among Chinese Christians." Unpublished PhD Dissertation. University of Massachusetts.

Bebbington, David W. 1989. *Evangelicalism in Modern Britain: A History from the 1730s to the 1980s*. London: Unwin Hyman.

Becker, Howard S. 1960. "Notes on the Concept of Commitment." *American Journal of Sociology* 66(1): 32–40.

Benton, Gregor., and Terence. Gomez, Edmund. 2008. *The Chinese in Britain, 1800-Present: Economy, Transnationalism, Identity*. UK: Palgrave Macmillan.

Bielo, James S. 2009. *Words Upon the Word: An Ethnography of Evangelical Group Bible Study*. New York: New York University Press.

Cao, Nanlai. 2013. "Renegotiating Locality and Morality in a Chinese Religious Diaspora: Wenzhou Christian Merchants in Paris, France." *The Asia Pacific Journal of Anthropology* 14(1): 85–101.

Cao, Nanlai. 2005. "The Church as a Surrogate Family for Working Class Immigrant Chinese Youth: An Ethnography of Segmented Assimilation." *Sociology of Religion*, 66(2): 183–200.

Chinese Church in London. 2000. "Fifty Years of Growth." London: Chinese Church in London (CCIL).

COCM. 2010. *Reaching the Chinese to Reach Europe – COCM 60th Anniversary Album*. Milton Keynes: Chinese Overseas Christian Mission.

Coleman, Simon. 2003. "Continuous Conversion? The Rhetoric, Practice, and Rhetorical Practice of Charismatic Protestant Conversion." In *The Anthropology of Religious Conversion*, edited by Andrew Buckser and Stephen Glazier, 15–27. Oxford: Rowman & Littlefield Publishers, INC.

Dickson, Andrea Deborah Claire. 2013. "Coming Home: A Study of Values Change Among Chinese Postgraduates and Visiting Scholars Who Encountered Christianity in the UK." Unpublished PhD Dissertation. University of Nottingham.

Fiedler, Katrin. 2010. "China's 'Christianity Fever' Revisited: Towards a Community-Oriented Reading of Christian Conversion in China." *Journal of Current Chinese Affairs* 39(4): 71–109.

Fowler, James W. 1981. *Stages of Faith: The Psychology of Human Development and the Quest for Meaning*. San Francisco: Harper and Row.

Fowler, James, W., and Lynn. Dell, Mary. 2006. "Stages of Faith from Infancy Through Adolescence: Reflections on Three Decades of Faith Development Theory." *The Handbook of Spiritual Development in Childhood and Adolescence.*, no. 2004: 34–45.

Gennep, Arnold van. 1960. *The Rites of Passage*. Edited by B Vizedom, Monika and L Caffee, Gabrielle. Translated. London: Routledge and Kegan Paul.

Gooren, Henri. 2010. *Religious Conversion and Disaffiliation: Tracing Patterns of Change in Faith Practices*. Basingstoke: Palgrave Macmillan.

Guest, Kenneth J. 2003. *God in Chinatown: Religion and Survival in New York's Evolving Immigrant Community*. New York: New York University Press.

Hall, Brian. 2006. "Social and Cultural Contexts in Conversion to Christianity among Chinese American College Students." *Sociology of Religion* 67(2): 131–147.

Huang, Yuqin. 2017. "Becoming Missionaries: Gender, Space and Subjectivities in Chinese Christian Communities in the UK." *Asia Pacific Journal of Anthropology* 18(3): 211–27.

Huang, Yuqin, and I-hsin Hsiao. 2015. "Chinese Evangelists on the Move: Space, Authority, and Ethnicization among Overseas Chinese Protestant Christians." *Social Compass* 62(3): 379–95.

Jindra, Ines W. 2014. *A New Model of Religious Conversion: Beyond Network Theory and Social Constructivism*. Brill.

Jindra, Ines W. 2008. "Religious Stage Development Among Converts to Different Religious Groups." *International Journal for the Psychology of Religion* 18 (May): 195–215.

Jones, Douglas. 1987. "The Chinese in Britain: Rebirth of a Community." *Journal of Ethnic and Migration Studies* 14 (1–2): 245–47.

Klein, Thoralf. 2011. "Conversion to Protestant Christianity in China and the 'Supply-Side Model': Explaining Changes in the Chinese Religious Field." *Religion* 41(4): 595–625.

Li, Daguo. 2012. "Out of the Ivory Tower: The Impact of Wider Social Contact on the Values, Religious Beliefs and Identities of Chinese Postgraduate Students in the UK." *Race Ethnicity and Education* 15(2): 241–58.

Liu, Garland Ching-Mui. 1992. "A Sociological Study of the Chinese People in Aberdeen and Elgin, With Special Reference to the Catering Business." Unpublished PhD Dissertation. Aberdeen University.

Madsen, Richard, and Elijah Siegler. 2011. "The Globalization of Chinese Religions and Traditions." In *Chinese Religious Life*, edited by David A. Palmer, Glenn Shive, and Philip L Wickeri, 227–40. Oxford: Oxford University Press.

Mannheim, Karl. 1952. "The Sociological Problem of Generation." In *Essays on the Sociology of Knowledge*, 163–95. UK: Taylor & Francis.

Marcus, George. 1995. "Ethnography in/of the World System: The Emergence of Multi-Sited Ethnography." *Annual Review of Anthropology* 24: 95–117.

McGuire, Meredith B. 2008. *Lived Religion: Faith and Practice in Everyday Life*. Oxford: Oxford University Press.

Nyhagen, Line and Beatrice Halsaa 2016. *Religion, Gender and Citizenship: Women of Faith, Feminism and Gender Equality*. Basingstoke: Palgrave Macmillan.

Nyíri, PÁL. 2003. "Moving Targets: Chinese Christian Proselytizing among Transnational Migrants from the People's Republic of China." *European Journal of East Asian Studies* 2(2): 263–301.

ONS. 2015. "2011 Census Analysis Index." London. https://www.ons.gov.uk/census/2011census/censusanalysisindex#ethnicity-national-identity-language-and-religion. Accessed 1 June 2019.

Rambo, Lewis, Ray. 1993. *Understanding Religious Conversion*. Yale University Press.

Rao, Xinzi. 2017. "Revisiting Chinese-Ness: A Transcultural Exploration of Chinese Christians in Germany." *Studies in World Christianity* 23(2): 122–40.

Smith, Christian. 2007. "Why Christianity Works: An Emotions- Focused Phenomenological Account." *Sociology of Religion* 68(2): 165–78.

Snow, David, and Richard, Machalek. 1984. "The Sociology of Conversion." *Annual Review of Sociology*, no. 10: 167–90.

Streib, Heinz. 2005. "Faith Development Research Revisited: Accounting for Diversity in Structure, Content, and Narrativity of Faith." *The International Journal for the Psychology of Religion* 15(2): 99–121.

Wang, Yuting. 2004. "Religious Conversion to Christianity Among Students from the People's Republic of China." San Francisco, California. http://hirr.hartsem.edu/sociology/wang.html. Accessed 1 June 2019.

Wang, Yuting, and Fenggang Yang. 2006. "More than Evangelical and Ethnic: The Ecological Factor in Chinese Conversion to Christianity in the United States." *Sociology of Religion* 67(2): 179–92.

Weller, Paul. 2008. *Religious Diversity in the UK: Contours and Issues*. London & New York: Continuum International Publishing Group.

Wong, Lai fan. 2006. "From Atheist to Evangelicals: The Christian Conversion Experiences of Mainland Chinese Intellectuals in the U.S.A." Boston University.

Woodhead, Linda. 2016. "The Rise of 'No Religion' in Britain: The Emergence of a New Cultural Majority." Journal of the British Academy 4 (December): 245–61. https://www.thebritishacademy.ac.uk/documents/1043/11_Woodhead_1825.pdf.

Xiang, Biao. 2013. "Multi-Scalar Ethnography: An Approach for Critical Engagement with Migration and Social Change." *Ethnography* 14(3): 282–99.

Yang, Ching-Kun. 1961. *Religion in Chinese Society: A Study of Contemporary Social Functions of Religion and Some of Their Historical Factors*. California: University of California Press.

Yang, Fenggang. 1998. "Chinese Conversion to Evangelical Christianity: The Importance of Social and Cultural Contexts." *Sociology of Religion* 59(3): 237.

Yang, Fenggang. 1999. *Chinese Christians in America: Conversion, Assimilation, and Adhesive Identities*. University Park, Pennsylvania: Pennsylvania State University Press.

Yang, Fenggang, and Joseph B Tamney. 2006. "Exploring Mass Conversion to Christianity among the Chinese: An Introduction." *Sociology of Religion* 67(2): 125.

Yuval-Davis, Nira. 2006. "Belonging and the Politics of Belonging." *Patterns of Prejudice* 40(3): 197–214.

CHAPTER 6

Chinese Christian Community in Germany

Home-Making and Chineseness

Jie Kang

1   Introduction

This chapter describes the interaction between ideology and practice among Chinese Christians in Germany, and how this is affected by ethnic enclaves, transnational connections and cultural differences among the Chinese. It presents a contrasting picture of home-makers (missionaries) and home-seekers (believers) in the Chinese diaspora. The article also illustrates how the transnational Chinese Christian community is well connected globally yet relatively isolated within German society.

An event that throws into relief this multilayered interaction of ideology, expectation, practice, and global versus local position is the Easter Chinese Christian Camp, held over five days and four nights every year in March or April. It expresses both the overall solidarity of Chinese Christians in Germany and their relative isolation from wider Germany society and German Christianity. However, beneath this expression of solidarity are the differences referred to above. This camp is the most important occasion for Chinese Christians in Germany to meet one another. As a brother named Sun told me, "It is the biggest party for Chinese Christians [in Germany]." Indeed, there are 300 to 400 participants each year, who usually gather in a youth hostel in one of the big German cities for four days: for example, Berlin in 2018 and Frankfurt in 2019. Before 2012, the camp was promoted among all the Chinese Christian fellowship groups and churches in Germany. In recent years, some well-established churches, such as the Chinese Christian Congregation Berlin, have organized their own camps. The aim of the Easter Camp is to create an opportunity for Chinese Christian fellowship groups to meet and a place to establish a collectively solemn, emotional and sacred atmosphere of worship for all Chinese Christians in Germany. Some believers speak of the burning, heartfelt passion that they experience when attending, in contrast to the "cooler" emotions of everyday life away from the camp. Believers describe the event as "a spiritual shot or gas station," which boosts and deepens their faith. They talk, moreover, of how affected they are by living closely with both believers and invited seekers over four days. At a meeting after the event, many believers shared the view that the atmosphere is warm and moving, making them feel at home and belonging in a big family. The event has a full and tight schedule from 7 am to 10 pm, covering teaching on Christian beliefs, a retreat involving total immersion in three sermons per day (over 10 in all), morning Bible group study, evening discussion of sermons, and time for believers and seekers to ask questions about Christian beliefs. Workshops discuss how Christian beliefs can be applied to everyday issues concerning family, marriage, friendship, love relationships and money and time management.

The accommodation also fosters solidarity and connectedness. It is common for four to five people to share a single room in the youth hostel chosen by the camp organizers, who must take into account the needs for low costs and large enough facilities for the huge number of attendees. Commenting on how these few days together encourage mutual enhancement of faith and the building of networks among Chinese Christians, Brother Sun said, "When we go to the camp and reside with other young male believers, we usually talk about our lives and our faith until very late at night. The experience makes us very close to each other." Recently, more than 200 Christians from all over Germany accepted Brother Chen's invitation to attend his wedding in a small town in the middle of the country. Asked how he knew so many people, he replied that it was because he had attended annual camps over the past 10 years while studying in Germany. The Easter Camp is also important in recruiting converts. Invited seekers become the focus of group persuasion as believers ply them with questions about why they haven't yet converted. Already moved by the sermons, singing of psalms and expressions of love and concern, they report how easy it is to yield to such pressure.

The considerable organization needed to host this major event is shared by several church leaders, church members, the Friends of Mission to the Chinese in Germany and the Chinese Library in Germany. Speakers at the Easter Camp are usually pastors or theological seminary teachers invited from Chinese-speaking countries or regions such as Taiwan, Singapore or Hong Kong. There are no speakers from mainland China, because the leadership network of the Chinese Christian church in Germany comprises people from Hong Kong or Taiwan and descendants of such people.

Despite taking place in Germany, this huge event is organized entirely by the Chinese, for the Chinese. Hardly any Germans are involved, except for the service staff at the hostel. There are approximately 150,000 people of Chinese origin or descent in Germany, including 60,000 students,[1] of whom Christians are a small proportion – about 5 percent, according to Oblau (2011:148).

---

[1] Interview with an officer of the Chinese embassy in Berlin, 2 February 2019.

Christian and non-Christian Chinese in Germany have the same range of origins, from recently arrived mainlanders to those drawn earlier from Taiwan or Hong Kong. Although sharing a common sense of "Chineseness," these groups display subtle cultural and political differences.

At first we might see this as a case of Chinese multicultural diversity, given the intermingling of peoples of different origins, customs and activities who have come in successive migratory waves to Germany: it reflects the internal diversity among Chinese and not the transcultural encounter between Chinese and non-Chinese Germans. This because the Chinese in Germany constitute an extreme case of a self-contained sociocultural enclave, which is isolated from the surrounding society.

However, the more established Chinese Christian fellowships in Germany can be seen as significant strands of the transnational ethnic non-mainland Chinese Christian network or diaspora covering Southeast Asia, North America and Europe. More-recent migrants from mainland China may eventually return home but are meanwhile sought out as possible converts to Christianity by pastors of mainly Hong Kong and Taiwanese origin. They are invited to church fellowships and to the Easter Camp.

2 Transnationalism and Ethnic Enclave

The Chinese Christian community in Germany is both part of a transnational religious network covering Southeast Asia, North America and Europe *and* an isolated ethnic enclave exclusively focused and based on Chinese. "Ethnic enclave" broadly refers to a geographic space with a high concentration of people from a recognized and distinctive sociocultural grouping. It is commonly based on economic activity including business and entrepreneurship, as found, for example, in Chinatowns or Wenzhou villages in various cities (Zhou and Logan 1989; Zhou 1992; Guest 2003; Cao 2005). However, the Chinese Christian community in Germany has created a different type of enclave, neither a geographical nor a physical concentration of Chinese living and working together. Rather, it is a discursive network of people connected through their shared faith, expressed in regular Sunday meetings and through workshops and Bible study. The church's physical space is a contact zone where lasting interpersonal bonds can be established and maintained. As a close-knit network built on trust, loyalty and kinship-like relationships, the Chinese Christian community provides emotional and physical support and the opportunity to exchange useful information. At the same time, as *net* suggests, this can also mean that individuals get caught up in it and become isolated from the rest of society. The Christian network is thus strongly inclusive in its emotional and social hold but exclusive in circumscribing believers' wider social involvement.

Transnationalism, according to Vertovec (2009:139), is "the actual, ongoing exchanges of information, money and resources – as well as regular travel and communication – that members of a diaspora may undertake with others in the homeland or elsewhere within the globalized ethnic community." The Chinese Christian network certainly comprises cross-border connections through which resources of human and capital constantly flow. However, previous studies have shown that the main features of the Chinese Christian network are its ethnocentricity (Yang 2002; Nyiri 2003; Huang and Hsiao 2015) and its independence of and relative isolation from other international Christian organizations, so its exchanges and linkages involve mainly ethnic Chinese rather than non-Chinese Christians. This may be because of the highly distinctive nature of Chinese language, culture and self-perception, which have the same isolating effect in non-Christian Chinese formal and informal social networks.[2] There is also a preference to have full control over their organization and their missionary expansion and church. Moreover, the major linkages of the Chinese Christian transnational network are made through individuals and based on personal rather than institutional connections. As Yang (2002:135) points out, "The most prominent transnational ties between [the Houston Chinese Church] and Hong Kong are those linking pastors." As this article will show, Chinese Christian transnational ties between Canada, the United States, Taiwan, Hong Kong and Germany are indeed strongly dependent on individual pastors and missionaries.

The Chinese Christian community in Germany differs from most other transnational religious networks, whose connections are mainly and directly between the homeland and the host country: the resources of the Chinese community in Germany are from neither mainland China nor Germany but rather Southeast Asia and North America, with mainland students being the target of evangelization. The dynamic underlying this process within the Chinese Christian community in Germany is the fact that church leaders are

---

2 Denominations do not play an important role in contemporary German Christianity where the division between churches has become largely irrelevant since the ecumenical movement of the early nineteenth century. Chinese churches or fellowship groups often borrow or rent German churches from different denomination randomly, including Lutheran, Baptist or Reformed churches, mainly depending on the cooperative willingness of individual German church leaders with regard to lending or renting a place to the Chinese church. Thus, neither German nor Chinese churches are preoccupied with denominational differences.

missionaries originally from Taiwan or Hong Kong, while church members are from the Chinese mainland.

Compared with Chinese migration to the US and UK, Chinese migration to Germany is relatively new. Since 2004, these migrants are predominantly young, first-generation students, the largest group among foreign students in German universities. This is unlike the situation of Chinese university students in the US, of whom about half were born there (Hall 2006). Over the past 10 years, an increasing number of Chinese students have obtained the legal status to live and work in Germany upon graduation, becoming white-collar middle class with stable incomes. While Chinese migrants to Germany tend to be relatively well-educated students and workers, those who earlier migrated to the US and other parts of Europe were often undocumented, illegal and socially marginalized, coming from particular areas of China such as Wenzhou, Fujian and Canton, speaking distinctive dialects and living in very localized ethnic enclaves, for example Chinatown in New York (Cao 2005; Cao 2013; Guest 2003). By contrast, the later Chinese migrants to Germany come from across the Chinese diaspora and use only Mandarin with one another at the church. Unlike the situation in France and Italy, there aren't many Wenzhou Christians in Germany. The few Wenzhou Christians, who are mainly Chinese restaurant owners, are usually unable to actively engage in church activities which are largely run by highly educated Chinese students. The huge gap between them of culture and education generally deters Wenzhou Christians from becoming regular church-goers. These different migratory and settlement contexts condition religion's function for each group.

Yang (1999:9) notes that Chinese Christian immigrants in the US have three identities: Christian, American and Chinese. He argues that the Chinese Christian church helps its members assimilate to US society while preserving their adherence to many aspects of traditional Chinese culture. By contrast, the church in Germany doesn't aim to secure German sociocultural and political identity for Chinese immigrants, who are already empowered by their education, legal status and working experience in German society. Besides, since they live and work legally in Germany, it is neither obligatory nor necessary for them to assimilate socioculturally, because they may, through the Chinese Christian church, secure a home in the diaspora, together with spiritual, emotional and practical support. As the Hongkonger Pastor Tian told me, "I don't feel that I actually live in Germany. I often say that I am here to work among Chinese. Basically, we live in a Chinese environment… Every day we work and serve Chinese people. I don't have time and language capacity to engage with German society. To be honest, I am in Germany but working for Chinese. Therefore, I can't assimilate into German society." Although Pastor Tian may be an extreme case because he and his wife don't have children, who could be agents of their integration into German society, Chinese missionaries and followers there do generally lack a substantial connection to Germany. Moreover, the enormous time and energy they put into supporting church activities limits believers' opportunities for contact with Germans and thus for learning German.

Cao (2013:90) portrays Chinese Christians in Europe as "embedded in a unique transnational Chinese space," which mainly refers to the religious connection between mainland China and the host society (see also Nyiri 2003). The Chinese Christian community in Germany has also created a distinctive Chinese space, which is part of an ethnoreligious network of Chinese Christians spanning Taiwan, Hong Kong and North America. There is no direct, institutionalized transfer of personnel and resources between mainland China and Germany, owing to Chinese political constraints on Christianity.

3 The Chinese Christian Network in Germany

Huang and Hsiao (2015) nicely illustrate this overarching, transnational ethnoreligious network: the gospel has been disseminated in a historical evangelical circle "beginning in mainland China, moving to Taiwan, Hong Kong and Southeast Asia, then on to North America, and finally back to mainland China" (386). Since 2000, Europe has become an important "Gospel transit point" in bringing Jesus back to mainland China, due to the increasing number of Chinese students and scholars who go there, especially to the UK, France and Germany.

The person most responsible for setting up the Mandarin ministry in Germany is Reverend Siegfried Glaw, a German member of the Overseas Missionary Fellowship (OMF) who speaks fluent Chinese and worked in Taiwan from 1966 to 1978. He is the founder of the Chinese Lending Library (DLL) currently located in Hannover and was the first president of the Friends of Mission to Chinese in Germany (FMCD). The FMCD was founded in 1985 and provides legal documents and logistical assistance for missionaries who come to work among Chinese in Germany (Nagy 2014). It also functions as a hub of the Chinese Christian network in Germany, organizing regular missionary meetings and annual regional and transregional Christian camps. Currently, there are 18 major cities with at least one Chinese Christian fellowship connected with the FMCD. However, despite its importance, the FMCD mainly assists and plays a supporting rather than a controlling or managerial role.

The Chinese Christian network in Germany "displays a low degree of institutionalization" (Oblau 2011:149), with members and entities not consistently following or being tied to specific institutions. Even congregations connected to the FMCD display diverse denominational backgrounds, reflecting the missionaries' varied cultural and theological backgrounds. Other fellowships and churches either are connected to other German Christian organizations through which they acquire legal missionary documentation, such as the Christian and Missionary Alliance, or, in some rare cases, organize the documentation themselves. For instance, the Chinese Christian church in Nuremberg, one of the few Chinese churches to have purchased its own building, is run by the churchgoers themselves. Four gifted brothers without theological training give the sermons at Sunday worship. That said, most Chinese Christian fellowships are led by missionaries sent and supported by churches or missionary societies outside Germany.

Moreover, all Chinese Christian fellowships operate fully independently of German institutions financially: their money comes largely from churches and from the contributions of congregations outside Germany. Thus, despite being physically located in Germany, the Chinese Christians there are resourced by the transnational ethnic Chinese Christian network. We may ask how this flow of material and human resources has been transmitted over long- and short-term missionary work. Missionary-led church operation is in fact the main feature of the Chinese church in Germany. Countless ethnic Chinese missionaries have devoted their lives to developing the Chinese Christian community there from a collection of informal, small Bible study groups into a large, more formalized community of faith.

4 Chinese Sunday Worship

In 1980 the early, small Chinese Bible study groups in Germany consisted of only a few, irregularly attending, mainly Taiwanese participants. There were hardly any mainland students or migrants going to Germany then. Since 2000 there has been a massive influx of such students, very few of whom were Christian before then. Taiwanese Christians thus pioneered Chinese Christianity in Germany, and although the increasing number of mainland Christians has since made them a minority, their founding contribution isn't forgotten. As the mainlander Brother Liu affectionately told me, "Taiwanese Christians contributed greatly to the evangelical work among mainland Chinese" in Germany.

Before 2000, hardly any pastor or preacher worked full-time among Chinese Christians in Germany, who therefore depended on "irregulars" instead. Brother Liu, from a German university town, told of his great effort to persuade Pastor Wang from Canada to settle in his small town. Brother Liu's Bible study group had a small, fluctuating membership, from two to a dozen people, with no one qualified to teach the Bible or give spiritual guidance on theological or practical problems, such as those concerning premarital sex faced by young Chinese students in Germany.

At best, a pastor from a nearby big city would come once a month to preach a sermon and lead Sunday worship. But Brother Liu's fellowship mostly had to either attend a German church or do without Sunday worship. Because they neither fully understood nor deeply related to sermons and hymns in German, it mattered greatly that these believers later acquired their own Sunday worship in Chinese. Many such Christians recount how moved they were when they first had their own Chinese Sunday worship and were able to sing Chinese songs and hear Chinese sermons. Pastor Tian told me of the emotionality of the first Chinese Sunday worship he led in a small northern town: "The Holy Spirit worked greatly on that very day, and many brothers and sisters were moved to tears, since they had waited a long time for this day." Such events marked the transition from irregular to regular Chinese Sunday worship.

Socioeconomic change in mainland China has also greatly affected the Chinese ministry in Germany. As China's economy has grown, Chinese students studying in Germany have become wealthier. Their demands have changed, from work to pay for living expenses to a more comfortable lifestyle (i.e., enjoying tourism and eating out), which they could never afford before 2000. In those days they were grateful to be invited to meals at either the pastor's home or church. The church thus now finds it harder to attract Chinese students, a situation exacerbated by competition with the better funded, Chinese-government-organized Chinese Students and Scholars Association (CSSA).

5 The Church versus the Chinese Students and Scholars Association (CSSA)

In recent years, the Chinese government has reinforced its influence on the Chinese in Germany through the Chinese embassy there, which supports the CSSA in targeting Chinese scholars and students in universities. The embassy also encourages Chinese migrants to establish associations in German cities to meet the needs of Chinese immigrant families. The CSSA in most German universities has thus become more powerful than Chinese Christian churches in attracting Chinese students and fulfilling their needs, for two main reasons:

1. The CSSA provides a programme of welcome to newcomers from China and circulates information to official WeChat groups on such topics as studying and living in Germany, registering at a city hall or university, getting a visa

extended, applying for a bank account, renting an apartment or student dormitory and buying or selling household items, and even news about jobs offered by Chinese universities and companies. This information is much more detailed than what the relatively small Christian fellowship provides, which focuses on faith and a more limited range of practical issues.

2. As foreigners seeking a supportive and secure "official organization" (*zuzhi*), Chinese students tend to regard the CSSA as reliable and trustworthy, owing to the support and official recognition it gets from the Chinese government, with embassy personnel at most CSSA activities, including welcomes at many German universities' orientation programmes. The CSSA is, moreover, well connected to Chinese companies and the Confucius Institute in Germany. The annual Chinese Spring Celebration, a major CSSA event, is often sponsored by a Chinese tourist company in Germany. The CSSA also collaborates with the Confucius Institute in organizing such events as Chinese concerts and academic presentations.

Thus, while the Christian church provides a spiritual home and presents a more international image, the CSSA is a national political organization representing the Chinese Communist government through its provision of useful services and official connection with the homeland. Its strong political character particularly appeals to students and scholars who intend to climb the ladder of a career in Chinese government once they have finished studying in Germany. The CSSA provides an opportunity for practicing social skills among Chinese and, more important, a platform for networking across a wide range of contacts useful for a future career in China, including embassy officials and representatives of Chinese universities and companies.

Acting like a small "party branch" in many German universities, the CSSA can be seen as Chinese-government outreach. A key aim of the Chinese embassy is to protect immigrant Chinese. According to an official in the Berlin embassy, there are six or seven cases of unnatural death each year among Chinese in Germany. Every chairperson of a CSSA branch (of which there are over 100 in Germany) acts as a counsellor-protector for Chinese students and scholars in that university. For example, in 2018 the embassy ordered the CSSA chair in a small university city to look after three Chinese doctoral students who were suffering from severe depression, a task he regarded as outside his competence despite its being among his duties as the chair.

The instrumental nature of the CSSA contrasts with the more approachable psychological help proffered by the church, to which, according to Pastor Tian, students turn with really serious life problems, especially concerning marriage and parenting. These can be discussed with experienced, university-trained counsellors provided by church, often with success. While the CSSA and the church have different relationships to overseas Chinese, there is still some overlap in what they do, and they are thus in competition for students' affiliation.

Although the church was the first to work among and successfully attract Chinese students in Germany, the CSSA has now broadly usurped this role. For instance, in 2013 about 100 people attended the church welcome program in a small university town in northern Germany, but in 2018 fewer than 10 students participated. In contrast, the CSSA WeChat groups in that town now include almost 2,000 members.

As shown above, although the Chinese Christian community is indeed ethnocentric, it is also separate from, independent of and to some extent even opposed to Chinese-state-promoted global and national projects. There are two reasons for this. First, each Chinese Christian group prioritizes its own sociopolitical concerns, weakening the wider national sentiment needed to unify the Christian faith within the community. Second, their resources don't come from the mainland and so don't reinforce and aren't the basis of a shared sentiment of common origin. As I will now show, "Chinese" is in fact a broad and diverse concept encompassing a range of meanings.

6   From Diversity to Difference

Research on Chinese-migrant churches in the US and Europe describes subtle sociocultural differences between mainland Chinese and other ethnic/cultural Chinese, often identified by the terms *huaren* (for cultural Chinese, officially referring to diaspora Chinese who lack a Chinese passport), *zhongguo ren* (mainland Chinese) and *huaqiao* (overseas sojourners who hold a Chinese passport; this term isn't used much in everyday interactions but is still important officially, such as at Chinese embassies). Yang (1999:166–67) observes that a Chinese church in the US changed its national and political identity from *zhongguo ren* to *huaren* to avoid divisiveness among members from different backgrounds. He claims that the longer a Chinese migrant stays in the US, the weaker their *zhongguo ren* identity becomes. I now build on this work by analyzing developments in the deconstruction and reconstruction of "Chineseness" among Chinese Christians following the expansion of China's economic and political power.

In Germany the Chinese Christian community mainly comprises Chinese-speaking people from mainland China, Hong Kong, Taiwan, Singapore and Malaysia. Most congregants are from mainland China, while church leaders are usually missionaries from Hong Kong, Taiwan, the US and Canada. Despite all speaking "standard" Chinese (*zhong wen*) – along with their regional tongues – and recognizing some ethnic, cultural and political commonalities, they see themselves as differing according to their political and cultural backgrounds. The names, mentioned in the previous paragraph, that these groups use for themselves express significant if broad differentiation. There might be some overlap in these designations, but mixing them up can cause serious problems. For example, *zhongguo* has become a political category referring only to mainland China, so unlike in the situation described by Yang, rather than a decreasing use of *zhongguo ren*, in Germany has seen a clear division between it and *huaren*, the self-identification of Chinese speakers who aren't from mainland China. Thus, despite its small size, the Chinese Christian community in Germany has sometimes conflicting underlying dynamics between Christians (both leaders and congregants) from different countries and regions.

This isn't evident at first glance, since churches try to avoid public conflict. However, the various subgroups from Taiwan, Hong Kong and Southeast Asia are visibly separate and close-knit, often because their standard Chinese normally isn't as fluent as that of mainland Chinese, with the partial exception of Taiwanese, so they feel excluded during rapid talk and, for instance, jocular exchanges. There are three other reasons for this separation.

First, as mentioned above, the ethnic subgroups' different political backgrounds shape their identities and interactions with one another. Many Chinese Christian fellowships in Germany began as Bible study groups organized by a Taiwanese in the 1980s. In recent years, however, some Taiwanese Christians have begun emphasizing their Taiwanese identity and diluting their Chineseness, with even the notion of *huaren* becoming problematic for them. For instance, a Taiwanese brother insisted on changing the name of his fellowship from Huaren Jidu tu tuanqi (Chinese Christian fellowship) to Huayu Jidu tu tuanqi (Chinese-language Christian fellowship), since he doesn't wish to identify as *huaren*, despite the fact that Taiwanese chose the original name. This transformation is a result of the Taiwanization, including de-Sinicization, in Taiwan since 2000. While young Taiwanese question the notion of *huaren*, ethnic Chinese from Hong Kong and Southeast Asia normally accept the designation. It should be noted that Hongkongers often express love for the Chinese people but dislike the Chinese Communist government. However, they object to being regarded as *zhongguo ren*, with young Hongkongers especially sharing with Taiwanese a strong nationalistic sentiment and denial that they are part of China.

Second, by contrast, mainland Chinese display little concern for or consciousness of living in a multicultural environment. Growing up surrounded by the political discourse of unity and harmony advanced by the Chinese

Communist government, they are taught to deem the Taiwanese as *Taiwan tongbao* (Taiwanese compatriots) and other ethnic Chinese as *haiwai qiaobao* (overseas Chinese compatriots), since all belong to the big Chinese family. Therefore being friendly in Germany to their "compatriots" from Taiwan and Hong Kong, they are hurt when unexpectedly confronted by rejection and social distance.

On the other hand, mainland Chinese may unintentionally hurt ethnic Chinese when proudly expressing Chinese national pride with such phrases as "we Chinese people" (*women zhongguo ren*), implying that all ethnic Chinese belong to the political category of *zhongguo ren*.

Mainland Chinese often even regard all ethnic Chinese as children of China, eager to return to their "homeland" one day, despite having lived in their own countries for many years, they are thought to still possess "Chinese hearts" and deep feelings for China. The song "My Chinese Heart" vividly illustrates this idea. It was first performed by the Hong Kong singer Cheung Ming-man, at the CCTV New Year's Gala in 1984, and made him a national superstar. The song won numerous prizes and was popular until the 1990s in both mainland China and among overseas Chinese. With government encouragement, Cheung sang it at the 2012 CCTV New Year's Gala, but by then it had minimal effect.

> Mountains and rivers are only in my dreams
> I've not set my foot in the old country for ages
> Yet nothing can convert
> My Chinese heart
>
> Though I rig myself out in a foreign suit
> My heart is still Chinese
> My ancestors branded every inch of me
> With the Chinese mark
>
> Great Yangtze, Great Wall
> Yellow Mountain, Yellow River
> Weigh so heavily on my bosom
> Whenever or wherever I am
> You are always dear to me
>
> The blood surging in my heart
> Echoes, "China, China"
> Even though I was born in an alien land
> Nothing can convert my Chinese heart

The song may resonate for both mainlanders and nonmainlanders with echoes of past Chinese suffering. This doesn't alter the hurt of mutual misunderstanding. While nonmainlanders resent and even feel threatened by being classified as part of the mainland, mainlanders cannot understand why their friendly, innocent overtures are rejected by "compatriots," especially church leaders. Brother Sun told me, "It really pained me deeply when a preacher from Hong Kong said, 'I don't regard myself as *zhongguo ren*.'" His feeling of exclusion was made worse by the frustrated expectation that a church leader should be above political views and should instead promote unity.

Finally, disharmony may have grown in response to the recent expansion of Chinese state power and status, which, while reinforcing mainlanders' national pride, increases the threat felt by ethnic Chinese and their wish to remain distant from China. The rising tension is also evident in church leaders' discouragement of political talk at church, although at other times they might be willing to express confidences. For instance, while interviewing Pastor Tian, I hesitantly raised a sensitive question concerning his identity as a Hongkonger, yet, to my surprise, he was happy to answer me clearly and forthrightly: "The very day that we decide to become a missionary working among Chinese, we there and then give up our background. ... No matter how bad our Mandarin is, we need to learn so that we are able to communicate with Chinese. We need to learn the Chinese way of thinking. We decide to never criticize nor judge problems in China. We don't have the right to judge. You can condemn something, but we won't say anything. It is like if I come to your house as a guest. No matter how bad your house is, I have no right to blame your parents. ... At our church, there is no difference between Taiwan, Hong Kong and mainland China. ... In church, everybody must forget his or her political background. Forget you are Chinese, forget you are Taiwanese, forget you are Hongkonger. ... If anyone were to bring their political views to church, I would kick him or her out."

Pastor Tian neither denies his identity as a Hongkonger nor accepts becoming "Chinese." Rather, he is willing to give up his political, cultural and historical background for the sake of proselytizing Chinese students and as an indication of his humility. To convert mainland Chinese, he and his wife try to understand them, by living with them, helping them, cooking for them and listening to their stories. Pastor Tian said, "This matches the teaching of the Bible: 'The Word was made flesh, and dwelt among us' [John 1:14]. 'The Word was made flesh' means that God himself was made in the likeness of men. If we want to win over a certain group of people, we should be made in their likeness." Asked why she cooks *liangpi*, a popular, special northern Chinese noodle-like dish, which is difficult and unusual for a Hongkonger to make, Pastor Tian's wife answered, "Because of love. Chinese students like it so much. We can win their hearts by cooking this particular kind of food. I had never heard of this food before coming to Germany."

While Pastor Tian and his wife cultivate mainland Chinese students by downplaying their Hong Kong background, other ministries claim that Hongkongers have an advantage: their international status and connections help them build bridges between mainland and ethnic Chinese, integrating and unifying them. Trying to overcome the differences between ethnic and mainland Chinese may be seen as evidence of missionaries' wish to create trust between them. Some ethnic Chinese are willing to come to Chinese churches in Germany partially because the leaders aren't from mainland China. Conversely, as Preacher He told me, many mainland Chinese trust her precisely because she is a Hongkonger: she doesn't share their small Chinese social network, so they feel safer opening up to her than to other Chinese.

Despite occasional and often unintended conflicts between mainland and ethnic Chinese, the Chinese Christian congregation in Germany prioritizes mutual love and support across cultural and political backgrounds, with the church as a platform and contact zone where Christians can meet and try to overcome bias and misunderstanding through direct communication and close interaction.

7 Battlefield and Home Away from Home

As mentioned above, many Chinese Christian fellowships in Germany are led by missionaries from Hong Kong (like Pastor Tian), Taiwan or even Chinese-speaking Canadian or American churches.[3] For such missionaries, Germany is the frontier of the ministry, a "battlefield" where they strive to convert Chinese to Christianity. The main tactic is to create a homelike base for them or, as Pastor Wang puts it, "a home away from home." Similarly, Pastor Tian noted that "everything was started from the home" in his work among Chinese students, with a small Bible study group at his place. It is quite common for pastors and preachers to set up such groups, of up to 20 people, in their own houses, where students can feel "at home," perhaps moving elsewhere when the group grows larger.

These missionaries also draw on the crucial Chinese family ritual of regularly eating together at home, which Pastor Wang and his wife began to do with students immediately on arriving in a small university town in northern Germany, despite lacking resources, thus ensuring close relationships with their guests. At Christmas, Pastor Tian and his wife share dinner at home with Chinese

---

3 Note here the general contrast between churches led by missionaries sent from outside the locality and churches led by pastors who have grown up in the area that they serve.

students, who welcome the homelike atmosphere and delicious meals. In their church, this couple proudly displayed the renovated, professional-standard kitchen, able to provide warm food for hundreds.

Lonely away from home, Chinese students turn to missionaries for guidance and even express disappointment if they aren't reprimanded for wrongdoing, as their parents would do. If church is family, then the missionaries are family heads (*jiazhang*), and young Chinese converts rely on them, lacking the experience and authority to lead churches themselves.

A successful pastor therefore has different kinds of "parental" responsibilities: providing advice and pastoral care, organizing the church, teaching, preaching, training and leading worship. Pastors' wives cook, organize Sunday school for second-generation children, lead choirs, and counsel women with family and parenting issues. A church's development and style depend on its leaders, who are role models for believers: the hard work and devotion of the pastor and his wife foster the healthy growth of their church, while the opposite leads to loss of fellowship and members.

Pastor Zhang's wife remarked that "students don't have the burden of many family chores, and therefore it's easier to bring about change among them" – meaning obedience to church leaders. This is counterbalanced by the fact that Chinese students who neither have a stable income nor can stay in Germany after graduation cannot provide stable membership or financial contributions to the church. Missionaries aiming to establish a church in Germany need more families and professionals to become members, pay tithes and volunteer regularly. Brother Li, a deacon at a big Chinese church in northern Germany, said, "A family also has a lot of work. It's not an exaggeration to say that serving in church is like a form of work."

Germany is a battlefield of missionary work for missionaries working hard among Chinese migrants and students. They must also work to secure continuing support from their sending church or missionary society, especially given the high taxes and other expenses in a welfare society like Germany. They usually return every two years to report on their achievements and meanwhile send prayer letters to the brothers and sisters who support them. However, congregants in Germany are normally unaware of who their pastor's sending church or missionary society is, and of their missionaries' double identities and commitment to both sides. Short missions from the sending country, sometimes invited and hosted by pastors in Germany, can fill this knowledge gap, while creating personal contacts between Chinese Christians in Germany and the overseas church.

Organizing such missions is arduous, including accommodation and transportation schedules between fellowships. Each team member invests considerable time and energy and must pay for travel, accommodation and some organizational expenses. But the receiving congregation doesn't always welcome such missions joyfully, because the specially prepared programme of sermons, Bible study and testimony interrupts the normal church programme, especially if the notice or the interval between visits is too short. This kind of reception and the visit's brevity preclude the development of close relationships. Moreover, missionaries' pushy attempts at conversion can be counterproductive. A Chinese student said he felt uncomfortable when some members of a recent Canadian mission asked him why he hadn't yet converted and what kind of bias he had against conversion. In addition, short-term missionaries can come across as patronizing benefactors, sermonizing in a superior way to the receiving church.

The solution to these problems is seen as churches in Germany being able to pay pastors' salaries themselves. However, to do this, as Pastor Zhang observed, a church needs "at least 5 to 10 Chinese families who have settled down in Germany, with stable incomes and, most important, a willingness to commit to the church." It is much harder for Chinese students to find a job and settle down after graduation in a small university town than in Hamburg or Berlin. This is one reason why missionaries tend to move to bigger German cities, where Chinese students have better employment and family prospects, though even in a big city, an adequate church membership is difficult to achieve. Pastor Tian's church is a success story, regarded as due to his and his wife's many years of hard work, wise management and efforts in connecting with other German cities, all of which continues even though their church can now provide them with a stable income. This couple stands apart from pastors who isolate their church from others once it's established and focus on only its growth: seeing other Chinese Christian fellowships as competition, they reject possible collaboration. For example, a Chinese church in a big city in east Germany, where the pastor rejected a connection with other Chinese church leaders in the same city, because the church is firmly established and has become financially independent based on the large number of congregations making regular contribution. That said, most Chinese Christian churches continue to work together and support one another, as evident in the collaboration shown at the annual Easter Camp with which this article began.

8   Conclusion

At the most abstract level of ideology, Chinese and other Christians in Germany are aware of themselves as members of a common Christian community, but in practice they have little to do with one another, with the Chinese Christians preferring to operate independently. Chinese Christians in Germany see themselves as part of the wide transnational Chinese community, but this perspective is challenged by the community's internal sociopolitical differences, coinciding with those of geographical origin: mainland China, Hong Kong, Taiwan, Singapore, Malaysia and even North America. The Chinese Christians and their social organizations in Germany reflect these divisions, with pastors largely from Hong Kong and Taiwan and congregants, mostly students, predominantly from mainland China. The pastors, moreover, see themselves as Christian missionaries in Germany supported by church organizations in Hong Kong, Taiwan and North America. One of their major tasks is converting Chinese students in Germany to Christianity, which they attempt to do by persuading these students to regard their church in Germany as a "spiritual home" providing the security, well-being and advice that they would normally get in their own homes in mainland China. The missionaries hope that the students will carry the message of Christianity to other Chinese migrants in Germany and continue to practice and evangelize as Christians on their return to mainland China. These Chinese missionaries have met the emotional and other needs of Chinese students in Germany by providing them with care, advice and practical contacts and so attracting and attaching them to the church. However, the Chinese state's increasing influence on Chinese students in Germany has undermined this success in recent years, through its German embassy's state-sponsored Chinese Students and Scholars Association (CSSA), which offers services and facilities greater than what the churches can provide. Chineseness is thus constructed, deconstructed and negotiated in a diasporic Chinese Christian community that is institutionally completely separated from mainland China and unintentionally positioned in competition with the Chinese-state-led overseas organization the CSSA.

References

Cao, Nanlai. 2005. "The Church as a Surrogate Family for Working Class Immigrant Chinese Youth: An Ethnography of Segmented Assimilation." *Sociology of Religion* 66(2): 183–200.

Cao, Nanlai. 2013. "Renegotiating Locality and Morality in a Chinese Religious Diaspora: Wenzhou Christian Merchants in Paris, France." *Asia Pacific Journal of Anthropology* 14(1): 85–101.

Guest, Kenneth. 2003. *God in Chinatown: Religion and Survival in New York's Evolving Immigrant Community*. New York: New York University Press.

Hall, Brian. 2006. "Social and Cultural Contexts in Conversion to Christianity among Chinese American College Students." *Sociology of Religion* 67(2): 131–47.

Huang, Yuqin, and I-hsin Hsiao. 2015. "Chinese Evangelists on the Move: Space, Authority, and Ethnicisation among Overseas Chinese Protestant Christians." *Social Compass* 62(3): 379–95.

Nagy, Dorottya. 2014. "Envisioning Change in China: Evangelical Missionary Work among Chinese Students in Germany." *Social Sciences and Missions* 27: 86–115.

Nyiri, Pal. 2003. "Moving Targets: Chinese Christian Proselytizing among Transnational Migrants from the Peoples' Republic of China." *European Journal of East Asian Studies* 2(2): 263–301.

Oblau, Gotthard. 2011. "Chinese Christian Communities in Germany." *Religions and Christianity in Today's China* 1(2): 147–51.

Vertovec, Steven. 2009. *Transnationalism*. London: Routledge.

Wang, Yaohui, and Guofu Liu, eds. 2014. *Annual Report on Chinese International Migration*. Beijing: Social Sciences Academic Press.

Yang, Fenggang. 1999. *Chinese Christians in America: Conversion, Assimilation, and Adhesive Identities*. University Park, PA: Pennsylvania State University Press.

Yang, Fenggang. 2002. "Chinese Christian Transnationalism: Diverse Networks of a Houston Church." Pp. 129–48 in *Religion across Borders: Transnational Immigrant Networks*, edited by Helen Rose Ebaugh and Janet Saltzman Chafetz. Walnut Creek, CA: AltaMira.

Zhou, Min. 1992 *Chinatown: The Socioeconomic Potential of an Urban Enclave*. Philadelphia: Temple University Press.

Zhou, Min, and John R. Logan. 1989. "Returns on Human Capital in Ethnic Enclaves: New York City's Chinatown." *American Sociological Review* 54: 809–20.

CHAPTER 7

Going Global and Back Again
The Transformation of Chinese Christian Networks between Southeast Asia and China since the 1980s

Chris White and Jifeng Liu

1   Introduction

The extensive ties between South Fujian and Chinese communities in Southeast Asia have played vital roles in the revival of religion in reform era China. Inbound financial contributions and the desire of local officials to court investment opportunities from overseas Chinese has resulted in their intimate involvement in the resurgence of local religious practices in South Fujian. Branch temples in Southeast Asia, eager to reconnect with founding temples in China, have organized tours and arranged for deities to visit religious sites in coastal provinces. Overseas Chinese wanting to renew relationships with relatives and ancestral homelands have financed the rebuilding of ancestral tombs and lineage rituals. Most research on this topic has centered on the resurgence of traditional Chinese religious practices, such as folk religion or ancestral veneration (Dean 2010; Dean and Zheng 2010; Kuah-Pearce 2011). But it is not only traditional Chinese religions that have benefitted from the transnational ties to overseas Chinese, Protestant churches have also resumed connections with Chinese Christian communities in Southeast Asia (Liu 2017; Liu and White 2019).

This research asks to what extent and how overseas Chinese in Southeast Asia have contributed to Protestantism in China, and how this involvement has changed over the course of the reform era. As a global religion, research on Christianity commonly involves transnational dimensions, but this is often framed as missionary-sending (usually Western) and missionary-receiving (usually non-Western) cultures. This current analysis is transnational, but is firmly located in an Asian context. It deals with overseas Chinese, often referred to as *Huaqiao*, located in Southeast Asia, and Protestant congregations in China, specifically in South Fujian, the ancestral home of many overseas Chinese. Strictly speaking, the term *Huaqiao* refers to Chinese citizens living in nations all over the globe, but those in Taiwan, Hong Kong, and Macao are not officially considered *Huaqiao*. In this chapter, however, we focus on overseas

Chinese in Southeast Asia, and include those in Taiwan, Hong Kong, and Macao, since in practice Chinese (including *Huaren*, or Chinese with nationalities or citizenship in other countries) in these regions are often grouped together by the government. This study argues that *Huaqiao* influence in Chinese Christianity has been vital to many church congregations in coastal southeast China during the reform era, but that this involvement has experienced a shift due to the changing economic conditions, as well as the rise of second and subsequent generations of *Huaqiao*. We treat the structuring of religious networks and how they are used as a dynamic process that has been reshaped by China's rise and the consequently evolving relations between the Chinese communities in Southeast Asia and South Fujian.

This chapter will first review the role of *Huaqiao* in the cultural and religious life of China. This background is given to contextualize the following discussion of the contributions of *Huaqiao* to Protestant congregations during the first three decades of reform. Specifically, the construction of large churches in *qiaoxiang*, or ancestral hometowns which produced a large number of immigrants, in the 1990s and early 2000s often depended on donations from *Huaqiao*. The subsequent section frames such contributions as remittances, arguing these donations are often considered as support from ethnic Chinese compatriots rather than foreign funding. Finally, this chapter analyzes how *Huaqiao* support has shifted in two significant ways in recent years. First, *Huaqiao* funding of church-building projects has transitioned to support for theological training programs. Second, instead of narrowly focusing on ancestral hometowns, *Huaqiao* are increasingly spreading support for Protestant endeavors throughout China.

2 Linking Southeast Asia and China: *Huaqiao* as Bridges

For centuries, Chinese along the southeast coast of China have ventured to the "South Seas" in search of economic opportunities. Interaction with local and Western peoples in Southeast Asia eventually carved out an important niche for Chinese to serve as brokers, mediating economic and cultural matters and provided an important link for outside traders to access the Chinese market, which was largely closed to foreigners (Kwee 2013). Imperial China, especially during the Ming (1368–1644) and early Qing (1644–1911) dynasties, felt uneasy about interactions with outsiders. Emperor Qianlong's famous letter to King George in 1793 in which he explains that China does not desire or need British products is indicative of the disdain and distrust of outsiders manifested by Chinese officials. In fact, at various times, maritime bans were promulgated by imperial governors that attempted to eliminate coastal Chinese residents from traveling overseas or interacting with foreigners. Despite such measures, coastal communities, especially in Fujian, continued to take to the seas.

Historian of Fujian, Hugh Clark (2006), has referred to the coast as a "membrane" that helped moderate outside influence, but it may be more accurate to think of it as a conduit, linking Chinese in coastal regions with native town fellows residing in Southeast Asia. As Philip Kuhn (2008: 28) summarizes, "Instead of being a boundary, the seacoast was a connection." The connection was especially strong because many of the Chinese who left their houses in coastal China were sojourning rather than migrating. The idea was to temporarily venture to Southeast Asia for business or labor opportunities, but to eventually return home, ideally with profits to support relatives and strengthen the family in China. Sending young male sojourners, then, was a strategy many lineages relied upon, and not without risk. Not only was the travel by ship dangerous, there was always the possibility that the sojourner would not return, or even worse, would cut off any connection with the family in China. To mitigate such risks, a number of mechanisms were developed, including requiring wives (and possibly children) to remain in China (Shen 2012). *Huaqiao* communities in Southeast Asia also kept sojourners connected to their ancestral homes and kept tabs on family members abroad.

The result, according to Kuhn (2008), was that sojourning actually strengthened lineage ties. The mechanisms and networks that carried Chinese to Southeast Asia actually *increased* the connectedness with the hometown. *Huaqiao* communities in Southeast Asia, then, can be thought of as extensions of the ancestral village in China. Julie Chu (2010: 11), who researched how more recent immigrants from Fujian continue to influence the space of the natal village, offers a similar argument: "While mobility has typically been framed as a state of instability and dislocation, ... it [is] actually *immobility* that was experienced as the definitive form of displacement."[1] According to Chu, transnational mobility was so common in Fujian that not participating in this, or at least having access to it (through close relatives), was and is lamentable.

More visible than the familial sentiments that sojourning conjured was the economic support *Huaqiao* provided to ancestral towns. Construction of family houses, temples, ancestral halls, schools, or other philanthropic endeavors transformed *qiaoxiang* and were tangible manifestations of *Huaqiao* ties. Much more significant than the economic support for lineages in coastal China were new cultural practices and values and political ideas that *Huaqiao*

---

1 Italics in original.

spread in China (Zheng 2010). For instance, numerous modernization projects in Xiamen, the principal city in South Fujian, including roads, a railway, and new forms of banking, were spearheaded by *Huaqiao* and financed with investments from Chinese communities in Southeast Asia (Cook 2006).

While *Huaqiao* connections substantially changed *qiaoxiang*, they were not always appreciated by imperial rulers. In general, sojourning Chinese were traditionally considered traitors who had deserted their home country and were not trustworthy. However, by the last quarter of the nineteenth century, a new attitude of greater pragmatism began to dictate how Chinese authorities viewed *Huaqiao*. In fact, beginning in the 1870s, the Qing began to actively court Chinese *Huaqiao*, sending emissaries to Chinese communities in Southeast Asia and even selling imperial titles to those willing to contribute to China (Yen 1970).

The benefits of *Huaqiao* support were also apparent to reformers and revolutionaries, including Sun Yat-sen, and overseas Chinese played pivotal rules in the eventual overthrow of the Qing regime. The new cultural, political, and religious ideas embraced by many *Huaqiao* meant that these connections often overlapped with Protestant ties and church networks were successfully used by reformers and revolutionaries to bring about political changes in many regions of coastal southeast China in the early twentieth century (Dunch 2001; White 2017a).

In the 1930s, a National Salvation Movement was established that enlisted the support of *Huaqiao* in Southeast Asia, united against the common enemy of Japan. Campaigns such as this began to shift the focus of attention from regional, or ancestral homes, to the new nation-state of China. According to Glen Peterson (2005), philanthropic support from *Huaqiao* after the establishment of the People's Republic of China (PRC) experienced a shift from "culturalism to nationalism." The ancestral hometown was no longer the only magnet for the loyalty of Chinese abroad; Chinese ethnicity began to transcend the native place and the dialect ties that had predominantly linked *Huaqiao* communities together. It is not unrelated that this shift occurred as Mandarin, the "national language," rose in popularity within China, and even within Chinese communities abroad.

But the victory of the Communist and the establishment of the People's Republic of China in 1949 drastically changed China's relationship with *Huaqiao*. Some Chinese who were abroad, either studying or sojourning, at the time of the founding of the PRC returned to help build a new China. Other *Huaqiao* who experienced increasingly antagonistic relationships with peoples in their Southeast Asian countries of residence also took the chance to return to China in the early years of the PRC. China's leaders expressed support for any

Huaqiao who wanted to return, and even whole swaths of land were devoted for resettling these sojourners onto "*Huaqiao* farms" in Fujian and other provinces (Li et al. 2003; Li 2010). But the majority stayed in their adopted homes, though many tried to preserve contact with their relatives in China. During the heightened political campaigns of the Maoist era, however, overseas connections became increasingly burdensome, and many families had little contact and even less financial support.

The 1980s witnessed a resumption of the channels connecting *Huaqiao* and ancestral hometowns. These reconnected links provided a vital spark igniting the fire of economic reform, particularly in South Fujian. The city of Xiamen on China's southeast coast was one of China's first Special Economic Zones (SEZs), a trial region that offered special privileges, such as tax breaks, to entice investment in new factories and businesses. Portions of Xiamen were allocated as a SEZ beginning in 1980, particularly with the goal of attracting funds from *Huaqiao* with roots in the region. The strategy worked. Funds came flooding in and helped revitalize the whole region with investment in manufacturing and other industries. From 1980–1985, Xiamen's GDP grew at an annual rate of over 15 percent (Beijing Review 1986). *Huaqiao* provided capital not only for economic development, but also for cultural and religious purposes, including support for Chinese churches, which we will now discuss in more depth.

3 *Huaqiao* Contributions to Church Building

This section will show how *Huaqiao* were integral to Chinese church construction in South Fujian in the reform era, but it may be helpful to first provide historical background for this involvement. *Huaqiao* engagement in South Fujian church affairs in the reform era was not new but rather a resumption of the connections between Chinese churches in South Fujian and in Southeast Asia. By the early nineteenth century, as the tentacles of the Protestant missionary enterprise expanded from Western Europe and North America beyond Africa and India, they came against the closed doors of China proper. Though Robert Morrison is considered the first Protestant missionary to gain a foothold in China in 1807, the country remained officially closed to proselytizing until the opening of five ports as part of the treaty ending the Opium War in 1842. The fact that China was off-limits to missionary efforts during the early decades of the nineteenth century did not mean that "Chinese" were off-limits. On the contrary, Chinese residing outside of China were a major target of evangelism by early Western missionaries in the first half of the nineteenth century (Su 2010). As John King Fairbank (1985: 13) remarked,

"Protestant missions began a flank attack on China through the soft underbelly of expatriate overseas Chinese communities in Southeast Asia." To be sure, the earliest Chinese converts to Protestantism were made in Singapore, Malacca, and Bangkok, where Chinese from the southeastern coastal provinces of Fujian and Guangdong had gathered for decades (Smith 1970; Lee 2001; White 2012). When China was finally pried open to Western missionary endeavors, the majority of missionaries and mission agencies working among the Chinese in Southeast Asia moved to China proper, often taking Chinese assistants with them.

Thus, it was natural that a close relationship between Chinese Christian communities in Southeast Asia and coastal China developed. Since the early nineteenth century, this relationship has been mutually supportive (White 2012). Human resources, in the form of preachers and pastors, have been cultivated and sent by Christian groups in Fujian and Guangdong while monetary resources were sent back to Christian families and congregations from workers and business owners in Southeast Asia. As *Huaqiao* communities in Southeast Asia grew in terms of numbers and economic strength in the early decades of the twentieth century, they were a stabilizing force and source of support for the chaos experienced by the numerous wars waged in mainland China. The various preaching tours by John Sung (Song Shangjie) further connected Christian communities in coastal China with co-religionists overseas Chinese in Southeast Asia. Sung, originally from Putian, Fujian, was a charismatic evangelist whose sparked revival through his preaching in China and throughout Southeast Asia, in places such as Malaysia, the Philippines, and particularly Singapore (Ireland 2012).

Historical records are littered with stories of church representatives from coastal south China traveling to *Huaqiao* communities in Southeast Asia hoping to raise funds for specific building projects, such as schools, hospitals, or churches. For instance, Chen Qiuqing, an influential pastor in Xiamen who served as the head of the national Church of Christ in China for much of the 1940s, was selected to travel to the Philippines in 1941 to report to *Huaqiao* there on the situation of the church and collect funds for church programs. While there, the Japanese began their occupation of the Philippines and Rev. Chen was imprisoned in a concentration camp. He was not released until 1945, when he returned to Xiamen. Rev. Chen was practicing what many other church leaders from South Fujian had done for decades – seeking support from *Huaqiao* Christians in Southeast Asia.

Such connections were so important for the church that even foreign missionaries tapped these well-established networks to gather funds for evangelistic efforts. One Presbyterian Church of England publication states:

> Mr. Slater [a PCE missionary] paid a visit to the Straits Settlements and collected a large sum for the building of a new boys' school [in Quanzhou] … During the same year, Miss Reynolds [another PCE missionary], on her way back from furlough, paid a similar visit and raised another large sum of money, which, with other funds available, will provide a new building for the girls' school.[2]

However, soon after the establishment of the PRC in 1949, the financial links between *Huaqiao* and Christian communities in China were severed. The contribution drives from Chinese individuals or Christian congregations moving through Chinese communities abroad stopped and evangelistic or expansion projects by churches in China were phased out. Remittances to family members did, in some instances, continue during the early decades of the PRC, but monetary support for church buildings or activities did not.

By 1949, the city of Xiamen housed many church buildings, some of them dating back to the mid-nineteenth century. As religious services were resumed in the early years of the reform era, these buildings were gradually returned to Christian congregations. The number of Christians in Xiamen, and in China as a whole, grew rapidly in the 1980s, leading to the overcrowding of the old church buildings. Permission for a new church building – the first large church to be built in the city since 1949 – was finally obtained in the 1990s by Rev. Wen Yihan (pseud.),[3] the pastor of an influential church in the city and head of the local *lianghui*, or "two committees."[4] The Jiangtou Gospel Church would be a landmark project, a mega-church that would project Xiamen as a modern, cosmopolitan city. The Christian community was excited and relieved that they had secured the cumbersome approvals for such a project. The last remaining challenge in constructing the church, was how this building project would be financed. The city agreed to provide the land, but the church community

---

2 Report by Mr. F. H. Hawkins on his visit to China (1928: 70–71). School of Oriental and Asian Studies archives, CWML L169.
3 For an ethnographic study of Rev. Wen and his church, see Liu and White, 2019.
4 The first of these is the National Committee of the Three-Self Patriotic Movement of the Protestant Churches in China (TSPM, *Sanzi aiguo yundong*). It was founded in the 1950s as a non-denominational Protestant organization. The TSPM functions as a liaison organization between the state and registered (and therefore officially recognized) churches. The second government-acknowledged Christian organization, the China Christian Council (CCC), was established in 1980 as a partner to the TSPM, its task being to oversee theological activities and train church leaders. The leaders and missions of these two organizations have often overlapped. On account of their close relationship, they are referred to as the *lianghui* (literally meaning "two committees").

needed to raise funds for the construction of the church, often referred to as the "ark" because of its dominating appearance.

The Christian community in Xiamen resorted to the age-old practice of relying on the extensive *Huaqiao* ties in raising support for the construction of the Jiangtou Church. Rev. Wen led numerous contribution drives, visiting Chinese churches in Southeast Asia to collect funds for this project. Of the eight million yuan spent on construction of the church,[5] seven million came from donations from *Huaqiao* Christian communities in Southeast Asia. A particularly effective strategy was when Rev. Wen led a group of choir members from his church in Xiamen on a tour of Chinese churches in the Philippines, Singapore, Malaysia, and other regions with large populations of South Fujian immigrants. The pianist for the choir, a blind Christian from Xiamen who had memorized the popular South Fujian hymnal, as well as Rev. Wen's charismatic preaching in the South Fujian dialect and the choir's professional singing, drew large crowds of *Huaqiao*, many of whom were born in or around Xiamen and retained strong sentiments to their hometowns. The saying, "When the church needs money, it's time for Rev. Wen to take Sister Cai [the pianist] to Southeast Asia," captures the successful approach the church in Xiamen used to gather support, particularly for building projects. It is not only in Xiamen that local churches have relied on *Huaqiao* funding for church building projects. This tactic has been employed by churches throughout South Fujian and in other *Huaqiao*-producing regions.

The church in the small town of Banzai, for instance, was reestablished in 1982, after being closed for two decades during the Maoist years. In 1993 Su Ziqing, a prominent doctor in Hong Kong who grew up in Banzai, approached local leaders about erecting a new church building. Dr. Su negotiated that he would also donate funds for the building of a new medical clinic if permission was granted for the construction of a church. Local authorities, eager to cultivate good ties with *Huaqiao*, readily agreed to this request. Today, the church and clinic stand next to each other and both prominently display plaques in recognition of the support they received from these "overseas" connections.

To be sure, in Southern Fujian, the 1990s and early 2000s witnessed numerous church building projects with significant funding coming from Chinese in Southeast Asia. While it would be nearly impossible to track down all church building projects with substantial funding from *Huaqiao*, one way we can see such contributions is in church commemorative booklets that are often

---

5 Based on the exchange rate in 1995, the eight million yuan cost of the church was approximately $960,000 USD.

printed in conjunction with major anniversary celebrations. It is common for such events to be combined with dedication services for new buildings and these publications often have a section detailing the financial support received for building projects. In fact, many list out each individual contribution, including the amount and name or village of the donor. Over the last decade of fieldwork in South Fujian, we have collected over 50 church anniversary booklets and the role of *Huaqiao* in the building of churches throughout the region, especially in the 1990s and early 2000s, is quite apparent.

It may be helpful to illustrate how *Huaqiao* contributions are evident in church commemorative booklets. The church in Xiaozha, a small town in Huian county, celebrated its 124th year anniversary in May of 2015. The congregation received approval for the construction of a new church building in 2006, but the project was not completed until 2012. Even before gaining approval for the new building, though, the church had been collecting donations for years. This anniversary celebration was a culmination of the building projects (in addition to the church, a new parsonage was also erected) and a chance to formally celebrate the construction of the new church. To help mark the occasion, a commemorative booklet, over 100 pages in length, was compiled to record the history and report on the activities and finances of the church. At the end of this volume, which was passed out to all attendees of the anniversary ceremony, columns listing the individual donors' names, amount of contribution, and home village/city are recorded. In total, nearly 500 names are listed, grouped according to their home village. Included near the end of this list are 15 *Huaqiao*, residing in places like the Philippines, Taiwan, and Hong Kong. The sum of all the donations collected was over 4.6 million yuan, but nearly 2.2 million of this amount came from the 15 *Huaqiao* donors. The vast majority of this portion, over 2 million yuan, came from one Filipino-Chinese, Wang Jinbing, a wealthy businessman and church elder who supported many churches in Huian county. In fact, the first interior page of the commemorative booklet features a stone stele placed on the wall of the new church that specifically highlights the contributions of this "compatriot sojourner to the Philippines."

Similarly, the commemorative booklet for the Yiban Church in Huian clearly shows the role of *Huaqiao* in the construction of the church's new building. Here, we see that overseas donations accounted for over 282,000 yuan of the 624,000 yuan cost of the new building. Local members of the Yiban church, in comparison, donated 196,000. "Domestic contributions" (referring to donations from members of other churches in China) accounted for most of the balance (over 127,000). The support from *Huaqiao* is further listed in the volume, showing that 14 individuals from Singapore donated nearly 250,000 yuan, and other donations were collected from *Huaqiao* in Taiwan, Indonesia, and the Philippines. In addition to these funds for the main construction of the church, a Christian *Huaqiao* in the Philippines further donated 130,000 yuan for a gate, wall surrounding the property, and bars for the windows.

The large churches scattered around South Fujian, such as those found in Xiaozha and Yiban mentioned here, have transformed the appearance of many towns and villages in the province. Michel Chambon (2017) argues that such structures play a spiritual role in that their verticality contradicts religious norms and traditional temple architecture. He details how large churches in Fujian act upon the surrounding society and both reflect and shape local Christian values. The construction of large, conspicuous churches in coastal China with *Huaqiao* funding is similar to the large, domineering houses erected in rural Fujian studied by Julie Chu. Multi-storied houses, referred to as *Meiguoke*, or "American guest" mansions, often with few or no residents, began popping up in regions surrounding Fuzhou, the capital of Fujian, in the 1990s. In Chu's field site (which she terms Longyan), approximately 70% of the town's income came from money sent from abroad, and two-thirds of this went to the construction of houses and temples (Chu 2010: 35). Immigrants from these villages, many of whom went to the US illegally, transported by snakeheads, or gangs of human smugglers, relied on extensive family and native place networks to find employment and protection overseas, especially working in Chinese restaurants. After years of labor, enough funds were accumulated for a large house to be erected in the natal village, despite the fact that the immigrants typically remained abroad. These houses, which often stand largely empty, serve as tangible representations of the family's transnational connections, just as *Huaqiao*-funded churches serve as statements to the surrounding society.

The large churches found throughout Fujian, similar to the *Meiguoke* mansions described by Chu, exhibit a competitive spirit, each trying to outdo neighboring churches in size and conspicuousness. But the erection of large churches in Fujian does more than just garner pride for the religious community or face for the substantial donors, this is also understood as a spiritual act. Just as expensive temple construction reflects how *ling* or efficacious a deity is, large churches are tangible proof of God's blessings on the religious community. The converse of this – small, shabby churches reflect spiritual weakness – is also a common assumption. *Huaqiao* contributions to church construction projects, then, often entail multiple significant motivations, including ancestral connections, a chance for enhanced prestige, and even evangelistic desires.

4 "Foreign" Support? *Huaqiao* Contributions as Remittances

One way we may be able to understand the monetary contributions by *Huaqiao* to church construction projects in China is as a form of remittance. As mentioned above, remittances, or money sent from immigrants to family members back in China, have played a key role in the economy of many cities and villages in southeast China. While portions of earnings were sent back from sojourners to family members in China, the allocation of these resources was typically managed not by the *Huaqiao*, but rather by family elders. That is to say, while the young worker made the money, he did not decide how it was spent.

Remittances have been a major topic of research for scholars studying overseas Chinese (e.g., Lin et al. 1999; Benton and Liu 2018). Khun Eng Kuah-Pearce's (2011) study on how Chinese immigrants in Singapore financially supported relatives in Anxi, a mountainous county in South Fujian, reveals that remittances were much more than monetary donations. Kuah-Pearce analyzes how the monetary resources offered by the Singaporean relatives allowed them to play a major role in reviving the religious traditions in their ancestral villages. While they provided the Chinese side with needed financial assistance, they also bestowed honor and face on the donors and offered prestige and privilege to the relatives in China.

The role of remittances, therefore, is often much more than an economic, one-way exchange. Research on remittances in China has shown that *qiaopi* or the letters sent back with the money transfer slips, were important means of communication and links between the immigrant and his (almost always male) family back in China (Benton and Liu 2018). Similarly, the donations from *Huaqiao* for church building projects were important ways for the immigrant community to remain involved in the religious life in ancestral towns. In her research on Dominican immigrants in Boston, Peggy Levitt (1998; 2001; and Levitt and Lamba-Nieves 2011) coined the phrase "social remittances" to describe how the contributions immigrants made to their home communities extended far beyond economic matters but included things such as fashion, consumption habits, and ways of thinking.

A major reason we suggest considering *Huaqiao* involvement in church construction within the framework of remittances is because such contributions were typically thought of as local, family fiscal matters. They were not regarded as outside help, but rather internal support. If sojourners were expected to one day return to the town, the funds sent back to the natal village were as much for them as for their relatives. While it is not expected that *Huaqiao* today immigrate back to their ancestral home, the mindset of support for the village or town as a natural family or local affair persists. This is important because the history of Chinese Christianity has been tainted with the brush of Western imperialism. The substantial financial resources the foreign mission enterprise generated for the Chinese church has provided fodder for critics of the church since the nineteenth century.

A major criticism of the Chinese church has been that converts were "rice Christians" who joined the church for the material benefits afforded by affiliating with foreigners. The Chinese Communist Party (CCP), in its early years, pointed to the substantial land, housing compounds, and property owned by foreign missions and the Chinese church to prove their charges of economic imperialism. The links to foreign monetary support allowed were most tangible in the well-built and often centrally located churches, Christian schools, and hospitals. Many of these structures were appropriated by the CCP, both before and after 1949 (White 2017b). All this to say that the historical links to "foreign money" have proved problematic for the Chinese church.

The official or registered church organization in China today is known as the Three-Self Patriotic Movement (TSPM), indicating that Chinese churches are self-supporting, self-propagating, and self-administrating. While this organization did not begin until 1951 (initially Three-Self Reform Movement; it added "Patriotic" to the title in 1954), by that time the three-self concept had been around for nearly a century (Shenk 1990). In fact, early missionary efforts by the Reformed Church in America (RCA) and English Presbyterians resulted in the establishment of a Chinese church in South Fujian that largely followed the three-self ideals in practice, if not in name (Cheung 2004).

A fixation on limiting the "foreign" funding of Chinese churches was not only a concern of Chinese authorities, "self-support" was also a goal of mission agencies and donors in the West. Examples of Chinese congregations raising funds for construction projects or evangelistic efforts were regularly published in mission periodicals to prove that a reliance on foreign economic support was meant to be temporary. For missionary societies at work in South Fujian,[6] foreign support for Christian schools and hospitals was typical, but individual congregations were expected to financially cover church expenses, including pastoral salaries. When foreign mission efforts were formally curtailed in the early 1950s, financial support from Western churches was completely removed.

Today, TSPM churches are restricted from receiving funds from foreign sources. Document 19, a CCP document first released in 1982 that outlines the party's view of religion in the reform era, has specific regulations prohibiting

---

6 There were three main mission groups active in South Fujian, the RCA, London Missionary Society, and English Presbyterians (White 2017a).

religious groups from accepting "foreign" funds. Section XI of this document states:

> All religious organizations and individuals must be educated not to make use of any means whatsoever to solicit funds from foreign church organizations, and religious persons and groups in our country as well as other groups and individuals must refuse any subsidy or funds offered by foreign church organizations for religious purposes. As for donations or offerings given in accordance with religious custom by foreign believers, overseas Chinese, or compatriots from Hong Kong and Macao to temples and churches within our territory, these may be accepted. But if it is a question of large contributions or offerings, permission must be sought from the provincial, urban [directly administered cities], or autonomous-area governments or from the central government department responsible for these matters before any religious body can accept them on its own, even though it can be established that the donor acts purely out of religious fervor with no strings attached.[7]

While this document represents the party's position on "foreign" money in religious affairs, it is less than clear in what is considered a "large contribution." The most recent regulations on religious affairs, which came into effect in 2018, are more precise, indicating that any donation over 100,000 yuan must be reported to county-level authorities and approved before being accepted. Such regulations are meant to preserve the independence of religious organizations and help ensure that foreign influences are not "using the cloak of religion" to sow political or social discord, a common fear of the ruling party. While these regulations cover all religions in China, the "foreign" religions of Christianity (both Protestantism and Catholicism) and Islam are particularly scrutinized for foreign connections. Buddhism, and to some extent Daoism, have successfully gathered millions of yuan in donations abroad, especially from *Huaqiao* individuals and groups.

Despite the regulations to report large donations, in practice, this does not always happen. One pastor of a church in a *qiaoxiang* explained that he never reports large donations from *Huaqiao*, but that the church would only accept such funds if they come with no strings attached. *Huaqiao* may suggest what the funds are used for, as in a specific construction project, but these donations

---

[7] The whole document can be found at: https://www.purdue.edu/crcs/wp-content/uploads/2014/08/Document_no._19_1982.pdf.

cannot limit or influence what is taught within the church. This same pastor explained that one large donation from a *Huaqiao* for a church construction project met with some resistance from local government officials. These officials were disappointed that such a large donation was going to the church, rather than another social program. However, this particular *Huaqiao* had previously built a private kindergarten and agreed to give this over to the town to manage (and own), which mitigated the criticisms of the large donation to the church.

As this chapter shows, Protestant congregations in Fujian, witnessing the success of Buddhist and Daoist groups, have also gathered substantial funds from *Huaqiao*. What is of interest for our discussion here is that such funds are not typically considered "foreign," or at least not in the same way as "Western" money. It is interesting to note that in the quote from Document 19 above, "foreign believers" and "overseas Chinese" are two different categories. The overview provided in the previous section helps explain why *Huaqiao* financial support is not thought of as "foreign." If the overseas Chinese community in Southeast Asia is an extension of the ancestral village, and *Huaqiao* are sojourners, as the historical mindset would have it, gathering funds from *Huaqiao* for church construction can be considered an "internal" or local affair. We suggest that the self-support, both historically and today, is not an aversion to foreign funding, but rather "Western" funding. Both before 1949 and again in the early decades of the reform era, contributions from *Huaqiao* have not been framed as contrary to the principle of self-support. Just as remittances were not thought of as foreign investment, but rather a normal survival strategy for families, churches receiving donations from *Huaqiao* was, and is, not considered as selling out or relying on foreign support. The decision-making power is still with the church, and regardless, the funds are not considered "foreign."

Historically, even mission agencies' real consideration regarding self-support tended to be *not* relying on mission funding, rather than a genuine concern with funds coming from one particular congregation. Mission reports praise Chinese churches in Fujian for being "self-supporting," even when portions of this funding came from outside of China. For example, the church in the Fujian prefectural town of Tingzhou was referred to as "self-supporting" in one London Missionary Society publication in 1938, even though much of the funds were gathered "through the help of Chinese friends in Singapore and other places" (Hutley 1938: 8).

The "three-self" idea, then, may more accurately be considered "2½ self" in practice for many Chinese churches in South Fujian. The funding of churches, particularly church construction, is rarely only collected from within the congregation. Though an in-depth discussion of this topic is beyond the scope of this chapter, this critique of "self-support" could be furthered by interrogating the concept of "self." Even churches that may not have *Huaqiao* connections often raise funds, especially for building projects, by seeking donations from other congregations, some of which may be far away in other provinces or regions of the country. This leads to some interesting, though difficult, questions to ponder, such as: Does the "self" in "self-support" refer to the local congregation? To China? To (ethnic) Chinese? Such questions could also be used to interrogate the other two branches of the three-self idea. For example, in the current digital age where much evangelism may occur in cyberspace, can one local congregation be truly "self-propagating"?

5 Theological Investment: *Qiaoxiang* and Beyond

5.1 Economic and Generational Shifts

It is obvious that the resurgence of religious activity in reform-era South Fujian has been greatly boosted by various transnational networks the region has fostered. Nevertheless, *Huaqiao* involvement in the religious life in coastal southeast China in recent years has witnessed significant shifts in the relationship between overseas Chinese and local Chinese religious communities. This section will discuss how some of these changes have particularly affected the role of *Huaqiao* in Chinese Christianity.

Over the last two decades, with the sustained economic development of China, the financing of the religious revival by *Huaqiao* has greatly diminished. A number of overseas Chinese of South Fujian origin were affected to a greater or less degree in the aftermath of the Asian financial crisis and consequently were forced to cut their financial contributions to the religious recovery in their ancestral homeland. China's economy, on the other hand, was relatively unscathed; it continued to develop and South Fujian has become one of China's most economically prosperous regions. This considerable change in economic situations has substantially reshaped the transnational ties and geopolitics of the region. It has also influenced the involvement of *Huaqiao* Christians in local Chinese churches.

As previously noted, in the construction of Xiamen's Jiangtou Gospel Church in the mid-1990s, nearly 90 percent of the costs were borne by overseas Chinese churches and individuals, the majority in Singapore and Malaysia. However, currently under construction in the eastern part of Xiamen is a new, large, landmark church. The estimated expenses for the construction of Eastern Church (*Dongbu tang*) total over 200 million yuan (or more than 30 million USD). Funding for this large project has come almost entirely from local Christians. It is not only in urban churches of South Fujian that economic contributions from *Huaqiao* have been less prevalent, construction of rural churches in recent years have been typically completed without significant funding from overseas Chinese.[8]

5.2 *Theological Investment: Social Remittances of Southeast Asian Chinese*

While the economic support from *Huaqiao* for church construction projects has dissipated, overseas Chinese churches have initiated other channels to engage in the South Fujian church. Foremost among these is the training of clergy and church workers for both registered and unregistered churches. Instead of making economic contributions, Southeast Asia is now becoming increasingly influential in the South Fujian church in terms of theology and leadership training. Since the late 1990s, the Fujian provincial *lianghui* has sent almost a dozen young pastors and preachers to pursue their master's degrees at Trinity Theological College (TTC) in Singapore, an institution that began its cooperation with China's national *lianghui* in 1991. Many of them have returned to become influential leaders in the church hierarchy. Meanwhile, through unofficial channels unregistered churches (better known as "house churches") have sent preachers to Singapore Bible College (SBC), an institution that gives great prominence to opposing liberal theology (targeting China's *lianghui* churches and TTC). These examples are not to say that the transnational networks of officially sanctioned churches and independent churches are necessarily sharply divided. For instance, one seminary in the Philippines is directed by a *Huaqiao* whose family is from the Xiamen region. This school has trained a large number of church workers for *both* registered *and* unregistered churches.

To be sure, seminaries and theological training programs catering to mainland Chinese students are found throughout Southeast Asia. Singapore, the Philippines, Indonesia, and Malaysia, in addition to Hong Kong and Taiwan, all host growing theological education programs targeting students from China. Most of these programs are subsidized by *Huaqiao* churches or provide monetary support for individual students from China to participate in such programs. Though statistics on the number of seminaries which enroll students from China or the number of such students do not exist, it is clear that there

---

8 One notable exception is the construction of a large mega church in the town of Jinjing. This new church, completed in 2018, cost over 40 million yuan. In 2017, when one of the authors visited this church, 32 million yuan had already been spent on construction efforts. Half of these funds came from *Huaqiao* in the Philippines, Taiwan, Hong Kong, and Macao. Most (about 12 million yuan) came from one donor in the Philippines.

are dozens of such seminaries and more Chinese students enrolled outside of China than in the state-approved, TSPM schools within China.

In addition to seminaries on China's borders catering to mainland students, there are numerous unsanctioned theological training opportunities, or even whole degree programs, carried out within China. Not all of these involve foreign actors, and those that do may not necessarily include *Huaqiao*, but many of these are initiated or supported by overseas Chinese who serve as teachers or interpreters. Whether it be through Chinese-language seminaries in Southeast Asia or short-term theological training programs conducted within China, there has been a noticeable shift in *Huaqiao* support, from building churches to theological training.

Strict controls on the number of official seminaries and students within China is a major factor in the proliferation of Protestant training programs for Chinese students outside of the official church structure. The imbalance in the amount of Christians and the number of pastors or trained clergy is stark. Exact numbers are impossible to pin down, but within registered churches and seminaries, we can offer some estimates. There are over 70,000 registered TSPM churches in China, but the 24 government-sanctioned seminaries in China graduate less than 1,000 seminarians each year. Unregistered churches are faced with similar shortages of trained leaders. This imbalance is found all over China (Vala 2009).

The turn to support for theological education can be considered a form of "social remittance" discussed by Levitt (1998; 2001; and Levitt and Lamba-Nieves 2011), but it also reflects another major shift in *Huaqiao* involvement in the Chinese church. While the vast majority of church building projects that included significant contributions from *Huaqiao* are found in *qiaoxiang*, the new focus on theological training is not constrained to these regions. The limited number of students from *qiaoxiang* means that the vast majority of theological students at the numerous seminaries founded and funded by *Huaqiao* are from other regions of China.

One large seminary in the Philippines, for example, offers full (bachelor) degree programs (three years) in Chinese to students from the mainland. Approximately 100 students, from both registered and unregistered congregations in China, study at the school each year. Only a handful of these, however, are from South Fujian. Despite the fact that the vast majority of *Huaqiao* in the Philippines trace their heritage back to South Fujian and the South Fujian language is often *lingua franca* within Chinese communities in the Philippines, this seminary only offers instruction in mandarin and English and actively recruits students from all over China. This is not to say that the traditional links to South Fujian have vanished. On the contrary, this seminary works with church leaders in Fujian to offer a master's degree program to students in Xiamen and up until 2018, ran an unsanctioned bachelor's degree program with a registered church in South Fujian. About half the students in this program came from the local region and the other half from other areas of China.

The generational change, however, seems to be more significant in the geographical expansion of *Huaqiao* involvement in Chinese Christian churches. A high proportion of the *Huaqiao* who donated to church construction projects in the early decades of the reform era were elderly, first-generation immigrants. Many were born in China and held fond memories of their ancestral villages. While they did not fulfill the traditional idea of moving back to China in their older years, many were happy to contribute for a new church in their ancestral hometowns. For the majority of second and subsequent generations of *Huaqiao* in Southeast Asia, though, the connection to the ancestral hometown is not as visceral. The virtual closure of China from 1949–1979 has meant that a large proportion of the current generation of adult *Huaqiao*, unlike the previous generations, do not associate very closely with the Chinese hometown of their forefathers. The Chinese ethnic pride is often strong among such individuals, but it is rarely localized like in previous eras.

This situation is not only apparent in Christian connections with *Huaqiao*. Recent scholarship has shown that the heavy restriction of travel and communication between Chinese in Southeast Asia and in China proper after the establishment of the PRC in 1949 has led to the weakening of ties between *Huaqiao* and their Chinese hometowns (Yow 2005; Ding 2006; Kuah-Pearce 2011). The erosion of these links have also been apparent in the religious connections as the rituals associated with ancestral worship and popular religion, which are closely tied to kinship and native-place networks, have declined in popularity and importance (Ding 2006; Kuah-Pearce 2011). The vast majority of *Huaqiao* in Southeast Asia today were not born in China and have less connection to their ancestral town, even if they do, however, tend to identify as ethnically "Chinese."

This shift is similar to the transition from localism to nationalism that occurred among *Huaqiao* in the first half of the twentieth century. As mentioned above, nation-building projects slowly took precedence over targeted support of the ancestral village. Many in the current generation of *Huaqiao* Christians do not have the cultural connection to or personal experience with a specific hometown in China that can be translated into significant social capital. In other words, donating a large sum for a church construction project for many of these younger *Huaqiao* Christians would not result in an increase in valuable social prestige. Even if their "face" or reputation for such a noble contribution would be enhanced in the ancestral village, since the link to this hometown is not as strong (as preceding generations), the value of such prestige for these individuals is low.

However, unlike the scholarship referenced above, we argue that the decrease in contributions from *Huaqiao* to church construction projects has not resulted in a disengagement with the Chinese church, but rather has led to a different form of engagement: theological training. *Huaqiao* involvement, therefore, should be thought of as dynamic and flexible. This is particularly so in the case of Christianity, a global, highly-institutionalized religion with evangelical tendencies. The shift to *Huaqiao* support for broader, pan-China efforts is more reasonable for such a religion.

It is not just in the links with ancestral hometowns that *Huaqiao* Christianity has experienced a transition. In general, the regional or sub-ethnic identity within global Chinese Christianity has weakened as pan-Chinese Christian organizations, such as the Chinese Coordination Center for World Evangelism (CCCOWE), and the influx of new Chinese immigrants have shifted many *Huaqiao* congregations to either Mandarin-speaking or English (Nagata 2005; Tam 2019).

An example of the recent theological influence of *Huaqiao* can be found in Stephen Tong (Tang Chongrong), a world-renowned evangelist who was born in Xiamen and migrated to Indonesia at the age of nine. Since the 1990s there has been a resurgent interest in Calvinism among the well-educated in the big cities of eastern and central China (Chow 2014). The influence of Tong's Reformed theology is not limited to Xiamen, but is attractive to a large number of Christians across China. His promotion of Reformed theology is giving an impetus to the recovery of the Reformed tradition in the mainstream church in South Fujian. Since the turn of the new century, a growing number of Christians in South Fujian have professed their denominational background to be the historical Reformed missions (Liu 2017).

6   Conclusion

The advancement of Christianity in China has historically been intimately connected to Southeast Asia. Many of the initial Protestant missionaries hoping to enter the country first evangelized Chinese in Southeast Asia and it was among the Chinese populations in this region where many missionaries retreated after the establishment of the PRC in 1949. Since the reform era, initiated in the late 1970s, Chinese in Southeast Asia have again played an important role in Chinese Christianity.

This research reveals that their involvement progressed from providing funding for the (re)building of churches in the 1980s and 1990s to theological training for Chinese, both in China and in Southeast Asia, in more recent years. The sentimental ties of overseas Chinese to their ancestral hometowns have weakened over the generations, but in the case of evangelical Chinese church leaders and educators, this has not necessarily led to a reduction in involvement or concern for churches in mainland China, but has rather freed these individuals and institutions up to provide training not just in their ancestral homes, but throughout the country.

Some scholars have argued that, alongside the passing away of the first-generation migrants from South Fujian, in general, subsequent generations of Southeast Asian Chinese have distanced themselves from their ancestral homeland in China and are becoming increasingly rooted in the countries in which they were born and reside. Consequently, the cultural links between *qiaoxiang* and overseas Chinese cannot be effectively maintained. However, most of these studies are concerned with the diffused practices of communal worship and popular religion that largely depend on kinship and regional ties. It thus seems understandable for those scholars to reach such a conclusion, given the fact that the younger generation of overseas Chinese may find it pointless to appreciate the homeland of their ancestors. We suggest that the generational transition has clearly affected the involvement of *Huaqiao* in Chinese Christianity, but that it has evolved, rather than disappeared.

It is also worth noting that alumni networks resulted from the transnational religious education are emerging and will likely have profound effects on religious ties in the near future. Several Southeast Asian seminaries have trained a large number of clergy and church workers who constitute respective alumni networks that have a marked impact on the Christian community not only in South Fujian but also throughout the country.

The transformation of the well-established networks linking overseas Chinese with church groups in China is not simply a religious phenomenon, these ties also produce and reflect transnational mobility and the spread of theological knowledge. By reviewing the shifting strategies overseas Chinese have used to influence the church in China, this chapter has framed Christianity as a Chinese religion with global implications that extend beyond religion.

6.1   Acknowledgements

An earlier version was presented at the Workshop on Southeast Asian Society and Culture from the Perspective of Everyday Life organized by the Center for Southeast Asian Studies of Xiamen University in November 2019. The authors wish to thank Tan Chee Beng and Kuah Khun Eng for their helpful comments.

6.2 *Funding*

This research was supported by the National Social Science Fund of China (grant number 18CZJ012).

References

Beijing Review. http://www.bjreview.com.cn/CIFIT/2009-08/10/content_211416.htm, accessed 21 July 2019.

Benton, Gregor and Hong Liu. 2018. *Dear China: Emigrant Letters and Remittances, 1820–1980*. Berkeley: University of California Press.

Chambon, Michel. 2017. "The Action of Christian Buildings on their Chinese Environment." *Studies in World Christianity* 23(2): 100–21.

Cheung, David (Chen Yiqiang). 2004. *Christianity in Modern China: The Making of the First Native Protestant Church*. Leiden: Brill.

Chow, Alexander. 2014. "Calvinist Public Theology in Urban China Today." *International Journal of Public Theology* 8(2): 158–75.

Chu, Julie Y. 2010. *Cosmologies of Credit: Transnational Mobility and the Politics of Destination in China*. Durham: Duke University Press.

Clark, Hugh. 2006. "The Religious Culture of Southern Fujian, 750–1450: Preliminary Reflections on Contacts across a Maritime Frontier." *Asia Major* 19(1/2): 211–40.

Cook, James A. 2006. "Reimagining China: Xiamen, Overseas Chinese, and a Transnational Modernity." Pp. 156–94 in *Everyday Modernity in China*, edited by Madeleine Yue Dong and Joshua Goldstein. Seattle: University of Washington Press.

Dean, Kenneth. 2010. "The Return Visits of Overseas Chinese to Ancestral Villages in Putian, Fujian." Pp. 254–75 in *Faiths on Display: Tourism and Religion in Contemporary China*, edited by Tim Oakes and Donald Sutton. Lanham, MD: Rowman and Littlefield.

Dean, Kenneth and Zheng Zhenman. 2010. *Ritual Alliances of the Putian Plain*. 2 vols. Leiden: Brill.

Ding Yuling. 2006. "Fujian chuantong qiaoxiang minjian zuzhi de juese zhuanbian" [The Changing Roles of Civil Organizations in Fujian Traditional *Qiaoxiang*]. Pp. 345–64 in *Kuaguo wangluo yu Hua'nan qiaoxiang: wenhua, rentong he shehui bianqian* [Transnational Networks and South China *Qiaoxiang*: Culture, Identity and Social Change], edited by Tan Chee-beng, Ding Yuling and Wang Lianmao. Hong Kong: Zhongwen daxue chubanshe.

Dunch, Ryan. 2001. *Fuzhou Protestants and the Making of a Modern China, 1857–1927*. New Haven: Yale University Press.

Fairbank, John King. 1985. "Introduction." Pp. 1–18 in *Christianity in China: Early Protestant Missionary Writings*, edited by Suzanne Wilson Barnett and John King Fairbank. Cambridge, MA: Harvard University Press.

Hutley, Kate. 1938. *Ordeal in Tingchow.* London: The Livington Press.
Ireland, Daryl R. 2012. "Becoming Modern Women: Creating a New Female Identity through John Sung's Evangelistic Teams." *Studies in World Christianity* 18(3): 237–53.
Kuah-Pearce, Khun Eng. 2011. *Rebuilding the Ancestral Village: Singaporeans in China.* Hong Kong: Hong Kong University Press.
Kuhn, Philip A. 2008. *Chinese among Others: Emigration in Modern Times.* Lanham, MD: Rowman and Littlefield.
Kwee, Hui Kian. 2013. "Chinese Economic Dominance in Southeast Asia: A *Longue Duree* Perspective." *Comparative Studies in Society and History* 55(1): 5–34.
Lee, Joseph Tse-Hei. 2001. "The Overseas Chinese Networks and Early Baptist Missionary Movement across the South China Sea." *The Historian* 63(4): 753–68.
Levitt, Peggy. 1998. "Social Remittances: Migration Driven Local-Level Forms of Cultural Diffusion." *International Migration Review* 32(4): 926–48.
Levitt, Peggy. 2001. *The Transnational Villagers.* Berkeley: University of California Press.
Levitt, Peggy and Deepak Lamba-Nieves. 2011. "Social Remittances Revisited." *Journal of Ethnic and Migration Studies* 37(1): 1–22.
Li, Minghuan. 2010. "Collective Symbols and Individual Options: Life on a State Farm for Returned Overseas Chinese after Decollectivization." Pp. 250–70 in *iChina: The Rise of the Individual in Modern Chinese Society,* edited by Mette Halskov Hansen and Rune Svarverud. Copenhagen: NIAS Press.
Li Minghuan, Yu Yunping, Liu Zhaohui, and Sun Sheng. 2003. "Shehui renleixue shiye zhong de Songping Huaqiao Nongchang" [A Study on Songping Overseas Chinese Farm from the Perspective of Social Anthropology]. *Huaqiao huaren lishi yanjiu* 2: 1–25.
Lin Jiajin, Luo Rucai, Chen Shusen, Pan Yining, and He Anju. 1999. *Jindai Guangdong qiaohui yanjiu* [Remittance in Modern Guangdong]. Guangzhou: Zhongshan daxue chubanshe.
Liu, Jifeng. 2017. "Retrieving the Past Glory: Social Memory, Transnational Networks and Christianity in Contemporary China." Ph.D. dissertation, Leiden University.
Liu, Jifeng and Chris White. 2019. "Old Pastor and Local Bureaucrats: Recasting Church-State Relations in Contemporary China." *Modern China* 45(5): 564–90.
Nagata, Judith. 2005. "Christianity among Transnational Chinese: Religious versus (Sub)ethnic Affiliation." *International Migration* 43(3): 99–130.
Peterson, Glen. 2005. "Overseas Chinese and Merchant Philanthropy in China: From Culturalism to Nationalism." *Journal of Chinese Overseas* 1(1): 87–109.
Shen, Huifen. 2012. *China's Left-Behind Wives: Families of Migrants from Fujian to Southeast Asia, 1930s-1950s.* Singapore: NUS Press.
Shenk, Wilbert R. 1990. "The Origins and Evolution of the Three-Selfs in Relation to China." *International Bulletin of Missionary Research* 14(1): 28–35.
Smith, Carl T. 1970. "A Register of Baptized Protestant Chinese, 1813–1842." *Chung Chi Bulletin* 49: 23–26.

Su Ching. 2010. *Jidujiao yu Xinjiapo Huaren 1819–1846* [Christianity and the Chinese in Singapore 1819–1846]. Xinzhu: Guoli qinghua daxue chubanshe.

Tam, Jonathan. 2019. "Renegotiating Religious Transnationalism: Fractures in Transnational Chinese Evangelicalism." *Global Networks* 19(1): 66–85.

Vala, Carsten T. 2009. "Pathways to the Pulpit: Leadership Training in 'Patriotic' and Unregistered Chinese Protestant Churches." Pp.96–125 in *Making Religion, Making the State: The Politics of Religion in Modern China*, edited by Yoshiko Ashiwa and David L. Wank. Stanford: Stanford University Press.

White, Chris. 2012. "Waves of Influence across the South Seas: Mutual Support between Protestants in Minnan and Southeast Asia." *Ching Feng* N.S. 11(1): 29–54.

White, Chris. 2017a. *Sacred Webs: The Social Lives and Networks of Minnan Protestants, 1840s-1920s*. Leiden: Brill.

White, Chris. 2017b. "Appropriating Christian History in Fujian: Red Tourism Meets the Cross." *Studies in World Christianity* 23(1): 35–50.

Yen, Ching-Hwang. 1970. "Ch'ing's Sale of Honours and the Chinese Leadership in Singapore and Malaya (1877–1912)." *Journal of Southeast Asian Studies* 1(2): 20–32.

Yow, Cheun Hoe. 2005. "Weakening Ties with the Ancestral Homeland in China: The Case Studies of Contemporary Singapore and Malaysian Chinese." *Modern Asian Studies* 39(3): 559–79.

Zheng Zhenman. 2010. "Guojihua yu difanghua: jindai Minnan qiaoxiang de shehui wenhua bianqian" [Internationalization and Localization: Social and Cultural Changes in *Qiaoxiang* in Modern Southern Fujian]. *Jindaishi yanjiu* 2: 62–75.

CHAPTER 8

The Ironies of Bringing Christ to the Motherland
The Interaction Ritual Chains of Chinese-Canadian Evangelicals over Short-Term Missions to China

Jonathan Tam

1   Introduction

This chapter addresses the question "how do the experience of short-term missions (STMs) to China affect the social solidarity among Chinese-Canadian evangelical (CCE) youths?" I specifically interrogate the intersections of their ethnic (i.e. Chinese), religious (i.e. evangelical), and national (i.e. Canadian) identities by examining how they give meaning to their STM experiences by applying interaction ritual chains (IRC) theory (Collins 2004).

My findings reveal that youths negotiate complex meanings to their transnational STM experiences. Several interconnected contradictions emerge, what I call "ironies." First, by being in China, the participants are forced to negotiate their Chinese and Canadian identities; that is, to come to decide the extent they are Chinese or Canadian. Second, while claiming solidarity with Christians in China under the global umbrella of Christendom, they struggle to come to terms with their Canadian socioeconomic privilege compared with the people they serve abroad. Third, despite the STMers' desire to "experience God" to strengthen their faith, this motivation is inherently based on modern Enlightenment values of empirical verification. By examining these ironies, theoretical insights emerge.

Below, I first introduce what STMs are and how it is relevant to our understanding of social solidarity in the sociology of religion. I follow by outlining IRC theory and my methodology in this paper. In presenting my data, I go through each of the ironies, followed by a discussion of how our understanding of social solidarity should be based on a revision of IRC's theory "chains" to "entangled chains." I conclude by discussing its implications to sociology's ongoing study of social solidarity.

2   Situating Transnational Short-Term Missions in Modernity

STMs are service trips, typically lasting from one week to a few months, which entails an individual travelling to a distant place to engage in a type of voluntary social service, often in tandem with proselytization. Given the rapid increase of STMs since the 1980s in tandem with the global infrastructure for tourism, these trips have arguably become a rite of passage for devout evangelicals (Howell 2012). Churches that commit themselves to STMs send teams annually.

Churches often subsidize the expenses of STMers because they see it as a worthwhile enterprise. In an age where conservative congregations are looking to stave off the threat of secularism (Almond, Appleby, & Sivan 2003; Ammerman 1987), STMs have been regarded one of the most compelling religious experiences available to the Protestant laity (Priest & Howell 2013).[1] As a result, conservative congregations like the evangelicals may willingly invest in STMs because it purportedly boosts the religiosity of its participants.

Since Warner's call for the study of the "New Paradigm" (Warner 1993), many social scientists of religion have placed their attention on immigrant congregations in North America, with some having studied second-generation Chinese Christians. However, most of these studies have been focused on the American experience (e.g. Chen 2008; Yang 1999). Among the studies of transnational religious linkages, many have prioritized connections with populations in the Global South (e.g. Jenkins 2012; Levitt 2007), with relatively fewer having examined the Chinese from a transnational frame (e.g. Tam & Hasmath 2015; Tam 2019; Yang 2002). This emphasis also applies to the research of STMs (see Priest 2008; Priest, Dischinger, Rasmussen, & Brown 2006; Priest & Howell 2013). Furthermore, compared to adults, youths have been an understudied demographic in the sociology of religion for immigrants. Given this study involves Chinese Canadian evangelical youths as transnational religious actors, it addresses a lacuna in the literature.

The act of missions is a core tenet of Christianity. It calls believers to action and to spread their faith to bring about the return of Christ, based on the soteriological (i.e. the doctrine of salvation) position that God's kingdom will not arrive on Earth until all have heard the gospel (Matthew 24:14). Therefore, STMs are an important enterprise for many stripes of conservative Christians. Previous studies of transnational engagements have found that traveling around the world to be embedded in unfamiliar contexts is a powerful way

---

1   From a religious economies' perspective, STMs can be a compelling emotional product for the religious consumer.

to snap people out of their mundanity, juxtapose their assumptions to other worldviews, and force its participants to confront their inherent beliefs and values (Levitt & Waters 2002; Louie 2004). STM s are thus ideal cases to study the mechanisms of social solidarity.

This paper engages the inherent ironies that emerged from my observation of STM teams going to China and Taiwan in 2015. How did the CCE youths who participated in STM s:

1. Make sense of their Chinese and Canadian identities?
2. Justify their socioeconomic privilege when doing missionary work under the global umbrella of Christendom?
3. Negotiate their desire to "experience God" as a form of empirical verification?

By focusing sociological attention on the meaning-making processes CCE youths engage in on STM s, we can uncover the mechanisms of social solidarity for the next generation of believers.

3 Theoretical Framework

This paper applies Collins' (2004) interaction ritual chains (IRC) theory to examine how people give meaning to their social world. Collins defines rituals as, "a mechanism of mutually focused emotion and attention producing a momentarily shared reality, which thereby generates solidarity and symbols of group membership" (Collins 2004: 7). This shared reality shapes the emotional landscape in how people navigate their social world.

He maintains that an individual's change in behavior, feeling, thought, and belief can be attributed to one situation shifting to another because of prior ritual experiences, a link within the "chain" of interaction ritual (IR s). The history of an individual's "chains" is charged with emotions that inform their preference for seeking out situations in the future.

IRC theory explains that the fundamental motivation of individuals' behavior lies in their search for emotional energy (EE) from one situation to the next. An individual's evaluation of whether a situation is attractive or not is based on whether they anticipate the IR could successfully supply EE. In effect, IR s can be understood using rational choice theory in that it operates as markets that compete for the participation of the individual (Collins 2004: 149–58). Collins summarizes the main thrust of IRC theory,

> The central mechanism of interaction ritual theory is that occasions that combine a high degree of mutual focus of attention, that is, a high degree

of intersubjectivity, together with a high degree of emotional entrainment – through bodily synchronization, mutual stimulation/arousal of participants' nervous systems – result in feelings of membership that are attached to cognitive symbols; and result also in the emotional energy of individual participants, giving them feelings of confidence, enthusiasm, and desire for action in what they consider a morally proper path.

Collins 2004: 42

Thus, the extent rituals can successfully charge EE in the symbolisms to carry from one situation to the next becomes a "full-scale social psychology" that explains behavior and cognition (Collins 2004).

Short-term emotional experiences are crystallized as long-term emotional outcomes through symbols. The short-term emotional product of IRs is from the intensification of emotions, leading to what Durkheim (1912: 46) defines as "sacred time." It is a "sort of electricity" that the group experiences in its state of "collective effervescence," and it can lead to the intensification of any emotion. From these moments, individuals inject EE into symbols that serve to engrave its significance into their minds and memories. This results in long-term emotions. Symbols are often nouns, ranging from objects (e.g. flags, emblems), people (e.g. the Pope), icons (e.g. the hammer and sickle), and songs (e.g. the national anthem), to ideas (e.g. fundamentalism) – the point is that a symbol can effectively serve as a vessel to hold EE.

Once charged with positive EE, symbols can become sacred, whereas their defamation (e.g. the burning of a national flag) may trigger outbursts of moral indignation (Durkheim 1912).[2] IRC theory argues that groups fundamentally differ because of their symbols. For example, Protestants are different from Catholics because the Protestant Reformation stripped away many of the Catholic symbols (e.g. the crucifix, liturgy, the Pope).

Symbols can be created or pass into irrelevance. When the EE in symbols is no longer sustained by ritual practices, these symbols can fade into a memory, eventually rendering them dead. In the same way, new rituals can lead to the creation of new symbols that are charged with EE.

IRC theory is suited to examine social solidarity because people are driven by emotions. The chains of previous experiences determine the emotional energy charged in the symbols, thus delineating what people hold to be sacred and profane. This then informs their course of action in terms of the

---

2 This is the same mechanism for people expressing moral outrage and resort to shaming or even violence when social or moral norms are violated (Elster 2009).

interaction rituals and communities they will seek out. Thus, the chains in IRC theory essentially define social solidarity.

4   Methodology

I applied IRC theory to understand how STMers gave meaning to their STM experiences. I adopted a multi-sited ethnographic approach by following four CCE STM teams from Christian and Missionary Alliance churches from Canada to China and Taiwan in the summer of 2015. Each of these churches shared similar characteristics in that they were medium- to large-sized churches (i.e. more than 250 church members), predominantly Cantonese-speaking, and were in the major cities across Canada. Semi-structured interviews were conducted before departing for the STM, shortly after the STM ended, and between 8 to 10 months after the STM. This way, I was able to track the participants' expectations before they departed for the STM, their immediate reactions and commitments immediately after the STM ended, and whether these sentiments held up after a year. For one of the STM teams, I observed its sending church Eastern Chinese Alliance Church (pseudonym) over the course of two years just north of the Greater Toronto Area.

I conducted 48 case studies consisting of 23 youths (14 to 30 years old)[3] and 25 adults (above 40 years old),[4] with most participants having completed all three interviews (i.e. pre-departure, immediately after the STM, and 8 months after the STM). Pseudonyms were used for both individual and institutional identities and extra care was made to ensure that no identifiable information would be linked to the participants involved. Observations and interviews with the youths under Canada's legal adult age of 18 were conducted with informed parental/guardian consent.

5   Irony 1: Chinese vs. Canadian

Homeland visits informs subjects on their ethnic and national identities; that is, when juxtaposed in a homeland situation, subjects come to realize how "Chinese" or "Western" they really are (Levitt & Waters 2002; Louie 2004).

---

[3] This is a common age range to describe youths. For example, the United Nations defines youth to be between 15 and 24 years of age. Furthermore, those in their late 20s would qualify for what Smith and Snell (2009) calls "emerging adults".
[4] There was only one STMer between 30 to 40 years old in my study.

These types of experiences are relevant given previous scholarship has identified ethnic identification to be an important variable to one's religiosity (Tam 2018; Wong, Tam, Hung, Tsui, & Wong 2018; Yang 1999)

The Canadian STM youths I observed varied in their degree of "Chinese-ness" before embarking on the mission. By "Chinese-ness," I refer to their ability to speak the language (i.e. Cantonese or Mandarin) and their familiarity of Chinese symbols. In contrast, all of the youth STMers were fluent in their "Canadian-ness." I draw on examples to illustrate three ideal types of STMers negotiating their ethnic identities: the non-Chinese, the tourist Chinese, and the learning Chinese.

Some STMers regarded themselves as strictly Canadian and not Chinese at all. For example, before departing for China, I asked Edith (19) why she chose her church's China STM over the Mexico one.

J: From your perspective, if [your church] does STMs this summer and one is going to Mexico and other to China, which one would you go to and why? Or does it not matter?
E: For me personally, no, it doesn't really matter as long as I am doing it for the right reasons.
J: What would you say are the right reasons?
E: Going to share the gospel with the people and be the light of the world.

For Edith, despite being ethnically Chinese, an STM to China did not carry any extra significance compared to going to other countries.

The tourist Chinese are those STMers who approached China using a "tourist gaze," where they are "directed to features of the landscape that, which separate them off from everyday experience. Such aspects are viewed because they are taken to be in some sense out of the ordinary" (Urry 1992). As a result, they see what they expect to see. For example, James (18) was exhilarated by the possibility of eating dog because he felt it was part of "Chinese culture." During the STM, he met someone from *Yulin* and found out they were famous for their annual dog-eating festival. James told Roland, an adult in the team, about this discovery and suggested for the team to go try eating dog to experience "Chinese culture." Roland challenged James' notion of "Chinese culture." He asked James, "If you go back to Canada and tell your friends that you had a Chinese experience by eating dog food, you are reinforcing the idea that eating dog is part of Chinese culture. It's not." He maintained that other cultures such as Indian or Korean also eats dogs. "There are some Chinese people that eat live monkey brains but 99.999% have never even seen it before. This food doesn't represent China." James insisted it is for a cultural experience, but Roland was adamant to not take James.

I interviewed Roland later and asked why he did not want to take James to try dog meat. He explained that it is important to learn to appreciate the broader culture. Focusing on only the exotic side of Chinese cuisine would only reinforce stereotypes. Roland gave the example that Chinese culture gets watered down in Western culture and used the example of the Dragon Boat Festival.

> Dragon boat races in China are both a race and an art. There are people on the dragon boats who specialize in pushing up and down on the boat to create the illusion of the dragon riding the waves ... In Canada, the art is lost, and it is just Westerners muscle-racing. Even though they may imitate the appearance of the dragon boat race, it's not the same.

However, despite his own longing for China, he acknowledges home is Canada for the next generation of CCEs and they would be, at best, exposed to a watered-down version of Chinese culture.

The last group were those who wanted to learn more about their ethnic culture rather than focus on the exotic aspects of it. For example, one STM team visited a cultural center where they had an exhibit on a variety of Chinese festivals. After the team did a quick tour and was ready to depart to do more sightseeing, Jess (21) was visibly reluctant to leave and wanted to stay to learn more. When immediately after the STM, Jess explained:

> There were two exhibits that I wanted to go to, one of them was the arts and crafts one and the other one is the culture one. In general, I am interested in other cultures but for Chinese, while it's kind of familiar, there are many things that I don't know. Things like the Dragon Boat Festival, you eat *zongzi* (glutinous rice wrapped in bamboo leaves), but I don't know why you do it ... But just knowing some of the things I did as a kid ... China was always very distant to me, because I was like yeah, I am Chinese, and I identify myself with some cultural aspects. But I've never been to China; I always felt myself as very Canadian, so coming here was cool. I feel I want to learn more about and just connect more, it makes me want to ask my grandparents what was like living here ...

The impact seemed to last because a year later, Jess still held the same sentiments:

> Before I was like, "I'm Chinese, but I'm Canadian," you know? My cultural background is Chinese and most of my friends are Asian, I speak Chinese

at home, and I eat Chinese food, but I feel like I didn't have a connection with China itself. Maybe with only the culture. But now I feel like I'm still very Canadian, but now I know what China is like. I was only there once, but it's more concrete.

STMers like Jess embraced the opportunity to build on their existing knowledge of China.

Where the youth fit in the non-Chinese, tourist Chinese, or learning Chinese ideal types depended on their mastery over the Chinese language and culture *before* even stepping into China. From an IRC theory perspective, the more EE the STMers had charged in Chinese cultural symbols, the more knowledge STMers had to build their new experiences upon.

The irony is that while going to China will increase your knowledge of Chinese-ness, but how much you can actually absorb was determined well before the STM.[5] Much of ethnic inheritances such as language and cultural acquisition occurs at home, and the child-rearing practices of how immigrant families reinforce Chinese-ness in one's childhood will frame the child interpretation of their transnational experiences. As a result, youth with varying degrees of familiarity with Chinese symbols will inevitably generate different meanings from their experiences.

6   Irony 2: Global Christendom vs. Neo-Colonialism

There is something inherently contradictory with the picture of STMers flying halfway around the world to serve poor orphans and spending a week telling them how much Jesus loves them, declaring that they are brothers and sisters in Christ, only to fly back to Canada and leave the children to their own devices. Monikers such as "voluntourism" (Occhipinti 2016) and "McMissions" (Adeney 1996) have been used to criticize the consumerist nature of STMs.

The STM teams I examined actively sought out disadvantaged situations to conduct their mission. One team leader compared the second STM city they went to on the same trip as being too privileged:

> The sanctuary seats 450 people with sound and lighting. Two projectors. Professional microphones and lighting system. [Classrooms] are air

---

[5] This is an outcome to what social psychologists call the "Dunning-Kruger effect" (Dunning 2012).

> conditioned (which was not the always the case on other STMs). And the food there was better than a lot of the restaurants I had in China. They covered the cost of the food too ... The camp we went to previously was basically steamed buns and vegetables everyday... In fact, next time we go back again, I told them to cut back on the meat but they wanted to keep the kids interested ... we got duck, chicken, beef, you name it, we got it.

The team leader insisted that STM teams should be there to help the less fortunate.

> There has to be a reason for me to be there ... the reason is to have [the local churches] become independent ... Actually, the day we arrived, they just finished off another camp. Why do they need resources from our church when they already had resources from another camp? These are questions I have to ask right? They can "over-program" too right? From what I see they are reasonably well off ... All these questions have got to be analyzed.

From the perspective of STM leaders, seeking out hosts that have a greater need makes sense because the whole point of sending an STM team is to provide support to those who need it.

As a result, the socioeconomic contrast between the STMers and the local Chinese becomes a common pre-condition of STMs. Some STMers like Sylvia played down the significance of this wealth disparity:

> J: You are saying we are brothers and sisters in Christ even though we are so far apart and in different places but at the same time, their background is much less privileged than our background. How do you make sense of that disparity in terms of our privilege and material wealth? You are brothers and sisters in Christ, but at the same time, you could spend thousands of Canadian dollars to fly there to meet them. Meanwhile they are struggling to make ends meet ...
>
> S: Yeah, I don't think it's necessarily that that's happening, but it's also the organization that you go with and how you go about it. But definitely going in with a humble heart and we didn't go there and flash all our houses or the expensive things we have, and we shared a whole bunch of things. And I think in the end too, we never focused on our wealth. I don't think I've ever talked to anyone during our trip about how much we have versus how much they have but like how much we have together as in, how filled we are in Christ. How He has given us so much stuff and just being so

grateful for everything. You know ... I could see where that could come in from [a secular] perspective ... But for myself, going into this STM, I never thought about that ... I think it depends on the context of the STM as well, I know some STMs help with transitioning into a community, it's not like, "Oh, we are bringing everything in, and we fly over here and do our work and just leave." Like there is continuity in a lot of mission trips. And like follow-up with that. It really depends on who's the leader.

From Sylvia's perspective, the wealth disparity can largely be mitigated by the intentions and goals of the mission. For her, focusing on commonalities between brothers and sisters and being grateful for a faith communion should be the focus.

However, some people feel that negative outcomes can occur even with the best of intentions. One of the strongest criticisms to the STM practice was levied by Francis (18), who actually left his church shortly after his mission. Francis reflected back on his time going to the same site for three years and felt guilty for participating. He attributed his new perspective to maturing outside the church's influence and graduating from the International Baccalaureate (IB) curriculum that emphasizes responsible "global citizenship."

F: You're forced to say stuff, even the smallest, like even when I was here, I would say stuff like "Even the smallest seed, like you sow it and it's going to grow," stuff like that. And it's like, really optimistic talk, to validate ourselves. It's optimism ... I definitely started questioning it ... when I started to explore these ideas of whether I am actually there for something bigger. This summer I am not going ... because I actually don't support this anymore ... I'm just trying to be 100% honest with my feelings.

J: I think what you are trying to say is it's got a very neo-colonial dimension where you have rich successful people going to a developing country to help them out and also make themselves feel good at the same time.[6]

---

6 While this may appear to be a leading question, Francis and I actually had conversations about neo-colonialism before the interview on the STM over our conversations about the International Baccalaureate (IB) program. I was formerly an IB teacher and Francis and I connected quickly given he was finishing his IB diploma at the time. A core part of the IB program is a Creativity, Activity, and Service (CAS) component which required students to conduct 150 hours of service, and Francis was using the STM to log the hours. When we met, I shared with him that the international Christian school I previously worked at also used mission trips for CAS hours and the students came back to school annually to show pictures of them with poor kids in less developed regions in the school-wide chapel. This led the conversation to neo-colonialism through topics like Rudyard Kipling's "The White Man's Burden"

F: Yeah, you know the whole story about Europe and Africa right? That's like, basically it. Neo-colonialism you know.

J: Isn't it slightly different though? I mean, you're Chinese, how can you be neo-colonial when you are Chinese doing it to your own motherland? You're not even born in Canada, you're China Chinese, right?

F: There is a play, *Things Fall Apart* by some black African playwright ... It talks about neo-colonialism ... I feel that way, like that son, from the African tribe, right ... You are actually a dangerous tool because you are [an African] who [locals] can look up to, but you are not [the same as them] ... [The local Chinese] can actually look up to you and say "Oh you are a Chinese guy," but I have all these American traits about me ... Because we just think we are being ourselves [but we were] really just becoming as gods for these kids. It's terrible.

J: What's so dangerous about it?

F: Well one danger of it, in terms of the Christian religion aspect, is that they actually do end up worshipping you and not God. That's one danger, and the more social-cultural danger, is that these kids start to worship that culture, and thinking, "Oh I'm living here. I'm living in such a shitty lifestyle, look at these guys. They want fans, they get fans. They think it's too hot, so they just go into an [air conditioned] room" ... I just think, these kids will end up hating on themselves when they are older. Right now, they may think they are funny; it may be a good time to play. But when they get older, they are hating themselves for being in this society because they can't be like us. I just see that happening.

J: So, it's like you show them a little bit of the West, and they realize what kind of dump they live in?

F: Yeah.

Throughout the interview, he was hypercritical about the STM enterprise and the neo-colonial consequences of entering China, looking *like* a Chinese, but actually not *being* Chinese inside. He cited the literary masterpiece *Things Fall Apart* that he took in his International Baccalaureate English class to illustrate his position.

The irony of the wealth disparity between the STMers and the missionized is difficult to untangle. STMers leverage Canadian wealth to fly over to support needy Chinese children. However, instead of spending the several thousand

---

(i.e. often taught in the English curriculum) and the history of missionaries in China (i.e. missionaries coming over on opium-filled gunboats). My statement here was just revisiting an old topic.

dollars on global travel, what if the STMers simply donated the money to those they were visiting? Are the youths simply going for a form of religious voluntourism or McMissions? On the contrary, if they do not go, will they even be aware of the situation to even consider giving donations? Sylvia believes the intent and goals is the emphasis. For Francis, good intent can lead to bad results.

7 Irony 3: Fundamentalism vs. Modernity

The necessity for STMs, and missionary work in general, can be traced to the fundamentalist movements at the turn of the 19th century. It was not a coincidence that the birth of fundamentalism overlapped with that of sociology, as both began with concerns about the rise of modernity. By "modernity" or any of its variants (e.g. modern, modernism), I follow Kumar's (1995) definition of a society that carries the hallmarks of Western 18th-century advances that prioritizes the working philosophies of rationalism and utilitarianism.

Modernity is tied to the rise of secularism, a body of principles that value rational knowledge and experience over the supernatural (Bellah 1964). The secularization of society necessitated the rejection of the absolute submission to the authority of religion. Furthermore, the rapid changes in society at the turn of the 19th century gave rise to pluralism; and pluralism requires that the application of the ideologies of modernism be prioritized.

Given that modernism prizes change over continuity, quantity over quality, and commercial efficiency over traditional values (Lawrence 1989: 27), Christian fundamentalism is a religiously-based cognitive and affective orientation of the world characterized by protest against modernism (Antoun 2001: 3). In other words, fundamentalism is the other side of the secularism diode, one that protests against the changes wrought by modernity.

STMers saw the trips as an opportunity to "experience God." This phrase or variations of it (e.g. seeing God, see for myself what God is doing) came up in all the interviews. Renee (16) is an example of a youth who sought support her "head knowledge" with religious experience. Renee started attending her church in middle school and was learning the ropes of how to be a Christian in her community. She felt she had acquired a lot of head knowledge and explained to me that she hears all these incredible stories of how people experience their faith.

> I see people that are really strong in their faith ... Sometimes I hear all these testimonies and things but then I don't know if I can do it or if the same thing will happen to me because even today when I was listening

to [a pastor's sermon about a supernatural experience], I feel like a lot of things sounds fictional to me ... A part of the purpose of why I'm going on STM is I want to experience God out of what I know, and I want to see if that will give me any answers.

Renee's reason for going on an STM resonated with many other STMers. She wanted to set apart a "sacred time" dedicated to God to affirm her faith.[7] Many STMers shared a similar desire to affirm whether the faith tradition in which they were raised is the real deal.

STMers also recognized the benefits of STMs helping them grow as individuals and believed there might be opportunities to be blessed by God through their sacrifice. Jason (23) recently graduated from reputable university with a degree in engineering and had been job-searching for several months to no avail. When I interviewed him in 2015, the province he lived in was undergoing a recession and he was growing frustrated with his job-search ordeal. He explained that past STMs had really allowed him to experience God. He hoped that by drawing closer to God through the STM, he would make it possible for God to guide him in the near future, especially in terms of starting a career.

JA: You know how at the very end there is an "altar call" (to formally convert people) ... So, I went through teaching for the whole week, and I thought to myself, "I don't know if the youths got the message or what they would think." And so ... 23 people rose their hands (to accept Christ) out of like 50 or 60? I was thinking like 5 would be really amazing already ... "Wow, God can do miraculous things!" ... So, to me it's like ... [God] does miracles, but you never really experience it here in Canada ...

J: So, it's strengthens your faith because you see God doing things that otherwise you would not see here.

JA: Yeah. So, finding a job is really worrisome to me. So, I guess also going to STM is, like you said, to strengthen my faith. Like here's my life and then whatever job you want me to do ...

J: The way I am hearing this is before taking a step on any of these paths, you are just going to give it up to God, offer yourself, get close to God, and let Him to lead you to wherever He wants you to go.

JA: Yeah, exactly. And hopefully I'll find some answers.

---

7 The application of the term "sacred time" is especially befitting considering it echoes Durkheim's (1912) distinction between profane time and sacred time.

Jason was aware that his perspective was in politically incorrect territory for his faith community, since expecting a reward for one's sacrifice can be interpreted as self-seeking (Protestant theology is based on Jesus' grace and not acts as the basis for salvation). Nonetheless, there is certainly a discourse of being blessed for proper sacrifices within Christianity (e.g. 1 Corinthians 4:1–2).

When I conducted my final interview with Jason in 2016, he had been unable to find a job for a whole year and had to choose between continuing his job search or participating in another STM that summer. He committed to the STM on the condition that he would opt out if he found employment before the STM, and even bought a non-refundable plane ticket to China. He eventually secured a job, so he did not go on the STM. He believed that securing the job was not necessarily God rewarding him, but rather, "It's more like a [process] of I'll trust in Him and He'll provide. Maybe it was a test [of faith]?"

Conservative branches of Christianity preach an embattled state of their faith and demand a return to core religious values through a strict adherence to their interpretation of the scripture (Ammerman 1987; Lawrence 1989). If one challenges a conservative Christian on how they should test their faith, many would cite Jesus' words from Luke 4:12, "Do not put the Lord your God to the test." I have even heard some CCEs preach that we should have "faith like children," referring to Luke 18:17, and believe unconditionally.

The innate tension between empirical verification and belief imbued within each of the STMers' expectations inevitably causes tension in their faith. The observations regarding the tension between science and religion have been observed in other studies (Almond et al. 2003; Ammerman 1987), so it is not surprising to see it come up in the STM experience. However, science in this case slips in surreptitiously, as it is the scientific method of empirical verification that is of consequence. Thus, the irony is that the STMers' faith draws validity and strength from the tools of the very enemies of modernity they seek to ward off.[8]

---

8 Berger's (1967) application of the term *nomos* highlighted the tension between science and religion. Meaning meaning*ful*ness, *nomos* contrasts with Durkheim's (1897) *anomie*, which is meaning*less*ness. Berger argues the *nomos* of religion performs a world-building function that offers a particular script for actors to adopt. He maintains, "viewed historically, most of man's worlds have been sacred worlds ... it can thus be said that religion has played a strategic part in the human enterprise of world-building" (27). In contemporary societies, he argues that modern science fulfills the function of providing *nomos*. The STMers, socialized in the *nomos* of evangelicalism and modernity, are forced to grapple with these entangled meanings.

8 Discussion: Entangled Chains

Groups are fundamentally constituted by individuals. Therefore, group solidarity depends on individual decisions towards sustaining cohesion. Theoretical insights emerge when examining situations imbued with inherent tensions. In this paper, scrutinizing the ironies in the youths' engagement on the STMs reveals a rich entanglement of symbols and emotions. The first irony highlights the tension between Chinese-ness and Canadian-ness. The second irony reveals the tension between global Christendom, religious philanthropy, and neo-colonialism. The third irony uncovers the conflict between contemporary fundamentalist Christianity versus modernity's penchant for empirical verification.

It is important to note that almost all of the youths in the study have spent most of their lives in Canada and have been socialized in a worldview different from their parents in Canada. In comparison, many of the adults are first-generation immigrants who moved to Canada for work. Therefore, the youths are the ones who have a richer diversity of symbols and are thus more likely to experience the above ironies.

Each of the three ironies essentially reflect two conflicting sacred symbols. For example, Edith felt her Canadian-ness trumped Chinese-ness in emotional valence. For Francis, his beliefs on neo-colonialism outweighed his ethic of global Christendom. In the case of Jason, he had to tenuously balance experiencing God between empirical verification and childlike faith. From an IRC theory perspective, each individual had emotional energy invested in both ends of the spectrum. I maintain this is not a false dichotomy because irrespective of the EE invested in symbols, at the end of the day, people can only carry one course of action. This course of action can lie at either ends of the spectrum or fall somewhere in the middle as a form of compromise.

IRC theory maintains that people make decisions because of how the "IR market" operates (Collins 2004: 141–182); an individual prefers to participate in IRs that they anticipate will generate the highest EE output. However, in a world where an individual may hold multiple conflicting symbols to be sacred, people face an increasingly complex EE calculus. Others have made similar observations; for example, it was previously suggested by Summers-Effler (2006) that Collins' imagery of chains may be too linear.

I suggest a modest modification in the form of "entangled chains" by reconceptualizing interaction ritual chains as sequences of links, with plasticity resembling elastic bands. To illustrate, each chain link of the elastic band is a symbol that carries emotional energy for an individual. A chain of links represents a history of emotional energy of a slowly evolving symbol over time (i.e. what "evangelicalism" means to a 7-year-old would be different when they become 40). The emotional strength of the chain is measured by the strength of the individual links. These chains of individual symbolic links are intertwined and messy.

The chains are malleable, and can be connected, stretched, bent, and twisted in a variety of ways. Like elastic bands, these links can come in a various sizes and densities. Smaller and denser bands carry more emotional energy, are more resilient, and have a stronger pull against adjacent bands. In contrast, looser and thinner bands carry less EE, are less resilient, and have a weaker pull. In fact, they can even snap if tugged upon too strongly.

My empirical material has shown that people's sense of identity involves more than linear chains of two discrete symbols (e.g. Chinese or Canadian); rather, it includes many intertwined symbols that is in constant negotiation (e.g. considering the ethics of how one can fly from Canada to China without perpetuating neo-colonial norms). Through the visualization of elastic-like entangled chains, the IR market principles as originally conceptualized by Collins still apply. It supplements a dynamic image explaining the rise of new symbols and the fall of previous ones. The elastic nature of entangled chains also resonates with the current findings on neuroplasticity.[9]

9 Conclusion: Entangled Chains in Modernity

The imagery of entangled chains benefits contemporary discussions in the sociology of religion. Current studies in how people continue to apply religion to their daily lives have found that people selectively integrate aspects of religiosity yet reject others, and these decisions are clearly not entirely based on rational explanations (e.g. Ammerman 2014; Smith & Snell 2009; Thiessen

---

9 LeDoux warned that while terms like emotion, cognition, perception, and memory are necessary for analytical purposes, they do not have clear boundaries nor dedicated regions in the brain. "The various classes of emotions are mediated by separate neural systems that have evolved for different reasons. There is no such thing as the emotional faculty and there is no single brain system dedicated to this phantom function" (LeDoux 1996: 16). The neural networks are intricate and multiple regions become active when facing decisions. This also explains why the classification of emotions is so difficult, resulting in untenable categories like mixed emotions (e.g. being simultaneously happy and envious of a friend's success) or secondary emotions (e.g. variations of primary emotions such as fear)(Franks 2014; Thamm 2006). The plasticity of the brain that allows different parts to evolve to execute different functions also make it difficult to separate emotion from cognition (Franks 2014).

2015). A sociological explanation using entangled chains accounts for why people accept or reject certain aspects of religion.

The STMer youths that I studied each had a different take on the three ironies. How Chinese does one have to be to attend a CCE church? What does it even mean to be Chinese? Do missions to China perpetuate global western hegemonies or reinforce global Christendom? To what extent should CCEs rely on childlike faith versus empirical verification to back up their "head knowledge"? These are conflicting positions that individuals have to sort out.

Each individual develops unique chains of experiences in their lives that charge up EE in their symbols, resulting in different conflicting sacred symbols that become entangled. Over time, because of these entangled symbols, people will choose to join certain groups and reject others based on what they share to be sacred. In a rapidly changing world where the growing impact of globalization, the Internet, and migration is the dominant trend, this has long-term implications to the future of social solidarity in modernity.

References

Adeney, M. 1996. "McMissions." *Christianity Today*. http://www.christianitytoday.com/ct/1996/november11/6td014.html, retrieved 30 June 2019.

Almond, G.A., Appleby, R.S., & Sivan, E. 2003. *Strong Religion: The Rise of Fundamentalisms Around the World*. Chicago: University of Chicago Press.

Ammerman, N.T. 1987. *Bible Believers: Fundamentalists in the Modern World*. New Brunswick, NJ: Rutgers University Press.

Ammerman, N.T. 2014. *Sacred Stories, Spiritual Tribes: Finding Religion in Everyday Life*. Oxford: Oxford University Press.

Antoun, R. 2001. *Understanding Fundamentalism: Christian, Islamic, and Jewish Movements*. Walnut Creek, CA: Altamira Press.

Bellah, R. 1964. "Religious Evolution." *American Sociological Review* 29(3), 358–374.

Berger, P. 1967. *The Sacred Canopy: Elements of Sociological Theory of Religion*. Garden City, NY: Doubleday.

Chen, C. 2008. *Getting saved in America: Taiwanese immigration and religious experience*. New Jersey: Princeton University Press.

Collins, R. 2004. *Interaction Ritual Chains*. New Jersey: Princeton University Press.

Dunning, D. 2012. "The Dunning–Kruger Effect." *Advances in Experimental Social Psychology* 44, 247–296.

Durkheim, É. 1897. *Suicide: A Study in Sociology*.

Durkheim, É. 1912. *The Elementary Forms of Religious Life*. Oxford University Press.

Elster, J. 2009. "Norms." Pp. 195–217 in *The Oxford Handbook of Analytical Sociology*, edited by P. Hedstrom & P. Bearman. Oxford, UK: Oxford University Press.

Franks, D.D. 2014. "Emotions and Neurosociology." Pp. 267–282 in *Handbook of the Sociology of Emotions*, 2nd ed., edited by J.E. Stets & J.H. Turner. New York, NY: Springer.

Howell, B.M. 2012. *Short-Term Mission: An Ethnography of Christian Travel Narrative and Experience*. Downers Grove, IL: IVP Academic.

Jenkins, P. 2012. *The Next Christendom: The Coming of Global Christianity*, 3rd ed. New York, NY: Oxford University Press.

Kumar, K. 1995. *From Post-Industrial to Post-Modern society: New Theories of the Contemporary World*. Oxford, UK: Blackwell Publishing.

Lawrence, B. 1989. *Defenders of God: The Fundamentalist Revolt Against the Modern Age*. San Francisco, CA: Harper & Row.

LeDoux, J. 1996. *The Emotional Brain: The Mysterious Underpinnings of Emotional Life*. New York, NY: Simon & Schuster.

Levitt, P. 2007. *God Needs No Passport: Immigrants and the Changing Religious Landscape*. New York, NY: The New Press.

Levitt, P., & Waters, M.C. eds. 2002. *The Changing Face of Home: The Transnational Lives of the Second Generation*. New York, NY: Russell Sage Foundation.

Louie, A. 2004. *Chineseness Across Borders: Renegotiating Chinese Identities in China and the United States*. Durham, NC: Duke University Press.

Occhipinti, L. 2016. "Not Just Tourists: Short-term Missionaries and Voluntourism." *Human Organization* 75(3), 258–268.

Priest, R.J., ed. 2008. *Effective Engagement in Short-term Missions: Doing it Right!* Pasadena, CA: William Carey Library.

Priest, R.J., Dischinger, T., Rasmussen, S., & Brown, C.M. 2006. "Researching the Short-term Mission Movement." *Missiology 34*(4), 431–450.

Priest, R.J., & Howell, B.M. 2013. "Introduction: Theme Issue on Short-Term Missions." *Missiology: An International Review 41*(2), 124–129.

Smith, C., & Snell, P. 2009. *Souls in Transition: The Religious and Spiritual Lives of Emerging Adults*. Oxford, UK: Oxford University Press.

Summers-Effler, E. 2006. "Ritual Theories." Pp. 135–154 in *Handbook of the Sociology of Emotions*, edited by J.E. Stets & J.H. Turner. New York, NY: Springer.

Tam, J., & Hasmath, R. 2015. "Navigating Uncertainty: The Survival Strategies of Religious NGOs in China." *Journal of Civil Society* 11(3), 283–299.

Tam, J. 2019. "Renegotiating Religious Transnationalism: Fractures in Transnational Chinese Evangelicalism." *Global Networks* 19(1), 66–85.

Thamm, R.A. 2006. "The classification of emotions." Pp. 11–37 in *Handbook of the Sociology of Emotions*, edited by J.E. Stets & J.H. Turner. New York, NY: Springer.

Thiessen, J. 2015. *The Meaning of Sunday: The Practice of Belief in a Secular Age*. Montreal, QC: McGill-Queens University Press.

Urry, J. 1992. "The Tourist Gaze 'Revisited'." *The American Behavioral Scientist* 36(2), 172–186.

Warner, S.R. 1993. "Work in Progress Toward a New Paradigm for the Sociological Study of Religion in the United States." *American Journal of Sociology* 98(5), 1044–1093.

Wong, E., Tam, J., Hung, K., Tsui, T., & Wong, W. 2018. *Listening to Their Voices: An Exploration of Faith Journeys of Canadian-born Chinese Christians.* Toronto, ON: CCCOWE Press.

Yang, F. 1999. *Chinese Christians in America: Conversion, Assimilation, and Adhesive Identities.* University Park, PA: Penn State University Press.

Yang, F. 2002. "Chinese Christian Transnationalism: Diverse Networks of a Houston Church." Pp. 129–148 in *Religion Across Borders: Transnational Immigrant Networks*, edited by H.R. Ebaugh & J.S. Chafetz. Walnut Creek, CA: Altamira Press.

CHAPTER 9

Between Cultural Reproduction and Cultural Translation

A Case Study of Yiguandao in London and Manchester

Hung-Jen Yang

Among "salvationist movements" or "redemptive societies" appearing in Republican China as a wave of religious movements, Yiguandao (一貫道) is the most important one that adapts well to the conditions of modernity and spreads actively to many different cultures.[1] Yiguandao started its proselytizing actions in North China in the early 1930s, and its network was expanded almost all over mainland China in the late 1940s. In the 1950s, although both the governments in mainland China and in Taiwan put the "sectarian" label on Yiguandao and proclaimed it to be an illegal religion, Yiguandao still paved its way to the world. In the end of the 1980s, the number of Yiguandao followers in Taiwan grew to a significant scale, and in the process of democratization, the government in Taiwan finally legalized Yiguandao (Mu 2002; Lu 2008). Nowadays Yiguandao has established its public temples or family prayer halls in more than 80 countries. Indeed, the globalization of Yiguandao is a significant phenomenon, which demands an analytic discussion.

Since the 1990s, several Yiguandao branches from Taiwan, Malaysia, and Singapore have reorganized their preaching work in some English-speaking countries, especially in the UK. The spread of Yiguandao around the world can be characterized by two approaches, that is, "cultural reproduction" and "cultural translation." These two approaches are exemplified by two types of Yiguandao public temples in the UK. The first type of Yiguandao temple was established for the diasporic Chinese in London, mainly a group of refugees from Vietnam in the 1970s. After the Yiguandao temple was established, these diasporic Chinese reclaimed the traditional Chinese folk religion, with a set of

---

1 In response to the western religious hegemony, a wave of religious movements emerged in North China in the early Republican era (1911–1949), and some researchers have named these religious organizations as "redemptive societies" (Duara 2001; Palmer 2011). Several "redemptive societies" believe that five different religions share the same origin and thus urge their followers to learn the core teachings from the founders of the five religions (Confucius, Laozi, Buddha, Jesus, and Muhammad).

familiar symbols, beliefs, and practices located in the migrant enclave. Also, as a result of this religious revival, ethnic identification among these diasporic Chinese followers was strengthened. This phenomenon can be analyzed by the concept of "cultural reproduction."

The second type of Yiguandao temple was built up for the non-Chinese western followers in the 2000s, including a public temple in suburban Manchester and another one in North East London, where the proselytizing cadres from Taiwan and Malaysia endeavored to create a new style of gathering space for these westerners. People of different ethnicities and different religions started to gather in the western-style Yiguandao public temples and what appealed to them was mainly the topic of self cultivation. Gradually, the interpretive flexibility of Dao emerged. Through the teachings that "Dao is not a religion" (道不是教), "Five religions, one origin" (五教同源), and the relevant ritual practices in the Yiguandao public temples, the followers from the Anglican church, Christianity, Catholicism, Judaism, and Islam were quick to grasp the specific meaning of "the encompassing of the contrary" in Dao (Dumont 1980: 240; Sangren 1987: 132–140). The concept of "cultural translation" can be applied to the analysis of this cross-cultural phenomenon.

With the two types of Yiguandao public temples in the UK, it is observed that Yiguandao has been adjusted on the route of its spread around the world. Based on my one-year fieldwork in London and Manchester in 2012, I seek to examine how the two approaches, "cultural reproduction" and "cultural translation," work to engage Yiguandao followers.[2]

1 Cultural Reproduction and Cultural Translation

In most situations, rather than deliberately adopting either the approach of "cultural reproduction" or "cultural translation," the pioneering staff of Yiguandao from Taiwan, Malaysia, and Singapore make different arrangements in the process of proselytization to cope with totally different social and cultural conditions, which nevertheless brings about unintended consequences, especially what Yiguandao means.

Since Yiguandao has a strong mission of saving people from the suffering world, earnest followers are urged to invite their family, friends, colleagues, acquaintances, strangers, and even people of different ethnicities to "receive

---

[2] The author was granted a fellowship to be a visiting researcher in Imperial College London in 2012, allowing him to conduct one-year participant observations in Yiguandao public temples in London and Manchester.

Dao" (求道). Undergoing the rite of initiation (傳道儀式), neophytes will receive from an initiator (點傳師) the "three treasures" (三寶), namely "Heavenly Portal" (玄關), "Divine Mantra" (口訣), and "Hand Seal" (合同) (Song 1983; Jordan & Overmyer 1986; Lu 2008). Among the three treasures, the "Heavenly Portal," a spot below the forehead, allows of plural interpretations. Once the "Heavenly Portal" is "opened" by the initiator endowed with heavenly mandate (天命), the soul or the true self will be on the right way connecting with heaven and protected by the deities when disasters occur. Besides, if followers can cultivate themselves by applying the "heavenly portal" and keep themselves from evil and greed, they will transcend the cycle of life and death.

According to the core doctrines of Yiguandao, all people are living in a period of the imminent apocalypse of the world, and the only way to halt destructive disasters is that everyone can cultivate themselves as well as help other people's conversion and cultivation. Once the majority of human beings in the world receive Dao and cultivate themselves well, the advent of the savior Maitreya Buddha (彌勒佛) will occur and bring salvation to the world. Therefore, earnest followers of Yiguandao have to introduce people as many as possible to receive Dao, which will also accumulate a lot of invisible "merits" (功德) for introducers and their family members. As the savior Maitreya Buddha has his wish of no more killing in the world, even including animal killing, followers are positively encouraged to accept the "vegetarian vow" (清口愿) for their whole life.

It is generally believed that Yiguandao is characterized by interpretative flexibility that leads to distinction in the way of proselytizing between the Chinese lifeworld and the western lifeworld. When Dao is transmitted in the Chinese societies, the teachings from Confucianism, Buddhism and Daoism would be centered. On the other hand, in the western societies, where Yiguandao is faced with diverse religions, such as Christianity, Islam, and Judaism, the doctrines of "Dao is not a religion" and "Five religions, one origin" require reinterpretation so as to fit in different conditions.

The concepts of "cultural reproduction" and "cultural translation" explain how Yiguandao is interpreted differently.[3] Cultural reproduction suggests that the existing structures impose too much constraint on the actors, whereby the

---

3   The concept "cultural reproduction" is inspired by Pierre Bourdieu's "Genesis and Structure of the Religious Field" (1991), while the other concept "cultural translation" is related to Bruno Latour's "Welcoming the Beings Sensitive to the Word" in An Inquiry into Modes of Existence (2013), but the author does not follow these two scholars' concepts strictly. The author constructs and contrasts these two concepts for the purpose of the empirical research of Yiguandao in London and Manchester.

actors are forced to choose among restricted selections and thus the flexibility of interpretation is limited. In my case study of the Yiguandao public temple located in the Vietnamese Chinese refugee community, the social and cultural conditions of the ethnic refugees incline them to adopt the already familiar symbols, beliefs, and practices from their original tradition. Misrecognition may occur when the original religious framework is appropriated and applied to a new one and vice versa. In the transnational religious field emerging from the connection between the Vietnamese Chinese ethnic group and the pioneering missionaries of Yiguandao in the UK, the process of symbolic struggle makes Yiguandao reduce itself into a kind of traditional folk religion in the Vietnamese Chinese community (Bourdieu 1991; Sangren 2000; Verter 2003; Rey 2007).

On the other hand, cultural translation points to another transnational religious field with much more dynamic interactions between the religion on the move and the religions in the western lifeworld. Religion should be viewed "not as a package, stable set of beliefs and practices rooted in a particular bounded time and space, but as a contingent clustering of diverse elements that come tighter within to-be-determined spaces riddled by power and interests. The resulting assemblages made up of actors, objects, technology, and ideas, travel at different rates and rhythms, across the different levels and scopes of the social fields in which they are embedded" (Levitt 2013: 160). In the globalization of Yiguandao from Taiwan to the world, the dimension of cultural border-crossing becomes more manifest than before (Yang 2015; Broy, Reinke & Clart 2017; Billioud 2020). Not only does the travelling religion convert believers of existing religions, but it itself is also reassembled into a new appearance (Yang & Ebaugh 2001; Tweed 2006; Cao 2013; Latour 2013).

2   Three Stages of the Yiguandao Mission in the UK

Since the early 1990s, the most significant "Yiguandao missionaries" in the UK have been the pioneering staff from Taiwan and Malaysia. In the mid-1970s, different branches of Yiguandao in Taiwan started to proselytize in Malaysia; among them, the Baoguang-Jiande (寶光建德) branch was the largest one. Two decades later, in Baoguang-Jiande branch, some of the second-generation Chinese followers in Kuala-Lumpur made a decision to go to the UK for two purposes, to pursue further studies and to preach Yiguandao to the western countries. In 1990, one of the examples was a female Malaysian Chinese student in Kuala-Lumpur, Ms. Ng, who got admission to St. Mary's Hospital Medical School and with a good command of English, served as a medical translator in some hospitals in London. By means of medical translation, Ms. Ng quickly made connections with a number of overseas Chinese from different countries. In 1993, aiming to introduce the overseas Chinese to Yiguandao, Ms. Ng invited a senior temple member, a leading initiator (領導點傳師) Mr. Ho, based at the headquarter in Central Taiwan belonging to the Baoguang-Jiande branch, to visit London. Mr. Ho used to be one of the early pioneering staff who transmitted Yiguandao to Kuala-Lumpur in the mid-1970s. Mr. Ho accepted the suggestion by Ms. Ng and then rented a condominium to be a temporary temple of Yiguandao in North West London near the medical school and some hospitals. This marked the "beginning stage" of Yiguandao Baoguang-Jiande branch's proselytizing efforts in the UK.

From 1993 to 2000, the first group of overseas Chinese who were introduced to "receive Dao," that is, to participate in the initiation ceremony of Yiguandao, were the Chinese immigrants from the previous British colony, Mauritius. Beginning with the participation of the Mauritian Chinese, the temporary Yiguandao public temple continued to draw Vietnamese Chinese followers and language was the key factor. Because of their common language, Cantonese, the Malaysian Chinese medical translator, Ms. Ng, communicated with the Mauritian Chinese without language barriers, and then the latter in turn introduced the Vietnamese Chinese into the newly established social network. Among the Vietnamese Chinese, one old lady performed an essential role. Not long after the connection between Ms. Ng and the old lady was made, the temporary temple of Yiguandao in North West London was frequented by new followers, all Vietnamese Chinese. To cope with the daily work of temple operation, and to conduct the initiation ceremony of Yiguandao smoothly, the leading initiator, Mr. Ho, launched a program of missionary rotation when he returned to Taiwan. Ultimately, several groups of Taiwanese pioneering staff were arranged to stay in London for three months through this rotation program till 2000.

With the missionary rotation program, the pioneering staff from Taiwan offered missionary service side by side with Ms. Ng. In comparison with Ms. Ng, a college student from Malaysia, the temple staff from Taiwan did not have much strength in terms of language and mobility in the mission of spreading Yiguandao. They were not able to speak English fluently and neither could they speak Cantonese, since their mother tongue was Hokkien and they received education in Mandarin-speaking schools. Also, in the 1990s, the Taiwanese were not eligible for visa-exempt entry to the UK, which resulted in their limited mobility from Taiwan to the UK. Nevertheless, they had unshakable faith in Yiguandao, accepting the vegetarian vow or even setting up a family prayer hall for quite a long time. With many years of religious practice and training, the temple staff from Taiwan were ready to preach Yiguandao despite their weakness.

Notwithstanding its contribution, the rotation program failed to create a stable team, which caused a bottleneck in the missionary work. Every time the Taiwanese staff left London, the remaining Malaysian Chinese staff, often two to three in total, had a hard time managing all the sacred and secular affairs by themselves. Especially around 1997, the temple staff encountered a new task when the above-mentioned old Vietnamese Chinese lady suggested that the temple move to the Vietnamese Chinese community in South East London. To carry out the plan of establishing another public temple of Yiguandao definitely required more staff. Thus, in 2001, the headquarter in Central Taiwan arranged a fifty-year-old initiator to reside in London and take charge of all the activities, which brought the rotation program to an end, and the Yiguandao mission entered the second stage led by this resident initiator, Mr. Wang.

Thereafter, the second stage can be called the "Chinese-enclave stage," roughly from 2001 to 2008, with only two Taiwanese and three Malaysian Chinese working together to preach Yiguandao to the Vietnamese Chinese in South East London. The Taiwanese staff included the middle-aged initiator, Mr. Wang, and his wife, also a Yiguandao lecturer, who opened a vegetarian café to earn their living while sustaining the temple activities. The three Malaysian Chinese staff included two young women, Ms. Ng and Ms. Gan, who came to the UK to study for a degree in the early 1990s, and one middle-aged lady Ms. Leong, who has already lived in London for over thirty years. Ms. Leong, serving as a nurse and a medical translator in some hospitals in London, was introduced to receive Dao by a Mauritian Chinese patient who just attended the Yiguandao initiation ceremony in the original temporary temple. In this stage, under the training of the resident initiator, the three Malaysian ladies became not only earnest but also adept adherents of Yiguandao; also, the three Malaysian ladies translated what the initiator taught into Cantonese, so that the Vietnamese Chinese could follow the rituals and learn the basic lessons of Yiguandao without unnecessary misunderstandings.

The year 2007 marked a major turning point in the Yiguandao mission, as three couples of bilingual Malaysian Chinese immigrants joined the pioneering staff. The initiation of the first couple into Yiguandao resulted from a coincidental encounter with the initiator Mr. Wang. After closing the unprofitable vegetarian café, Mr. Wang started a fortune-telling business in "Mind, Body, and Soul Exhibitions." A couple of middle-class Malaysian immigrants came to the exhibition and unintentionally encountered the initiator. In this encounter, Mr. Wang told them about their life and future, which was not just convincing but more importantly an experience of epiphany to the couple and eventually led them into Yiguandao. While the husband of this couple was a senior lecturer in a famous business college in London, the wife Mrs. Chan, already trained to be an interpreter in the church in Malaysia at her early age, acquired the ability to translate the Bible into Chinese and later served as an interpreter in the Yiguandao temple. After the middle-class Malaysian couple received Dao, the social network of the Malaysian Chinese was formed. Another young couple Mr. and Mrs. Tse, who had received Dao in different branches of Yiguandao in Malaysia and wanted to stay in London to start their own business, were also introduced to the temple. Almost at the same time, still another young couple Mr. and Mrs. Poh, who just got their master degrees, joined the temple staff as well. The formation of the Malaysian Chinese network ushered in the third stage of Yiguandao mission, called the "western follower stage," at which the staff's multi-lingual capacity made Yiguandao spread beyond the overseas Chinese community.

From the "beginning stage" to the "Chinese-enclave stage" and the "western follower stage" of the Yiguandao mission in the UK, while the initiator Mr. Wang and his wife were the organizational center of the doctrines, rituals, and activities of the Yiguandao temple, all the Malaysian Chinese immigrants were the new blood added to the temple staff. With their bilingual or even multi-lingual capacity, the Malaysian Chinese staff contributed to Yiguandao proselytization not only among the overseas Chinese but also among English-speaking westerners.

However, a phenomenon is quite remarkable as we compare the Vietnamese Chinese followers with the western followers.[4] When the Yiguandao missionaries, consisting of the Taiwanese and the Malaysian Chinese, proselytized to the Vietnamese Chinese, no followers accepted the vegetarian vow, which signified strict religious adherence to Yiguandao. On the other hand, when the same Yiguandao missionaries interacted with the western followers, the vegetarian adherents emerged gradually. What were the mechanisms that made the western followers convert to Yiguandao so thoroughly, yet the Vietnamese Chinese just wanted to worship in the temple but hesitated to transform themselves further by accepting the vegetarian vow or setting up their own family prayer halls? The following sections will focus on how the public temples in

---

4   Although there are some publications on the global spread of Yiguandao, there is no publication specifically about the comparison between the Vietnamese Chinese followers and the western followers. For more details on the global spread of Yiguandao, see Broy, Reinke & Clart (2017) "Migrating Buddhas and Global Confucianism: The Transnational Space Making of Taiwanese Religious Organizations."

London and Manchester were adjusted, facing followers of different ethnicities and cultures.

3 Cultural Reproduction: The Vietnamese Chinese Followers of Yiguandao in London

In the 1970s, different groups of Vietnamese Chinese refugees were settled in suburban areas of South East London. Indeed, in the proselytization of Yiguandao in London, the Vietnamese Chinese community occupied a significant place. When the first Vietnamese Chinese old lady was introduced to the temporary Yiguandao temple in North West London, she learned that the ritual of "receiving three treasures" (求三寶) meant the same as the "Guanyin mind-dharma" (觀音心法). Of course, this was not the core meaning of Yiguandao. But rather than proclaim itself as Yiguandao, it was a compromising rhetoric to avoid the stigmatized images of "sectarian groups" made by the two governments across the Taiwan Strait. Following the old lady back to the Vietnamese neighborhood in South East London, the Yiguandao missionaries noticed that these Vietnamese Chinese shared a close kinship, and they all worshiped a specific "Guanyin temple" (觀音堂) organized by a senior temple host in the neighborhood. In terms of religious market and religious competition, Yiguandao was unintentionally put in the competitive field of "Guanyin worship" (Stark & Finke 2000). Afterwards, the Guanyin-Yiguandao followers in the Vietnamese Chinese enclave designated a new kind of religious schedule and religious map, so that they made an arrangement about when and which temple to attend.

However, the strategies that the Yiguandao missionaries applied to attract the Vietnamese Chinese rendered the subsequent conversion process more difficult. On the one hand, by relating itself to or even appropriating the major religion, Guanyin belief, which the Vietnamese Chinese followed, Yiguandao quickly erected its foundation in the ethnic enclave. On the other hand, the Yiguandao public temple was mistaken for a similar kind of Guanyin belief. Thereby the Yiguandao missionaries were not able to encourage the followers in the Vietnamese Chinese enclave to convert to Dao cultivation (修道), which involves much more than worshiping the deities on the first and fifteenth days of every lunar month and praying for safety, health and wealth.[5] One of the senior male members was especially trained to be the temple staff, but in the

---

5 Besides, according to research field-work in Taiwan, it is indicated that the notion of "efficacy of deity" occupies a pivotal position in the traditional Chinese folk religions (Sangren 1987, 2000).

end he still could not take the vegetarian vow, which signaled a retreat from his potential commitment and remained just a common worshiper in a variety of Chinese folk temples.

Indeed, to appeal to the Vietnamese Chinese followers, the arrangements of the gathering space, worshiping days, sacred beings, sacred words, and the interpretation of core rituals were made (Tweed 2006; Levitt 2013). First, the appropriation of the spatial arrangement of the gathering hall was started with a pioneering staff member from Taiwan. This earnest temple staff, who was also an owner of a small-and-medium enterprise in Taiwan, made a decision to buy property in South East London as a response to the proposal of setting up a permanent public temple in London. Considering he could also send his children abroad to study in the UK, this entrepreneur eventually bought a house in the area where Vietnamese Chinese resided, a three-story house in the complex of the connected "council houses" constructed for the refugees. The pioneering staff transformed the second floor into a public temple of Yiguandao, reserving the first floor for a reception hall and a kitchen, the third floor for the private living space of the temple staff and their family. The layout of the second floor was almost a transplantation of a traditional Chinese worship hall (神明廳). While half of the space on the second floor was designated for the lecturing of Yiguandao lessons, the other half was designed for an altar with some Buddhist statues in front of the portrait of Bodhisattva Guanyin, and dozens of kneeling boxes were placed on the floor.

Second, the adoption of the same worshiping days was also an imitation. Following the same sacred days in the Chinese tradition as the Guanyin worship, the temple staff scheduled the gathering worship on the first and fifteenth days of every lunar month, symbolizing the birth and the fulfilment of everything in the world according to the cycle of the changing moon. However, different from the folk religions in the Chinese lifeworld, Yiguandao emphasized moral teachings in the process of worship; hence, the lessons of how to be a good person in everyone's family and community were reiterated. The teachings from Confucius, Shakyamuni and Laozi were also introduced to the Vietnamese Chinese through some historical cultivators' stories, with a view to cultivating faith of these diasporic immigrants. The gathering worship was arranged before dinner, so that these followers could still worship the existing Guanyin temple in the morning or at noon on the same days without time conflict.

Third, the imitation of the arrangement of sacred beings was also evident. For the purpose of attracting the Vietnamese Chinese without barriers, the major sacred image was Guanyin and the sacred statues included Maitreya Buddha, Kuan Kung (關公), and Lu Dongbin (呂洞賓), all familiar to them. To make these followers have more faith in Yiguandao, the staff highlighted the importance of Guanyin as well as other famous deities in the traditional Chinese folk religions.

Next, the sacred words presented in the Yiguandao public temple in the Vietnamese Chinese community deliberately centered on Guanyin belief rather than syncretism of teachings attributed to Confucianism, Buddhism, and Daoism. More specifically, on both sides of the sacred image of Guanyin, the sacred words were framed and hung. On the right were the words referring to the sacred place where Guanyin got enlightened, and on the left were the words of salvation in the pure land.[6] Clearly, the sacred words did not allow much interpretive space for the essential syncretic teachings of Confucianism, Buddhism and Daoism, not to mention the major western religions such as Christianity, Catholicism, Judaism and Islam.

Finally, one of the core rituals of Yiguandao, "opening the heavenly portal" (點玄關), was interpreted in a way that highlighted its association with the Guanyin worship. According to legend and folklore in the traditional Chinese society, Bodhisattva Guanyin was a princess in an ancient kingdom and after her enlightenment, she always carried a small jar with willow branches to spray the sacred water healing the sufferings in the world. The Guanyin legend was already familiar to the Vietnamese Chinese and thus when they were initiated into Yiguandao, the meaning of the core ritual was simplified and reassembled by connecting the "heavenly portal" to Guanyin's jar and willow branches. To illustrate this significant ritual in the cultivation practice of Yiguandao, which symbolizes opening the portal of one's soul, the temple staff would explain that opening the portal would allow the soul to find its way even back to heaven after death, similar to the idea of "opening Guanyin's jar lid." As Yiguandao's core ritual was associated with Guanyin's legend, new Vietnamese Chinese followers could readily comprehend and accept the signification when the initiator conducted the ritual, pointing to the most crucial spot below their forehead.

Obviously, to proselytize Yiguandao in the Vietnamese Chinese community, the pioneering staff adopted elements from the new followers' existing religious belief. In doing so, the core ritual of Yiguandao was situated in the process of the symbolic struggle and appeared to win over the Guanyin worship (Bourdieu 1991; Rey 2007). Nevertheless, although the central doctrines of "Dao is not a religion" and "Five Religions, One Origin" were conveyed frequently in the Yiguandao temple, the core meaning of Yiguandao cultivation was at

---

6   On the right, "Without evil thought, everywhere is like the Southern Sea, the land of enlightenment" (思無邪何處非南海); on the left, "With Dao, home is the Western Heavens, the land of purity" (志於道吾家即西天).

stake, almost on the verge of being submerged in the appropriation of Guanyin belief.

4 Cultural Translation: The Western Followers of Yiguandao in London and Manchester

Diverging from the adoption or imitation of religious elements in the "Chinese-enclave stage," the mechanism of cultural translation was applied in the third, "western follower stage." Cultural translation refers to the cultural border-crossing of Yiguandao in London and Manchester, which could be traced back to the early 2000s, when a number of westerners introduced by a Taiwanese lady were initiated into Yiguandao. This Taiwanese lady, Ms. Chen, forty-year-old and unmarried, decided to give up her teaching job as well as the chair position in the International Trade Department of a college in central Taiwan. As a second-generation follower of Yiguandao in Taiwan, Ms. Chen wanted to introduce more people to receive Dao in order to offer "merits" to her mother, who just passed away in 2000. After several waves of students were introduced to receive Dao in her family prayer hall, Ms. Chen could not find any more followers at that time. In her search for solutions, a friend of hers suggested that she ask the efficacious deity of Guan Gung in a famous temple in central Taiwan. The answer was beyond her imagination, as the message from Guan Gung was that she ought to go aboard to the UK to complete the sacred mission.

Being a teacher in the International Trade Department, Ms. Chen was able to speak English better than the other pioneering staff from Taiwan. When Ms. Chen arrived in Manchester in 2000, she tried to apply for admission to the doctoral program of education in order to stay longer in the UK, while performing Tai Chi (太極拳) in downtown Manchester to attract westerners who got interested in it. Not long after her continuing performance of Tai Chi, some westerners followed Ms. Chen to learn Tai Chi as an informal group. With trust established, Ms. Chen contacted the initiator Mr. Wang in London, who in turn organized the pioneering Malaysian Chinese staff to help the initiation ceremonies of Yiguandao in Manchester. At this point, a public temple was temporarily set up in the condominium rented by Ms. Chen, where the first group of western followers attracted by Tai Chi teaching subsequently received Dao.

The remarkable difference of the public temple in Manchester was the ethnic composition of the followers with 70% westerners living near Manchester downtown and 30% overseas Chinese, mainly business immigrants and students from mainland China. As the majority of the followers were English-speaking westerners, translation was required. Indeed, with the translation of

Ms. Chen and the Malaysian Chinese staff, the English preaching of Yiguandao worked well. More importantly, these new western followers all belonged to mainstream religions in the UK, including Christianity, Anglican Catholicism, Judaism and Islam; as a result, the Yiguandao preaching emphasized the doctrines of "Dao is not a religion" and "Five regions, one origin" much more naturally than before. The western followers were encouraged to study their familiar religious classics, such as the Bible and the teachings of Muhammad, in comparison with what Confucius, Buddha and Laozi taught. The major theme was indeed turned into an encounter with the western religions; therefore, the interpretation of the core rituals and "the meaning of receiving three treasures" were also reassembled to fit in the totally different context. The first treasure, called "Heavenly Portal," was interpreted to be the way leading to the paradise, symbolizing the "true self" of every human being. A unique kind of dynamic syncretism was experimented through the Dao-receiving process, in which the westerners participated.

In 2009, a thirty-two-year-old western follower in Manchester took the vegetarian vow, and three years later, he opened a family prayer hall in his living room without any Buddha image or statue on the minimalist altar. During the opening days of this family prayer hall, another western follower, a white lady in her early forties who was also a spiritualist and an animal protector, decided to take the vegetarian vow.

Besides the public temple in Manchester, another example of cultural border-crossing of Yiguandao in the UK occurred in the public temple in North East London, established in 2009. Indeed, this public temple itself was an illustration of cultural border-crossing par excellence.

In 2007, the chief leader of Baoguang-Jiande branch arrived in the UK to inspect the development of Yiguandao for the first time. The chief leader was a very mature entrepreneur and initiator, and he was also one of the pioneering staff who transmitted Yiguandao to Singapore and Malaysia in the early 1970s. When the chief leader visited the public temple located in the Vietnamese Chinese neighborhood, he quickly noted that all the staff in this public temple were very earnest in the proselytization of Yiguandao with hundreds of Vietnamese Chinese followers gathering together in the small temple and listening to his teaching for several hours without any complaint despite the limited space. In the end of this inspection, the chief leader commanded the initiator Mr. Wang to find a larger building in another location for the use of public temple in London. Also, the chief leader noticed that a team of bilingual or multi-lingual temple staff were already organized, and thus, it was time to take the next step, that is, to set up a new temple in the mainstream neighborhood to attract western followers.

Spending several months searching for a suitable building in London, the initiator Mr. Wang and the staff finally made a suggestion to the chief leader in Taiwan to buy the Old Town Hall in Zone 3 of North East London, the usage of which was restricted to educational or religious purposes. After a long period of preparation, including real estate transaction, association registration, and interior decoration, the opening day was scheduled in May 2009. On the opening day, the chief leader invited several senior initiators from Taiwan and Hong Kong to help the rituals of the initiation ceremony; a group of bi-lingual Chinese adept staff from Singapore served as the lecturers of Yiguandao's core rituals and the Malaysian Chinese missionaries as the ritual operators in the ceremony. To their surprise, over one hundred neophytes received Dao on the opening day, and the ethnic composition of these neophytes was almost the same as in Manchester public temple, with 70% westerners and 30% overseas Chinese. Till now, thousands of Yiguandao followers have received Dao in the public temples in Manchester and London, and the ethnic composition remains unchanged.

Compared with the proselytizing experience in the Vietnamese Chinese enclave in South East London, the conditions of the public temple in North East London were totally different in five dimensions, including the gathering space, the worshiping days, the sacred beings and the sacred words inside the temple, and more importantly, the unique interpretation of Yiguandao's core rituals.

First of all, the spatial arrangement of the public temple in North East London was based on innovation from scratch. According to the government regulations, the original appearance of the Old Town Hall, a historical building converted into a public temple of Yiguandao, had to be maintained. The Old Town Hall was completed in 1876 in the Victorian style. Entering through the heavy wooden door, one would get into the reception area with two spacious lounges on both sides, and the spiral staircase in the center led to the second and the third floors. The second floor was remodeled into a capacious dining room with a multi-functional kitchen, where Taiwanese, Malaysian, Indian, or British vegetarian meals could be served conveniently. The design of the third floor was the focal point of the historical building. In addition to reserving all the Victorian style of wall edge decorations, there were two crystal chandeliers hung from the ceiling, and thousands of small-sized, golden Maitreya Buddha statues were put on the surrounding wall shelves.

In terms of the sacred beings and the sacred words, several differences could be noted. Only one Buddha statue was set up on the sacred table, which was a middle-sized statue of Maitreya Buddha made of white jade, with three Buddha lights supported by white-jade lamp holders. Four Chinese characters

"明明上帝" (Ming-Ming Shang-Di), meaning "Enlightening God," were inscribed on the central board painted golden. Moreover, the other set of sacred words were inscribed on the golden boards on both sides, highlighting two Confucian classics, "the Great Learning" (大學) and "the Doctrine of the Mean" (中庸).[7] In front of the sacred table, there lined up dozens of kneeling boxes wrapped in white. All in all, the Yiguandao temple in the Old Town Hall was characterized by solemnity with a style of minimalism, and the color tones of the space, the sacred beings, and the sacred words were unified into a composition of golden and white colors. At first glance, no one would recognize it as a traditional Chinese temple, where green, yellow, red, white, and black colors are usually used to constitute the basic color system following the traditional belief of "five elements" (五行).

Besides, the worshiping days were rearranged on the weekends. There were approximately 40 to 80 regular attendants among Yiguandao followers in the Old Town Hall every weekend. Not a few westerners would still go to church after receiving Dao. These new western followers made a schedule to attend Yiguandao temple on Saturday and go to church on Sunday, since upon receiving Dao, they were told that "Dao is not a religion" and "All religions are searching for the same Dao." In other words, these western followers did not feel uneasy or conflicted about retaining their original belief while attending the Yiguandao temple.

In such different social and cultural conditions, the interpretation of Yiguandao's core rituals was also transformed. Generally, the term "translation" has dual signification; one indicates the translation of different languages and the other points to the translation of different cultures. The lady Mrs. Chan who was trained to be an interpreter in the church in Malaysia translated what the initiator and the Yiguandao lecturer taught into Biblical language and meanwhile interpreted the western attendants' questions or opinions into Chinese. The scene of cultural border-crossing often took place. One of the examples could be found in the initiator Mr. Wang's preaching. Adept at the major classics of Confucianism, Buddhism, and Daoism after learning from many senior initiators for dozens of years in Taiwan, Mr. Wang was able to respond to the western followers' questions and offer suitable answers based on teachings from classics and transcending cultural and religious differences. No matter what questions were posed, he would relate them to the essence of Dao, emphasizing that all religions are searching

---

7 On the right, "Dao of the Great Learning as an eternal golden mirror" (大學道千秋金鑑); on the left, "Doctrine of the Mean as immortal faith" (中庸理萬古丹青).

for the same Dao and that continuous use of three treasures in one's self-cultivation would lead to more understanding of Dao. In this way, the initiator Mr. Wang brought western followers into the context of Dao rather than reduce Dao to western religions. Another example, in the gathering on Easter Day, the Yiguandao lecturer Mrs. Wang, related Jesus's sacrifice to the sacrifice of the Yiguandao female founder (師母); in doing so, this association helped the westerners better understand Yiguandao. Further, Mrs. Wang explained the meaning of Karma by asking the westerners to imagine what motivated Jesus to carry the cross, so that they could understand that the same motivation compelled the Yiguandao female founder to carry the Karma of human beings. The ideas of "Sin" and "Karma," despite their different denotations, were syncretized and translated into different religions. Hence, in the process of "cultural translation," cultural border-crossing occurred frequently, and the discourses, "Dao is not a religion" and "five religions, one origin," acquired new interpretation.

5 Conclusion

Since the early 1930s, as one of the "redemptive societies" emerging in North China, Yiguandao has encountered totally diverse social and cultural conditions in different countries; at the same time, Yiguandao has adapted to the plural faces of modernity. As the case study of public temples in London and Manchester has shown, with the different arrangements in five dimensions, including sacred space, worshiping days, sacred beings, sacred words, and interpretation of core rituals, Yiguandao was either misrecognized as a kind of traditional Chinese folk religion in the Vietnamese Chinese enclave or reconstructed to be a kind of universal religion claiming that all religions are searching the same Dao in the western lifeworld.

While the diverse social and cultural conditions determine the scope of interpretative flexibility of Dao, the core doctrines and rituals of Yiguandao also render it a mutable religion. The religious discourses of "Dao is not a religion" and "All regions are searching for the same Dao," together with the rituals of "opening the heavenly portal," encourage the Yiguandao missionaries to face the mainstream western religions with confidence, and by means of cultural border-crossing mechanisms, the Yiguandao missionaries along with the western followers transform Yiguandao to fit in with the multiple conditions of modernity. All in all, in the process of globalization, a number of westerners are converted to Yiguandao, which is also converted into a new face.

References

Billioud, Sébastien. 2020. *Reclaiming the Wilderness: Contemporary Dynamics of the Yiguandao.* Oxford University Press.

Bourdieu, Pierre. 1991. "Genesis and Structure of the Religious Field." *Comparative Social Research* 13: 1–44.

Broy, Nikolas, Jens Reinke, and Philip Clart. 2017. "Migrating Buddhas and Global Confucianism: The Transnational Space Making of Taiwanese Religious Organizations." *Working Paper Series des SFB 1199 an der Universität Leipzig,* 4, pp. 1–36.

Cao, Nanlai. 2013. "Renegotiating Locality and Morality in a Chinese Religious Diaspora: Wenzhou Christian Merchants in Paris, France." *The Asia Pacific Journal of Anthropology* 14(1): 85–101.

Duara, Prasenjit. 2001. "The Discourse of Civilization and Pan-Asianism," *Journal of World History* 12(1):99–130.

Dumont, Louis. 1980. *Homo Hierarchicus: The Caste System and its Implications.* Translated [from the French] by Mark Sainsbury, Louis Dumont, and Basia Gulati. Chicago: University of Chicago Press.

Jordan, David K. and Overmyer, Daniel L. 1986. *The Flying Phoenix: Aspects of Chinese Sectarianism in Taiwan.* Princeton, N.J.: Princeton University Press.

Latour, Bruno. 2013. *An Inquiry into Modes of Existence.* Cambridge & London: Harvard University Press.

Levitt, Peggy. 2013. "Religion on the Move: Mapping Global Cultural Production and Consumption." Pp.159–176. In *Religion on the Edge: De-centering and Re-Centering the Sociology of Religion,* edited by Courtney Bender, Wendy Cadge, Peggy Levitt, and David Smilde. Oxford University Press.

Lu, Yun-Feng. 2008. *The Transformation of Yiguandao in Taiwan.* Lexington Books.

Mu, Yu (慕禹). 2002. *An Outline of Yiguandao* (一貫道概要). Tainan (台南): Tianju shuju (靝巨書局) (in Chinese).

Palmer, David. 2011. "Chinese Redemptive Societies and Salvationist Religion: Historical Phenomenon or Sociological Category?" *Journal of Chinese Theatre, Ritual and Folklore* (民俗曲藝) 172: 21–72.

Rey, Terry. 2007. *Bourdieu on Religion: Imposing Faith and Legitimacy.* London; Oakville, Conn.: Equinox.

Sangren, P. Steven. 1987. *History and Magical Power in a Chinese Community.* Sanford, Calif.: Stanford University Press.

Sangren, P. Steven. 2000. *Chinese Sociologics: An Anthropological Account of the Role of Alienation in Social Reproduction.* London: Athlone Press.

Song, Guangyu (宋光宇). 1983. *Exploring the Way of Heaven: Research Report about Yiguandao* (天道鈎沉：一貫道調查報告). Taipei: Yuanyou (元祐出版社) (in Chinese).

Stark, Rodney and Roger Finke. 2000. *Acts of Faith: Explaining the Human Side of Religion.* Berkeley: University of California Press.

Tweed, Thomas. 2006. *Crossing and Dwelling: A Theory of Religion.* Cambridge: Harvard University Press.

Verter, Bradford. 2003. "Theorizing Religion with Bourdieu against Bourdieu." *Sociological Theory* 21(2): 150–174.

Yang, Fenggang and Helen Rose Ebaugh. 2001. "Religion and Ethnicity among New Immigrants: The Impact of Majority/Minority Status in Home and Host Countries." *Journal for the Scientific Study of Religion* 40(3): 367–378.

Yang, Hung-Jen (楊弘任). 2015. "Syncretism and Translation: An Actor-network Analysis of the Yiguandao Community in the UK." Pp. 235–274, in *Current Religion in Everyday Life: Religious Individualization and Relational Being,* edited by Ying-Kuei Huang (黃應貴). Taipei: Socio Publishing Co., Ltd. (群學出版社) (in Chinese).

CHAPTER 10

Global Dao

The Making of Transnational Yiguandao

Nikolas Broy

1   Introduction[1]

Among the various religious groups that utilized the increasing global connectedness of East Asian societies since the end of the nineteenth century there were also a group of so-called "redemptive societies," i.e., allegedly modern religious organizations that grew from traditional sectarian and moral groups, to spread beyond their countries of origin.[2] As one of the most successful and persistent "redemptive societies", Yiguandao 一貫道 ("The Way of Pervading Unity") spread beyond the Chinese Mainland particularly since the mid-1940s, when the earliest activists[3] went to Hong Kong, Japan, and Korea (Mu 2002: 130, 134–136; Broy, Reinke, and Clart 2017: 23). Already its "parent tradition" Xiantiandao 先天道 ("Way of Former Heaven") was able to utilize migration movements in order to establish significant presences in Chinese diasporas in Vietnam, Thailand, Malaysia, and Singapore already since the 1860s (Topley 1963; You 2011; Wei 2015; Show 2018). Thus, while it may be overstated to call Yiguandao "China's first religious export to the world" (Song 1983: 206) – particularly because some indigenous Chinese Christian evangelists engaged in transnational enterprises at about the same period of time (cf. Yang, Tong,

---

1   I would like to thank Yang Fenggang and the reviewers of the Annual Review of the Sociology of Religion for their helpful comments and suggestions to an earlier draft version. It goes without saying that all remaining errors are entirely mine.
2   The term "redemptive societies" was coined by historian Prasenjit Duara to describe the Republican-era (1911–1949) new religious movements. It was soon taken up by many Chinese studies scholars afterwards more broadly to replace the concept of "sectarianism" that many thought to not fit the Chinese religious landscape. Despite its strength in highlighting the novelty of these groups, however, it is theoretically flawed in suggesting a discontinuity between late imperial era and modern groups. Cf. Duara 2001: 117–126; Palmer 2011; Broy 2015.
3   I use the word "religious activists" not to assume any political engagements, but to highlight how missionary zeal and a sense of eschatological urgency dominate these actors' entire private and business lives, and thus to distinguish them from ordinary and occasional practitioners.

and Anderson 2017) – it nevertheless can be considered one of the most important and large-scaled ones besides two other Taiwanese organizations, i.e., the "Compassion Relief Foundation" (Ciji gongdehui 慈濟功德會) and "Buddha's Light Mountain" (Foguangshan 佛光山) (for a concise summary of research related to these two organizations, see Broy, Reinke, and Clart 2017: 6, 14–17).[4]

This essay traces the global spread of Yiguandao from three different angles: The first section sketches the overall development of Yiguandao's global proselytization from the mid-1940s to the present. I argue that we can distinguish three periods with their respective characteristics, many of which are related to specific political, economic, and social circumstances. Section two takes a micro look at the history and activities of a particular "Buddha hall" (*fotang* 佛堂) belonging to Andong division 安東組 and located in Vienna, Austria from its inception in the early 1990s to the present day. Drawing on this case study the last section analyzes six patterns of transnational development and transculturation. While there are much more factors and elements that could be explored, this essay follows an inductive approach informed by fieldwork experiences and which suggest these six modes and patterns as particularly insightful regarding spatial and transcultural aspects of religious globalizations. Finally, the conclusion summarizes the findings of the essay.

2   The Global Spread of Yiguandao: Periods of Transnationalization

As far as we can tell from internal documents, Yiguandao leaders claimed global relevance already during the early 1880s when it was still a marginal religious group in Shandong Province 山東省 in northern China, proclaiming that their teachings would "save [people] at home and abroad" (*pudu hainei haiwai* 普渡海內海外). Likewise, the 1937 catechism *Answers to Doubts about the Unity Sect* claims that the active dissemination of the Dao will come to an end only when it has united the entire globe under the utopia of the "Great Unity" (*datong* 大同) (Broy, Reinke, and Clart 2017: 21). Based on Lin Wanchuan's 林萬傳 (pen name Mu Yu 慕禹) meticulous research and other available material (Mu

---

4 The research that led to this publication was part of a larger project on the global spread of Taiwanese religious organizations conducted at the Collaborative Research Centre (SFB) 1199: "Processes of Spatialization under the Global Condition" at Leipzig University, 2016–2019. It was funded with a grant from the German Research Foundation (DFG). For a programmatic introduction, see Broy, Reinke, and Clart 2017.

2002: 60–227; Lin 2009; 2011), the global spread of Yiguandao can be divided into three primary phases:

1. 1945–1950: Except for small-scaled earlier missionary efforts in Hong Kong (1936) and Japan (1944), this period marks the factual beginning of deliberate and committed transnational proselytization. Most probably, it was the end of WWII and the restoration of international travel in East Asia that enabled Yiguandao leaders to dispatch missionaries, first to East and Southeast Asia.

2. 1950s-1970s: The beginning of this period is marked by the founding of the People's Republic of China (PRC) in 1949 and subsequent mass campaigns to eradicate the allegedly reactionary sect Yiguandao during the early 1950s, a political movement that led to the incarceration and death of tens of thousands of activists and practitioners (cf. Hung 2010). Nevertheless, religious activities in East and Southeast Asia continued, were intensified, and reached new destinations such as the Philippines, but this time organized from headquarters that were established in Taiwan, Hong Kong, and Southeast Asia by missionaries and refugees. The relationships to former religious centers on the Mainland, however, were completely severed. One of the only non-Asian countries Yiguandao was brought to during this phase is Brazil where the earliest activists arrived already in the early 1950s. This example highlights the transnational character of Yiguandao already at this time as most activists who came to Brazil during the 1950s arrived via the Mainland, Hong Kong, or Japan (Mu 2002: 212–215). The end of this period marks the beginning of the last and most recent phase, when Yiguandao finally evolved into a truly global religion in terms of geographical dispersion. Thus, one of the earliest "Buddha halls" (fotang 佛堂) to be established in a Western country was founded in 1968 in New York City by the Hong Kongese Jichu division 基礎組 (Mu 2002: 201).

3. Since the 1970s: The increasing turn to Australia and New Zealand (1980s), South Asia (1990s), North America (particularly since the 1970s), South America (1980s), South Africa (late 1980s), and Europe (particularly since the early 1990s) marks the emergence of Yiguandao as a geographically global religion. Yet, judging from existing case studies and the author's fieldwork, the majority of Yiguandao's activists and practitioners is still predominantly "Chinese,"[5] as their proselytization and activities

---

5 In this essay, I shall use "Chinese" in a broad understanding to refer to individuals and communities who trace their origins back to Chinese ancestry and share Chinese cultural notions and practices, such as the Chinese language, but without indicating any national identities of

primarily cater to the Chinese diasporas worldwide. Moreover, national and global aspirations were institutionalized through the establishing of national Yiguandao associations (the first was set up in Taiwan in 1988) and the "World I-Kuan Tao Headquarters" (*Yiguandao shijie zonghui* 一貫道世界總會, official abbreviation WITH) in Los Angeles in 1996. According to official numbers, the movement claims thirty million followers worldwide, who are organized in fourteen registered national religious associations as well as more than thirty similar but nominally non-religious institutions.[6] Moreover, Yiguandao begins to appear as a global player by engaging in transnational political and social activities, such as campaigns related to global warming, vegetarianism, interfaith dialogue, and world peace.[7]

Despite its short duration, the first period had a serious impact on Yiguandao's global spread for several reasons: first, following the unstable period of government persecution in China and internal disputes resulting from the untimely death of paramount leader Zhang Tianran 張天然 (1889–1947), Yiguandao began to split into numerous and quite independent divisions and branches, which developed independently from each other. Moreover, Yiguandao consists today of at least twenty-six divisions and branches that are dispersed not only in Taiwan, but also in Hong Kong and in the United States.[8] Second, while there was a modest degree of cooperation between different divisions and branches in Taiwan, – many communities that were originally established in East and Southeast Asia during this period by Mainland activists often developed independently from the new Taiwanese centers. Some of these communities remained closer to the "original" Yiguandao. Others were keener to adapt to local circumstances and indigenized. For instance, a congregation established in late 1940s Nagoya soon evolved into an entirely autonomous Japanese enterprise under the appellation "Assembly Hall for Morality" (J. Dōtoku kaikan 道徳会館) that began its own transnational proselytization in the mid-1980s and runs chapters in Myanmar, Thailand, Mongolia, India, the Philippines, Brazil, and the United States (Broy 2019b). Similarly, the Korean counterpart "International Morality Association Yiguandao" (K. Gukje Dodeok Hyeophoe Ilgwando 國際道德協會一貫道) became a Koreanized version with

---

individual members of these communities. Instead, I will use "Taiwanese" or "PRC/Mainland Chinese" to further distinguish them.

6 Interview with Li Yuzhu, present chairman of WITH, March 2017, Taipei.
7 For Yiguandao's global activism, see recent coverages in its mouthpiece *Yiguandao zonghui huixun* 一貫道總會會訊.
8 Interview with Li Yuzhu 李玉柱, present chairman of WITH, March 2017, Taipei.

its own globalization projects in Japan, France, and the United States (Lee 2014: 157–160).

Until the end of the second phase (1970s), proselytizing appears to have remained confined primarily to East and Southeast Asia. This observation seems to reflect the economic and political circumstances at that time as well as the socioeconomic statuses of Yiguandao adherents, as the island was still a predominantly agricultural society during the 1950s and experienced rapid industrialization, urbanization, and a boost in general education only since the 1960s (Clart 1995/1996: 129). Accordingly, most followers did not have many resources left in order to travel or migrate. In addition, Taiwan's emigration policy and restrictions imposed on migrants in many countries (such as the United States, Australia, and Canada) were another factor in restraining outmigration and missionary activities (Song 1996: 429–432; Chen 2008: 18–20). Finally, until its legalization in 1987 Yiguandao was banned by the Kuomintang government, which also had a hampering effect on organizational capacities for the pursuit of large-scale globalization projects. On the other hand, Yiguandao's turn to the Americas, Australia, New Zealand, Europe, and Africa particularly since the 1980s appears to have been a direct consequence of Taiwan's political and socioeconomic transformation that facilitated international travel, migration, business investments, and mission. In addition, the implementation of new immigration policies for highly educated Asians since the 1970s, particularly in North America and Australia, led to increasing numbers of Taiwanese business migrants and students to these countries (Chen 2008: 19–23), many of whom also took their religious faiths with them.

To conclude this first section, we can see how external factors, such as political and socioeconomic circumstances, migration patterns, and cultural proximity have channelled Yiguandao's global activities from geographically and culturally proximate in the early years to distant in the recent phase. Moreover, particularly the past decades of intensified global connectedness have witnessed a quantitative and qualitative increase in its transnational proselytizing activities. Because of continued repression in China (since 1949) and Taiwan (until 1987), individual aspirations, and limitations in cross-branch interaction, many divisions and branches developed quite independently from each other, some of which even turned into entirely autonomous religious organizations. Therefore, Yiguandao today is a highly decentralized, heterogeneous, and transnational religious movement with various divisions and hubs that are dispersed not only in Taiwan, but also in Hong Kong, Korea, Southeast Asia, the United States, and Brazil. In my understanding of a religious movement, I follow Barend ter Haar's conceptualization of the historic White Lotus tradition of the Song period (960–1279) – as to be distinguished from the later derogatory label "White Lotus," which was applied by Confucian historiography to popular religious sects – as a set of religious groups that share a number of distinctive religious convictions and practices, but not necessarily a common organization (1999: 12–13).

3   A Case Study of Andong Division's Transplantation to Vienna, Austria

Following this rather sketchy outline, this section looks at the example of an Yiguandao community belonging to Andong division 安東組 in Vienna, Austria in order to analyze the processes of transnationalization and transculturation in detail. Unless stated otherwise, the data are based on ethnographic fieldwork conducted by the author in June 2016 (including informal conversations and interviews), and they are supplemented by an analysis of published Yiguandao materials.

The first private Buddha hall in Austria was established in 1992 by a Taiwanese mother who accompanied her two daughters studying musicology in Vienna.[9] While her husband stayed behind until retirement in order to earn money for the couple, he tried to visit his family as often as possible. Usually accompanied by a "transmitting master" (*dianchuanshi* 點傳師) – a high-ranking member assigned by Yiguandao elders with the task of conversion – they utilized every visit to proselytize in Austria and neighboring countries. In order to attract followers among Vienna's Chinese community, the couple opened a Chinese-style café that served as a meeting point to enjoy Chinese snacks, to socialize, and to attract possible converts. In 2002, the Honghang fotang 宏航佛堂 was founded and only four years later transformed into Vienna's first public Yiguandao temple. Because the growing demand appears to have exceeded the existing capacity of 200 square meters, the community bought an old industrial facility in the suburbs that is altogether nine times the size

---

9 This description synthetizes the following accounts in Yiguandao journals: *Pingjiang zhukan* 萍江竹刊 (*Pin Jiang Magazine*), #138 (2012/9), "Haiwai chuanzhen wenhua xinchuan shengsheng bu xi de zaiti he baozheng 海外傳真 文化薪傳 生生不息的載體和保證"; #143 (2013/7), "Haiwai chuanzhen kaihuang xinsheng lixiang gongming 海外傳真 開荒心聲 理想共鳴" (these issues can be viewed online at http://www.andong.org.tw/index.php/2009-09-30-07-23-17/2011-04-19-07-05-39.html, last retrieved 7 July 2016); *Yiguandao zonghui huixun*, #289 (2015/10), special report "Yiguandao Andong daochang Ouzhou daowu zhongxin, Aodili Weiyena Honghang gonggong fotang, kuojian luocheng qiyong 一貫道安東道場歐洲道務中心，奧地利維也納宏航公共佛堂，擴建落成啟用", no pagination.

of the old Buddha hall. After having been entirely refurbished in 2015, Honghang fotang serves not only as the seat of the Austrian Yiguandao Association. Founded in 2007 and intended to coordinate activities in the country, it was the first of its kind in Europe. In addition, the temple also represents the European hub of Andong as it is the only branch temple on the entire continent with a permanently residing *dianchuanshi*. In addition, the branch has also established one public temple in Linz (approximately 180km west of Vienna) in 1998, which is named Hongshu fotang 宏恕佛堂. Altogether, Andong claims to have followers in each federal state of Austria.

Honghang's turn to a larger facility demonstrates the growing success of the community in attracting followers. According to data provided by the temple in June 2016, they claim to have initiated approximately 2,500 individuals, with roughly two-thousand (eighty percent) being Chinese. Since being initiated is a mere ritual act – which is called "seeking the Dao" (*qiudao* 求道) – that does not require a high level of individual commitment, most initiands did not turn into regularly practitioners afterwards. While there are no accurate figures available, fieldwork experience suggests that regular events attract about twenty to thirty practitioners and participation peaks at large events such as Chinese New Year. In addition to the large altar room that can easily accommodate about two-hundred practitioners, the temple also houses a dining room, a shop for Taiwanese products and food, a storage for ancestor tablets (*huai'entang* 懷恩堂), class rooms, kitchens, a library, upstairs dormitories for visitors, and a shrine dedicated to Huang Daxian 黃大仙 (see below). The community obtains the food products from a Taiwanese wholesale company based in the Netherlands without any surcharge, which is why their prices are below that of ordinary Asian supermarkets in Vienna. Since there is no specifically demarcated Chinese quarter or Chinatown in the city, financial considerations appear to have played a major role in finding the right place for the new temple, as it is located in a rather industrial area in the southern part of the city. Similar observations have been made among many migrant religious communities in the US (Ebaugh and Chafetz 2000a: 43–45), where there was no organic relationship of the migrant religious community to its immediate neighborhood whatsoever..

While this research found that funds are usually raised locally (Ebaugh and Chafetz 2000b: 49), at least the reconstruction of the new Honghang fotang demonstrates a global network of capital. Thus, a list of 348 donors displayed in the dining room of the temple includes individuals, Buddha halls, and private businesses in Austria, Taiwan, Hong Kong, Southeast Asia, and the United States. Likewise, Vienna's Yiguandao community in general is integrated into transnational financial networks that contribute to humanitarian aid in China,

Taiwan, and other places. For instance, posters displayed in the temple and articles in the Austrian Yiguandao bulletin appeal to visitors to safe one Euro per day in order to contribute to charities.[10] In 2008, Honghang fotang and the three Viennese Buddha halls mentioned above also contributed financially to an official PRC fundraising project for the victims of the Great Sichuan Earthquake.[11]

As noted by many scholars, migrant religious congregations tend to adopt the "community center model," thus offering an array of cultural and social services for the migrants that include activities related to the home culture, nonreligious classes, mutual help, guidance, recreation, and sport (Ebaugh and Chafetz 2000b: 55–59; Yang and Ebaugh 2001: 275–276). Very much the same holds true for Honghang fotang:[12] for instance, practitioners come to the temple to meet compatriots, talk in their native tongue, enjoy Chinese food, buy Taiwanese products and groceries, or to undergo treatments in traditional Chinese medicine (TCM). In addition, the temple offers a variety of classes, such as classics reading classes for children that focus on traditional didactic tracts such as *Sanzijing* 三字經 (*Classic in Three Characters*) and *Dizigui* 弟子規 (*Rules for Disciples*), but also on the Yiguandao text *Baixiaojing* 百孝經 (*Classic on the Hundred Forms of Filial Duty*) that are intended to nurture moral sentiments and Confucian values. Thus, informants at the temple pointed out to me how they regard Austrian society as lacking proper morals, and why they believe to transmit these values is immensely important. As pointed out by Sébastien Billioud and the late Joël Thoraval in their study of the Confucian grassroots revival, these traditional scriptures (except for the *Baixiaojing*) are ubiquitous in traditionally minded education and Confucian circles in Chinese communities worldwide (2015: 20, 83; cf. Billioud 2020: 189-194). For adults, the temple also provides a separate class for reading and discussing the Confucian *Analects* (*lunyuban* 論語班), while those interested in rather physical aspects may participate in a Taijiquan (*Taiji yangsheng ban* 太極養生班) or fitness class. In addition, Honghang community particularly emphasizes the "happy family class" (*xingfu jiating ban* 幸福家庭班) – a model established by Gao Weiyang 高維陽,

---

10   *Pingjiang ouxun* 萍江歐訊, #159 (2015/12), pp. 4–5.
11   See the list of donors displayed on the website of the PRC Embassy in Austria: "Sichuan dadizhen lü Ao huaqiao huaren ji shehui gejie jiezhenzai juankuan xianjin tongjibiao 四川大地震旅奧華僑華人及社會各界賑災捐款現金統計表." (http://www.chinaembassy.at/chn/xwdt/P020080723568424535772.xls) (last retrieved 17 June 2016). Honghang fotang's contribution is mentioned in its bulletin *Pingjiang zhukan*, #155 (2015/7), "Gan'en chengdan sheng xinxin nuli shixing chuangxinji 感恩承擔生信心　努力實行創新機".
12   This section is based on my fieldwork as well as on *Pingjiang ouxun*, #160 (2016/2), p. 2.

grandson of longterm Andong leader Gao Binkai 高斌凱 (1924–2008), who envisions it as a safe environment for parents and their children to enhance mutual understanding in order to maintain a joyful and untroubled family life. Finally, the temple also offers German classes for adults and Chinese ones for children – apparently designed to assist first-generation migrants to adapt to life in Austria as well as to help Austrian-born/raised children to connect to their Chinese heritage. Most probably in response to general rhythms of work, these classes are usually scheduled from Friday afternoon to Sunday – a finding, which also holds true among migrant religious congregations in the US (Yang and Ebaugh 2001: 275–277). While attendance in the classes is for free, participants tend to pay a certain amount of "earnest money" (*baozhengjin* 保證金) in order to assure the classes are being held.

Some members of Honghang community are extraordinarily committed to the promotion of traditional Chinese culture and Yiguandao teachings – which for most of them is basically the same. For instance, one Chinese Austrian informant who grew up in Vienna for most of his life experienced the practice of Chinese martial arts and the encounter with an Yiguandao community (that was located in the vicinity of his parents' house) during his youth as the primary portal to engage with traditional Chinese culture. Having been a committed activist for several years, he and his fellow Chinese Austrian wife have established a private academy dedicated to the study of traditional Chinese culture in 2014 in their new hometown of approximately 49,000 inhabitants. Located near the Swiss border and named after Lake Constance (which is called "*Bodensee*" in German, and *bodenghu* 博登湖 in Chinese), the Bodeng xuetang 博登學堂 offers classes in Chinese language, Qigong, Taijiquan, and meditation. Besides spreading Chinese culture, the couple also utilizes this endeavor to invite interested peers into their private Buddha hall, which enabled them to recruit a limited number of Chinese adherents in their hometown. Currently, they also stage weekly meditation retreats for non-Chinese speakers, where they also discuss the Buddhist *Platform Sūtra*.[13]

On the other hand, Honghang community provides a set of meditation practices that not only appeals to Chinese adherents, but which also attracts a considerable number of non-Chinese practitioners. According to data provided by the temple in 2016, roughly twenty percent (overall number approximately five-hundred individuals) of all initiands since 1998 are not of Chinese heritage – figures that according to my fieldwork experience are above

---

13   See the newly established German-language website "Weg der Einheit," which is a translation of "The Way of Unity", see https://wegdereinheit.net/events-veranstaltungen/, accessed 14 February 2020.

average. Unlike most other Yiguandao branches (Lu 2008: 102–107), Andong is well-known for its emphasis on meditation (officially termed "mind method of the three treasures," *sanbao xinfa* 三寶心法, but colloquially called *jingzuo* 靜坐, "quite sitting") that is generally attributed to the aforementioned leader Gao Binkai. For several years, the temple offers weekly classes in meditation that are supplemented by annual meditation camps, which usually last three to seven days and are scheduled in August, which is a usual period for vacation and recreation. Because the number of participants sometimes exceeded the capacities of the earlier Honghang temple (in one year up to eighty people), the community sometimes needed to rent other facilities, such as a high school in Salzburg, which was vacant during the summer break.

The summer camps are usually supervised by Cai Shuifa 蔡水發, a senior Andong leader and primary promoter of Yiguandao meditation in Taiwan, who travels to Vienna specifically for this event. Because he is not able to speak German, his advices are interpreted by a bilingual member who grew up in Austria. Usually, two or three additional transmitting masters – including the local master as well as one from Taipei and one from Thailand – oversee smaller groups. In 2015 and 2018, the meditation camps attracted approximately forty to fifty practitioners (in 2018 with fifty percent female practitioners) from diverse places including Vienna, Salzburg, Linz, Vorarlberg (near the Swiss border, which is also the location of the Bodeng xuetang), and northern Italy.[14] Because of the remarkable ratio of non-Chinese practitioners – fifty percent in 2015 (twenty-five individuals) and twenty-four in 2018 (ten individuals) – it is perhaps not surprising that the camp features a variety of practices that Western audiences would expect of such an event. Thus, besides the Yiguandao technique (which is usually practiced sitting), participants also engage in walking meditation and Yoga – which is not a usual component of Andong meditation in Taiwan. In both years, these activities were supervised not by Chinese members or Taiwanese leaders, but by two non-Chinese Austrian experts, both of whom have participated in this event for many years.[15] According to brief conversion accounts of six non-Chinese participants of the 2018 camp documented in Andong's official bulletin,[16] we can get a glimpse into how they became acquainted with the group and how they experience their

---

14 In addition to the information obtained in an informal interview, other data come from the local Andong journal: *Pingjiang ouxun*, #158 (2015/9), 2. For the 2018 data, see: *Pingjiang zhukan*, #174 (2018/9), 68.

15 See his blog entry: https://uebungswege.wordpress.com/2015/09/15/7-tage-in-stille/, last retrieved 24 June 2016.

16 This section is based on *Pingjiang zhukan*, #174 (2018/9), 68–77.

participation. Thus, most of them were recruited by Yiguandao activists during Taijiquan classes or services in TCM, and some expressed a profound interest in "Asian philosophies" and disdain for the Christian Church as their primary motivation to engage with Yiguandao. Yet others appreciate the camp as a "place of silence" (*Ort der Stille*) that enables one to leave everyday problems aside. What is remarkable about them is that there appears to be trend towards regular participation, as most interviewees stated to have participated at the camp for several years.

To discuss a last example of innovation that emerged from the community's transnational connections, Honghang temple may very well be the only Yiguandao facility outside of Guangdong Province 廣東省 and Hong Kong that houses a shrine dedicated to Huang Daxian 黃大仙 (Cantonese: Wong Tai Sin). This deity is particularly popular in this area and among Cantonese migrants, but except for some regions in Zhejiang Province he is next to unknown in most parts of the Mainland and in Taiwan (Chan and Lang 2015). The reason for the establishing of a separate shrine dedicated to the god lies in his special relationship with the local transmitting master who originally hails from Hong Kong. Thus, not only that his father was reported to have been saved by the deity (which was the reason why he was venerated by the *dianchuanshi* in the first place), but it appears that Huang Daxian has revealed himself to the master that he would like to seek the Dao and become initiated into the group. As I have been told at the temple, the ritual was performed successfully, and a shrine dedicated to the god was erected in Honghang temple. Similar procedures of initiating minor gods into the Dao can be traced back to the early history of Yiguandao in China. Still today, the deity and praying to him appears to be quite unknown to many visitors, as there are introductory pamphlets displayed right next to the shrine.

4 Adaptive Modes and Patterns of Transnationalization

This section analyzes six patterns and modes of Yiguandao's globalization that are specifically visible in the case of Honghang community. I do not claim them to represent an exhaustive list of possible factors and elements that might affect the transnationalization of religious groups, nor do I propose a full-fledged theoretical framework. Rather, following an inductive approach informed by fieldwork experiences in Taiwan, Austria, South Africa, California, and Japan I suggest the following six modes and patterns as particularly insightful in regard to spatial and transcultural aspects of religious globalizations.

First, Chinese migration represents the fundamental framework and infrastructure that channels Yiguandao's global spread (cf. Clart 2000: 137). Thus, basically all existing case studies demonstrate that the movement established presences wherever there are large Chinese communities, thus particularly in Southeast Asia and North America, which in 2009 made up 78.5 percent of all overseas Chinese (see Li and Li 2013: 20–25). In particular, Yiguandao's global spread is related to Taiwanese migration, as most high-ranking members are Taiwanese, and most headquarters are located there. Furthermore, it is important to note the intimate connection between Taiwanese business migration and Yiguandao proselytization (for examples from Singapore and Thailand, see Song 1997: 10–12, 19–23; Lin 2015: 62–63). Very much the same holds true for the Vienna case, where most activists – except for the transmitting master who hails from Hong Kong – migrated to Austria from Taiwan. Yet, among the practitioners one finds Chinese from various national backgrounds. Overall, most Chinese migrants in Vienna and Austria come from Qingtian County 青田縣 in Zhejiang Province – as it is the case in many other European cities. While there are no accurate statistics available, observers believe that seventy to eighty percent of all Chinese migrants in Austria are from Zhejiang, and seventy to eighty percent of those are from Qingtian (Kwok 2012: 94). However, because of limited data I am not able to verify if the majority of Honghang's followers are Qingtian migrants too. Yet, during my fieldwork I met a few of them.

Second, in terms of religious authority, administration, practice, and architecture, most overseas chapters embody a corporate identity, which is directed from the Taiwanese headquarters. In the case of Honghang community, it is very clear that the temple itself replicates religious symbols and emblems of Taiwanese Andong Buddha halls. For instance, the altar room displays a painting depicting eighteen Andong martyrs of the turbulent late 1940s and there is the characteristic "circle of limitlessness" (*wujiquan* 無極圈) placed above the altar as a representation of the supreme deity Eternal Venerable Mother, which is a typical feature of Andong and is rarely seen at other Yiguandao sites. In terms of religious authority and administration, we can also observe how Andong's headquarters in the northwestern Taiwanese city of Xinzhu 新竹 is the central point of reference and guidance. For instance, the name of the temple was not chosen randomly, but it reflects a deeply hierarchical understanding, as all local and regional hubs of Andong use the character *hong* 宏 within their names – as does the headquarters Hongzong shengtang 宏宗聖堂. More importantly, religious personnel are frequently sent to Honghang by the headquarters and Andong's leader Xie Dexiang 謝德祥 himself has visited the temple countless times. Likewise, Honghang members usually embark on short-time visits to the headquarters in order to participate in ceremonial events, training groups, and administrative meetings as well as to interact with fellow Andong members in more informal ways. Because the community is not entirely Taiwanese but there are Chinese from various national backgrounds involved – during my fieldwork I met Austrian Chinese (from Qingtian), Malay Chinese, and practitioners from Shandong Province, PRC – the eminent position of Andong headquarters and other Taiwanese Andong temples actually recontextualizes Taiwan's locality within the global arena as it is made into a site for pilgrimage and source of religious authority and inspiration (for similar findings regarding Ciji Foundation, see Huang 2003: 241).

Third, these seemingly unidirectional center-periphery relationships are transcended by individual transnational networks of people, within which religious personnel, ideas, artifacts, and money move. Many of these circulations are individually motivated and came into being through friendship or business interaction. At Honghang temple, there is frequent interaction with Lin Zhihong 林志鴻 – a transmitting master from Thailand who regularly participates in the meditation camp and other events – and with an Andong community in Sidney.[17] In addition, the funding for the new temple that opened in 2015 was neither only local nor subsidized by the headquarters, but it rather unveils a highly complex transnational network of individuals, families, temples, and businesses in Taiwan, Austria, Southeast Asia, and the United States. This attests to the fact that religious globalization is not a unilateral development from center to periphery, but it rather consists of multidirectional flows (Csordas 2009: 3–4) or reverse and cross flows that run from the seemingly subaltern to the dominant or without any dominant at all (Beyer 2006: 25). Here, I follow Peggy Levitt in contending that these networks are transnational in nature, rather than global. This is not to deny that Yiguandao groups have spread on a global scale, but it highlights the fact that the movement is nowhere near to becoming a deterritorialized religious network (Levitt 2007: 22), but rather that individuals, groups, temples, and institutions are usually very much rooted in particular places between which the density and intensity of ties differs with regard to the relationships between these places.

Yet, while the networks through which people, ideas, artifacts, and money move are transnational in nature – and thus are the religious groups or organizations behind them – actors themselves need not to be transnational or mobile at all in order to be involved in a transnational religious movement (cf. Levitt 2007: 23–24). On the one hand, many of those Yiguandao practitioners and activists who "stay behind" are also involved in border-crossing activities

---

17 On the Sidney connection, see Andong's bulletin *Pingjiang zhukan*, #160 (2016/5), 56–59.

in their respective local congregations. Thus, even middle-sized Buddha halls in Taiwan regularly attract visitors from afar, as most migrants usually like to return to their original native places, to partake in religious events and ceremonies, and to share experiences and insights from their lives. Hence, it is wrong to assert that overseas communities are the transnational ones while those in Taiwan are merely local. Rather, it appears that regardless of their location most Yiguandao temples may be considered "translocalities" – using a term coined by Arjun Appadurai (1996: 192) – where people, ideas, artifacts, and money from various places "cross and dwell" (to use Thomas Tweed's language, 2006: 73–79, 81–82) and where local practitioners are thus enabled to reach out to other places and people in these other places (inspired by Gielis 2009; Smith 2016; a similar observation about Yiguandao is made in Billioud 2020: 209-214). Thus, by listening to sermons of and meeting Yiguandao activists from all over the globe in a middle-sized Taiwanese Buddha hall is truly a transnational interaction.

Fourth, while we should be cautious not to overemphasize the transnational character of certain individuals (cf. Dietze and Naumann 2018), mobile actors are important factors in establishing and maintaining transnational networks. Based on the frequency of their boarder-crossings, we may distinguish "settlers" and "visitors": while settlers – i.e., long-term migrants who live in the respective countries – participate in a local Yiguandao community and their activities, visitors – usually highly committed activists, such as volunteers and religious specialists – travel to particular congregations for a limited time period and in order to assist the local communities. The case of Honghang community demonstrates how religious life in Vienna is an interplay of relatively immobile actors – settlers, i.e. the local community – and occasional as well as regular visitors, such as Cai Shuifa and Lin Zhihong, who come to Austria at least annually in order to operate the meditation camps. Judging from my own fieldwork experience, this integration of non-local expertise into local religious enterprises seems to be a typical pattern of how overseas Yiguandao communities operate (a similar point is made in Billioud 2020: 209-211). Yet, it needs to be clarified that many purportedly immobile settlers also return to Taiwan on a regular basis (mostly at Chinese New Year) or participate in religious events at fellow communities in other places but in the same country (for a case study of activist mobility in Thailand, see Lin 2016: 201–209). This interplay of local activists and travelling missionaries – as religious specialists who travel first and foremost for religious reasons – counters the intuition entailed in pattern one, namely that Yiguandao's global spread is merely a side-effect of economically motivated Chinese migration. While migration and business networks are in fact an important framework and infrastructure that channels Yiguandao's globalization, the example of Honghang fotang demonstrates how the specifically religious circulation of personnel is vital in its transcultural engagements.

Fifth, in regard to the participation of non-Chinese practitioners, it appears that Yiguandao teachings and practices are often perceived by non-Chinese as a version of Buddhism or Daoism, or most basically as "Oriental wisdom" or "Asian philosophies." Thus, many attendees of the meditation camp ascribed their original intend to participate in this and earlier events to their prior interest in Buddhist or Daoist philosophy. Similarly, others found their way into the movement through Taijiquan, Qigong, or martial arts engagements. Similar findings have been made by scholars in their research about Yiguandao in diverse places, such as Vancouver, London, Paris, Johannesburg, and Los Angeles (Clart 2000: 139; Yang 2015: 269; Billioud 2016; Broy 2019a: 31; 2020: 271–279). In some cases, Yiguandao activists also deliberately play with the expectations of non-Chinese practitioners by portraying Yiguandao as the only authentic form of Daoism or Buddhism, up to the point that some of them think that they are participating in a Daoist or Buddhist group.

For this religious appeal to unfold, there needs to be an existing ecology of understanding and familiarity, which made it possible for Yiguandao activists to invest on. The meditation camp example shows how the diffusion of Asian spirituality and bodily practices to Europe have fostered such an understanding and interest. Diffusion – as it is understood here – refers to the transmission of more or less disparate religious elements into other societies through books, movies, TV programs, and other media (following Finney 1991: 393–394). Thus, religious symbols, ideas, and artifacts are able to travel quite independently from real persons and the original religious institutions they were embedded in. Even though most non-Chinese may not have heard about Yiguandao, translations of Chinese classics into Western languages – in particular the *Daodejing* 道德經, which is the second-most translated book after the Bible (Siegler 2003: 314–317; Palmer and Siegler 2017: 15–17) – the widespread recognition of Chinese cosmological symbols such as Yin, Yang, and *qi* 氣, the concept of "Dao" (in Western discourses mostly "Tao") itself, and the popularity of Qigong and Taijiquan have led to the emergence of what David Palmer and Elijah Siegler have called an "instant Tao pop culture" (2017: 16–17), i.e. the appropriation and transculturation of Chinese cultural and religious symbols and practices in the North American religious landscape, in particular in New Age circles. This line of reasoning could easily be extended to include Buddhist – or specifically Zen Buddhist – elements, but the point is clear: cultural diffusions have set the stage for Yiguandao's – and other Chinese religious ventures, for that matter – proselytization. While it may be argued that despite its global presence Yiguandao is nowhere near to becoming a truly global religion as its heavy "Chinese baggage" is a hindrance towards this aim, it is also true that particular its emphasis of Chinese and purportedly "Asian" values, beliefs, and practices – such as mindfulness, spiritual conduct of life, and spiritualized bodily practices – that attracts a particular cohort of non-Chinese religious believers and spiritual seekers who seek for alternative attitudes towards human life, nature, spirituality, and moral cultivation. To a certain extent, the diffusion of Chinese religious elements into non-Chinese societies has created the demand for Yiguandao and similar religious movements.

Sixth, particularly when compared to age-old global religions that experienced centuries of various indigenizations, Yiguandao's relatively short duration of transcultural engagement – in most cases not more than a few decades – shows that despite goodwill intentions and engaged proselytization on the ground indigenization is still at a preliminary level of "work-in-progress," saying that non-Chinese represent a very tiny minority within the overall movement. Yet, different from other Taiwanese religious exports such as Foguangshan and Ciji, Yiguandao's earliest mission to Korea and Japan in the late 1940s have led to the emergence of nativized groups with high levels of adaptation, particularly in terms of leadership, membership, organizational structures, cultural and religious practices, and the use of language.

5 Conclusion

This essay has traced the global spread of Yiguandao from three different angles by (1) exploring its overall history and scope, (2) analyzing a case study of Yiguandao's Andong division in Vienna, Austria, and (3) synthetizing the findings from these two sections into a broader analysis of typical patterns and modes of Yiguandao's globalization. Thus, I have demonstrated that Yiguandao's global spread is intimately related to Chinese, and specifically Taiwanese, migration, but yet religious activities and interactions are created and maintained particularly by individually motivated circulations of religious personnel that cannot be reduced to economically motivated migration and that cut across unidirectional center-periphery relations. Furthermore, I have shown how Yiguandao is creating a global web of intersecting networks through which people, ideas, artifacts, and money move in multidirectional ways. Through its global engagement, Yiguandao temples have become translocalities, where practitioners are enabled to reach out to other places and people in these other places. Finally, the essay explored the nature of Yiguandao's outreach to non-Chinese practitioners. Even though their numbers may appear insignificant when compared to the majority of its Chinese followers,

Yiguandao is not only a transnational religious movement whose activities, organizations, and networks cross national boundaries, but its proselytizing also inherently aims at crossing cultural-ethnic boundaries and thus to become a truly "travelling faith" that transcends the original migrant community (cf. Wong and Levitt 2014). While these efforts are still a "work-in-progress," Yiguandao activists are nevertheless able to cater to a cohort of spiritual seekers and interested practitioners whose initial contact was prompted by the diffusion of Asian spiritualities to non-Chinese societies in the nineteenth and twentieth centuries.

References

Appadurai, Arjun. 1996. *Modernity at Large: Cultural Dimensions of Globalization*. Minneapolis: University of Minnesota Press.

Beyer, Peter. 2006. *Religions in Global Society*. New York: Routledge.

Billioud, Sébastien. 2016. "De Taïwan à Maison-Alfort, réflexions sur la globalisation du Yiguandao." La Religion des Chinois en France, Colloque international, Paris, 2016, May 18.

Billioud, Sébastien. 2020. *Reclaiming the Wilderness. Contemporary Dynamics of the Yiguandao*. Oxford: Oxford University Press.

Billioud, Sébastien, and Joël Thoraval. 2015. *The Sage and the People: The Confucian Revival in China*. New York: Oxford University Press.

Broy, Nikolas. 2015. "Syncretic Sects and Redemptive Societies: Toward a New Understanding of 'Sectarianism' in the Study of Chinese Religions." *Review of Religion and Chinese Society* 2(2): 145–85.

Broy, Nikolas. 2019a. "Maitreya's Garden in the Township: Transnational Religious Spaces of Yiguandao Activists in Urban South Africa." *China Perspectives* (4): 27–36.

Broy, Nikolas. 2019b. "Zhonghua Yiguandao biancheng Riben Tiandao: Guanyu 'Xiantian dadao xitong' zongjiao tuanti Ribenhua de yixie sikao 中華一貫道變成日本天道：關於「先天大道系統」宗教團體日本化的一些思考." In *Cong Taiwan dao shijie: Ershiyi shiji Yiguandao de quanqiuhua guoji xueshu yantaohui lunwenji* 從台灣到世界：二十一世紀一貫道的全球化國際學術研討會論文集. Taipei: Academia Sinica, Research Center for Humanities and Social Sciences.

Broy, Nikolas. 2020. "American Dao and Global Interactions: Transnational Religious Networks in an English-Speaking Yiguandao Congregation in Urban California." In *Transnational Religious Spaces: Religious Interactions in Africa, East Asia, and Beyond*, edited by Philip Clart and Adam Jones, 263–282. Berlin: De Gruyter.

Broy, Nikolas, Jens Reinke, and Philip Clart. 2017. "Migrating Buddhas and Global Confucianism: The Transnational Space Making of Taiwanese Religious Organizations."

Working Paper Series des SFB 1199 an der Universität Leipzig (4): 1–36. Download via: https://research.uni-leipzig.de/~sfb1199/publication/migrating-buddhas-and-global-confucianism/, last retrieved July 3, 2019.

Chan, Selina C., and Graeme Lang. 2015. *Building Temples in China: Memories, Tourism, and Identities*. London: Routledge.

Chen, Carolyn. 2008. *Getting Saved in America: Taiwanese Immigration and Religious Experience*. Princeton, NJ: Princeton University Press.

Clart, Philip. 1995/1996. "Sects, Cults, and Popular Religion: Aspects of Religious Change in Post-War Taiwan." *British Columbia Asian Review* 9: 120–163.

Clart, Philip. 2000. "Opening the Wilderness for the Way of Heaven: A Chinese New Religion in the Greater Vancouver Area." *Journal of Chinese Religions* 28: 127–144.

Csordas, Thomas J. 2009. "Introduction: Modalities of Transnational Transcendence." In *Transnational Transcendence: Essays on Religion and Globalization*, edited by Thomas J. Csordas, 1–29. Berkeley: University of California Press.

Dietze, Antje, and Katja Naumann. 2018. "Revisiting Transnational Actors from a Spatial Perspective." *European Review of History: Revue européenne d'histoire* 25 (3–4): 415–430.

Duara, Prasenjit. 2001. "The Discourse of Civilization and Pan-Asianism." *Journal of World History* 12(1): 99–130.

Ebaugh, Helen R., and Janet S. Chafetz. 2000a. "Environmental Impacts: Opportunities and Constraints." In *Religion and the New Immigrants: Continuities and Adaptations in Immigrant Congregations*, edited by Helen R. Ebaugh and Janet S. Chafetz, 31–48. Walnut Creek, CA: AltaMira Press.

Ebaugh, Helen R., and Janet S. Chafetz. 2000b. "Structural Adaptations to the Immigrant Context." In *Religion and the New Immigrants: Continuities and Adaptations in Immigrant Congregations*, edited by Helen R. Ebaugh and Janet S. Chafetz, 49–70. Walnut Creek, CA: AltaMira Press.

Finney, Henry C. 1991. "American Zen's "Japan Connection": A Critical Case Study of Zen Buddhism's Diffusion to the West." *Sociological Analysis* 52 (4): 379–396.

Gielis, Ruben. 2009. "A Global Sense of Migrant Places: Towards a Place Perspective in the Study of Migrant Transnationalism." *Global Networks* 9(2): 271–287.

Huang, C. Julia. 2003. "Sacred or Profane? The Compassion Relief Movement's Transnationalism in Taiwan, Japan, Malaysia, and the United States." *European Journal of East Asian Studies* 2(2): 217–241.

Hung, Chang-tai. 2010. "The Anti-Unity Sect Campaign and Mass Mobilization in the Early People's Republic of China." *The China Quarterly* (202): 400–420.

Kwok, Kim. 2012. "Chinese Immigrant Economy in Vienna in Transnational Era." doctoral dissertation, Sinologie, Universität Wien.

Lee Gyungwon 李京源. 2014. "Hanguo Yiguandao fazhan gaishu 韓國一貫道發展概述." *Huaren zongjiao yanjiu* 華人宗教研究 (4): 147–166.

Levitt, Peggy. 2007. *God Needs No Passport: Immigrants and the Changing American Religious Landscape.* New York: New Press.

Li, Peter S., and Eva X. Li. 2013. "The Chinese Overseas Population." In *Routledge Handbook of the Chinese Diaspora*, edited by Chee-Beng Tan, 15–28. London, New York: Routledge.

Lin Rongze 林榮澤. 2009. "Zhanhou Dalu lai Tai zongjiao de zaidihua yu quanqiuhua: yi Yiguandao wei li 戰後大陸來台宗教的在地化與全球化 – 以一貫道為例." *Xin shiji zongjiao yanjiu* 新世紀宗教研究 7(3): 1–47.

Lin Rongze 林榮澤. 2011. "Yiguandao de guojihua yu shijie daochang 一貫道的國際化與世界道場." In *Yiguandao zang: Shengdian zhi bu* 一貫道藏. 聖典之部. Vol. 10, edited by Lin Rongze 林榮澤, 3–28. Taipei: Lantai chubanshe.

Lin Yusheng 林育生. 2015. "Taiguo Yiguandao de fazhan yu jingji shehui bianqian 泰國一貫道的發展與經濟社會變遷." *Ya Tai yanjiu luntan* 亞太研究論壇 (61): 55–85.

Lin Yusheng 林育生. 2016. "Tai ni okeru Ikkantō no soshiki hatten to ningen no ryūdōsei タイにおける一貫道の組織発展と人間の流動性." *Higashi-Ajia kenkyū* 東南アジア研究 53(2): 189–216.

Lu, Yunfeng. 2008. *The Transformation of Yiguan Dao in Taiwan: Adapting to a Changing Religious Economy.* Lanham, MD: Lexington Books.

Mu Yu 慕禹. 2002. *Yiguandao gaiyao* 一貫道概要. Tainan: Tianju shuju.

Palmer, David A. 2011. "Chinese Redemptive Societies and Salvationist Religion: Historical Phenomenon or Sociological Category?" *Minsu quyi* 民俗曲藝 (172): 21–72.

Palmer, David A., and Elijah Siegler. 2017. *Dream Trippers: Global Daoism and the Predicament of Modern Spirituality.* Chicago: The University of Chicago Press.

Show Ying Ruo 蘇芸若. 2018. "Chinese Buddhist Vegetarian Halls (Zhaitang) in Southeast Asia: Their Origins and Historical Implications." *NSC Working Paper* (28): 1–51.

Siegler, Elijah T. 2003. "The Dao of America: The History and Practice of American Daoism." PhD dissertation, University of California, Santa Barbara.

Smith, Michael P. 2016. "Translocality: A Critical Reflection." In *Translocal Geographies: Spaces, Places, Connections*, edited by Ayona Datta and Katherine Brickell, 181–198. London: Taylor and Francis.

Song Guangyu 宋光宇. 1983. *Tiandao gouchen: Yiguandao diaocha baogao* 天道鈎沉：一貫道調查報告. Taipei: Yuanyou.

Song Guangyu 宋光宇. 1996. *Tiandao chuandeng: Yiguandao yu xiandai shehui* 天道傳燈：一貫道與現代社會. Banqiao: Sanyang.

Song Guangyu 宋光宇. 1997. "Zongjiao chuanbo, shangye huodong yu wenhua rentong: Yiguandao zai Xinjiapo de chuanbo yu fazhan 宗教傳播、商業活動與文化認同－一貫道在新加坡的傳播與發展." *Guoli Taiwan daxue wenshizhe xuebao* 國立臺灣大學文史哲學報, 47: 213–258.

ter Haar, Barend. 1999. *The White Lotus Teachings in Chinese Religious History.* Honolulu: University of Hawai'i Press.

Topley, Marjorie. 1963. "The Great Way of Former Heaven: A Group of Chinese Secret Religious Sects." *Bulletin of the School of Oriental and African Studies* 26: 362–392.

Tweed, Thomas A. 2006. *Crossing and Dwelling: A Theory of Religion.* Cambridge, Mass. Harvard University Press.

Wei Dingming 危丁明. 2015. *Shumin de yongheng: Xiantiandao ji qi zai Gang Ao ji Dongya diqu de fazhan* 庶民的永恆: 先天道及其在港澳及東南亞地區的發展. Taipei: Boyang wenhua.

Wong, Diana, and Peggy Levitt. 2014. "Travelling Faiths and Migrant Religions: The Case of Circulating Models of *da'wa* among the Tablighi Jamaat and Foguangshan in Malaysia." *Global Networks* 14(3): 348–362.

Yang Fenggang, and Helen R. Ebaugh. 2001. "Transformations in New Immigrant Religions and Their Global Implications." *American Sociological Review* 66(2): 269–288.

Yang, Fenggang, Joy K.C. Tong, and Allan H. Anderson, eds. 2017. Global Chinese Pentecostal and Charismatic Christianity. Boston: Brill.

Yang Hung-jen 楊弘任. 2015. "Zongshe yu zhuanyi: Yiguandao zai Yingguo de xingdongzhe wangluo fenxi 綜攝與轉譯: 一貫道在英國的行動者網絡分析." In *Richang shenghuo zhong de dangdai zongjiao* 日常生活中的當代宗教, edited by Yinggui Huang 黃應貴, 235–274. Taipei: Qunxue chubanshe.

You Zi'an 游子安. 2011. "Nijū seiki Sentendō no Kanton, Honkon kara Betonamu e no denbō to henyō 二〇世紀、先天道の広東・香港からベトナムへの伝播と変容." In *Ekkyōsuru kindai Higashi Ajia no minshū shūkyō: Chūgoku, Taiwan, Honkon, Betonamu, soshite Nihon* 越境する近代東アジアの民衆宗教: 中国・台湾・香港・ベトナム、そして日本, edited by Fusaji Takeuchi 武内房司, 47–82. Tōkyō: Akashi Shoten.

CHAPTER 11

Tension between the Chinese Government and Transnational Qigong Groups

Management by the State and Their Dissemination Overseas

Utiraruto Otehode and Benjamin Penny

In the past two decades, the Chinese government has been vigilant in monitoring qigong organizations within and outside China, implementing measures nationwide to suppress, and prevent the rise of, certain types of qigong organizations. At the operational level, it has adopted three different negative categories for qigong organizations. These are 'evil cults (*xiejiao* 邪教),'[1] 'harmful qigong groups (*youhai qigong zuzhi* 有害气功组织)' and 'problematic qigong groups (*cunzai wenti de qigong zuzhi* 存在问题的气功组织)'. According to information from the Chinese Anti-Cult Association (*fan xiejiao xiehui* 反邪教协会) website and documents from local government anti-cult activities departments, there are more than twenty 'evil cults'. The precise number and identifications of them varies from document to document: a consolidated list is provided below. In addition, there are fourteen 'harmful qigong groups' and also 51 'problematic qigong groups.' Most research to date has concentrated on Falun Gong and other 'evil cults,' (Penny 2012; Irons 2018) however, little is known about those considered under the latter two categories.

In this paper we will address two questions: what are the backgrounds for the emergence of these categories? Why are different qigong groups classified in different categories? To answer these questions, we need to look back at the Chinese government's activities *vis-a-vis* qigong groups between 1995 and 2005, when they greatly strengthened their management of qigong.[2] It was during this period that the positive categories of 'qigong for health (*jianshen qigong* 健身气功)' and 'qigong as medical treatment (*yiliao qigong* 医疗气功),' as well as the negative categories of 'evil cults', 'harmful qigong groups' and

---

[1] This term is more accurately translated "heterodox teachings" but "evil cult" has become the government's standard translation into English.

[2] The term and category 'qigong' was incorporated into the Chinese medical system in the 1950s. On qigong in the 1950s, see Otehode and Penny 2016. On the qigong fever of the 1980s, see Palmer 2007; Otehode 2009.

'problematic qigong groups' emerged. We proceed to give outlines of three of the negatively categorised groups – Falun Gong 法伦功, Puti Gong 菩提功, Tian Gong 天功 – which are listed as an evil cult, a harmful qigong group, and a problematic qigong group respectively, and analyse why they might have been placed in these categories.

1 The Chinese Government's Management of Qigong Organizations

From the early 1980s to the end of the 1990s, the Chinese government's management of qigong organizations was not systematic. Qigong groups were managed separately by several state departments and Communist Party organizations. At the same time, national-level qigong 'social organizations' and local qigong associations also played an important role in management. This ad hoc approach engendered many conflicts: between different qigong groups, between local qigong associations and qigong groups, and between qigong organizations and local government departments. Against this background, beginning in 1993, under instruction from the Ministry of Civil Affairs, local qigong associations were required to register with their local Civil Affairs department and with their local qigong association. However, the government did not explicitly classify qigong groups until 1995.

In December 1995, the Chinese Association for Research in Qigong Science (*Zhongguo qigong kexue yanjiuhui* 中国气功科学研究会), under the leadership of its chairman Huang Jingbo 黄静波, classified all qigong groups registered with them. They divided these groups into five categories, the third being groups that included 'superstitions (*mixin* 迷信)' or had the characteristics of 'secret societies (*huidaomen* 会道门)' (Palmer 2008a, 2008b). The qigong organizations in this category, including Falun Gong at that time, required rectification. Subsequently, the Chinese Association for Research in Qigong Science deregistered Falun Gong in December 1996 (He 2006).

In the same year, on August 5, 1996, seven ministries and commissions including the Propaganda Department of the CCP Central Committee, the State Sports Commission, the Ministry of Health, the Ministry of Civil Affairs, the Ministry of Public Security, the State Administration of Traditional Chinese Medicine, and the State Administration for Industry and Commerce jointly issued the 'Notice on Strengthening the Management of Social Qigong (*guanyu jiaqiang shehui qigong guanli de tongzhi* 关于加强社会气功管理的通知)'. The terms 'social qigong (*shehui qigong* 社会气功)', 'qigong for health' and 'qigong medical treatment (*qigong yiliao* 气功医疗)' were first defined in this notice. Thus:

> 'Social qigong' refers to the activities of 'qigong for health' and 'qigong for medical treatment' that involve many people in society. 'Qigong for health' refers to those qigong activities engaged in by the masses where participating in exercise is used for physical fitness and rehabilitation. Qigong that is used directly to treat other people's diseases or to teach other people to do so constitutes medical practice, and should be considered 'qigong medical treatment'.
>
> GUOJIA TIYU ZONGJU JIANSHEN QIGONG GUANLI ZHONGXIN 2004: 2

The notice also clarified that 'qigong for health' came under the jurisdiction of the State Sports Commission and 'qigong medical treatment' was managed by the Ministry of Health.

On this basis, the State Sports Commission released the 'Management Methods for Qigong for Health (*jianshen qigong guanli banfa* 健身气功管理办法)' and the 'Evaluation Methods for Ascertaining the Technical Level of Masters of Qigong for Health; Trial Implementation (*jianshen qigongshi jishu dengji shenping banfa*; *shixing* 健身气功师技术等级审评办法 试行),' on February 22, 1998. In the same year, on October 5, the General Administration of Sports approved 11 'qigong for health' groups. These were:

1. Huaxia Intelligent Gong *huaxia zhineng gong* 华夏智能功
2. Yan Xin Qigong 严新气功
3. Great Goose Gong *dayan gong* 大雁功
4. Ma Litang's Instructions on the Six Characters *Ma Litang liuzi jue* 马礼堂六字诀
5. Illumination of Wisdom Gong *huiming gong* 慧明功
6. Heart Gong *xin gong* 心功
7. Mount Pan Yin and Yang Gong *Panshan yinyang gong* 盘山阴阳功
8. Guo Lin's New Qigong *Guo Lin xin qigong* 郭林新气功
9. Empty Spirit Gong 虚灵功
10. Happiness Gong *xinfu gong* 幸福功
11. Yuanji Gong 元级功

One year later, on April 25, 1999, Falun Gong practitioners went to Zhongnanhai 中南海 to submit their collective petition aimed, in the first instance, at gaining the release of practitioners earlier detained in Tianjin. On July 22, the Ministry of Civil Affairs released a document identifying Falun Gong as an 'illegal organization (*feifa zuzhi* 非法组织)' effectively banning it. Shortly afterwards, it was additionally identified as an 'evil cult organization (*xiejiao zuzhi* 邪教组织)'. On October 9, the Supreme People's Court and the Supreme People's Procuratorate explained the issues concerning the specific application of the law in the handling and organization of crimes committed by 'cult organizations.' The legal definition of an 'evil cult organization' in China is as follows:

> The term 'evil cult organization' refers to illegal organizations established under the cover of 'religion', 'qigong' or other designations that deify their primary personage; that use, invent and spread superstitions, heterodox ideas, etc. to confuse and deceive others; that develop and control their membership; and that endanger society.
>
> GONGANBU GUONEI ANQUAN BAOWEIJU 1999: 8

While cracking down on Falun Gong, the Chinese government also defined the two other negative categories of qigong groups, namely harmful qigong groups, and problematic qigong groups. In reference to the former, in 2000, the General Office of the CCP Central Committee promulgated the 'Opinion of the Central Committee of the Chinese Communist Party on Handling Issues Related to Qigong Organizations that Harm Society (*guanyu chuli dui shehui you weihaide qigong zuzhi youguan wentide yijian* 关于处理对社会有危害的气功组织有关问题的意见)', and in 2002, the Ministry of Public Security issued the 'Notice of the Ministry of Public Security on Strengthening the Work of Combating Qigong Organizations that are Harmful to Society (*guanyu jiaqiang tongdui shehui you weihaide qigong zuzhi douzheng gongzuode tongzhi* 关于加强同对社会有危害的气功组织斗争工作的通知).'[3]

With the proviso mentioned above, that the categorisation of groups as evil cults is not completely fixed or stable, the following is a consolidated list of those groups so-designated:[4]

1. Falun Gong *falun gong* 法轮功
2. Shouters *huhan pai* 呼喊派
3. Disciple Society *mentuhui* 门徒会
4. Full Scope Church *quanfanwei jiaohui* 全范围教会
5. Lingling Sect *lingling jiao* 灵灵教
6. New Testament Church *xinyue jiaohui* 新约教会
7. Guanyin Method *guanyin famen* 观音法门

---

3 We have not been able to locate full versions of these two documents.
4 This list is widely circulated, although sometimes the order in which the groups is listed is different. The most recent government source we have been able to find is "The 23 Evil Cults Identified in Our Country *woguo rendingde ershisan zhong xiejiao* 我国认定的23种邪教," released by the 610 Office of Shiyan 十堰 City, Hubei Province on 6 July 2017, see http://zt.10yan.com/html/xiejiao/zhishi/1270_13484.html.

8. Lord God Sect *zhushen jiao* 主神教
9. Anointed King *beili wang* 被立王
10. Unification Church *tongyi jiao* 统一教
11. Three Grades of Servants *sanban puren* 三班仆人
12. True Buddha School *lingxian zhenfo zong* 灵仙真佛宗
13. Children of God *Tianfude ernü* 天父的儿女
14. Dami Mission *dami xuanjiaohui* 达米宣教会
15. World Elijah Gospel Mission Society *shijie yiliya fuyin xuanjiaohui* 世界以利亚福音宣教会
16. Church of Almighty God *quannengshen* 全能神 (Eastern Lightning *dongfang shandian* 东方闪电)
17. Bloody Holy Spirit *xueshui shengling* 血水圣灵
18. Mainland China Administrative Deacon Station *zhonghua dalu xingzheng zhishi zhan* 中华大陆行政执事站
19. Perfect and Sudden Enlightenment Method *yuandun famen* 圆顿法门
20. South China Church *huanan jiaohui* 华南教会
21. Teachings of Changshou *changshou jiao* 常受教
22. Mental Luminosity Method *xinlin famen* 心灵法门
23. Lotus Store School *huazang zongmen* 华藏宗门 (Huazang Gong *huazang gong* 华藏功)

The fourteen 'harmful qigong groups' identified by the Chinese government, are listed below:[5]

1. China Nourishing Life and Enhancing Wisdom Gong *Zhonghua yangsheng yizhi gong* 中华养生益智功 or Zhong Gong 中功
2. Shen Chang's Human Body Technology *Shen Chang renti keji* 沈昌人体科技
3. Fragrant Gong *xiang gong* 香功
4. China Nature Special Gong *Zhongguo ziran teyi gong* 中国自然特异功
5. Special Abilities Gong of Humanity and the Cosmos *renyu teneng gong* 人宇特能功
6. China Gong of the Female Spirit of Kunlun *Zhonghua kunlun nüsheng gong* 中华昆仑女神功
7. Sun and Moon Qigong *riyue qigong* 日月气功
8. Yuanji Gong 元级功[6]
9. Puti Gong 菩提功
10. Compassion Gong *cibei gong* 慈悲功

---

[5] This list derives from a document circulated to regional qigong organisations, which was distributed by the China Qigong for Health Association *Zhongguo jianshen qigong xiehui* 中国健身气功协会. It was obtained by Utiraruto Otehode in 2005.

[6] Yuanji Gong also appears as one of the 'qigong for health' groups in 1998.

11. Three Three Nine Ascending the Origin Gong *sansanjiu chengyuan gong* 三三九乘元功
12. 10,000 Methods Return to the Origin Gong *wanfa guiyi gong* 万法归一功
13. Yitong Health Method *yitong jiankang fa* 一通健康法
14. Lotus Store School *huazang zongmen* 华藏宗门 (Huazang Gong 华藏功)

The precise process for determining which groups were classified into this category is obscure as there is very little publicly available material that provides any explanation. According to one of the people in charge of a qigong association in Henan province interviewed by Utiraruto Otehode in 2005, the General Administration of Sports and the 610 Office (*liuyiling bangongshe* 610 办公室) solicited opinions from various local qigong associations from across the country which responded by identifying certain groups as 'harmful.'[7] For example, the person from Henan wrote a long document that identified various 'defects' in Xiang Gong 香功 and suggested that the central government should define it as an evil cult. Xiang Gong was eventually defined as a harmful qigong group rather than an evil cult but was nonetheless banned and suppressed. Clearly, such documents provided by local qigong associations were influential to the central government's decision-making. We can infer that the fourteen qigong organizations listed above were nominated by local qigong associations and related departments.

While these categories of qigong groups arose at a specific time and under specific circumstances, they are still current, and the Chinese government still actively suppresses 'evil cults' and 'harmful qigong groups'. On the other hand, some qigong organizations that have been savagely attacked in China have survived overseas. Falun Gong has a flourishing organization and practitioners in many countries around the world. Some of the 'harmful qigong groups' are still very active at home as well as abroad. In 2014, a local anti-cult website described the activities of some 'harmful qigong groups' as follows:

> After many years of sustained and effective suppression by government departments, Zhongguo Ziran Teyi Gong, Sansan Jiucheng Yuangong, Yitong Gong, and Cibei Gong have basically ceased activities. However, most of the activities of harmful qigong groups have not stopped and some of them are very active. This includes Zhong Gong (active in North China, Central China, Northeast China, and parts of East China), Puti

---

[7] The 610 Office is the security agency established on June 10, 1999 to coordinate and implement the persecution of Falun Gong. The information from the person in Henan came in a conversation with Utiraruto Otehode in 2005.

Gong (active in Northeast China, North China, Central China, and parts of East China) and Yuanji Gong (active in East China and Central China).
ZIYANGSHI FAN XIEJIAO WANG 2014

The third negative category of qigong groups – problematic qigong groups – is much harder to find information about. An internal document obtained by Utiraruto Otehode in 2005 from an official in a qigong association in Henan lists the 51 groups categorized this way. The heading on the document reads "List of 51 Problematic Qigong Organisations that have already been dealt with (*chuli* 处理)". Two other documents found on official government webpages use the same term and very similar locutions. The first, which does, however, label the 51 groups as 'harmful' rather than 'problematic', was published on 9 February 2009; the second on 26 May 2018:

> At present, fourteen harmful qigong methods have been banned in our country and 51 harmful qigong organizations have been dealt with.
> XIA 2009

> These [fourteen] harmful qigong organizations have been banned; another 51 qigong organizations have been dealt with appropriately.
> ANON 2018

Thus, there is consistent reference to both '51 groups' and the fact they have already been 'dealt with' from 2005 to 2018. Most of the 51 groups listed are relatively unknown; Tian Gong is probably the one with the highest profile and broadest reach.

2 Falun Gong, Puti Gong and Tian Gong

In this part of the paper we will introduce three groups, respectively categorised as an evil cult – Falun Gong – a harmful qigong group – Puti Gong – and a problematic qigong group – Tian Gong. The first, and best-known, is Falun Gong so we will devote less time to it than the other two groups.

Falun Gong was founded in 1992 by Li Hongzhi 李洪志, known as Master Li by his followers. Li is from near Changchun and when he started teaching there and shortly afterwards in Beijing, his was just one of many new qigong groups. In his authorised biography it says he was taught from boyhood by a succession of 28 masters from the Buddhist and Daoist traditions, and indeed Falun Gong writings are full of terms from these two religions but with new meanings for them. At first officially registered and supported by the qigong bureaucracy, their falling out occurred in 1995 (see above). Li's teachings include a description of a cosmos of many dimensions, including heavens of various sorts from which, he says, all humans originated. We were all 'Buddhas, Daos, or Gods *fo dao shen* 佛道神', in his terminology and fell step-by-step to the earth which he describes as a cesspool. His method of cultivation is the way we climb back up to our rightful places in the heaven we came from many lives ago. In his teachings, Li himself plays a crucial role as an all-seeing, all-knowing being who has a personal role in inserting a *'falun* 法轮' into a practitioner's abdomen (in another dimension), in protecting them in the form of his 'law-body *fashen* 法身,' and during their cultivation transforming their accumulated virtue (*de* 德) into merit (*gong* 功). Li migrated to the US in the late 1990s, prior to the Zhongnanhai incident and now lives in New York State.

Puti Gong 菩提功 was founded a year earlier than Falun Gong – in 1991 – by Di Yuming 狄玉明, originally, according to government sources, Di Yuwang 狄玉旺. Puti translates as "Bodhi", the Buddhist term meaning "enlightenment," the supreme and sublime understanding of the real nature of all existence. Within the group, Di is known (in English-language texts) as JinBodhi, and in Chinese as Supreme Chan Master Golden Bodhi (*Jin Bodhi chan shangshi* 金菩提禪上師). Originally based in Guangzhou, Puti Gong had centres in 26 Chinese cities at its peak and sold video and audio tapes, books, and various kinds of spiritualised water, tea, and blessed objects as well as training courses. Di claimed that his teachings derived from a tradition based in the Tibetan monastery of Kumbum (Taersi 塔爾寺) in Xining in Qinghai province in far western China. This claimed affiliation is not particularly obvious in the teachings and practices of Puti Gong, though it honours the Medicine Buddha (*yaoshi fo* 药师佛) or Bhaiṣajyaguru in its meditative practice. Although born in Hebei province in 1964, he moved to Qinghai with his parents in 1971 and grew up in a Tibetan region. He claims to have started practising when he was seven and to have 'come down from the mountain' in 1991, when he established Puti Gong. Claiming to possess 'extraordinary abilities *teyi gongneng* 特異功能' and to be able to cure otherwise incurable diseases, he maintained he was the descendent of the Tang official Di Renjie 狄仁傑, better known in English as Judge Dee (Bai 2013). As with Falun Gong, and many other forms of qigong from the 1980s and 1990s, Puti Gong stresses its convenience and applicability to modern life. It can be done, their texts stress, at anytime and anywhere and by practitioners of any age, sex, race, religion, education, or language. Practicing the Puti Gong cultivation method leads, they say, to improvements in health, the healing of disease, the acquisition of extraordinary abilities, and prosperity.

The founder of Tian Gong 天功 was Chen Letian 陈乐天, known to his followers as Letian Dashi 乐天大师, or Grand Master Letian. Like Li Hongzhi and Di Yuming, Chen now lives in North America, in his case San Francisco. His biography, as presented by the group, depicts him in typical terms for a qigong master: a sickly child he travelled from his home in Zhejiang to seek out different masters and cultivation techniques. Decades later, he gained 'sudden enlightenment (*dunwu* 顿悟)', a term that, in China, is typically associated with Chan Buddhism. From this point his wisdom came via transmissions from Cosmic Masters (*yuzhou dashi* 宇宙大师), not from the Chinese tradition but from Atlantis, Lemuria and Mu. Tian Gong is based on these transmissions. Unlike the two previous groups described here, Tian Gong celebrates its heritage in the qigong movement and the endorsements it received in the late 1980s and into the 1990s from official qigong organisations in China. In 1994, Letian Dashi emigrated to the US and in 1995 first spread his teachings in the US and Europe. In that year he also established the organisations that served to popularize Tian Gong: the grandly named World Tian Gong Federation (*shijie tiangong lianhehui* 世界天功联合会) and the Tian Gong International Foundation (*tiangong guoji jijinhui* 天功国际基金会). On the US Tian Gong website, the Tian Gong International Foundation was nominated as a 501c3 not-for-profit, non-religious, public service tax deductible organization (Tian Gong USA 2018). Apart from his links to qigong organisations, the official biography makes great play of Letian Dashi's connexions with sites generally associated with the western paranormal. In 1997, it says, he led his followers on cultivations journeys to 'over thirty countries, where they conducted paranormal research and studies of sacred and mystical regions of the Earth, relics of ancient civilizations, different civilizations from the past and from higher dimensions.' These places included Easter Island, the Pyramids in Egypt, Mayan sites in Mexico, the Bermuda Triangle, Fatima and Lourdes in Portugal and France respectively, etc. He also showed a particular interest in the relics of Joan of Arc. On a cultivation journey in 1999 to the Himalayas, Letian Dashi apparently underwent a 'test of life and death' and in doing so passed a crucial point in his cultivation.

Given such a pedigree, Tian Gong's actual practice seems rather tame and its claims are fairly standard among qigong groups. A practitioner will, Letian Dashi says, become healthy, have their spirit healed, gain wisdom and extraordinary abilities, and become youthful. He also claims, as do many qigong masters, that his practice is in fact, very old – in this case he claims descendance from the '1,400 year old Bronze Bell Qigong (*tongzhong qigong* 铜钟气功),' later abbreviated to 'Celestial Bell Qigong (*tianzhong qigong* 天钟气功)', and finally Tian Gong. This accounts for the logo of the movement featuring a stylized bell on a *taijitu* 太极图 or yin-yang symbol.

The fate of each of these three groups since 1999 is a story of expatriation, attempts to establish themselves in new territories, and continuing suppression in their homeland.

The situation of Falun Gong will not be rehearsed here as it is part of the public discourse around human rights in China. This is primarily due to the assiduous efforts of Falun Gong to keep itself in the headlines. In this context the most salient point is that Falun Gong has positioned itself as stridently anti-government with claims that appeal both to secular notions of rights, such as the torture and the alleged 'organ harvesting' of imprisoned practitioners, as well as to religious ideas, such as claims that communism itself is 'anti-nature' and that cosmic struggles between good and evil are currently being fought throughout the multi-dimensional universe.

In some ways the situation with Puti gong is similar but in one important feature the two groups are very different. According to Chinese government sources, Di Yuming migrated to Canada in 1998 – sources internal to Puti Gong say 1999 – and acquired Canadian nationality.[8] They also claim that he moved to Taiwan in 2009. Now based in Canada, it has established a physical presence in various countries around the world. There are currently three centres in Canada, six in the USA, five in Taiwan, five in South Korea, two in Hong Kong, two in Singapore, six in Malaysia, one in Indonesia, one in Australia and one in Myanmar.[9]

Just as important is the presence they have established on the Internet. The most important site is "Bodhi Meditation: For Health and Life" (https://www.puti.org/) which has versions in English, Korean, Indonesian, Burmese and Chinese (in traditional characters). This website has a full suite of offerings including introductions to the practice, a biography of JinBodhi, contact details of centres worldwide, details of the courses they offer, testimonials to the efficacy of the practice, galleries of photos and artworks, music, a 'youth' section and a shop selling books, DVDs, CDs and digital recordings, and 'Meditation Blessings sport wear'. One section also has a digital version of their hard copy magazine *Meditation and Health* (in English, Chinese and Korean), the first issue of which was published in Spring 2011. The most recent issue is number 27 from 2019.

---

8 See, for example, "Hebei anti-evil cult public lecture denouncing 'Puti Gong' for defrauding money and harming life (*Hebeisheng fanxiejiao dajiangtang kaijiang shoujie piancai haiming 'putigong'* 河北省反邪教大讲堂开讲 首揭骗财害命 '菩提功'), http://report.hebei.com.cn/system/2015/04/16/015351203.shtml.

9 This information is provided on the group's website, however Utiraruto Otehode has visited the centres in Hongkong and South Korea and Benjamin Penny has visited the centre in Taiwan.

At present, Puti Gong present themselves exclusively as a meditation group and JinBodhi as a "Meditation Master" dressed in saffron robes in many of the images. The opening paragraph on their introductory webpage reads:

> Bodhi Meditation was founded by Meditation Master JinBodhi in 1991. Our mission is to impart practical, effective meditation techniques as a way of strengthening the energy of the physical body, and to inspire the spiritual mind so as to bring greater health and joy to the world at large.
> BODHI MEDITATION FOR HEALTH FOR LIFE 2019

Puti Gong's status as a qigong group is completely elided. On the entire website, the word "qigong" appears only once and that is to distinguish Puti Gong from it (McClure 2013). Puti Gong also runs Facebook pages in English, Chinese and Korean for the group itself, for *Meditation and Health*, and one called 'Zen Crazy (*Chanfeng* 禪瘋)' based in Taiwan. It also has pages for downloading its materials, a discussion group page and a dedicated Youtube channel for its many videos.

Puti Gong's great point of difference from Falun Gong is that no mention is made of the status of the group in China on any of its websites or social media offerings. Despite being recognized as a 'harmful qigong group' by the Chinese government in 2000, with all its organizations and activities in China being banned, Puti Gong do not seem to be interested in integrating their suppression into their teachings as Falun Gong does, or to be involved in any protest activities. From Chinese reports, Puti Gong practitioners in China have apparently maintained contacts with the organizations abroad, with information flowing into China, and money and practitioners flowing out. Practitioners in China can obtain information about Puti Gong's activities abroad and JinBodhi's new teachings through the Internet. In terms of money flow, Chinese government sources claim that 108 Puti Gong practitioners from Cangzhou 沧州 in Hebei province collected Y600,000 (about US$95,000) to build a meditation hall in Canada in 2005 (Jin Xuan 2017). Chinese Puti Gong practitioners have also gone abroad to participate in meditation classes. For example, one Ms. Meng and her son Yue from Shuangyashan 双鸭山 in Heilongjiang Province visited Malaysia in 2013 and 2014 respectively to participated in Puti Gong classes. After Ms. Meng returned to China, she organized a Puti Gong class in her hometown (Liu 2014).

These international movements have heightened the official vigilance among Chinese agencies with media, local governments and local anti-cult associations warning that Puti gong is an evil cult (Ping'an Ningguo 2017; Zhengfawei 2017; Yan 2014). A 27-minute video criticising Puti Gong is available on the anti-cult network website *Zhongguo fanxiejiao wang* 中国反邪教网 and is widely circulated (Kaifeng wang 2017). There are also reports of continuing activities in China. For example, in March 2015, an illegal gathering of Puti Gong was uncovered in Ningjin 宁晋 County in Hebei Province (Changcheng wang 2015). The organizer was Qiao Jianzhong 乔建忠, a disciple of Di Yuming, who had gathered 120 activist practitioners (*gugan* 骨干)[10] and ordinary followers from Hebei, Heilongjiang, Liaoning, Jilin, Inner Mongolia and Jiangsu provinces for talks on health (Kaifeng wang 2017). However, to all intents and purposes, as far as their English-language followers are concerned, "Bodhi meditation" must appear simply as a Buddhist-style meditation group with a non-political, charismatic Chinese master.

The story of Tian Gong is different again. It was noted above that Letian Dashi moved to the US in 1994 and experienced a major challenge in the Himalayas in 1999. His biography next notes that in 2003 he received important transmissions from the Cosmic Masters while in Roswell, New Mexico, the alleged crash site of an alien spaceship. Thus, the tensions in the world of qigong in China from 1995 on and the cataclysmic events in 1999 pass without acknowledgment, even though, as we saw above, Tian Gong lays such stress on its links to the qigong movement.

The story of continuing transmissions goes through the 2000s with the teachings taking on a cosmic salvific role, first with the Roswell revelations passing on a method of cultivation that will allow a 'new type of human' to emerge for 'a new era of a universalized humanity.' Later that year – in Berlin – a transmission informed Letian Dashi that Tian Gong's cosmic role was to save the earth, save all life, and save the self. Finally, 'between 2004 and 2006' a cosmic history and Tian Gong's cosmic role was revealed to him. Apparently, people were first invited just to be 'guests (*keren* 客人)' on this planet by the 'Spirit of the Earth (*diqiu shen* 地球神)' but ended up staying permanently, becoming its owner or 'host (*zhuren* 主人)'. After the great damage we have inflicted on the earth itself and on other people, our world is moving towards annihilation and a great catastrophe for all humanity. Spreading and practicing Letian Dashi's teachings is the way these terrible events can be avoided.

It is relevant that the last entry on the website refers to 2006. At that time, Tian Gong indicated that its main centres were in Union City near San Francisco, Berlin and the Canary Islands. The Berlin centre was run by two sisters named Tianping 天萍 (whose original name was Yang Jianping 杨剑萍) and Tianying 天婴 (Yang Tianying 杨天婴, now also known as Tianyin 天音) who

---

10   The role of qigong activist practitioners is detailed in Otehode and Penny 2017.

had worked with Letian Dashi for some years. Tianying started learning Tian Gong in China in 1993 and Tianping, who had lived in Germany since 1989, was initially his German interpreter. The Berlin Tian Gong centre was established in 1999 but has since transformed into the Tian'ai 天爱 (or heavenly love) Qigong Institute. Letian Dashi's name is currently not mentioned on the website, which now proclaims a heritage going back to the Buddhist figure Bodhidharma. The Berlin Centre also has contact details for Tian'ai qigong activities in Spain and in Peru.

At the same time the Union City centre seems to have been taken over in 2010 by Mu Tianjia 牧天嘉 (or Cathy Mu), also formerly an interpreter for Letian Dashi. The website seems to have been active until about June 2013, advertising classes given by Mu Tianjia and then to have gone quiet. She now runs a qigong group called Pure Beautiful Healing which, she says, will help her students attain, 'abundance in health, wealth, joy, love, ever-lasting beauty, and happiness.' In her biography on that site, Mu says that, 'in 2008, at Berkeley, California, USA, she met a top Qi Gong Grandmaster whose teaching reached and healed millions (who preferred not to be mentioned by name any longer)'. This is presumably Letian Dashi, who appears to have ceased any public activities.

3   Conclusion

We have seen how the three categories of 'evil cult', 'harmful qigong group' and 'problematic qigong group' arose in a period of aggressive Chinese government management of qigong groups. We have also introduced one qigong group from each of these three categories. Can we say, then, why the different qigong groups were classified into these three categories?

Before making a tentative conclusion – tentative because the official documentation is not publicly available – it may be useful to note the partial *irrelevance* of one theory that has been raised to explain why the Chinese government has attacked qigong groups with such vigour. This explanation rests on the observation that the teachings of qigong groups are often concerned with matters spiritual, or at least non-materialistic. Thus, as far as the Party is concerned, they are spreading ideas that implicitly undermine the ideology of Communism and thus cannot be allowed in an authoritarian state with a claimed monopoly on the truth. This position may explain why those qigong groups that have developed and disseminated complex sets of ideas about how the cosmos is organised and the role of their respective teachings for the salvation of humanity have been labelled in a negative way. It does not, however, help us to explain why each of these three groups has been allocated to a different category of seriousness. All three, after all, seem to be equally antithetical to the Party's own teachings and each of the leaders seems equally spiritualised. Clearly, we must look elsewhere for an explanation.

Our conclusion is that, as in so much else, the answer lies in politics, and in particular to the perceived threat to the current form of the Chinese state. Ever since its suppression, Falun Gong has positioned itself as an unbending critic of the Chinese regime, even elevating anti-government activities to the status of obligatory religious tasks under the rubric of "Clarifying the Truth". It is also very clear that it has a strong organisation and a loyal following outside China (and possibly the remnants of one inside China as well). Falun Gong has also become adept at mobilising the support of non-practitioners in their struggle and has been active in lobbying governments around the world. It, thus, remains an ever-present threat and deserves inclusion in the most serious category of 'evil cult'.

Puti gong, while remaining active and apparently flourishing in some parts of the world and also maintaining contacts and support within China, has never presented itself as an anti-Chinese government or anti-Communist group. It has, as we have seen above, been much more concerned with recreating itself in a form attractive to westerners interested in Buddhism and meditation, and presumably making money and perpetuating itself thereby. By being so apparently apolitical, Puti Gong escapes the formal classification as an 'evil cult' and falls into the next category of 'harmful qigong group', though clearly the distinction between the two is sometimes not observed by local anti-cult associations and local media in China.

Finally, the explanation for why Tian Gong is classified only as 'problematic' despite having, perhaps, the most outlandish teachings of the three is clear. Its master has gone quiet. It has ceased to exist in the country he was last active in and the only remnant of his teaching network that remains has changed its name, does not acknowledge its originator publicly and appears not to refer to his teachings any more. It is reasonable that the government would not view it as a cause of concern.

References

Anon. 2018. "Naxie shi qigong youhai zuzhi? Naxie shi guojia tuiguangde gongfa?". http://www.rbw.org.cn/Article.aspx?i=B3P (uploaded onto https://www.weibo.com/ttarticle/p/show?id=2309404244015766707892). Retrieved 8 June 2019.

Bai Yi. 2013. "Jia Sa and Yi Dai Shen Qi of Bodhi Meditation" https://masterrehab.wordpress.com/2013/07/07/jia-sa-and-yi-dai-shen-qi-of-bodhi-meditation. Retrieved 8 June 2019.

Bodhi Meditation for Health for Life.2019. "Introduction to Bodhi Meditation." https://www.puti.org/en/introduction-about-bodhi-meditation. Retrieved 8 May 2019.

Changcheng wang. 2015. "Hebei sheng fan xiejiao da jiangtang kaijiang, shoujie piancai haiming puti ong." http://report.hebei.com.cn/system/2015/04/16/015351203.shtml. Retrieved 24 September 2020.

Gonganbu guonei anquan baoweiju. 1999. "Chajin qudi xiejiao zuzhi falü fagui." Beijing: Qunzhong chubanshe.

Guojia tiyu zongju jianshen qigong guanli zhongxin. 2004. "Jianshen qigong fudaoyuan peixun jiaocai (er)." Internal Document.

He Zi. 2006. "1996 nian Zhongguo qigong kexue yanjiuhui kaichule falungong." http://kaiwind.com/c/2006-07-04/733546.shtml. Retrieved 24 September 2020.

Irons, Edward A. 2018. "The List: Evolution of China's List of Illegal and Evil Cults." *The Journal of CESNUR*, 1, 33–57.

Jin Xuan. 2017. "Jingti pizhe fojiao waiyi de pianzi – puti gong." https://kknews.cc/fo/39rrrg8.html. Retrieved 24 September 2020.

Kaifeng wang. 2017. "Jiechuan puti gong de zhen mianmu." http://www.chengyang.gov.cn/n1/n6/n810/n827/180501172937312070.html. Retrieved 24 September 2020.

Liu Yi. 2014. "Shuangyashan pohuo puti gong feifa juhui anjian." www.kaiwind.com/c/2014-08-20/997715.shtml. Retrieved 24 September 2020.

McClure, Melia. 2013. "Peace, Inside and Out: A Bodhi Meditation Retreat." *Meditation & Health* 9. https://www.puti.org/en/meditation-health-no-09-12. Retrieved 8 May 2019.

Otehode, Utiraruto. 2009. "The Creation and Reemergence of Qigong in China." Pp.241–263 in *Making Religion, Making the State: The Politics of Religion in Modern China*, edited by Yoshiko Ashiwa and David L. Wank, Stanford: Stanford University Press.

Otehode, Utiraruto.and Penny, Benjamin. 2016. "Qigong Therapy in 1950s China." *East Asian History*, 40: 69–83.

Otehode, Utiraruto.and Penny, Benjamin. 2017. "Activist Practitioners in the Qigong Boom of the 1980s." *East Asian History*, 41: 15–24.

Palmer, David A. 2007.*Qigong Fever: Body, Science and Utopia in China.* New York: Columbia University Press.

Palmer, David A..2008a. "Les mutations du discours sur les sectes en Chine moderne. Orthodoxie impériale, idéologie révolutionnaire, catégories sociologiques." pp. 31–50 in *Archives de sciences sociales des religions*, 53e Année, No. 144.

Palmer, David A.2008b. "Heretical Doctrines, Reactionary Secret Societies, Evil Cults: Labeling Heterodoxy in Twentieth-Century China." pp. 113–34 in *Chinese*

Religiosities: Afflictions of Modernity and State Formation. Edited by Mayfair Mei-hui Yang. Berkeley: University of California Press.

Ping'an Ningguo. 2017. "Puti gong jiujin shige sha huose?" https://read01.com/Eegko7.html#.X21ayBcRXXX8. Retrieved 24 September 2020.

Penny, Benjamin. 2012. *The Religion of Falun Gong*. Chicago: University of Chicago Press.

Tian Gong USA. 2018. "Tian Gong USA" http://www.tiangongusa.org. Retrieved from www.archive.org. Viewed 8 June 2019.

Xia Leiming. 2009. "Jiji tuiguang youyi qigong zhenfeng xiangdui dizhi xiejiao". http://www.bohechashe.org/c/2009-02-09/804766.shtml. Retrieved 8 June 2019.

Yan Yin. 2014. "Puti gong xiejiao." http://paper.taizhou.cn/tzrb/html/2014-09/11/content_573354.htm. Retrieved 8 May 2019.

Zhengfawei. 2017. "Puti gong haile tamen." http://www.tongguan.gov.cn/zdzl/jkhcfzfxjbba/37923.htm. Retrieved 8 May 2019.

Ziyangshi Fan Xiejiao wang. 2014. "14 zhong youhai qigong de rending ji youguan qingkuang. " http://www.zysfxb.com/news/show-195.html. Retrieved 8 May 2019.

CHAPTER 12

To Be or Not to Be a Confucian

Explicit and Implicit Religious Identities in the Global Twenty-First Century

Anna Sun

1   The Puzzle: To Be or Not to Be a Confucian

Although Confucianism is usually associated with the greater China region (Mainland China and Taiwan), it has not been an exclusively Chinese religious tradition.[1] Historically, for over a millennium, it has been an important part of the ritual, cultural, political, economic, and social heritage of both Japan and Korea. They, along with China, form the so-called "Confucian East Asia" (Ivanhoe 2016; Paramore 2016; Deuchler 2015; Kim 2014; Tu 1996). Confucianism has also been a crucial part of everyday life in societies as diverse as Vietnam, Indonesia, and Singapore (Tran 2017; Kelly 2006; McHale 2003). At the turn to the twenty-first century, we see new developments not only in countries where Confucianism has traditionally left strong impressions, but also in other parts of the world, such as North America (Jeung, Fong, and Kim 2019; Neville 2000). With greater global mobility, Confucianism is now emerging in different regions of the world, made possible by people who carry Confucianism with them as their treasured foundation of ethics, rituals, social ties, and subjective meaning, a deep-rooted connection that evolves as they cross national borders (Long 2019; Song 2017).

---

1 This chapter began as a paper entitled "The Puzzles of Religious Identity in Contemporary China," presented at the Society for the Scientific Study of Religion 2018 annual conference. I thank Ann Braude, Catherine Brekus, Alan Copperman, Conrad Hackett, Jaime Kucinskas, Richard Madsen, Mark Mullins, Neha Sahgal, Bin Song, Brian Steensland, Chris White, Lawrence Whitney, Linda Woodhead, Fenggang Yang, among others, for insightful discussions about religious identity. I also thank colleagues at the "Urbanity and Religion" workshop at the Max-Weber-Kolleg at University of Erfurt, especially Asuman Laetzer-Lasar, Susanne Rau, Jörg Rüpke, and Emiliano Urciuoli, for conversations comparing the ancient Roman world with contemporary China. Last but not least, I thank Angela Lei Parkinson, Bin Song, Shumo Wang, and members of the MATAKIN in Indonesia, especially Budi Wijaya and Lany Guito, for agreeing to be interviewed and quoted, as well as for conversations about religious life in China and the Chinese diaspora.

However, global survey data on religion show that very few people claim a Confucian identity. Over and again we see very few people identifying themselves as Confucians in survey research; the number of Confucians in such data is so minuscule that Confucianism is mostly absent in the categories of major religions in the world – see, for instance, *The Global Religious Landscape: A Report on the Size and Distribution of the World's Major Religious Groups as of 2010* (Pew 2012). The highest number of Confucians appears to be found in South Korea (under 2%). There are very few who call themselves Confucians in Mainland China (0.2%), and the numbers are too small to be noted in Taiwan, Vietnam, or Japan (Sun 2013). The case of global Confucianism raised the sociological question of religious identity: Why do so few people identify themselves as Confucians? What are the sociological factors contributing to the self-identification of Confucians in certain societies, as well as to the lack of such identifications in others?

The distinction of weak and strong religious identities may not be sufficient in answering these questions (Lim and Putnam 2010; Hackett 2014). Based on ethnographic data I have collected from Mainland China, Taiwan, South Korea, Japan, Indonesia, and the United States, I argue that, in the case of transnational Confucianism, it is important to think of religious identities as *implicit* and *explicit*. I propose that Confucianism as a religious identity has been *implicit* both in the present and historically, especially in the case of China and South Korea. But it has become more *explicit* in certain societies today, such as Singapore and Indonesia, because religious identity in these countries is seen as an essential component of citizenship. In the end, to be or not to be a Confucian may be less a matter of religious choice than a reflection of the role religious identity plays in global and transnational modernity. Today we are all expected to be able to either have a self-avowed and clear-cut religious identity – "I am a Christian," or "I am a Buddhist" – or to fall into rather academic and abstract categories such as "I am an atheist" or "I am an agnostic."

But what are we missing when we focus solely on religious self-identifications that in effect privilege membership in institutionalized monotheistic religions? What are we missing when we take a self-avowed religious identity too much for granted, i.e. as a necessary component in individual religious life, even when exclusive or clear-cut religious identity has never been the norm in certain religious traditions? In the end, "to be or not to be a Confucian" may not be a matter of individual "religious choice." It may instead be a reflection of the role the epistemology and politics of religious identity plays in the global twenty-first century.

2   Religious Identity: Reconsidering a Concept

How should we understand the concept of religious identity? Is it something that comes naturally to people who participate in religious life? Is it something that one acquires consciously when one is part of a group of people who share similar religious beliefs and practices? Is it a universal aspect of people who consider themselves religious?

Since Hans Mol's *Identity and the Sacred* (1976), the concept of religious identity has moved from the margins of theories of religion to the forefront. In the field of sociology of religion, religious identity is often used to measure whether religion has a positive or negative effect in various aspects of social and individual life, such as Liam and Putnam's study of religiosity and life satisfaction, in which they discover that "people with a strong religious identity tend to have a higher level of life satisfaction even when attendance and congregational friendship are controlled" (Liam and Putnam 2010). But such studies tend to rely on a notion of religious identity as a clear-cut, either/or dichotomy. The more exciting work engages the concept of identity intersectionally, especially in terms of racial and religious identities (Ammerman 2006; Marti 2009).

In "A Cultural Sociology of Religion: New Directions," Penny Edgell stresses the importance of a "fluid and contextual approach to religious identity":

> Cultural approaches also call for us to recast our understanding of religious identity, emphasizing that such identity is always inherently fluid and intersectional, with boundaries that are actively made and defended (or blurred and changed). The relative boundedness of religious identities can vary across and within contexts, and the boundary-making process is a locus for simultaneous inclusion and exclusion. At the individual level, the meaning of religious identities may vary a great deal, and religion's influence on an individual's attitudes, beliefs, and actions may also vary across time or social location.
>
> EDGELL 2012: 258

To approach the study of religious identity as a contextual concept means that we must take history and politics into consideration. In her discussion of religion as identity-claim, Linda Woodhead draws our attention to the increasing politicization of religious identity:

> The concept of "religious identity" is often used not just for descriptive but for explanatory purposes as, for example, when it is said that the

increasing visibility of religion in even supposedly secular Europe has to do with a reassertion of religious identity, or when Muslims are said to be asserting their identity in the face of secularism. [...] On this account religion may be treated as a source of identity like ethnicity, gender, sexuality etc., and hence as being both a matter of social ascription and of personal choice (in how one appropriates and 'performs' that identity).

WOODHEAD 2011

If we agree with Woodhead that today religious identity is a concept often treated as akin to ethnicity or gender, we must also take into consideration the historical and political conditions under which religious identity is formed, disseminated, used, and reproduced as a conceptual category for scholarship as well as statecraft. This is a situation I have analyzed in depth in the context of the making of Confucianism as a world religion in the nineteenth and twentieth centuries (Sun 2013). And this is an issue receiving increasing urgent attention by social scientists today. As Fenggang Yang put it:

In the social scientific study of religion and spirituality in the Global East, a key problem is how to measure religion and religiosity. The existing measures commonly used in the West and around the world are primarily based on Judeo-Christian understandings of identity, membership, and attendance. To be more precise, in the Judeo-Christian context, it is assumed that religious identity is exclusive, that every religious person is a member of a local congregation that is part of a denomination or a distinct religion, and that regular activities include weekly attendance at a corporate worship service. However, East Asian religions have distinct characteristics: Religious identity is not necessarily exclusive, religious practice is not based on a weekly rhythm, individual devotion or practice is at least as important as corporate rituals, and the boundaries of religiosity and secularity are ambiguous or blurred.

YANG 2018

In the same vein, scholars of Chinese religion have been challenging the existing categories of religion, religious identity, and religious belonging. For example, Kenneth Dean suggests that we need to think about the "religious field" of Chinese religions, and Asian religions in general (Dean 2016), and Daan F. Oostveen advocates a new way of looking at religious belonging in the East Asian context, using the Deleuzian terms "rhizomatic belonging" to capture the multiplicity of the Chinese religious experience (Oostveen 2019). I have been using terms such as "the linked ecologies of the Chinese religious system" to address the non-monotheistic structure of religious life in Chinese society (Abbott 2005; Sun 2016; 2018).

Indeed, these reflections are very similar to the main critique of identity as a concept offered by Brubaker and Copper in "Beyond 'Identity'":

> Rather than stirring all self-understandings based on race, religion, ethnicity, and so on into the great conceptual melting pot of "identity," we would do better to use a more differentiated analytical language. Terms such as commonality, connectedness, and groupness could be usefully employed here in place of the all-purpose "identity".
> **BRUBAKER AND COOPER 2013: 20**

However, the issue of identity is not merely a scholarly concern, hence it cannot, alas, be resolved through rejection of problematic terms. There is constant social and political demand to quantify members of groups, from race to ethnicity to gender and religion. Such demands are intensified in our increasingly global information society.

For social scientists of religion, the matter is not only an epistemological one but also an empirical one. To translate these concerns into empirical terms, we need to find new measurements for religious identity that can give us a more accurate account of religious populations globally. In "Seven Things to Consider When Measuring Religious Identity," Conrad Hackett makes the following important recommendations:

1. Definitions and measures of religious identity shape knowledge about religious groups;
2. Variation in question wording leads to variation in responses;
3. Comparing results across surveys provides valuable perspective;
4. Incentives shape how respondents report their religious identity;
5. Religious identity may be liminal;
6. Salient identity categories are often unmeasured; and
7. Religious identity and religious practice may not seem congruent. (Hackett 2014: 397).

These insights are indeed crucial when we employ the concept of religious identity in empirical work such as survey research, for the consequences of this new awareness and the new measurements is significant. The kind of data collection Hackett has in mind is not only for scholarly analysis, but also for public consumption in popular media, as well as the formation of local and international policies regarding religion and politics.

But why is religious identity such a thorny concept for scholars to grasp? In Ian Hacking's discussion of the classifications of people, a topic that has long engaged the philosopher of science, he remarks:

> I have long been interested in classifications of people, in how they affect the people classified, and how the effects on the people in turn change the classifications. [...] I coined two slogans. The first one, "making up people," referred to the ways in which a new scientific classification may bring into being a new kind of person, conceived of and experienced as a way to be a person. The second, the "looping effect," referred to the way in which a classification may interact with the people classified.
> Hacking 2007: 285–6

Hacking lists five main aspects of the framework of "making up people," a social process
that can be found throughout human history:
a) The *classification* into kinds of people.
b) The *individuals and peoples* in the various classes [of different kinds].
c) The *institutions,* for example those that manage tribute, taxation and recruitment. They firm up the classifications.
d) *Knowledge* about the kind of people in question, their characteristics.
e) *Experts* in the administrations, local officers on the ground (288–9).

In this social production of classifications of people, we have larger categories such as gender, race, ethnicity, nationality, and sexuality, as well as smaller categories such as refugees, geniuses, the homeless, and the autistic. The most important insight of Hacking in this analysis is his view that not only the categories are socially produced and reproduced, but they also produce kinds of people, which is what he calls "the looping effect." Such an effect can be social, psychological, or even biomedical:

> We think of many kinds of people as objects of scientific inquiry. [...] Sometimes the aim is to organise and to help, but at the same time to keep society safe, as when prosperous people or the state aid the poor or the homeless. [...] Sometimes we study a kind of person just to admire, to understand, to encourage and perhaps even to emulate, as (sometimes) with genius. We think of these kinds of people as given, as definite classes defined by definite properties. [...] But it is not quite like that. They are moving targets because our investigations interact with the targets themselves, and change them. And since they are changed, they are not

quite the same kind of people as before. The target has moved. That is the looping effect. Sometimes our sciences create kinds of people that in a certain sense did not exist before. That is making up people.
HACKING 2007: 292–3

Among the many classification categories Hacking discusses, religion is not one of them. Although religion as a dynamic classificatory scheme is not new to epistemological analysis, religious identity as a concept has not been fully considered in terms of how it "makes up people." How does the process of the looping effect change the way people relate to religious identity? And how does it change – if it does – the way people relate to religion and religious experiences? In what ways are people with religious identities "moving targets"?

3 From Explicit Religious Identity to Implicit Religious Identity

I propose to focus on a pair of concepts for thinking about religious identity and its looping effect: Explicit and implicit religious identities. Explicit religious identity is the self-avowed identification of individuals with a specific religious tradition (in rare cases, multiple religious traditions). Explicit religious identity is manifested in people who recognize and acknowledge one or more religious traditions as central to their identity and to their conception of a meaningful life. Implicit religious identity, on the other hand, is salient in people who practice various religious rituals, beliefs, and ethics that are significant or even central to their identity and conception of a meaningful life, yet they do not necessarily acknowledge it as the source of a religious identity for cultural, historical, social, or political reasons.

The emphasis here is on the alignment – or discrepancy – between the act of religious self-avowal (identificational action) and the act of other forms of religious practice that produce observable patterns of behavior in different societies. In other words, what we are examining is not merely choices made by individuals, but the cultural, historical, social, and political conditions under which such alignment or discrepancy may be formed for large numbers of people in a given population. This is quite different from how David M. Bell defines these concepts. He states them in terms of the awareness– or the lack thereof – that individuals may have regarding her attachment to religious communities: "An explicit religious identity refers to an individual who consciously identifies with a religious community and/or supernatural entity. A person who has an implicit religious identity may be largely unaware of the attachments to a religious community" (Bell 2008: 138).

The notion of "implicit religion" – rather than "implicit religious identity" – is a very different concept, first suggested by Edward Bailey in 1968 and is continuingly gaining scholarly attention. For Bailey, "implicit religion" is akin to "secular faith," by which he refers to "those aspects of everyday life, the understanding of which may be enhanced if we ask whether they might have, within them, some sort of inherent religiosity of their own" (Bailey 2010: 271). Karen Lord believes that it is important to take "implicit religion" seriously because it is "a construct that connects the seemingly opposite and separate poles of the sacred and the secular and facilitates the understanding of how belief structures can span the entirety of human experience and exert influence in unexpected areas and in unanticipated ways" (Lord 44).

But the concepts I deploy here, namely implicit and explicit religious identity, is not about "implicit religion," which is invented to address religious experiences and activities that cannot fit easily into the existing categories of organized religion. Bailey's "implicit religion" is about how to *define religions*. But the concepts of implicit and explicit religious identity are about why there is *self-avowal identification* with a religion (or, rarely, religions) in some cases and not in others, even though people who don't avow may still be engaged in religious activities. This is about how to define people's *identification with religions*.

One may argue that explicit identity is a thin notion of religious identity, whereas implicit identity is a thick notion of religious identity:
a) Thin notion: religious identity as religious affiliation and religious self-identification;
b) Thick notion: religious identity as religious practices, religious experiences, and embodied religiosity.

As Hackett shows, religious identity (the thin notion) often is not congruent with religious practice (thick notion) in survey data, and the inconsistent ways in which these two aspects of religious life are measured and analyzed pose a real problem in survey research (Hackett 2014: 408–410).

Equally importantly, the concepts of explicit and implicit religious identity aim to point to the looping effect that people experience when their religious practices and beliefs are defined – both by themselves and by others – in a social and political context in which labels of religions have certain effects. When people start claiming explicit religious identities, they form new relationships with the religious traditions that they engage in, i.e. the looping effect of "making up people."

The dynamic definition of religion involves the following aspects:
a) *Religious traditions*: historical, theological, material, and institutional *social realities* that include religious practices, ethics, texts, and sacred sites;

b) *Classifications of religions*: socially constructed classification schemes of religions that are specific to given historical moments and social contexts;
c) *Religious actions*: religious actors' practices and beliefs expressed through prayers and other rituals according to different religious traditions, conducted by individuals as well as communities.

In this context, religious identity is the result of the interactions of these factors. I propose two modalities of religious identity:

a) *Implicit religious identity*: one may engage in *religious actions* belonging to a certain *religious tradition* (or multiple religious traditions) without having a self-avowed religious identity, due to the social conditions under which *classifications of religions* are constructed;

b) *Explicit religious identity*: one may engage in *religious actions* belonging to a certain *religious tradition* (or multiple religious traditions) and have a self-avowed religious identity (or, rarely, multiple religious identities), due to the social conditions under which *classifications of religions* are constructed.

Explicit religious identity is taken for granted in many religious worlds, such as predominately Christian or Muslim societies, in which to have a clearly defined religious identity is seen as a precondition of being religious. Indeed, in her discussion of "implicit religion," Karen Lord quotes Andrew Shanks' remark that "[a]ll religion is about identity – but which identity?" (Lord 44). As a result, we often think of religious identity as a necessary and intrinsic part of religious life.

The history of monotheistic religious traditions speaks of the necessity for Jews, Christians, and Muslims to define themselves as separate religious groups and draw clear boundaries among followers of different religious traditions, both monotheistic and polytheistic. For example, from the early days of Christianity, followers of the new religion have unambiguous identities to distinguish themselves from the followers of Judaism and various combinations of Roman religions. Nevertheless, the centrality of explicit religious identity is not something to be taken for granted.

I suggest that implicit rather than explicit religious identity is more prevalent in societies where non-monotheistic religious life is the norm, such as China. Only at the turn to the twentieth century, with the rise of the modern nation state and the classificatory imperatives as part of its statecraft, concurrent with the importation of Western monotheistic conceptions of religious identity, did the Chinese government begin to tabulate the embedded religious traditions as separate religions with adherents having separate religious identities. Illustrating the looping effect on a national scale, religions are treated as social and institutional forces and, as a result, become that (Goossaert and

Palmer 2011; Sun 2013). Indeed, this is when most Chinese – the ones who were not Christians or Muslims – began to encounter the social, institutional, and political realities of explicit religious identity. They were, in the past, merely followers of the interconnected traditions of Confucianism, Buddhism, and Daoism, living a meaningful life rich with religious ritual activities without having any explicit religious identity.

When Chinese religions become increasingly global and transnational, the dynamics of this transmutation from implicit to explicit religious identity emerges with greater clarity. This is why the case of transnational and global Confucianism is crucial to our analysis.

4 The Case of Global Confucianism: From Implicit Identity to Explicit Identity

Confucianism is an excellent example of the looping effect of the making of religious identity groups. Indeed, the case of Confucianism is a very useful test-case for several hypotheses regarding religious identity. Here are four hypotheses that are the most relevant to the gradual transmutation of Confucianism from implicit to explicit religious identity.

Hypothesis A concerns *religious identity and religious freedom*:
a) In a society where there is relatively more religious freedom, it is more likely for people to claim explicit religious identity, including ones that not accepted as mainstream or orthodox;
b) In a society where there is relatively less religious freedom, it is less likely for people to claim explicit religious identity other than what is mainstream or orthodox.

Hypothesis B concerns *religious identity and the monotheistic milieu*:
a) In a society where monotheistic religious traditions have been the norm of religious life, it is more likely for people to claim explicit religious identity, for being religious means to be a member of one particular religion in the monotheistic context;
b) In a society where polytheistic religious traditions have been the norm of religious life, it is more likely for people to have implicit religious identity, and less likely for people to claim explicit religious identity ("I am someone who conducts these rituals," rather than "I am someone who is a member of this religion").

Hypothesis C concerns *religious identity and religious activism*:
a) In a society where there are institutions, organizations, and individual actors who promote the recognition and spread of a certain religious

tradition, it is more likely for members of this tradition to claim explicit religious identity;
b) In a society where there are no or few institutions, organizations, and individual actors who promote the recognition and spread of a certain religious tradition, it is less likely for members of this tradition to claim explicit religious identity.

Hypothesis D concerns *religious identity and identity requirements of the state*:
a) In a society where registration of religious identity is a necessary part of the requirements of citizenship or residency, people are more likely to claim explicit religious identity.
b) In a society where registration of religious identify is a not necessary part of the requirements of citizenship or residency, people are less likely to claim explicit religious identity.

Hypothesis A refers to the well-documented phenomenon of the close relationship between religious identity and religious freedom (or religious repression), which has been discussed extensively in the case of China, with the "gray market" of religion theory being one of the most illuminating analyses (Yang 2006). This also has implications to the discussion of human rights and religious identity (Breskaya, Giordan, and Richardson 2018).

Here I focus on Hypotheses B, C, and D, which address the social and political conditions under which religious identities may turn from implicit to explicit. These hypotheses can shed light on the puzzle of why to be a Confucian is an explicit religious identity in some societies, and an implicit religious identity in others, especially in our age of globalization. In what follows, I discuss empirical cases of the current developments of Confucianism as a religion in Mainland China, Japan, South Korea, Indonesia, and the United States, primarily based on ethnographic fieldwork I conducted between 2008 and 2018.

Although these hypotheses are proposed with Chinese religions in mind, and with Confucianism as the main case study here, I believe they would also have bearings on other religious traditions. For instance, in the history of Roman religion and early Christianity, we see over and again how the practitioners of diverse religious traditions were caught between explicit and implicit religious identities. The Romans in late antiquity did not know that they are "pagans"; they were practitioners of various ritual actions who, for the most part, had implicit rather than explicit religious identities. Indeed, as Jörg Rüpke shows us, explicit religious identity is the opposite of what Roman religious life is about: "No unified 'Roman Religion' existed, but there were no independent religions either. To talk about Roman religion is to talk about cultural practices that fit our notion of 'religion'" (Rüpke 2013: 20). In other words, Roman religion should be understood not through the rigid categories that one may wish to impose on it, but through a heuristic consideration that finds in it the functional equivalent of what we think of as the essential elements of religious life.

Yet once clear-cut and often rigid religious identity becomes the norm, being both *explicit* and *exclusive* in monotheistic traditions, people whose religious lives are outside of such norm are considered "pagan," "heathen," or deviously irreligious. The Oxford Dictionary defines the word "heathen" as a derogatory term:

> A person who does not belong to a widely held religion (especially one who is not a Christian, Jew, or Muslim) as regarded by those who do: "my brother and I were raised, as my grandma puts it, as heathens."

This is how the Chinese have been regarded by many since the beginning of their encounters with the West, as in "the Heathen Chinee."[2] Even in the 1950s, we see a similar understanding in the popular imagination: "Of the many rich insights in this book [*The Soul of China* by Amaury de Riencourt], the most important are those that emphasize the profound differences between China and the West. [...] Instead of a war on nature, they have conducted a race-long love affair with it, though not with God: 'no civilization has been so consistently irreligious as the Chinese'" (Editorial 35). Such views still have traction today, both in popular thinking and in academic work, and our effort at rectification has to start from understanding the classification scheme we follow, as well as the process of "making up people," especially in the realm of religious identity.

5 Religious Identity and the Monotheistic Milieu

Hypothesis B, as listed above, concerns the differences between predominantly monotheistic societies (primarily those with Abrahamic religions such as Christianity, Judaism, and Islam) and non-monotheistic societies (the ones with non-Abrahamic and polytheistic religions). Here I use "predominantly monotheistic" to refer to societies such as the United States where Abrahamic religions represent the majority of its religious population, even though

---

2 "The Heathen Chinee" was a popular poem by Bret Harte published in 1870, which describes a Chinese laborer in the United States, Ah Sin, who cheats in a game of cards: "But the hands that were played/By that heathen Chinee/And the points that he made/Were quite frightful to see/ ... Then I looked up at Nye/And he gazed upon me/And he rose with a sigh/And said, "Can this be?/We are ruined by Chinese cheap labor,"/And he went for that heathen Chinee" (Harte 1870).

non-monotheistic religions are also part of the American religious landscape. I use "predominantly polytheistic" to refer to societies such as China where non-Abrahamic religions such as Confucianism, Buddhism, and Daoism represent the religious practice of the majority of its population, even though monotheistic Abrahamic religions such as Christianity and Islam also have a strong presence. The logic of monotheistic religions has been governing the understanding of religious life globally since the early modern period (Assmann 2009), and the consequences of this epistemological aberration are acutely felt in non-monotheistic societies such as China (Sun 2016).

There is the further issue of religious identities as either *singular* or *composite*. A singular religious identity mostly takes the logical form of *either/or*. Such religious identities are the norm in predominately monotheistic societies, where one's identity could be, for example, either an Orthodox Christian or an Orthodox Jew, either a Protestant or a Catholic, but never both.[3] A composite religious identity mostly takes the logical form of *and/and*. Such religious identities are the norm in predominantly polytheistic societies such as China, where people's explicit or implicit religious identities are often amalgams of more than one religious tradition, such as a blending of Confucianism, Buddhism, and Daoism; or a blending of Confucian tradition with Christianity or Islam, resulting in a Confucian Christian or Confucian Muslim (Wu 2016; Benite 2005).

There has been an ongoing discussion in the field of the sociology of religion on why it is so difficult to classify Chinese religions and to survey religious life using standard social scientific categories (Yang 2014, 2016; Sun 2013, 2016). This has to do with the fact that the categories we use as social scientists do not map well in Chinese society, which is a profoundly polytheistic world in which monotheistic religious – Christianity and Islam – also occupy important spaces. As an example, let us examine the following standard survey question for China:

Are you a member or believer of one of the following religions?[4]
Protestant Christianity
Catholicism
Islam
Buddhism

---

3   The one exceptional case is the increasingly visible composite identity of American "JewBu," or Jewish-Buddhist (Sigalow 2019).
4   This is a standard question about religious identity in surveys in China and East Asia, and similar versions can be found in World Values Survey, Pew surveys, and Horizon surveys, among others.

Daoism
Folk religion
Confucianism
I don't believe in any religion.
Other

To put it simply, almost every concept involved in this line of inquiry can be problematic in the context of China, unless the person surveyed is a Christian or Muslim. Such questioning implies that one should know *what one's religion is*. This view has two implied assumptions:

a) One *should* have a self-avowed religious identity;
b) one *should* have no more than one religious identity, with multiple identities being exceptional cases (i.e. a *singular* religious identity rather than a *composite* one).

These assumptions are deeply problematic for any society where monotheistic religious traditions are not the norm, and they are certainly wide of the mark for the Chinese case.

What does it mean to be a "member" of Buddhism, Confucianism, Daoism, or "folk religion"? We can examine the issues from the perspective of the pluralist nature of these traditions, such as analyzing the monothetic suppositions behind treating Daoism or "folk religions" as distinct religions with clearly demarcated boundaries, the way we assume clear boundaries between Christianity and Islam. But it is also important to understand the situation from the perspectives and lived experiences of religious practitioners.

Although a small percentage of Buddhists in China go through the official conversion process (*guiyi*) – no official statistics are yet available for this population – most practitioners of Buddhist rituals and ethics are comfortable with not having any official religious identity. In survey data, about 16–18% of Chinese say they are followers of Buddhism, even though, judging by my ethnographical interviews, the real number of practitioners of Buddhism must be a great deal higher (such as Horizon Survey 2007). With Daoism, historically there is no official conversion process for lay followers; only religious professionals, i.e. Daoist priests and priestesses, have the privilege of receiving initiation rituals.[5]

---

5 In my fieldwork in 2016, I conducted interviews in a Daoist temple in Shanghai which had just started holding conversion ceremonies for lay followers. The Daoist priests I interviewed explained that this was a new undertaking for their temple, and it was likely that this development was inspired by the Buddhist temples in Shanghai that were becoming increasingly successful in establishing formal conversion ceremonies for their followers, thus securing a core group of followers and supporters of the temples. However, this is highly

For Confucianism, it is important to note that there has been no official initiation process in its long tradition that is akin to a baptism. There is no conversion process *per se* to mark the boundary between being a Confucian and not being a Confucian; to become a Confucian is a lifelong process of cultivation and practice (Sun 2013). This is one of the reasons why there are so few Confucians in survey data. In the 2016 Horizon survey, only 12 out of nearly 7,000 (0.2%) surveyed identified themselves as Confucians, with the majority (78.1%) claiming no religious identity.

However, if we look at religious practice, we find that a large percentage of people surveyed (67.6%) conduct ancestral rites at least once "in the past year." Although ancestral rites may be a universal practice, the ritual expressions of ancestral activities in China is largely Confucian, especially the way they are infused with the Confucian ethical language of filial piety (Sun 2019). A similar case can be found in South Korea, where Confucian rituals for ancestral spirits are arguably the most important rituals practiced in South Korea today, especially the ones performed on the ritual day of Chuseok, even though very few South Koreans identity themselves explicitly as Confucians (Kim 2014).

6   Religious Identity and Religious Activism

Hypothesis C deals with the relation between religious identity and religious activism. I propose that, in a society where there are institutions, organizations, and individual actors who promote the recognition and spread of a certain religious tradition, it is more likely for members of this tradition to claim explicit religious identity.

There have been ongoing attempts by Confucian religious activists in Mainland China and Hong Kong to promote a Confucian religious identity, starting from the end of the 19th century. The most notable recent Chinese Confucian activists are Jiang Qing in Mainland China and Tang Enjia in Hong Kong (Sun 2013; Billoud 2015). However, their efforts to invent identity-making events such as conversion rituals have not been successful, and Jiang's revival of religious Confucianism is further curtailed by the changing political situation in China.

The more significant and successful cases of Confucian religious activism are in fact outside of the national boundaries of China. In *Boston Confucianism: Portable Tradition in Late Modern World*, Robert Neville makes the bold

---

unusual in the Daoist tradition, in which most conversion rituals have been reserved for Daoist professionals.

assertion that one need not be ethically Chinese to be a Confucian (Neville 2000). He argues that Confucianism as a philosophical and religious tradition has relevance to non-East Asian societies, and he shows that Confucianism as a world philosophy can guide the lives of ethnically diverse people in our "late modern world." Neville's position is a provocative one because this is not a position commonly taken up by people who think of themselves as Confucians – or as followers of the Confucian tradition – in China and the Chinese diaspora. Although this view is also long held in South Korea, where people do not subscribe to the view of Confucianism as an ethically *Chinese* heritage, they also tend to think of Confucianism as an East Asian tradition, and that the Koreans are the true inheritors of Confucianism in modern society, especially of its Neo-Confucian legacy.

Neville is one of the most active members of "Boston Confucians," which also include Tu Wei-Ming and John Berthrong. Neville sees the Confucian notion of rituals as having great impact on the implementation of values in individuals in any society, and he believes that it could be the basis of the formation of a good society in the contemporary world (Neville 2017). If the founding generation of the Boston Confucians consists of worldly philosophers who aim to include Confucian thought into a cosmopolitan system of ethical ideas and practices, the next generation of Boston Confucians, the members of the "Boston University Confucian Association" care as much about Confucian ideas as Confucian ritual practice, which includes both social rituals and religious rituals.

Bin Song, a scholar of Confucianism with a PhD in religious studies from Boston University, has been the driving force behind the establishment of the Boston University Confucian Association, which routinely has dozens of participants in its events. In addition to carrying out Confucian activities at Boston University, Bin Song is also an emerging Confucian public intellectual, with dozens of articles on Confucian ritual life and ethics published on the website the Huffpost. In 2016, Bin Song led a workshop in Boston on the history and practice of Confucius veneration and *tian* worship. The participants came from diverse backgrounds: Chinese and non-Chinese, and people who belong to different religious traditions, including Christianity. It was an event with clearly articulated Confucian religious rituals, with traditional ideas embedded in innovative format.[6]

Although the Boston University Confucian Association is still a small association, it has attracted interest and support from diverse communities, such

---

6   From interview with Bin Song, March 23, 2017, Boston.

as the participation of Dr. Lawrence A. Whitney, at the time the University Chaplain for Community Life at Boston University. Such examples show the robustness as well the agility of the development of Boston Confucianism. Instead of emphasizing the uniqueness of the Confucian tradition, it embraces cultural diversity; instead of treating Confucian religiosity as singular, it suggests religious pluralism, with critical views expressed side by side with new interpretations of classical Confucian ritual texts. It remains to be seen how far this development will go, but one cannot help but be optimistic about the vitality, strength, and creativity of the Boston Confucians.

The development of such Confucian activism ensures that Confucianism as a religion is becoming a reality in the United States. Angela Lei Parkinson, a Chinese-American who received her Master of Divinity from the University of Chicago Divinity School, is the founder of and advisor to "Confucian Commons," the Confucian student group at the Rockefeller Chapel at the University of Chicago, alongside religious and spiritual groups such as Baha'i, Buddhist, Christian, and Hindu.[7] She is affectionately known, among the racially and culturally diverse members of Confucian Commons, as the first "Confucian Chaplain."[8] This is indeed the first such group in an American institution of higher education, and very probably not the last.

On September 28, 2018, Shumo Wang, a Master of Divinity student at the Harvard Divinity School, organized and led the first ritual ceremony celebrating the birthday of Confucius at Andover Chapel, the space reserved for sacred rites for all religious groups at the Harvard Divinity School. The ceremony was structurally an amalgam of different ritual traditions, and it can be argued that the event showed how hybridity can be both authentic and creative. It consisted of opening music playing on a cello as participants entered into the chapel, which filled to capacity; a short liturgy in English that was based on canonical Confucian writings; a hymn written by Wang accompanied by the piano and a chamber group; and offerings of food and water to the spirit of Confucius, represented by a traditional wooden tablet, engraved with Confucius' sacred titles. Through it all, Wang led the ritual activities with sureness and precision, his commendable ability rooted in his deep learning of Confucian ritual knowledge as well as in his ongoing training in ministry at the Divinity School, which emphasizes – in a completely open, non-denominational way – the structure

---

7 The Confucian Common is listed under "Religious and Spiritual Groups" of the "Spiritual Life" website of the University of Chicago (https://spirit.uchicago.edu/get-involved/religious-spiritual-groups/confucian).
8 Interview with Angela Parkinson, September 28, 2019, Cambridge, Massachusetts.

of religious services that is often based on a Protestant model of communal worship.

Wang is a longstanding practitioner of Confucian ritual and ethical teachings, having followed for nearly a decade a Confucian teacher in Beijing, who is the founder of a "studio" (an informal association) of Confucian learning. There, Wang became well-versed in Confucian rituals, which took place under the rubric of "cultural activities." At the Harvard Divinity School, he promoted the religious aspects of the Confucian tradition and spoke of himself not just as a cultural but also as a religious Confucian. He envisions a future as a Confucian religious professional, i.e. as a Confucian chaplain, an explicit identity that in fact has not existed in China in the past, since Confucianism has not had a separate clergy in its long history.[9]

Unlike in Mainland China, where to organize a religious group often invites political scrutiny, to form a community around shared religious interests in the United States has long been treated as a cherished and even sacred practice of civic liberty. Religious freedom certainly has diverse consequences, not only in the United States but also globally. One of the significant consequences is perhaps the hyper articulation of explicit religious identity, not only the traditional ones but also newly invented identities.[10] Confucian activists can fully express their explicit religious identity in this context. But that is a step that the majority of practitioners of Confucian rituals and ethics in East Asia do not yet feel the need to follow.

7 Religious Identity and the Identity Requirements of the State

Hypothesis D deals with religious identity and the identity requirements of the state. I propose that, in a society where registration of religious identity is a necessary part of the requirements of citizenship or residency, people are more likely to claim explicit religious identity. Although sociologists have been paying attention to the issue of registration in religious life, they tend to focus

---

9 Interview with Shumo Wang, September 11, 2018, Cambridge, Massachusetts.
10 For example, in 2016 New Zealand recognized the legality of wedding ceremonies conducted by the pastor of the Church of the Flying Spaghetti Monster, or Pastafarianism, with the tagline "joined in holy macaroni" (The Times of Israel 2016). The struggle for the legal recognition of the religious identify of Pastafarians elsewhere – in Israel and in the United State, for instance – is still on the boil. Another case is the Iglesia Maradoniana (Church of Maradona) in Argentina, which treats the footballer Maradona as a figure of divinity. It has a sizable following and routinely conducts baptisms and religious weddings (Franklin 2008).

on the registration of religious institutions and organizations (Finke, Mataic, and Fox 2018; Yang 2018). What happens when the state mandates religious identity requirement to all of its citizens?

This brings us to the fascinating case of Confucianism in Indonesia. There is a highly visible, highly passionate grassroots organization for Confucianism in Indonesia today, and its development is a story of long-term political, social, and religious struggle (Chen 2012). As a minority religion in a country with the largest Muslim population in the world – according to Pew, Indonesia has 205 million Muslims in 2010, about 88% of Indonesian population – Confucianism becomes a test case for racial and religious tolerance in Indonesia. In fact, the Confucian community is "a minority within the minority," account for only "approximately 0.7% (about 1,365,000 persons) of the Indonesian population" (Heriyanto Yang and Yogyakarta 2005). But I suggest that it has also become a test case for the development of Confucianism as an explicit religious identity.

The MATAKIN, the "Supreme Council for the Confucian Religion in Indonesia," was founded in 1955, and it has become the central force in the promotion of Confucianism as a religion as well as the campaigning of a Confucian religious identity for Chinese Indonesians. Racial discrimination against the Chinese communities in Indonesia has a long and painful history, with the most violent episodes taking place during and after the Suharto "New Order" era (1966–1998), especially the racially motivated riots in May 1998, with many Chinese Indonesian communities as its targets.

The richness and innovativeness of the Confucian religious rituals in Indonesia belongs to a different paper. What I have learned from my fieldwork there – including interviews with more than a dozen current members of the MATAKIN and visits to two Confucius temples, one for formal Confucian ceremonies and one for weekly congregational worship – is that, although the mandate of the MATAKIN is primarily about the Confucian religion, it is important for us to understand it in the larger racial, political, religious, and legal context (Long 2019).

For example, the MATAKIN has been active in Confucian-Islamic dialogue, a necessary strategic move to establish the legitimacy of Confucianism as a religion. Several prominent Indonesian imams were invited to participate in the interreligious dialogue hosted by the MATAKIN at its festive annual conference in Jakarta in 2017, including Dr. Nasarudin Umar, the Grand Imam of the National Mosque, who in my interview with him expressed great admiration for Confucianism as a religious tradition in my interview with him. It speaks volumes that, when the United States Vice President Mike Pence visited Indonesia in 2017, the chairman of the MATAKIN, Dr. Uung Sendana Linggaraja, was invited to participate in an interfaith religious meeting with him at the Istiqlal Mosque, the National Mosque, along with Indonesian religious leaders of Islam, Hinduism, Catholicism, Protestantism, and Buddhism (White House 2017).

Such public recognition is the result of decades of prolonged legal fights for the legitimation of Confucian religious identity of Chinese Indonesians. The most famous case involved the validity of the Confucian wedding of Budi Wijaya and Lany Guito in 1985. All Indonesians are required to have religiously sanctioned wedding ceremonies, and for Budi and Lany, who married in their Confucius temple in Surabaya, their marriage was invalid because Confucianism was not recognized as a religion at the time. As a result, their marriage was not accepted by the state, and their two children were considered illegitimate. The case was eventually brought to the Indonesian Supreme Court, and the court ruled in the couple's favor.[11] As a consequence, Confucianism as a religion began to flourish more publicly in Indonesia.

But the key issue is the state requirement for the registration of religious identity. Since all Indonesian citizens must declare a religious identity, which is noted on the uniform identification card that everyone carries, it has become imperative for Chinese Indonesians to be able to have Confucianism to be legally recognized as a religion. During an interview, a Chinese Indonesian woman who is active in the MATAKIN showed me her ID card, which has a column for religion (*Agama*), and hers says *Khonghucu*, the Indonesian word for Confucianism. She told me that before they could list Confucianism, they had to choose from other existing categories. "But I am not a Buddhist or Hindu!" She said, "So I listed Muslim. Thankfully now I can state the truth, which is that I am a Confucian."[12]

The case of Confucianism in Indonesia is a good example of how external social and structural factors might affect the development of explicit religious identity, in this case of explicit Confucian religious identity. Here we see the central importance of the law and legal systems, and we also see the importance of the state apparatuses, as well as grassroots organizations. The example of Chinese-Indonesian Confucians will certainly have an impact beyond Indonesia. Their struggle for recognition may become a model for Confucian activists elsewhere, and their firmly held explicit Confucian religious identity may have a looping effect on others in different Confucian societies in East Asia and Southeast Asia, even though their own social and political circumstances are unique. And their claim to a explicit Confucian religious identity is

---

11 This case was widely covered in international media.
12 Interview, October 16, 2017, Jakarta, Indonesia.

certainly having an impact on the social scientific study of religion, not only in Indonesia but globally.

8 Transnational and Global Confucianism: The Future of Religious Identity

In "Kinds of People: Moving Targets," as mentioned earlier, Ian Hacking offers a definition of what he means by "making up people," the way scientific and social scientific inquiries often in the end "make up" social groups and group identities, from complex classifications of gender to race, from "multiple personalities" to "geniuses." His points are three-fold: a) our classification scheme, or the categories of "kinds of people," are socially constructed; b) these categories of groupness often produce "looping effect" in people, because "our investigations interact with the targets themselves and change them"; c) the consequence is that our inquiries and classificatory efforts might in the end "create kinds of people that in a certain sense did not exist before" (Hacking 293). In this process, the human sciences – such as sociology, psychology, medicine – are propelled by what he calls the "engines of discovery," imperatives that drive the classification of kinds of people: to count, quantify, create norms, correlate, medicalize, biologize, geneticize, normalize, bureaucratize, and reclaim identity (305–6).

As a philosopher, Hacking's interest in the question of classification is in what ways it is "a species of nominalism": "I would love to place them in the grand tradition of British nominalism, of Ockham, of Hobbes, of Locke, of Mill, or Russell, of Austin" (293). However, Hacking also offers the following acknowledgement: "All this may seem closer to sociology than to philosophy" (293). The issues of "making up people" – of groups, of group identity, of looping effect of categories of identities – are indeed in the realm of sociology. What is beyond the scope of philosophy is where sociology starts, such as examining the interactions not only between classificatory categories and people, but also between social institutions and people, between state policies and people.

What's more, what we are seeing in the case of Confucianism is how its transnational and global realities are changing the existing parameters of "engines of discovery." The process of classification, quantification, norm-creation, normalization, bureaucratization, and identity reclamation is now conducted internationally by social scientists as well as state agencies who interact through their collection and analysis of global data, including the counting of groups of people with different religious identities.

These transnational engines of discovery, through measurements such as survey research, are now meeting the challenge of implicit religious identity in polytheistic societies such as China. The challenge that polytheistic societies pose is to the normative assumptions of explicit religious identity. In the meantime, political and social demands, both formally and informally, are making religious identities increasingly explicit for individual religious actors. This is at the heart of the modern practice of administrative statecraft, or normalizing governmentality, which treats "population" as social phenomena and variables that can be governed through statistical data (Foucault 2009 [1977–78]). This phenomenon, the transformation of the implicit into the explicit, in turn affects or even inspires practitioners in other societies to reshape their sense of what is possible, what is essential, and what is desirable in the articulation of their own religious experiences. We see this in the cases of Confucianism in the United States and in Indonesia, and increasingly in China as well.

In cases not discussed in this paper, such as the religious "none" phenomenon in North America and Europe, we see how its development may be pointing to the other direction, namely from explicit religious identity to no religious identity or implicit religious identity. According a Pew Research Center report of a 2014 survey, the "nones" refers to "a category that includes people who self-identify as atheists or agnostics, as well as those who say their religion is 'nothing in particular,'" and the "nones" "now make up 23% of U.S. adults, up from 16% in 2007" (Lipka 2015). But data also suggest that this may not be clear evidence for the decline of religious life. In the same survey, 61% religious "nones" said that they "believe in God or universal spirit," 37% "pray at least monthly," and 9% "attend religious services at least monthly" (Lipka 2015). How do we classify people who do not have any explicit religious identity yet are certainly not secular?

For social scientists who cannot avoid using the concept of religious identity, it may be necessary to start distinguishing explicit religious identity from implicit identity. It may also be necessary to examine the actual practice of the individual actors being studied. Originally posed in abstract terms by philosophers, the questions surrounding the phenomenon of religious identity can now be analyzed and better understood sociologically. To be or not to be a Confucian may not be an existential question, but it is certainly a question of empirical significance in our global age of the transmutation of religious identities.

References

Abbott, Andrew. 2005. "Linked Ecologies: States and Universities as Environments for Professions." *Sociological Theory* 23 (3): 245–274.

Ammerman, Nancy. 2006. "Religious Identities in Contemporary American Life: Lessons from the NJPS (National Jewish Population Survey)," *Sociology of Religion* 67:4.
Assmann, Jon. 2009. *The Price of Monotheism*. Stanford: Stanford University Press.
Bailey, Edward. 2010. "Implicit Religion." *Religion* 40: 271–278.
Bell, David M. 2008. "Development of the Religious Self: A Theoretical Foundation for Measuring Religious Identity." In Abby Day, ed. *Religion and the Individual: Belief, Practice, Identity*. London: Routledge, 127–143.
Benite, Zvi Ben-Dor. 2005. *The Dao of Muhammad: A Cultural History of Muslims in Late Imperial China*. Cambridge, MA: Harvard University Press.
Billioud, Sébastien, and Joël Thoraval. 2015. *The Sage and the People: The Confucian Revival in China*. Oxford: Oxford University Press.
Breskaya, Olga, Giuseppe Giordan, and James Richardson. 2018. "Human Rights and Religion: A Sociological Perspective." *Journal for the Scientific Study of Religion* 57(3): 419–431.
Brubaker, Rogers and Cooper, Frederick. 2000. "Beyond 'Identity'." *Theory and Society* 29(1):1–47.
Chen, Yong. 2012. *Record of a Twenty-Eight-Day Visit of Confucianism in Indonesia* (in Chinese). Singapore: Chinese Heritage Center.
Day, Abby. 2016. Ed. *Religion and the Individual: Belief, Practice, Identity*. London: Routledge.
Dean, Kenneth. 2016. "Conditions of Mastery: The Syncretic Religious Field of Singapore and the Rise of Hokkien Daoist Master Tan Kok Hian." *Cahiers d'Extrême-Asie* 15: 219–244.
Deuchler, Martina. 2015. *Under the Ancestors' Eyes: Kinship, Status, and Locality in Premodern Korea*. Cambridge, MA: Harvard University Press.
Edgell, Penny. 2012. "A Cultural Sociology of Religion: New Directions," Annual Review of Sociology (38): 247–265.
Editorial. 1958. "*The Soul of China* by Amaury de Riencourt". *Life Magazine*, September 15, 1958.
Finke, Roger, Dane Mataic, and Jonathan Fox. 2018. "Assessing the Impact of Religious Registration." *Journal for the Scientific Study of Religion* 56(4):720–36.
Foucault, Michel. 2009. *Security, Territory, Population: Lectures at the College de France, 1977–78*. New York: Palgrave Macmillian.
Franklin, Jonathan. 2008. "Diego Maradona: He Was Sent from Above." *The Guardian*, November 11, 2008.
Giordan, Giuseppe. 2014. "Introduction: Pluralism as Legitimization of Diversity," in *Religious Pluralism: Framing Religious Diversity in the Contemporary World*, edited by Giuseppe Giordan and Enzo Pace. New York: Springer.
Giordan, Giuseppe and Enzo Pace, eds. 2008. *Mapping Religion and Spirituality in a Postsecular World*. Leiden and Boston: Brill.

Goossaert, Vincent and David A. Palmer. 2011. *The Religious Question in Modern China*. Chicago: University of Chicago Press.

Hackett, Conrad. 2014. "Seven Things to Consider When Measuring Religious Identity," *Religion* (44) 3: 396–413.

Hacking, Ian. 2007. "Kinds of People: Moving Targets." *Proceedings of the British Academy* 151: 285–318.

Harte, Bret. 1870. "Plain Language from Truthful James." *The Overland Monthly Magazine*.

Horizon Survey. 2007. "The Spiritual Life of Chinese Residents Survey." The Association of Religion Data Archive.

Jeung, Russell M, Seanan S. Fong, and Helen Jin Kim. 2019. *Family Sacrifices: The Worldviews and Ethics of Chinese Americans*. Oxford: Oxford University Press.

Kelley, Liam. 2006. "Confucianism in Vietnam: A State of the Field Essay." *Journal of Vietnamese Studies* 1(1–2): 314–370.

Kim, Song-Chul. 2014. "Who Are Venerated in Contemporary Domestic Ancestral Rites? An Aspect of Ritual Change among Urbanites in Korea." *Korea Journal* 54(1): 85–104.

Kim, Sungmoon. 2014. *Confucian Democracy in East Asia: Theory and Practice*. London: Cambridge University Press.

Lim, Chaeyoon and Putnam, Robert D. 2010. "Religion, Social Networks, and Life Satisfaction," *American Sociological Review* 75(6) 914–933.

Lipka, Michael. 2015. "Religious 'Nones' Are Not Only Growing, They're Becoming More Seclar." *Fact Tank*, Pew Research Center

(https://www.pewresearch.org/fact-tank/2015/11/11/religious-nones-are-not-only-growing-theyre-becoming-more-secular/)

Long, Nicholas J. 2019. " 'Straightening What's Crooked'? Recognition as Moral Disruption in Indonesia's Confucian Revival." *Anthropological Forum* 29(4): 335–355.

Lord, Karen. 2008."Implicit Religion: A Contemporary Theory for the Relationships between Religion, State, and Society," *Journal of Contemporary Religion* (23)1: 33–46.

Marti, Gerardo. 2009. "Affinity, Identity, and Transcendence: The Experience of Religious Racial Integration in Diverse Congregations." *Journal for the Scientific Study of Religion*. 48(1): 53–68.

McHale, Shawn Frederick. 2003. *Print and Power: Buddhism, Confucianism, and Communism in the Making of Modern Vietnam*. Honolulu: University of Hawaii Press.

Mol, Hans. 1978. *Identity and Religion*. Beverly Hills: Sage Publications.

Neville, Robert C. 2000. *Boston Confucianism: Portable Tradition in Late Modern World*. Albany: State University of New York Press.

Neville, Robert C. 2017. *The Good is One, Its Manifestations Many: Confucian Essays on Metaphysics, Morals, Rituals, Institutions, and Genders*. Albany: State University of New York Press.

Oostveen, Daan F. 2019. "Religious Belonging in the East Asian Context: An Exploration of Rhizomatic Belonging," *Religions* (10)182: 36–46.

Oostveen, Daan F. 2018. "Multiple Religious Belonging and the "Deconstruction" of Religion." *Exchange: Journal of Contemporary Christianities in Context* 47 (1): 39–52.

Paramore, Kiri. 2016. *Japanese Confucianism: A Cultural History*. London: Cambridge University Press.

Pew Research Center. 2012. *The Global Religious Landscape: A Report on the Size and Distribution of the World's Major Religious Groups as of 2010*. Washington DC: Pew Research Center.

Rüpke, Jörg. 2013. *Religion: Antiquity and Its Legacy*. Oxford: Oxford University Press.

Sigalow, Emily. 2019. *American JewBu: Jews, Buddhists, and Religious Change*. Princeton: Princeton University Press.

Song, Bin. 2017. "A Catechism of Ruism (Confucianism): A Chart of Ruist Virtues." *Huffpost* (onlin magazine) (https://www.huffpost.com/entry/a-catechism-of-ruism-conf_4_b_11607540).

Sun, Anna. 2013. *Confucianism as a World Religion: Contested Histories and Contemporary Realities*. Princeton: Princeton University Press.

Sun, Anna. 2016. "The Study of Chinese Religions in the Social Sciences: Beyond the Monotheistic Assumption," in *Religion and Orientalism in Asian Studies*, edited by Kiri Paramore. London: Bloomsbury, 51–72.

Sun, Anna. 2018. "Contemporary Confucius Temples Life in Mainland China: Report from the Field," in *Varieties of Confucian Experience*, edited by Sebastian Billioud. Leiden: Brill, 205–234.

Sun, Anna. 2019. "Turning Ghosts into Ancestors in Contemporary Urban China." *Harvard Divinity School Bulletin*, Spring 2019: 49–59.

Times of Israel. 2016. "New Zealand Gets First 'Pastafarian' Pastor." *The Times of Israel*, March 1, 2016.

Tran, Anh Q. trans. *Gods, Heroes, and Ancestors: An Interreligious Encounter in Eighteenth Century Vietnam*. Oxford: Oxford University Press.

Tu, Weming. 1996. *Confucian Traditions in East Asian Modernity: Moral Education and Economic Culture in Japan and the Four Mini-Dragons*. Cambridge, MA: Harvard University Press.

Yang, Fenggang. 2006. "The Red, Black, and Gray Markets of Religion in China." *The Sociological Quarterly*. 47: 93–122.

Yang, Fenggang. 2014. "What about China? Religious Vitality in the Most Secular and Rapidly Modernizing Society." *Sociology of Religion*, 2014, 75:4.

Yang, Fenggang. 2016. "Exceptionalism or Chinamerica: Measuring Religious Change I he Globalizing World Today," *Journal for the Scientific Study of Religion*. 55(1):7–22.

Yang, Fenggang. 2018. "Religion in the Global East: Challenges and Opportunities for the Social Scientific Study of Religion," *Religions* (9), 305.

Yang, Fenggang. 2018. *Atlas of Religion in China: Social and Geographical Contexts*. Leiden: Brill.

Yang, Heriyanto and Yogyakarta. 2005. "The History and Legal Position of Confucianism in Post-Independence Indonesia." *Marburg Journal of Religion*, (10)1.

White House, Statements and Releases. 2017. "Readout of the Vice President's Meeting with Interfaith Religious Leaders, April 20, 2017" (https://www.whitehouse.gov/briefings-statements/readout-vice-presidents-meeting-interfaith-religious-leaders/).

Woodhead, Linda. 2011. "Five Concepts of Religion," *International Review of Sociology* (21)1: 121–143.

Wu, Albert Monshan. 2016. *From Christ to Confucius: German Missionaries, Chinese Christians, and the Globalization of Christianity, 1860-1950*. New Haven: Yale University Press.

CHAPTER 13

Diverse Religious Experiences among Overseas Chinese in the United Arab Emirates

Yuting Wang

1   Introduction[1]

Facilitated by robust global trade and commerce, and accelerating development in telecommunication and transportation, the flow of people across national borders and continents has continued an upward trend in the last decade.[2] One of the most important consequences of continuous population movement is the growing religious diversity, not only in immigrant receiving countries, but also in the sending countries given the transnational ties fostered by increased mobility. The changing religious landscape has met with varied responses from state governments. In some cases, secular states impose strict regulations on religious activities, creating a hostile environment for followers of either a particular religion or all religions (such as France and China). In contrast, the principle of religious freedom is deeply ingrained in some other societies (such as the United States), which produces a vibrant religious market and a myriad of new religions. There are certainly cases where the dominant religion in a society, often empowered by the state, suppresses religious minorities.

The divergent attitudes toward religious diversity reflect the shifting demography and the mounting challenges to deal with "religious others" in the era of globalization. As the fastest growing religion in the world, Islam is often portrayed as an insulated system of beliefs and practices. Such impression about Islam and Muslim societies is not completely unfounded. In their struggle against colonialism and westernization, Islamic fundamentalism has garnered much support. While there are ample examples in history where

---

[1] Earlier versions of this chapter were presented at the 1st EASSR conference in Singapore in July 2018 and a conference titled "Dialogues between Arabic and Chinese Civilizations" held in Abu Dhabi in Oct. 2019. I would like to thank colleagues at these events for their insightful comments. All remaining errors in the paper are my own.
[2] Department of Economic and Social Affairs, United Nations, *The International Migrant Stock 2019*, Sept. 2019, https://www.unmigration.org.

religious minorities in Muslim countries were granted freedom to practice their chosen beliefs and the Qur'an in various places sanctifies religious pluralism within certain parameters (Emon 2012), the rise of Islamic extremism since the end of the 20th century have inflicted horrendous violence on both Muslims and non-Muslims. Economic stagnation and political precariousness that characterize many Muslim societies today have strengthened the appealing of political Islam, an effective ideological currency to boost the power of state (Esposito 1997; Mandaville 2007). As the process of urbanization and the expansion of transnational ties further shake the roots of family and community structure that have sustained Muslim societies throughout the millennia, rejecting "others" becomes a means of self protection.

Situated in a turbulent region plagued by sectarian violence and religious extremism, the United Arab Emirates (UAE) – a small monarch in the Arabian Gulf, has made itself a champion of peace and tolerance. In 2016, the UAE introduced the post of Minister of Tolerance to the Cabinet and subsequently established the Ministry of Tolerance, which is tasked to eradicate ideological, cultural and religious bigotry in the UAE society through creating a social environment that values diversity and difference.[3] Following the declaration of 2019 as the "Year of Tolerance,"[4] the Ministry of Tolerance spearheaded a number of high profile events inside the country and abroad. Notably, the UAE became the first country in the Arabian Peninsula that hosted the official visit of a Pope. The plan to build the Abrahamic House of Fraternity, a complex containing a Jewish Synagogue, a Christian church, and an Islamic mosque, further demonstrates UAE's vision of religious pluralism (MacMillan 2019). Although the UAE continues to exercise close surveillance on religious activities, social hostility toward religion is relatively low in the country.[5]

In contrast, the People's Republic of China, a strategic partner of the UAE, has been heavily criticized for its clampdown on religions, especially Christianity and Islam. Based on a study by Pew Research Center, China implements the highest level of restrictive policies on religion among all 198 countries included in the study (Mamjudar 2019). Chinese government has banned a number of religious groups and detains a large number of clergies and activists. By demolishing religious structures with pronounced "non-Chinese"

---

3   For official statements on tolerance issued by the UAE government see https://www.government.ae/en/about-the-uae/culture/tolerance/tolerance-initiatives.
4   For more information on the Year of Tolerance see https://www.government.ae/en/about-the-uae/culture/tolerance/tolerance-initiatives.
5   "Trends in Global Restrictions on Religion," Pew Research Center, 2016, accessed on Feb. 28, 2017 at http://www.pewforum.org/2016/06/23/trends-in-global-restrictions-on-religion/.

characteristics – particularly the Christian cross and Islamic dome, the government seeks to "Sinicize" all religions in order to combat religious extremism and separatism. A month after its announcement of stricter new rules on religion on Feb. 1, 2018, the Chinese Communist Party (CCP) dissolved its long existing Religious Affairs Bureau and merged it into the United Front Work Department, indicating the growing importance of religion in overseas Chinese management. In a white paper released in April 2018, the government insists that religious groups and religious affairs in China are not to be interfered and influenced by foreign entities.[6]

Despite these differences in terms of sociocultural context and policies, the UAE and China have recently upgraded their relationship to a "comprehensive strategic partnership," a phrase used to refer to the highest level of bilateral relationship between China and any foreign country. The geopolitical importance of the UAE within China's Belt and Road network has made the country, particularly its global city – Dubai, highly attractive to Chinese businesspeople and professionals. Over the last two decades, the UAE government has already cultivated a friendly environment for Chinese companies, investors, expatriates, and visitors. The newly signed agreements further facilitate the influx of Chinese companies and individuals. The number of Chinese expatriates has increased sharply from around 2,000 in the early 1990s to more than 270,000 by the end of 2018, creating vibrant Chinese spaces in the Emirates.[7]

The encountering between Chinese migrants and Islam is not a new subject for research. However, studies on this topic largely fall within Southeast Asian studies. We know very little about the experiences of Chinese migrants in other Muslim-majority context due to the historical patterns of Chinese emigration. Chinese are highly eclectic when comes to beliefs and practices related to the sacred (Yang 1961). Dynamic and flexible, Chinese religiosity is deeply influenced by the cross-fertilization between indigenous traditions – Confucianism, Daoism, and folk religions, and imported teachings – Buddhism, Christianity, and Islam. Such hybridity is particularly pronounced in the case of Islam in China. Nevertheless, cultural differences and politically motivated conflicts have also produced wide spread Islamophobia in Chinese societies.[8]

---

6 The Chinese government issued a white paper on April 3, 2018, titled "China's Policies and Practices on Protecting Freedom of Religious Belief." Full text is available online at http://english.www.gov.cn/archive/white_paper/2018/04/04/content_281476100999028.htm.
7 Data obtained from the Chinese Consulate General in Dubai.
8 There has been long-existing conflict between Muslim minorities and the Han majority in Chinese history. The separatist movement since the 1990s and subsequent riots throughout the last two decades in Muslim majority Uyghur Autonomous Region in China's Northwest have further intensified the conflict since 2016.

Studying the religious experiences of overseas Chinese in the UAE, therefore, is both timely and meaningful.

This paper provides a glimpse of the vibrant religious lives of the Chinese expatriates in the UAE. I consider the characteristics of Chinese religiosity and the varied levels of visibility of different Chinese religious or quasi-religious groups in the country. While focusing primarily on Chinese Christians, Muslims, and Buddhists, I also pay attention to the cases of folk religions and syncretic New Religious Movements (NRMs). By delineating the contour of religious spaces produced and maintained by Chinese expatriates in the UAE, this paper serves three goals: first, it adds to our knowledge of the diverse religious experiences of overseas Chinese, especially the post-2000 migrants who differ significantly from the previous cohorts; second, it sheds light on the impact of Chinese state policies on overseas Chinese communities; third, it deepens our understanding of Muslim societies' responses toward religious pluralism.

2   Locating Overseas Chinese Community in the UAE

Home to nearly 9 million global migrants from a wide range of national, ethnic, and religious backgrounds, the UAE is the 6th largest immigrant receiving countries in 2019.[9] Since the founding of the federation in 1971, the UAE, especially its global city – Dubai, has experienced unprecedented growth and emerged as a new global hub of transportation, investment, and tourism. To maintain its competitive edge, the UAE's decision makers embrace a policy of tolerance and welcome diversity. Religious pluralism is central in the public discourses. Data from Pew-Templeton Global Religious Futures Project show that about 76.9 percent of the population in the UAE are Muslims, 12.6 percent are Christians, 6.6 percent are Hindus, 2 percent are Buddhists, and the rest practice other religions or are unaffiliated.[10] While remaining a Muslim-majority environment, the city of Dubai is touted as "a spiritual oasis" in the region (Thomas 2009). It is home to the largest evangelical Christian church in the Middle East, the largest Catholic parish in the world, one of the most prominent Malankara Orthodox Churches, and two wards of the Church of Jesus Christ of Latter-day Saints. More than a dozen churches in Bur Dubai and Jabel Ali run regular programs on weekends and hold a variety of events on

---

9   Source: Department of Economic and Social Affairs, United Nations.
10   Source: Global Restriction on Religion Studies, accessed on April 6, 2017 at http://www.globalreligiousfutures.org/countries/united-arab-emirates#/?affiliations_religion_id=0&affiliations_year=2010&region_name=All%20Countries&restrictions_year=2014.

weekdays. In addition, congregations that have yet to build churches of their own have the permission to hold weekend services in hotel ballrooms. It is also no secret that many Bible study groups meet regularly in private homes. Despite Islam's disapproval of polytheistic traditions, a Hindu temple built with the blessings of Sheikh Rashid – Dubai's former ruler, has existed for many decades and is now a popular place for worship as well as tourism. To accommodate the growing South Asian population, another Hindu temple and a Sikh gurudwara have recently been constructed in Jabel Ali on land donated by the ruling family. In fact, except Ajman and Umm Al Quwain, two small emirates in the north, there are more than forty church buildings and places of worship in every emirate, catering to believers from a variety of linguistic and cultural backgrounds and denominations. In addition, followers of Judaism, Baha'i faith, and Buddhism have also created their own spiritual homes in the country (Thompson 2019).

The amount of diversity exists in the UAE is the product of rapid economic development and construction boom since the discovery of oil. To address the issue of labor shortage, the Gulf countries have adopted policies to attract foreign guest workers (Longva 1997; Winckler 1997; Kapiszewski 2001; Gardner 2010; Kamrava and Babar 2012). While these countries have the highest net migration rates in the world, their immigration laws are among the most restrictive, offering neither citizenship nor permanent residence. Foreign population is largely managed by a *kafala* system,[11] which has produced a sense of "permanent impermanence" (Ali 2010). Hence, the approach toward diversity is not assimilation or acculturation, but peaceful co-existence – in another word, tolerance.

Chinese are among the newest additions to the diverse foreign population in the UAE. In the city of Dubai alone, the number of Chinese migrants has increased from around 2,000 in the early 1990s to 270,000 in 2018,[12] creating a significant overseas Chinese presence in a new location. Unlike other Chinese immigrants in North America and Europe, the majority of Chinese migrants in the UAE are part of the cohort of post-2000 "new migrants" who answered the

---

11 *Kafala* system is the sponsorship system implemented in the Gulf Arab countries to monitor temporary foreign guest workers. Under this system, only nationals or corporate entities can obtain legal visas and residency permits for foreign guest workers. Since the Arab Spring and the recent drop in oil price, GCC countries have been considering changing the *kafala* system. Qatar became the first Gulf state to abolish the *kafala* system on Dec.13, 2016. See "Qatar Abolishes 'Kafala' Labor System," *Arab News*, Dec. 13, 2016, accessed on Nov. 16, 2016 at http://www.arabnews.com/node/1023416/middle-east.
12 Data provided by Chinese Consulate General in Dubai.

Chinese government's call of "Going Out" and headed to the less desirable destinations in the Global South. They come from divergent backgrounds, from employees of large Chinese state-owned companies, owners of small businesses, to highly educated professionals in Fortune 500 companies. In addition to those in real estate, investment, commerce, and hospitality industries, there are also teachers, artists, physicians, engineers, and lawyers. At the lower end, there are shopkeepers, hairdressers, masseuses, and construction workers.

In the eyes of UAE residents, the religious beliefs and practices of Chinese are at best a mystery. Even those who have some knowledge about China would assume that Chinese in general do not have any religious beliefs since atheism is the underpinning doctrine of CCP, the ruling party. While Hindus, Sikhs, and Christians have become a common sight in the city's worship places, Chinese are largely absent from the religious scene. The lack of historical connection between China and the Arabian Gulf, the peculiar characteristics of Chinese religiosity, and the primarily economic concerns of Chinese migrants have all contributed to the absence. Therefore, the increasing appearance of Chinese faces in mosques, churches and other religious congregations in recent years has taken many by surprise. At the meantime, the diverse forms of Chinese folk religions, Buddhist sects, and pseudo- or quasi-religions are mostly hidden behind closed doors and practiced in private spaces. Nevertheless, the UAE government's liberal attitude toward cultural diversity has from time to time made it possible for some of these groups to display their religions in the public space.

3   Chinese Christians in the "Spiritual Oasis"

In Islam, a strict monotheistic tradition, the oneness of God is quintessential and an uncompromised pillar of faith. The concept of religious pluralism, although has been practiced from the early age of Islamic civilization, is mostly confined within the box of Abrahamic traditions. Despite the fact that Judaism, Christianity, and Islam have fought ruthlessly against each other throughout the millennia, peaceful co-existence of Muslims, Christians, and Jews within a single political system has been observed in history and at present.

In the last few years, the UAE has emerged as an enthusiastic advocate of the spirit of inclusiveness. Christians in the UAE enjoy considerable freedom to congregate. Each weekend, tens of thousands of worshipers from various ethnic groups gather together in churches and worship centers constructed on land donated by the ruling families in each emirate. Some congregations without a physical address would gather in banquet or conference halls in centrally located hotels on Friday mornings. Bible study groups frequently meet in private homes during weekdays. Easter and Christmas are also widely celebrated. Compared to the Christians in Mainland China who have been facing intensifing government restrictions,[13] their counterparts in the UAE seem to enjoy more religious freedom than many of them had expected from a predominately Arab Muslim society. Although it is illegal for Christians to proselytize in the UAE and religious publications are closely monitored and controlled, regular attendance of religious services and the formation of house churches do not jeopardize job security and personal safety. Individuals also have the opportunity to join certain denomination or sect that do not have legal status in China, such as the Church of Jesus Christ of Latter-Day Saints and the Pentecostal Church. According to Mr. Huang, who converted to Christianity in Dubai and attends an inter-denominational church,

> Having faith in God is a good thing for oneself and the society. When you have faith, you have disciplines. When you know who is the Lord of the World, you will not be afraid. People who have faith are more trustworthy. Muslims like to do business with religious people. They'd rather do business with a Christian than an atheist. Muslims consider Christians "People of the Book." Christianity and Islam come from the same root. My Muslim friends have no problem that I am a Christian. They are happy that I believe in God too.

There are roughly two groups of Chinese Christians in the UAE. One is comprised of well-educated professionals who exhibit "the predisposing conditions of tension, religious problem-solving perspectives and religious seeking" (Yang and Abel 2014). They have wide social networks, can communicate in English at ease, and are able to initiate meaningful interactions with people from different racial/ethnic and religious backgrounds. Some have already converted to Christianity in China, North America or Europe, while others converted in Dubai. Some conversions take place outside the Chinese Christian network. While some of them attend international churches, others become members in Chinese Christian Church of Dubai (CCCD), an evangelical organization founded by a group of Chinese Americans and maintains a close relationship with US embassy and consulate.

---

13   Kuo, Lily, "In China, They're Closing Churches, Jailing Pastors – and Even Rewriting Scripture," *The Guardian*, Jan. 13, 2019, accessed on Jan. 15, 2019 at https://www.theguardian.com/world/2019/jan/13/china-christians-religious-persecution-translation-bible.

The other group are recruited by friends and acquaintances associated with CCCD and other international evangelical organizations. Although proselytizing is prohibited for religions other than Islam, religious communities, especially evangelical Christians, continue to seek potential converts discreetly through personal connections. Dubai government rarely interferes with religious events that take place in private spaces. CCCD organizes a number of events throughout the year to reach out to the Chinese expatriate community, such as social gatherings on Christmas Eve, Chinese New Year, and Mid-Autumn Festival. It also arranges visits of prominent preachers from US, Canada, Malaysia, Hong Kong, and elsewhere to deliver sermons and to meet with Church members and potential converts. Although CCCD is housed in Dubai Evangelical Church Center in Jabel Ali, it has nourished a wide Christian social network and sustains a Christian space for the Chinese expatriates, whether they are long-term residents or newly arrivals.

CCCD also maintains close contact with international Christine organizations – such as Hong Kong 611, a Charismatic evangelical group based in Hong Kong. The Chinese-concentrated International City in Dubai is an important node on the Chinese Christian network in the country. While weekly services and other large events organized by CCCD usually take place in Jabel Ali's[14] church district, Bible Study groups are held weekly in the residential complexes of Dubai International City catering to the Chinese residents, especially those who work in the nearby Dragon Mart – the largest Chinese commodities center outside China. On weekdays, gatherings usually begin after 10pm, when the shops in Dragon Mart close. Religious meetings and social gatherings help new converts to strengthen their faith and form new social ties.

The size of Chinese Christian community has been growing steadily. CCCD performs baptism about four to five times a year and each time anywhere between a handful and dozens of new converts become baptized at the church. A new meeting place in Dubai International City for the Chinese evangelical Christian community opened its door in late 2017, providing a more convenient and permanent location for Chinese Christians to gather more frequently and build stronger bonds. WeChat groups and public accounts ensure smooth communication among members and enable new Christians or potential converts to stay in touch with clergies and religious scholars in Dubai and elsewhere.

---

14 Jabel Ali is a district in the South of Dubai, which houses many Christine churches and a Sikh Gurudwara.

4 Chinese State and Its Muslim "Qiaomin"(僑民)

It is estimated that China's Muslim minorities – including Hui, Uyghur, other ethnic Muslim minorities, and Han converts – count no more than 10 percent of the total population of Chinese expatriates in the UAE. Most of them concentrate in the city of Dubai. Chinese Muslim families – easily distinguishable by their clothing – are frequently sighted in Dubai International City, where more than a dozen Hui and Uyghur restaurants dotted the neighborhoods. A number of other businesses owned by Hui people and Uyghurs have also emerged over the last decade, particularly tour agencies specialized in arranging "halal tours" for Emiratis and other Muslim expats who are interested in visiting China for business or leisure. Although Chinese Muslims remain numerically small within the overseas Chinese community in Dubai, only a handful of other cities in the world outside China may be comparable in terms of the level of concentration of Chinese Muslims in a single location.

While the status of Chinese Muslims has shifted from a religious minority to majority as the result of migration to the UAE – a Muslim-majority society, the experiences of Chinese Muslims is more complicated than commonly assumed. As a new destination for Chinese migrants, Dubai is an unfamiliar and transitory place. Given the religious affiliation, cultural tradition, and Arabic skills of Chinese Muslims, Dubai government has relied on them to help mediate disputes and resolve conflict within the Chinese expatriate community. Many of these Chinese Muslims were either trained as clergy or Arabic translators, who later entered other professions including trade and legal services. Chain migration strongly characterizes the flow of Chinese Muslims into Dubai, which has in many ways reproduced the traditional structure of ethnic businesses and new employment opportunities for Chinese Muslims (Wang 2018.

A large number of Chinese Muslims are attracted to the UAE for both economic and religious reasons. Once settled, they are able to fully participate in all the religious activities with little hindrance. Their children have the opportunity to grow up in a Muslim society where all schools provide Islamic education and Arabic lessons. However, the prevailing Sunni Islamic tradition in the UAE follows the Shafi'i school of theology, which to some extent constrains the religious activities of other Islamic sects. In terms of religious beliefs and practices, Chinese Muslims often report a period of adjustment, and sometimes major shift in their understanding of Islamic teachings. Islam has a long history of more than a thousand years in China. Some long-existing practices and beliefs that characterize Chinese Muslim communities have met with strong criticisms and are even rejected as unorthodoxy. The UAE government also exercises considerable control over religious education and activities in the country, creating a more or less standardized form of religious life for Muslim expatriates.

More importantly, unlike Christians, overseas Chinese Muslims are affected by the rippling effect of tightening religious control in China. The affairs of overseas Chinese Muslims, no matter their ethnic backgrounds, are managed under the framework of "Qiaomin" (僑民) or "Huaqiao" (華僑), a term that suggests the existence of "a single community with a considerable solidarity" regardless the spatial and temporal distance created as the result of migration (Wang 1991). In the case of Hui people, or the Chinese-speaking Muslims, it makes some sense to use the term "Qiaomin" or "Huaqiao," since they have indeed acquired many unmistakable Chinese characteristics. However, using "Qiaomin" or "Huaqiao" to refer to the Turkic-speaking Uyghurs illustrates Chinese state's policy toward ethnic minorities living within its borders and the nonnegotiable principle of sovereignty and territorial integrity. The affairs of overseas Chinese are managed through five government agencies and vital to the missions of China's political apparatus. Like other overseas Chinese, China's Muslim minorities are not only expected to facilitate the realization of "Chinese Dream" wherever they are, but also closely monitored at various levels (Wang 2020). Due to the absence of naturalization in the current immigration policy of the UAE, unless overseas Chinese Muslims can manage to obtain a third-country passport, they still fall under the jurisdiction of Chinese authority. The forced repatriation of Uyghurs from the UAE, the frequent visits of Overseas Chinese Affairs Office, a variety of events organized by the office to create a strong sense of nationalism, and the increasing attention from the Chinese diplomatic missions in the UAE in the last few years clearly demonstrate the growing penetration of Chinese state power in overseas Chinese communities.

There are two major Chinese Muslim organizations in the UAE: one is comprised of the Chinese Islamic Cultural Center (CICC) – a Da'wah organization established in 2007, and the Dubai Chinese Community Mosque, both overseen by a well-respected Chinese clergy – Mr. Han, or Iman Han; led by Iman Ma, an employee of the Department of Islamic Affairs and Charitable Activities (IACA), the other organization functions under Kalemah Center, a Dubai-based non-profit Da'wah organization. IACA has employed a number of well-trained Chinese clergies to coordinate educational programs and organize social activities aiming at creating a sense of community for Chinese Muslims and spreading Islam to non-Muslims within the larger Chinese community in the UAE. Both organizations provide a wide range of free courses, including Arabic lessons, Islamic studies, Mandarin Chinese lessons, as well as martial arts lessons on both weekends and weekdays, open to both Chinese and non-Chinese expatriates.

Beyond these formal Chinese Islamic spaces, a number of active Chinese Muslims from Hui, Han, and Uyghur backgrounds, have devoted much effort in promoting mutual understanding between China and the UAE. Through organizing lectures, conferences, art exhibitions, and other inter-faith activities, they create temporary Chinese Islamic spaces in art galleries (exhibitions of Chinese Islamic calligraphy and paintings by Chinese Muslim artists), auditoriums (Chinese martial art show), conference centers (inter-faith dialogue events and academic conferences) in five-star hotels. These activities have expanded the traditional space of Chinese Muslim community centered on mosques, Islamic centers, and ethnic halal restaurants. Despite the temporality, these spaces provide platforms for meaningful social interactions and exchanges between Chinese Muslims and Muslims expatriates of diverse nationalities.

Connected by mosques, schools, Muslim-run businesses, cultural events, and various social activities, Chinese Muslims in the UAE have established a close-knit social network, providing much needed information and assistance to potential converts, new Muslims, and new migrants from China's Muslim concentrated areas. WeChat groups, a number of public accounts, together with important Chinese Muslim websites create a virtual space that further connect Dubai's Chinese Muslim community with Chinese Muslim social networks in China, Southeast Asia, North America, and elsewhere. Within these overlapping networks, whether virtual or face-to-face, Chinese Muslims continue to negotiate their unique hyphenated identity.

5 Making Buddhist Space in Dubai: Beyond Orthodoxy and Orthopraxy

While the two monotheistic traditions – Islam and Christianity – actively recruit converts either publically or in private, Buddhism also exerts its influence in the UAE's Chinese expatriate community. In Chinese societies, Buddhism is deeply intertwined with Chinese culture itself. The mutual influence of Confucianism, Buddhism, Daoism, and folk religions have produced generations of Chinese Buddhists who are only loosely connected through a highly fluid and flexible system of beliefs and practices. Most lay followers of Mahayana Buddhism do not strictly follow strict vegetarian diet and practice rigorous meditation. Buddhism is imbued in people's lives through ancestor worship, funeral rites, and temple visits. It has been more a cultural tradition than a religion that requires clear definitions of orthodoxy and orthopraxy. Although many Chinese do not identify themselves as Buddhists, they still believe in the circle of Karma. In Chinese society, Buddhism is often an embedded religion, rather than an explicit faith like Christianity and Islam (Chen 2002).

While there are around a dozen meditation centers across the UAE, there is only one Buddhist temple in the country. It is a Theravada Buddhist center maintained by the Sri Lankan community. Mahayana Buddhism followed by the Chinese has been kept alive through private devotions of individual followers. Some of them adhere to Buddhism because it is a family tradition, while some have developed deeper knowledge in Buddhism through studies. Unlike Christians and Muslims, congregational prayers are not required of Mahayana Buddhists. To policy makers in the UAE, Buddhism is either a religion that involves a pantheon of deities or is not a religion at all. Although expatriates are not prohibited from practicing Buddhism and Buddhist meditation enjoys considerable popularity among Western professionals, Buddhism is largely invisible in UAE's public space.

Several Buddhist groups exist in the Chinese expatriate community in the UAE. Since there is no membership system, it is difficult to know the exact number of followers in these groups, which are often based on provincial origins and operate without clear affiliation with established Buddhist organizations in China and the Chinese diaspora. The participants are loosely connected through social networks. Gatherings usually take place in private homes or Chinese restaurants, where rituals may be performed in collectivity. These Buddhist groups have gained some publicity within the Chinese community in recent years. For example, they organized charitable events to collect donations for Nepal after the earthquake in 2015, and for Syrian refugees. A group of Chinese Buddhists visited Syrian refugee camps in Amman, Jordan to hand over the donations. These activities have helped to create a positive image of Chinese Buddhists in the circle of philanthropists in the UAE. Although these Buddhist groups have little inter-group collaborations, they all hope to establish a Buddhist center in the UAE in the future.

A number of Buddhist sects have also made their inroads into the UAE through Chinese social networks. Combining Buddhist languages and concepts with a variety of folk religious practices, these offshoots of Buddhism are often denounced by mainstream Buddhist organizations as unorthodox, or even cultic. They are part of the New Religious Movements that are syncretic in nature. Facilitated by the Internet and social media, they spread very fast among certain segments of the population. Xinling Famen (心靈法門), or Guan Yin Citta Dharma Door, is such an organization.

A Buddhist sect founded by Juhong Lu (盧軍宏), a Charismatic Chinese Australian who claims to possess the power to read one's totems in heaven,[15] Xinling Famen has attracted allegedly more than seven million followers around the world. The members are predominately immigrant Chinese. Unlike the mainstream Buddhism, Xinling Famen borrows the organizational structure of Protestantism. The worship style at its rallies resembles that of some Pentecostal churches and charismatic healing cults. Master Lu presides large conventions held in major global cities around the world to perform healing miracles in front of hundreds of thousands of followers with their arms stretched out and bursting in tears at the sight of Master Lu. Lu himself is a prominent figure in Australia's Chinese immigrant community. According to various promotional videos posted on youtube, the mission of Xinling Famen is to "promote Chinese culture and the essence of Buddhism, explore the world of Totem and cultivate Confucianism." Followers are instructed to read different combinations of sutras from Buddhist canons printed on papers that can be folded into a "small house." These "small houses" may be downloaded and printed from Master Lu's website. These pages contain different combinations of Buddhist sutras that have been meticulously arranged by Master Lu himself to help the followers to get ride of bad Karma. The practitioners may write down the names of people, to whom they would like to dedicate the "small houses," such as miscarried fetuses, deceased relatives, sick family members and friends, even people who have hurt them before, and people they wish to maintain good relationships with. It is recommended that the followers read as many "small houses" as they can every day. After finishing reading, one must follow prescribed rituals to burn the "small houses" at a Buddhist altar. There is also a long list of specific rules that the practitioners must follow in order to maximize good Karma.

The status of Xinling Famen within Buddhism is highly controversial. It has been criticized for appropriating Buddhist terms to mobilize a cultic movement that involves the worship of a single person – a self-declared reincarnation of Buddha. Master's Lu's divine power to see a person's past, present, and future is called bogus and a complete fabrication. Master Lu, nevertheless, claims his orthodoxy by creating a Buddhist Association of Chinese in Australia and pledges his commitment to spread Buddhism. In the last two decades, Xinling Famen has grown at an astonishing speed despite controversies and criticisms. It has developed a strong foothold in Indonesia and Singapore and has spread to France (Ji 2014).

---

15   Here, totem refers to Chinese zodiac signs, the symbolic animal associated with one's time of birth.

Xinling Famen reached Dubai around the year of 2012 and 2013. Unlike mainstream Buddhism, joining Xinling Famen does not require any training. One does not need to understand the complicated Buddhist philosophy and the how-to tutorials are easy to follow. Members are also encouraged to practice together in collectivity. These characteristics have generated some converts and produced a sense of belonging for new members. The first altar was set up in the home of a Chinese woman in Dubai International City, who later moved the altar to another apartment she rented to accommodate the growing number of believers. When the members complete reading from the "small houses," they visit the altar to burn the papers. These visits often result in social gatherings, where the members bond with each other.

The followers of Xinling Famen in Dubai are well connected to a global network of devotees through the Internet. The global appearance of Xinling Famen and lack of local attachment differentiate Xinling Famen from other Buddhist groups in Dubai. Despite its small size (around twenty members at the time of writing), Xinling Famen is well known among Chinese expatriate community, mostly due to the participation of several individuals who are highly active and well known in Dubai's Chinese community. Followers of Xinling Famen have established more altars in private homes in the last several years. They continue to meet regularly to practice in collectivity. They are also keen to establish a Buddhist center in Dubai. It would be interesting to see if any of the Buddhist groups would eventually dominate the process, or if these Buddhist groups would be able to reconcile the status quo to work together and construct a unified Chinese Buddhist space in the UAE.

6   Folk Religion and Quasi-Religious Spaces

Like their compatriots in China, many Chinese expatriates either do not consider themselves religious, or feel reluctant to identify with any religion. Chinese religions are diffused and difficult to measure based on the standard of monotheistic traditions. A myriad of locally grown beliefs and practices related to the sacred or supernatural experiences across China are often referred to as folk religions. The lack of clear organizational structure and the ambiguous nature of these practices make it much harder to observe and record to what extent folk religions exist in the UAE's Chinese community. In a lavishly staged public celebration of Chinese New Year's Day of 2018 in Downtown Dubai attended by His Highness Sheikh Mohammed Al Maktoum, the ruler of Dubai, and members of the royal family, ministers, and local dignitaries, a large statue of Ma-tsu (媽祖) appeared in the procession. Invited by Fujian

Business Association through an elaborate ritual from a famous Ma-tsu temple in Meizhou (湄洲), the presence of this statue is a clear sign of the existence of folk religions in Dubai's Chinese community.

Taking the advantage of a liberal business culture in the UAE, a variety of spiritual counseling businesses have also found their ways into the Chinese expatriate community. Create Abundance[16] was such an organization that claims to provide fast, effective, and scientific solutions to soul and spiritual growth. Presenting itself as a private club for social networking and personal growth, the "soul coaches" organized lectures, workshops, as well as webinars on a variety of topics, such as how to restore harmonious relationships in marriage and family life, how to make fortune and accumulate wealth, how to improve public relations for business owners, and ultimately how to achieve better health and happiness. All the classes were based on books written by Zhang Xinyue (張馨月), the founder of this organization, who was described as a scholar with double doctoral degrees in economics and psychology and was on study tour around the world to continue learning and pondering on philosophical questions. The books draw on theories and concepts from psychotherapy, teachings of major world religions—particularly Buddhism, as well as metaphysics, offering people who feel trapped in life's vicious cycles a way to connect with positive energy waves transmitted from outer space, to transform life, to make the impossible possible, and to make miracles happen. Until the authority banned it for fraud and illegal operation in 2017, the organization operated private clubs in major cities across China and in global cities in North America, Europe, Australia, and the Middle East. These private clubs were all located in the most expensive neighborhoods in the cities and are decorated exquisitely. Free lectures and workshops were regularly offered to attract a large audience invited through expansive social networks of coaches and existing members. The attendees were then encouraged and persuaded to purchase advanced course packages offered by "soul coaches" of higher ranks and eventually the founder herself. The organization also organized week-long luxurious cruise tours along some of the world's most popular routes, during which the participants would enjoy beautiful scenery, establish new friendships, and attend intensive lectures on soul growth to connect with coaches

---

16   Create Abundance is known as Chuangzao Fengsheng (創造豐盛) in Chinese. It was established in 2002 and banned in 2017. For report on the alleged illegal activities of this organization, see "Wodi Shenxinling Peixun: Lianjie Yuzhou Nengliang? (臥底身心靈培訓：鏈接宇宙能量？)" *Sina News*, April 17, 2016, accessed on Nov. 13, 2017 at http://news.sina.com.cn/c/zg/2016-04-17/doc-ifxriqqx2837457.shtml.

with high-level energies. The cost of these course packages ranged between 10,000 and 500,000 US dollars per person.

Create Abundance opened a private club in a villa located in the expensive Jumeirah district of Dubai in the summer of 2016. The person in charge claimed to be a well-trained spiritual counselor with medical background and a certificate in clinical psychology. The organization did not claim itself as a religious organization, but an organization that promotes scientific methods in helping members to achieve soul development. The organizational structure and recruitment procedure, however, resemble that of cultic groups with a flavor of secrecy. The organizers frequently evoke religious vocabularies and claim to provide ultimate solutions to various problems members experience in personal lives, career development, and businesses. The venture in Dubai had some success at the beginning. By offering free lessons, it recruited several dozens of participants between 2016–2017. Social media apps, videos, and audios are the major tools these soul coaches use to encourage continued participation in paid courses.

Create Abundance may be short lived, however, during my research, I have met with a number of Chinese expatriates who continue to pursue their own spiritual paths. Notably, these individuals are highly educated and often employed in large multinational corporations. Empowered by their professional status, overseas experiences, and language skills, they maintain close contact with the diverse expatriate community in the UAE, which allow them to connect with a variety of alternative healing methods and spirituality other than established religions. In turn, private homes in upper-class neighborhoods have become important spaces for meditation and in some cases, the practice of hypnotherapy.

7   Conclusion: Chinese Religious Spaces in a Cosmopolitan Muslim Society

Human migration and the geographic diffusion of religion have long been closely intertwined. Religion plays an important role in anchoring individuals and communities; whether they are forcefully uprooted from home or voluntarily seek better opportunities away from home. Migration has also strongly shaped religious beliefs, practices, organizational structures, as well as individual religiosity and identity. The diverse religious experiences of Chinese migrants in the UAE are evidently molded by their movement from China – an officially atheist country ruled by the Chinese Communist Party that exercises highly restrictive policies on religion, to the UAE – a Muslim-majority society with an overwhelmingly diverse foreign population and a benevolent sheikhdom that embraces a policy of tolerance.

Followers of religions that are suppressed in China, particularly Christians and Muslims, have highly positive experiences in the UAE. The latter has certainly benefited from living in a Muslim-majority social environment, although the Chinese flavor might fade away gradually given the dominant Islamic teaching in the Gulf region. The Chinese Christian community in the UAE began to take shape in the early 2000s with the influx of Chinese migrants to the region. The rapid growth of Christianity in China and within the Chinese diaspora, coupled with Islam's acknowledgment of Christians as "people of the book," have contributed to the resilience of the Chinese Christine congregations in the UAE. The superior organizational structure and advanced "marketing techniques" of evangelical Christianity backed by the expansive transnational networks of evangelical Christian organizations further enhance the vitality of the Chinese Christian community in the UAE.

Through their participations in religious activities or events, Chinese expatriates in the UAE also help to enrich the religious lives in a society that has acquired certain cosmopolitan characteristics. The activities of Chinese Muslim communities have created different types of Chinese Islamic spaces, from traditional ethnic businesses to cultural venues. The introduction of distinctive Chinese Islamic artistic forms, such as Chinese Islamic calligraphy, has stimulated much interest in China's Islamic legacy and facilitated cross-civilizational dialogues.

The presence of Buddhism, folk religions, and controversial quasi-religious phenomena within the Chinese community in the UAE poses some challenges to UAE's model of religious affairs management. Despite its enthusiasm to embrace religious pluralism, the status of polytheism and NRMs are largely unmentioned in public discourses. The framework of cultural diversity may provide a possible solution to the status of these non-monotheistic beliefs and practices in Muslim societies. However, more studies are needed to address the theological gap and to guide public policies.

The Chinese government is particularly concerned with NRMs, given the precedence of Falun Gong. While many NRMs have been banned in China, some of these groups have flourished in transnational spaces that the Chinese state is less likely to penetrate. Quasi-religious organizations may in fact face fewer obstacles in the UAE, since its guise as business entities rather than religious organizations. Yet, in the case of Create Abundance, the ban in China has clearly led to its demise in overseas Chinese communities.

Probably the most important issue that has emerged from the discussion is the growing influence of Chinese state in overseas Chinese communities, evident in the case of Uyghurs. While Chinese Muslims have enjoyed greater religious freedom living in a Muslim-majority country, Chinese state agencies have maintained its tight control of ethno-religious minorities – as long as they retain Chinese passports. The fact that the UAE and China have established close collaborations on all fronts, especially in the aspects of territorial integrity, security, and the fight against terrorism,[17] means that the Chinese government will have control over its overseas Chinese communities to a great extent.

References

Ali, Sayed. 2010. "Permanent Impermanence," *Contexts* 9(2): 26-31.
Ali, Sayed. 2000. *Dubai: Gilded Cage*. New Haven: Yale University Press.
Chen, Carolyn. 2002. "The Religious Varieties of Ethnic Presence: A Comparison Between a Taiwanese Immigrant Buddhist Temple and an Evangelical Christian Church," *Sociology of Religion* 63(2): 215–238.
Emon, Anver M. 2012. *Religious Pluralism and Islamic Law: Dhimmis and Others in the Empire of Law*. Oxford, UK: Oxford University Press.
Esposito, John. 1997. *Political Islam: Revolution, Radicalism, or Reform?* Boulder, CO: Lynne Rienner Publishers, Inc.
Gardner, Andrew M. 2010. *City of Strangers: Gulf Migration and the Indian Community in Bahrain*. Ithaca, NY: Cornell University.
Ji, Zhe. 2014. "Buddhist Groups among Chinese Immigrants in France: The Patterns of Religious Globalization," *Review of Religion and Chinese Society* 1: 213–235.
Kamrava, Mehran and Zahra Babar (eds). 2012. *Migrant Labor in the Persian Gulf*. London: Hurst & Company.
Kapiszewski, Andrzej. 2001. *Nationals and Expatriates: Population and Labor Dilemmas of the Gulf Cooperation Council States*. Reading: Ithaca Press.
Longva, Anh Nga. 1997. *Walls Built on Sand: Migration, Exclusion and Society in Kuwait*. Boulder, CO: Westview.
MacMillan, Arthur. 2019. "UAE Vision of Interfaith Harmony Takes Shape in Abrahamic House of Fraternity," *The National*, Sept. 21. Accessed on Dec. 10, 2019 at https://www.thenational.ae/uae/uae-vision-of-interfaith-harmony-takes-shape-in-abrahamic-house-of-fraternity-1.912931.

---

17   Wam, "UAE, China issue joint statement on 10-point comprehensive strategic partnership," *Khaleej Times*, July 21, 2018, accessed on Dec. 13, 2019 at https://www.khaleejtimes.com/nation/uae-china-week/uae-china-issue-joint-statement-for-comprehensive-strategic-partnership.

Majumdar, Samirah. 2019. "Recent Chinese Dealings with Faith Groups Reflect a Pattern of Government Restrictions on Religion," *Pew Research Center Fact Tank*, Oct. 11. Accessed on Dec. 13, 2019 at https://www.pewresearch.org/fact-tank/2018/10/11/recent-chinese-dealings-with-faith-groups-reflect-a-pattern-of-government-restrictions-on-religion/.

Mandaville, Peter. 2007. *Global Political Islam*. London and New York: Routledge.

Thomas, George. 2009. "Dubai: A Spiritual Oasis," *CBN News*, Dec. 9, 2009. Accessed on April 5, 2017 at http://www.cbn.com/cbnnews/world/2009/may/dubai-a-spiritual-oasis-/?mobile=false.

Thompson, Andrew (ed). 2019. *Celebrating Tolerance: Religious Diversity in the United Arab Emirates*. Dubai, Abu Dhabi and London: Motivate Publishing.

Wang, Gungwu. 1991. *China and the Chinese Overseas*. Singapore: Times Academic Press.

Wang, Yuting. 2020. "Being Chinese Muslims in Dubai: Religion and Nationalism in a Transnational Space," Middle East Center Paper Series (33), LSE Middle East Center.

Wang, Yuting. 2018. "The Making of China's 'Good Muslims': From Middleman Minority to Cultural Entrepreneurs," *The China Review* 18(4): 131–154.

Winckler, Onn. 1997. "The Immigration Policy of the Gulf Cooperation Council (GCC) States," *Middle Eastern Studies* 33(3): 480–98.

Yang, C.K. 1961. *Religion in Chinese Society: A study of Contemporary Social Functions of Religion and Some of Their Historical Factors*. Berkeley, CA: University of California Press.

Yang, Fenggang and Andrew Abel, 2014. "Sociology of Religious Conversion," pp. 140–163 in *The Oxford Handbook of Religious Conversion*, edited by Lewis R. Rambo and Charles E. Farhadian. New York, NY: Oxford University Press, p. 142.

CHAPTER 14

Chinese Muslim Diaspora Communities and the Role of International Islamic Education Networks
A Case Study of Dubai

Jacqueline Armijo and Shaojin Chai

1   Introduction[1]

On Friday, July 13, 2018, Imam Han officially inaugurated the first Chinese Muslim diaspora mosque in the Middle East, and perhaps the first of its kind in the world. The Chinese Muslim community of Dubai is currently estimated to number around 10,000 and is made up of primarily Hui, as well as Uyghurs, and Han Chinese who have converted to Islam. The *khutbah* (sermon) was delivered in Arabic, English, and Chinese, and those who attended the service were a reflection of the cosmopolitan nature of Dubai's international residents. As one Chinese who took part reported, the mosque overflowed with Muslims from "all directions". Located in "International City" an extensive housing development established in 2005, the mosque immediately became both the religious and social center to the rapidly growing Chinese Muslim population of Dubai, as well as the local neighborhood mosque attracting a range of foreigners, most from South Asian countries (primarily Pakistan, Afghanistan, and Bangladesh).

The mosque, known as the Hua Fang Mosque in Chinese, 华坊清真寺, *Huafang Qingzhensi*, was the culmination of many years of intensive work by the Chinese Muslim community of Dubai as a whole, but also one man in particular: Imam Han. Originally from Qinghai Province in northwest China, Han's journey to Dubai was almost as unlikely as the establishment of the

---

1   This chapter will focus on the Hui community of Dubai. Over the past few years, most Uyghur residents of Dubai have left, either returning to China when their Chinese passports were not renewed, or at the request of Chinese authorities. Some have sought asylum in other countries, most notably Turkey. In addition, except when discussing public figures, individuals' real names are not used. Recent events in China have led to the development of surveillance activities being carried out among Chinese Muslim diaspora communities around the world.

mosque itself and reflects the crucial role played by traditional Chinese Islamic networks of religious education and Dubai's increasingly important role as both a major trading partner of Dubai, but also a key transportation hub in China's massive Belt and Road Initiative (BRI).

Over the past 15 years China-Dubai economic and trade relations have increased dramatically. China surpassed both the U.S. and the E.U. to become Dubai's most important trading partner, with total trade expected to reach $70 billion in 2020. China has also become a major investor in Dubai real estate, as well as transport facilities. The number of Chinese tourists increased from an estimated 150,000 in 2015 to almost one million in 2019. Not surprisingly there has also been a several fold increase in the number of Chinese residents in Dubai, from an estimated 20–30,000 in 2006 to over a quarter of a million in 2019. Although in the early days, many of the Chinese working in Dubai were construction workers, these days most are shop owners, businesspeople, professionals in a range of fields, and students. Within this growing community of Chinese there has been a steady growth in the number of Chinese Muslims.

This chapter focuses on the Chinese Muslim community of Dubai, both the Hui community, as well as the growing number of Han Chinese who have converted to Islam. Special attention is given to the role of international Islamic education networks in facilitating migration to Dubai. The research for this chapter is based primarily on interviews carried out with Chinese Muslim residents in Dubai between 2008 and 2020, and also builds on earlier interviews carried out with Hui students studying at Islamic schools in China and overseas. Beginning with a brief overview of the history of Islam in China, the chapter then discusses the development of Islamic education in China and the role of networks in sustaining this body of religious knowledge as well as Muslim communities in China over the past millennium. The focus will then switch to the rapid development of Dubai into the world's most globalized city. The role of Dragon Mart in facilitating the influx of first Han Chinese and later Hui will be examined, followed by a discussion of different dimensions of the lives of Chinese Muslims in Dubai, and the potential impact of the growing number of converts and transnational marriages creating a new hybrid international Chinese identity.

2   Islam in China – a Brief Historical Overview

China's Muslim population today is conservatively estimated to number over 20 million. Although concentrated in northwest China, Muslim communities can be found throughout China, in every province and every major city

(Gladney 1996:27). Of China's 55 officially recognized minority peoples, ten are historically Muslim. The two largest groups are the Hui, who are spread throughout China, and the Uyghurs who primarily live in their historic homeland in present-day Xinjiang in northwest China.

The Hui are the descendants of the Muslim traders, craftsmen, officials, scientists, engineers, and soldiers who began settling in China from the earliest days of Islam. Beginning in the Tang Dynasty (618–907) the first communities of Muslims to settle in China were traders who traveled along the overland and maritime Silk Routes. Those who traveled by land were primarily from the Middle East and Central Asia and established communities in Chang'an (present-day Xi'an). Those who traveled by sea were mostly from the Persian Gulf region, and established communities first in Guangzhou and later in Quanzhou along China's southeastern coast. In both of these regions, the foreign Muslim traders (as was the case with all foreign traders) lived in districts set aside for them, known as *fanfang* 蕃坊, or foreigners' quarters. It was not until 1998, with the discovery of an early 9th century shipwreck off the coast Indonesia, that the extent of this early trading network became evident. The ship, a *dhow*, originating in the Persian Gulf, was headed back home with tens of thousands of goods from China, primarily pottery and porcelain. The small ship, measuring only 60 feet in length, had over 70,000 objects neatly stacked in large ceramic urns, that were then stowed in layers of rows along the bottom of the ship. Analysis of the pottery, most of which survived intact, showed that these custom-designed mass-produced objects had been made in kilns from several different regions of China, for markets across the Persian Gulf region (Krahl 2010).

It was in the Mongol Yuan Dynasty (1279–1368) that hundreds of thousands of Muslims from the Middle East and Central Asia were recruited, as well as forcibly relocated, by the Mongols to China to help them establish, control, and develop their new empire. During this period, the Mongol Yuan emperors dispatched craftsmen to wherever they were needed in the empire and posted Muslim civil servants to government positions throughout China (Rossabi 1981).

The Mongol court also promoted and made major investments in trade across China, as well as Asia. Muslim traders were in a position to benefit from these investments, which they used to more fully develop their trade routes, thus expanding land and maritime Silk Routes. As these long-distance trade networks became even more entrenched, an ancillary development was the creation of trading posts that included inns and restaurants that met the needs of Muslim travelers. As A.D.W. Forbes explains, these early networks influenced the development of Muslim communities across China: "China's Hui Muslim population has long been associated with caravan commerce and related 'service' industries such as the provision of inns, *caravanserai*, *halal* restaurants, butchers, etc., and the nuclei of many Hui settlements from Sinkiang [Xinjiang] in the north-west to Heilungkiang [Heilongjiang] in the far north-east have formed around caravan termini, to be followed in the fullness of time by Hui women and children, mosque, *madrasa* and *imam*" (Forbes 1987:4).

3 Acculturation and the Development of Indigenous Islamic Education Systems

With the establishment of the Ming Dynasty in 1368, the Chinese empire was once again ruled by ethnic Han Chinese. Foreigners who had settled in China were allowed to stay, but in an effort to reclaim the empire's traditional Chinese cultural identity, foreign residents were expected to adopt Chinese names, dress in traditional Chinese clothing styles, and learn to speak Chinese. Many, if not most of the Muslim residents were already well acculturated, and there is no historical evidence of any resistance on their part to these new directives. If anything, in some respects, efforts to acculturate had been too successful. As more and more prominent Chinese Muslim families adopted elite traditional Chinese values and ambitions surrounding a classical education in preparation for taking the imperial civil and military service exams, fluency in Arabic and Persian began to wane.

Some Muslim religious scholars voiced concern that the loss of these languages used in religious texts would weaken communities' ability to sustain their faith. In response to this growing concern, a group of Chinese Muslim scholars who were fully versed in both the Chinese Confucian Classics, as well as Islamic religious texts, set about writing a series of works in Chinese on Islam and Islamic thought. Eventually these works were compiled into a collection that became known as the *Han Kitab* (*Han*, referring to the Chinese language, *kitab* being the Arabic word for book). James Frankel has described this process as follows: "These writings reflect a tacit attempt by the Chinese Muslim literati to portray themselves, their community and their faith as 'orthodox' in both Islamic and Confucian terms. Their purpose was to educate readers, both Sinicized Muslims and curious non-Muslim literati, about Islam. That they did so in the language of Neo-Confucianism reflects their dual heritage and history, in other words their 'simultaneity'." (Frankel 2008:425)

It was also during this time that Muslim scholars developed words in Chinese to represent important Islamic religious terms: Islam became known as

Qingzhen jiao 清真教 (the pure and true religion), God was known as *Zhenzhu* 真主 (the true lord), the Prophet Mohammed was referred to as a *shengren* 圣人(sage), and mosques became known as *qingzhensi* 清真寺, or temples of the pure and true.

The project to revive Islamic education in China proved effective, with texts from the *Han Kitab* used to develop curricula for Islamic schools across the country. Chinese Muslim religious teachers traveled to different regions to establish new schools and introduce the curriculum. As certain teachers became especially popular, students from different areas would travel to study with them. These education networks overlapped with the trade networks that crisscrossed China and were often dominated by Chinese Muslims. One of the results of this constant stream of Chinese Muslim traders, students, and teachers across networks linking communities across China, was that Chinese Muslims were in general well informed about what was happening in Muslim communities around the country, and therefore throughout China in general (Ben-Dor Benite 2005).

The establishment of the Qing Dynasty in 1644, resulted in "foreigners" once again ruling China. Unlike the Ming emperors who had developed strong policies isolating China from the rest of the world, the Manchu emperors sought to expand their new empire, thus reopening formerly closed trade and travel routes. Chinese Muslims who had been tied off from the Islamic heartland soon began traveling to the Middle East on pilgrimage and to study. Some Muslims who studied overseas brought back with them what they thought of as more authentic religious practices. As religious communities became divided and conflicts ensued, military intervention on the part of the state eventually led to major uprisings. Rebellions in the northwest led to the death and displacement of millions, with tens of thousands of Chinese Muslims fleeing to Czarist Russia (present day Kazakhstan, Kyrgyzstan, and Uzbekistan)(Lipman 1997). In southwest China, the influx of large numbers of Han Chinese settlers into what had been a frontier region led to conflicts over natural resources and property with local inhabitants, many of whom were Hui who had settled there in the Yuan Dynasty. A major multi-ethnic rebellion led by Du Wenxiu broke out (1856–1873), and in its aftermath, of the Hui who survived the government led massacres, many fled to neighboring Laos, Burma, and Thailand (Atwill 2005).

The next wave of Chinese Muslims to leave China occurred in the aftermath of the establishment of the People's Republic of China. Most of the Chinese Muslims who fled during this period had close ties with the defeated Nationalist government. Some fled to neighboring regions, especially in southwest China, but most fled to Taiwan, especially those in leadership positions (Cieciura

2018). In addition, a small but influential group were able to make their way to Saudi Arabia, where many of their descendants still live (Jeong 2016).

Initially, it appeared that the government would fulfill their promise of guaranteeing religious freedom. However, it was not long before political campaigns began first restricting (during the Anti-Rightist campaign that began in 1958) and then attacking religious practices. During the chaotic period of the Cultural Revolution (1966–1976) Chinese Muslims (together with all religious communities) experienced widespread intense and violent persecution. All forms of religious practice were strictly forbidden and all mosques (except for the one used by foreign Muslim diplomats in Beijing), were confiscated by local governments, severely damaged, and in some cases destroyed. Muslims were punished for any actions seen as religious, and often forced to take part in practices deliberately meant to offend and ritually pollute. These policies included forcing Muslims to raise pigs in their homes and mosques, and eat pork. Religious leaders were especially vulnerable to violent attacks by Red Guards (Armijo 2008).

In the years immediately following the Cultural Revolution, the Muslims of China lost no time in rebuilding their devastated communities. Their first priority was to rebuild their damaged mosques, thereby creating a space where Muslims could once again pray together as a community. Mosques also soon reasserted their roles as centers of Islamic learning. During this period wealthier Muslim communities (usually those in larger cities) began to make donations to more impoverished Muslim communities (usually in more remote villages) so that mosques could be repaired and imams hired.

Over the past 30 years, throughout all of China (except Xinjiang), most mosques have organized classes in Islamic and Arabic studies for all members of the community: from pre-school children to retirees. They have also revived and developed comprehensive Islamic studies degree programs that include the study of Arabic, Qur'an, Hadith, Islamic law, Chinese language and history, and more recently the history of Islam in China (Armijo 2009). According to government estimates, as of 2003 there were 35,000 mosques in China, 45,000 Muslim teachers, and 24,000 full-time students studying in private and government Islamic schools. (*People's Daily* 2003)

Around the same time, news was spreading throughout these communities of opportunities to study at Islamic colleges overseas. Initially, small groups of students set off for Abu Nur in Damascus, Syria, the International Islamic University in Islamabad, Pakistan, Madina University in Saudi Arabia, and Al Azhar in Cairo, Egypt. These early students, who were from different regions of China, encouraged both friends and family to join them. In addition, students began traveling to Indonesia, Iran, Malaysia, the Sudan, and Turkey (especially

Uyghur students, who speak a Turkic dialect). Many of the students married other students, often from different regions of China, further developing the networks amongst different Muslim communities in China.

Between 1998 and 2005 Armijo interviewed dozens of Hui students studying at Islamic universities in Damascus and Cairo, as well as those who had studied in Pakistan, Malaysia, Saudi Arabia, and Iran, after they had returned to China. Students were overwhelmingly positive about their experiences studying overseas. For these early groups of students, who remembered the hardships faced by Muslims during the Cultural Revolution, being able to live some place where they could fully practice their religion without any concerns, was an extraordinary experience.

Over the past twenty years Chinese Muslim diaspora communities have begun to appear in centers of Islamic learning, including Malaysia, Indonesia, Pakistan, Egypt, Saudi Arabia, and Syria (that is until the recent outbreak of the civil war there). Each of these communities has their own history and has faced their own challenges. In some cases, the Chinese Muslim students became part of earlier Hui diaspora communities that had developed during the different waves of Muslims that had fled China in the past. At this point in time however, the fastest growing Chinese Muslim diaspora community is in Dubai. What is interesting about the community in Dubai is that its development is quite different than the others. First, the UAE has never been a major center of Islamic learning, and second, as relatively young country (established in 1971) that only recently began to develop, in the past it had not been a place to seek a safe haven. So, the question arises, why have so many Chinese Muslims made their way to Dubai?

4 Dubai – the World's Most International City

Despite having a fraction of the land and natural resources of Abu Dhabi, the largest of the seven emirates that make up the UAE and the site of the nation's capital, Dubai has a larger and more diverse population, with residents hailing from more than 200 countries. With a total population of 10 million, and more than 85% of them being foreign born, the UAE has the highest net immigration rate in the world. Of the more than 8.5 million foreign residents, approximately 5.5 million come from the South Asian countries of India, Bangladesh, and Pakistan. (United Nations 2019)

The UAE's high rate of migrant workers dates back to the 1970s when the country began to develop with earnings from its oil and liquefied natural gas (LNG) resources. Initially most migrant workers came from other Arab countries, but by the late 1970s workers from South Asia formed the largest group. Over the next several decades, as the UAE in general, and Dubai in particular, diversified their economy and sought to develop themselves as both a trade and transportation hub, as well as a center for international business, the city attracted an extensive range of professionals from around the world.

Dubai is a city with not one culture, but many. Further complicating Dubai's multi-dimensional identity is the fact that of the millions of foreigners living there, only a very small handful have even a possibility of ever attaining citizenship. These restrictions regarding both citizenship, as well as permanent residency, however, do not appear to have in any way impeded the continuous flow of workers to the region. And although certain professionals are allowed to bring their families with them, their family must leave with them as soon as their work-based residence permit expires.[2]

The larger ex-pat communities have their own schools, as well as their own social clubs. What is not allowed or encouraged is any form of social or political activism. Churches for example, as well as temples, play important roles in many international communities, but proselytization efforts, at least among the local population, are not allowed. In addition to Shi'a and Ismaili mosques, there are Catholic, Protestant, Evangelical, Mormon, Greek and Coptic Orthodox churches, as well as Sikh and Hindu temples.

5 Dragon Mart – Where the World, or at Least the Gulf Shops

As was the case with many of the earlier waves of migrant workers from South Asia, most of the Chinese who first arrived in the late 1970s and early 1980s, were construction workers working for foreign companies. Several decades later, as Chinese construction companies began to work on major infrastructure projects in the UAE more Chinese workers arrived, including significant numbers of engineers and construction managers. More recently, however, Chinese construction companies have begun using lower salaried workers from other

---

[2] In 2019, the UAE introduced 5 and 10-year renewable residency programs for long-term residents who had already made significant contributions to the development of the country, as well as more recent residents who showed great promise. Although quite different than granting permanent residency, and still limited to only a few thousand being granted every year, the initiative was warmly received. Faisal Masudi, "UAE Golden Visa Gives Expats Security, Says Top Official," Gulf News [UAE], 5 February 2020. For a close study of the history of Dubai's Indian community, see Neha Vora's *Impossible Citizens: Dubai's Indian Diaspora*. Durham: Duke University Press, 2013.

countries. These days, many Chinese residents of Dubai are businesspeople, professionals from a range of industries, service sector and hospitality industry workers, and store owners. There are over 4,000 Chinese companies based in the UAE. The largest concentration of Chinese businesses is in Dragon Mart.

Today, once again, ships laden with rows and rows of containers filled to the brim with custom-made goods for different Middle Eastern markets are leaving China's ports and retracing the maritime Silk Route back to the Gulf. Many of these goods are headed to Dragon Mart, just outside Dubai, the largest Chinese retail center outside of China. Built in 2004 as a joint venture between Nakheel, the Dubai government's property development corporation and China's state-owned Chinamex Corporation, Dragon Mart rapidly gained customers from throughout the Gulf, the Middle East and Africa. In 2010 there were an estimated 20,000 visitors every day, and by 2019 the number had risen to 120,000, a five-fold increase. (*The National*, 5 February 2019)

Over three quarters of a mile in length, with nearly 4,000 vendors, Dragon Mart attracts both retail and wholesale customers with a dizzying array of goods: from furniture, cosmetics, construction machinery, bathroom and lighting fixtures, office supplies and traditional Chinese ceramics to *shishas* (hookas), and traditional Arab clothing. It is estimated that over a million different types of goods are sold at Dragon Mart, and that every year close to 2 million customers visit, spending billions of dollars.

6 Growing Presence of Chinese Muslims in Dubai

When Dragon Mart first opened in 2004, there were very few if any Chinese Muslims working there. However, over the next ten years the number of Chinese Muslims began to grow. When interviewed in 2013, several of them estimated that now as much as 25 percent of the workers were Chinese Muslims, primarily Hui with about 10% being Uyghurs from northwest China. Most of those interviewed had spent some time studying Arabic overseas, or at one of the many independent Islamic schools spread throughout China. Unlike the Han Chinese who, as is the case with most Chinese diaspora communities around the world, come predominantly from eastern coastal cities such as Wenzhou, the Hui come from different communities throughout China. But like the Han Chinese, many had either followed family members to Dubai, or persuaded them to join them there.

One of the first Hui that Armijo interviewed was Yusuf. Like many other Hui in Dragon Mart, he had first studied Arabic in China. He continued his Islamic education in Pakistan, and subsequently decided to try his luck doing business in the UAE. He worked there for several years before deciding to open a kiosk in Dragon Mart, where he sells traditional Chinese medical herbs.[3] During a later visit in October 2015, it was clear his small business had continued to prosper as a constant flow of customers approached him. In his particular line of business, the complex nature of traditional Chinese medicine required a high level of Arabic. Most Chinese merchants at Dragon Mart have very limited knowledge of Arabic, and a calculator serves as their main form of communication.

All the Chinese Muslims interviewed were positive about their experience in Dubai and appreciated the opportunity to live and do business in a Muslim country where they were allowed to freely and conveniently practice their religion. In many respects their descriptions of the benefits of living in a Muslim country echoed those of the Chinese Muslim students interviewed years earlier. But for the Chinese Muslims living in Dubai today, although they understand the possibility of permanent residency is almost non-existent, they do hope to live there for the near future and, if possible, convince friends and family to join them there. Many had already convinced their parents to move to Dubai, or at least spend a good portion of each year living there, to help take care of their grandchildren.

Unlike in certain Muslim majority countries, such as Indonesia or Malaysia (Hew 2018), there is no dominant local negative view of Chinese. In Dubai, the Chinese community as a whole is just one of several dozen large ex-pat communities. And although there is some negative stereotyping of Chinese, due to their prominent role in massage parlors and certain other illegal activities, the overall view of Chinese is either neutral or positive. Chinese Muslims, however, are generally viewed positively by local Muslims as they are seen as co-religionists, and by Han Chinese as they are seen as useful middlemen for both business and cultural interactions. In interviews, Hui Muslims generally say they feel respected by locals, and that the Han Chinese tend to treat them better there, than back in China.

One of the interesting developments associated with the growing number of Chinese Muslims working at Dragon Mart is the opening of several Chinese Muslim restaurants nearby in International City (a huge residential development with over 100,000 residents). As of February 2020, there were a dozen

---

3 Traditional Chinese Medicine is popular throughout the region, with small clinics found across the Gulf. Moxibustion, or cupping, known as *hijama* in Arabia, is especially popular as it is a practice associated with the Prophet Muhammad. In 2011, Tong Ren Tang 同仁堂, China's largest manufacturer of traditional medicine, opened a clinic and pharmacy in Dubai's Health Care City. China has also incorporated Traditional Chinese Medicine as part of the cultural and scientific exchange dimension of the Belt and Road Initiative.

different halal Chinese restaurants, most run by Hui from northwest China (primarily Qinghai, Gansu, Ningxia, and Xinjiang). In the past there were a few run by Uyghurs, but most of these have since closed or changed hands, as most Uyghurs have had to leave the UAE. These restaurants serve as both informal meeting places for Chinese Muslims and also provide job opportunities for the community. They have also proven quite popular, not only with Chinese Muslims, but with Han Chinese, locals, South Asians, and other foreign communities. Due to the increasing number of non-Chinese customers, and the relatively higher salaries demanded by Chinese Muslim workers, many of the restaurants have begun to hire English-speaking waiters from countries such as Pakistan, India, and Bangladesh.

7 The Role of Islamic Education Networks

Despite their relatively recent arrival, and the fact that they hail from different regions of China, the Chinese Muslims (both Hui and Han converts) of Dubai have managed to create a strong sense of community supported by several community centers and independent schools. In interviews carried out across several years, it became clear that it was primarily the Hui who had studied in Islamic colleges overseas who were the most prominent and active supporters of community projects.

Among the different foreign Islamic colleges that most Hui currently living in Dubai have graduated from are: Abu Nur in Damascus, Al Azhar in Cairo, the International Institute of Islamic Studies in Islamabad, and Madina University in Saudi Arabia. Other less well represented universities include ones in Indonesia, Malaysia, the Sudan, the UAE, Jordan, Libya, and Tunisia. Of those who settled in Dubai 15 to 20 years ago, many found professional jobs working as interpreters and translators; in some cases for different government offices, in others for private companies. Their contacts with government officials and business owners allowed them to gain a better understanding of the local society, which they often used to assist friends and relatives to move to Dubai. Others ended up working in small local businesses, or started ones of their own. Restaurants continue to be a popular business venture, and more recently with the huge influx of Chinese tourists to the region, several travel agencies geared towards them have been established, with a few that focus on what is now known has 'halal tourism'. In the past, most Chinese Muslims who traveled to Dubai were on their way to Saudi for the hajj pilgrimage, however, these days Dubai has become an increasingly popular tourist destination for Chinese Muslims.

One of the largest and most active groups of Islamic university graduates are the ones who studied at Abu Nur Islamic Institute in Damascus. Established by the Grand Mufti of Syria, Shaikh Ahmad Kaftaru, who was also the leader of Syria's large Naqshbandi Sufi Order, this particular Islamic college is known for being relatively progressive and inclusive. A favorite expression of Kaftaru was a reminder to his students "to be a doctor, not a lawyer," or in other words, the importance of caring for people, rather than arguing over laws and legal interpretations. Under the leadership of Shaikh Kaftaru (who died in 2004), Abu Nur attracted thousands of Muslims students from around the world. The Hui and Uyghur students who studied there were able to interact with Muslims from an wide range of backgrounds. Many were from the former Soviet Republics, and thus also familiar with living under restrictive government policies, and there were also students from across the Middle East, Europe, Southeast Asia, and different regions of Africa. It should not be surprising that so many of these students ended up in Dubai after graduating. In Dubai they found another Muslim society that was welcoming of both foreigners and Muslims from different traditions.

The path some had taken to Dubai was quite direct, whereas others had taken a more scenic route. One woman, for example, a Hui originally from central China, had first spent two years traveling to different regions of China to visit as many Islamic girls' schools as possible. She wanted to document best practices in different schools in order to develop a better understanding of the needs of Muslim girls in China, and the best way to meet them. What turned out to be her final stop was a famous girls' school in Yunnan Province in southwest China. There she met and married a local Hui and they subsequently decided to pursue advanced Islamic studies overseas. They both were accepted into a program at Al Azhar in Cairo and studied there for about ten years. When it came time to leave, Dubai came up as a good possible place to get jobs and a good environment to raise their children. When interviewed in 2015, at the small multi-lingual preschool she had opened in the China section of International City, Mariam spoke of the satisfaction she had from providing local Chinese and Muslim children lessons in Chinese, Arabic, and English. The teachers at the school were a mix of Chinese, Filipino, and Arab, and the students were from a range of backgrounds, including several who were mixed. As Mariam described the different children in her school, she made a point of identifying those that were from mixed families. She pointed out a young girl who had a Hui mother and a Somali father, noting how exceptionally beautiful she was. Her comments were striking as they revealed not simply an acceptance of mixed marriages, but a view of them as a positive development in Dubai's growing Chinese community.

Like almost all those interviewed, Mariam spoke very positively about her life in Dubai, and although clearly exhausted from running the language school, was quite content to stay there as long as possible. To her mind the only downside to living in Dubai was making sure that her children kept up their Chinese, but by starting the pre-school, she had helped address that problem.

Another Chinese Muslim who had studied overseas was a woman interviewed while working in the Islamic Cultural Center inside Dragon Mart. The center provides Arabic lessons and Islamic studies classes to the large number of Chinese and non-Chinese who work at Dragon Mart. When interviewed she had only been in Dubai a few months, having just graduated with a degree in Arabic literature from Al Azhar. She spoke very positively about life in Dubai, and her work at the center. She also made the observation that judging from what she had seen in terms of the number of conversions to Islam by Han Chinese, she speculated that in a few years most of the Chinese Muslims in Dubai might well be converts. And although no one else interviewed in Dubai made a similar claim, her comment does speak to the surprising number of conversions among the Han Chinese community.

8   Role of Converts

Throughout the history of Islam in China there was no significant history of Muslims actively proselytizing. Even when Chinese Muslim scholars developed the *Han Kitab* texts, although their audience was in part the Han Chinese Confucian elite, they were not seeking to spread their religion. As Frankel explains, their goal was rather to persuade the Confucian scholars of "Islam's compatibility with Chinese cultural norms to assuage any concerns that Muslims posed a threat to the Confucian social order" (Frankel 2017:501).

The two most common ways that Muslim communities increased their numbers (in addition to normal demographic growth) was through marriages, and through the adoption of children abandoned or sold by Han Chinese families. In the case of marriages, which were usually between Muslim men and local women, although the wife didn't necessarily have to convert, it was understood that the children would be raised as Muslim. While not encouraged in traditional Chinese society, the abandonment of babies and young children, especially girls during periods of extreme deprivation such as famine, was common. When possible, Muslim communities were known to adopt these children and raise them as family (Gladney 1996; Broomhall 1910). This willingness to incorporate the children of strangers into their families reflects both Islamic values regarding the importance of taking care of orphans, but also a flexibility and inclusiveness not found in many societies, and especially unusual in China where paternal lineage was, and to a certain extent continues to be, a cornerstone of filial piety and ancestor worship.

Despite the absence of any tradition of proselytization, over the past twenty years there has been a growing number of cases of Han Chinese (as well as other nationality groups in China) converting to Islam. Beginning in the 1980s as mosques around the country were once again allowed to offer classes in Arabic and Islamic studies young Han Chinese started to join these classes. Some had known that in the past their families had been Muslim, but had abandoned their faith, others had only just found out. As one imam in Kunming explained, these young people mostly showed up hoping to learn about their family's lost traditions, not necessarily with an interest in conversion.

The first time Armijo ever heard of Han Chinese without any familial connection to Islam converting was during fieldwork in a remote impoverished region of Yunnan province in the late 1990s. While interviewing female students at a village Islamic school she was approached by two girls who told her they were converts. The phrase they used was "*women shi jinjiaode* 我们是进教的," "we are those who have entered the religion."[4] They were both from poor families and had Hui neighbors who had treated them kindly and encouraged them to get an education. As even government schools, although technically free, now have increasingly onerous "fees", throughout China, especially in poor rural areas, young girls are less and less likely to be able to attend, let alone finish primary school. In this case the girls had decided to attend the local Islamic girls' school, which did not have fees, and later converted to Islam.

More recently however, it appears that conversions of Han Chinese from a range of backgrounds, are happening across China. At present there are only two known articles that focus on converts to Islam in China. One is a survey carried out by Ma Qiang (2013) of 71 converts from 25 provinces, Hong Kong, and Taiwan. The other is a close analysis of seven converts in Qinghai province interviewed by Alexander Stewart (2016).

Just as the term for converts has evolved over the past twenty or thirty years (see footnote 4), so has the term for Chinese Muslim. In the past the term *Hui* 回 was used to describe not just someone's ethnicity, but in fact their religion. For example, while carrying out research among the Hui in the 1980s and 1990s Armijo was

---

4 Over time different terms have been used to refer to Muslim converts in China. After *jinjiao*, other terms including, *xin Musilin* 新穆斯林 (new Muslim) and *Musilin Huaren* 穆斯林华人 (Muslim Chinese) began to be used. More recently in Northwest China the term *guixin* 归信 (return to faith/belief) is used. Currently in Dubai the most often used term is *guiyi* 皈依 (originally used primarily to refer to conversion to Buddhism), which is also written as *guiyi* 归依.

frequently asked, "Ni shi Meiguo Huizu ma?" 你是美国回族吗? (Are you an American Hui?) It was only after 2000 that one heard people ask if someone who was Hui, was *also* Muslim. Stewart noticed the changing dynamic of religious identity among Xining Muslims and noted that this "growing rejection of passive, inherited ethnic religiosity in favor of choosing and pursuing religious identity, and this atmosphere of religious fervor has helped arouse the curiosity of some members of the Han and other non-Muslim ethnicities as well." (Stewart 2016:205)

While reasons for their conversion varied widely, one observation made by both authors is that the converts, like converts the world over, were generally more disciplined when it came to the orthopraxy of their new religion. A few voiced disappointment in the somewhat lax approach taken by some of their co-religionists who had been born into the faith. Although most of the converts had first had regular interaction with Chinese Muslims, some had not, and became active in on-line forums developed for and by Han Chinese converts. Perhaps most interesting, both authors noted that for many of the converts one of the attractions of Islam was that it represented a cosmopolitan and inclusive ideology found around the world. Stewart concludes that for these converts, "conversion to Islam can be seen as compatible with, or even the product of, modern trends of increasing rationality, individual agency, and transnational identity" (Stewart 2016:201).

Dubai is not the only place where Chinese are converting to Islam. Research by Hew Wai Weng in both Indonesia and Malaysia has documented different reasons why individual Chinese have decided to convert to Islam. In the past, both of these countries have experienced periods of extreme anti-Chinese prejudice, including race riots. The Chinese and Indonesian, or Malay identities are generally considered almost mutually exclusive. Nevertheless, Chinese from a range of backgrounds are converting to Islam. The conversions upend longstanding ethnic/religious characterizations thus enhancing their significance. Converting to Islam no longer necessitates completely abandoning traditional Chinese values and practices, and by accepting Chinese converts, Islam in Indonesia is seen as being more cosmopolitan and transnational (Hew 2018).

Given the rise of Chinese converts in China, as well as among overseas Chinese communities, that the phenomenon should also be found in Dubai, should not come as a surprise.

9   Local Muslim Community Organizations in Dubai

In Dubai, there are three major local Islamic community organizations in which the Chinese Muslim community is active. Two of these organizations,

Kalemah Islamic Center and the Dubai Islamic Information Center, focus on charitable works in general, organizing activities and classes for non-Arab Muslims, and *da'wah* or religious outreach to non-Muslims. Kalemah organizes Arabic and Islamic studies classes in several different languages to meet the needs of Dubai's diverse communities. Classes are geared toward both recent converts and Muslims in general wishing to deepen their religious knowledge. Kalemah regularly organizes events in English, Urdu, Tagalog, Nepali, Indonesian, and Bengali.

In October of 2015, Kalemah organized "The New Muslim Summit," an event for recent converts that was billed as being the largest of its kind ever in the region. The event took place at the Cultural and Scientific Association's headquarters in Mamzar, Dubai. There were four large auditoriums, each of which could seat hundreds, with four simultaneous presentations: one in Chinese, one in English, one in Amharic (for the large Ethiopian community) and one in Nepali. The presentation in English appeared to be aimed at Filipino converts. The event was well organized and well attended, with volunteers who spoke all the relevant languages.

Although the event was billed as being for recent converts, in the auditorium designated for the Chinese speakers, at least half of the audience were Hui, with the rest being recent converts. The Chinese presentation had two speakers, one a Hui scholar from the community in Dubai, and the other a prominent imam visiting from China. The Hui scholar's presentation focused on Islam as a religious and belief system that fostered acceptance and inclusivity. The audience was encouraged to use their faith to improve themselves, help others, and make the world a better place. The lecture was one that could be appreciated and understood by both those who had grown-up Muslim and recent converts. The audience was enthusiastic and clearly understood and enjoyed the lecture immensely. The presentation by the guest speaker, however, was not as well received. The presentation was clearly aimed at Hui Muslims who had formally studied Islam, and was not nearly as universal or accessible as the earlier one. At first it seemed surprising that the prominent guest lecturer would not know how to connect with his audience, but in fact, why would he, since imams in China would have had little if any experience making formal presentations to large numbers of converts.

Although Kalemah offers weekly classes in several different languages, it is the ones geared toward the Chinese community that are the most popular. Every Friday morning[5] over a dozen classes are held at a local public elementary

---

5 As Friday and Saturday are the weekend in the UAE, the schools would normally be closed on those days.

school that has opened up its classrooms for the Chinese community. There are several levels of Arabic, Chinese language, and Islamic studies, for both children and adults. The teachers are almost all Hui who have studied overseas, or attended Islamic colleges in China. These classes are in many respects the heart of the Chinese Muslim community. The classes are all free and open to anyone who wants to attend. Many of the Chinese who attend the classes are not Muslim, and want to learn Arabic for practical reasons, such as to facilitate their work, or just for daily life and adapting to life in a foreign country. Others bring their children for the Chinese language classes to make sure they keep up their Chinese language skills since most of them attend schools in which the language of instruction is either Arabic or English. The classes have between eight to 24 students each. Snacks are provided during the break, which also serves as a good time for people to meet and for friends to to catch up with one another. At the end of the two-hour class period there is a lecture open to everyone. Usually the larger meeting includes about a hundred people, with the women sitting on one side of the auditorium, and the men on the other. It is a general lecture that includes both religious and non-religious topics. For example, one lecture attended in March 2015, focused on Arabic language drills involving the entire audience, an interesting lecture on astronomy, and a discussion about Islamic values. The presentation ends in time for those who want to, to head off for Friday prayers.

When it first opened in 2006, the Chinese Islamic Cultural Centre was a located in a small modest office in an out of the way corner of Dragon Mart. Over the years it grew in size, as well as the services it provided. Initially it focused on offering Arabic language classes, then as more people became interested in learning about Islam, Islamic studies classes were offered. Translation and interpretation services were then added, as was matchmaking, and guidance for those wanting to formally convert. From the beginning it had offered a place for Chinese Muslims meet and pray together on Fridays, even though the space was invariably too small for all those who wanted to take part. In 2018, however, the center acquired a more spacious and better designed home when it was incorporated into the structure of the new Chinese mosque.

The new setting has several offices, two classrooms, and a large meeting room. There are large displays throughout the center on different aspects of the history of Islam in China. And while the services it provides are the same as before, the staff has grown in size. In some respects, the diversity of the staff reflects Dubai. In a visit in 2019, in addition to about half a dozen Chinese Muslims (both Hui and converts), the staff and teachers also included: a *muezzin* (the person who performs the call to prayer) from India, a Qur'an teacher from Mauritania, a Rohingya receptionist, and an Islamic studies teacher from Tajikistan. The center also offers a range of Arabic and Islamic studies course, which are especially convenient for the large numbers of Chinese and Chinese Muslims who live in the neighborhood. Staff also organize various social and charitable activities for the community. The fact that the classes are free and open to anyone, comes as quite a surprise to recently arrived Chinese anxious to start adapting to life in their new home. According to several of the Chinese teachers there, they are often first asked "Really, there is no charge for the classes?" And then, "But you could make so much money by having fees?" The dedication and generosity of spirit of the Chinese Muslim teachers clearly provides an important opportunity for the community to share not just their knowledge, but their values.

10   A "Foreign Quarter 蕃坊 Mosque" Comes to the Middle East

In selecting 华坊清真寺, *Huafang Qingzhensi* (Chinese Quarter Mosque) as the name for their mosque, the Chinese Muslim community of Dubai ended up choosing a term that invokes a range of images: the historic Silk Routes, the early Muslim traders who settled in China, and the Dubai neighborhood where the mosque is located. Unlike traditional mosques in China whose architecture is highly influenced by classical Chinese design aesthetics, the Chinese Quarter Mosque in Dubai reflects local Middle Eastern building design. Had the design incorporated even a small amount of traditional Chinese mosque architecture it could have acted as an evocative and educational symbol of the history of Islam in China. Perhaps in the future a small museum could be incorporated into the mosque complex that relates that history.

During the month of Ramadan the mosque provides *iftar* meals to over a thousand people who come to the mosque as the sun is setting to break their daily fast. Local Chinese Muslim restaurants provide their traditional dishes, which have proved to be extremely popular among the other foreign Muslims living in the neighborhood. It is undoubtedly the only mosque in the Middle East that provides Chinese food for *iftar* during Ramadan. Many of those who joined in these evening meals, both the Chinese and other foreign Muslims, noted how it was an unusual and unexpected upending of traditional expectations. However, given the extraordinarily cosmopolitan nature of life in Dubai, no doubt, this seemingly unlikely twist on the usual, will soon become unremarkable.

As mentioned earlier, one person in particular has been instrumental in seeing this immensely important project through to its finish: Imam Han. In many respects his path to Dubai is reflective of those taken by so many Muslims from China. Raised in a traditional Hui village in Qinghai, Imam Han first went to Beijing in the early 1980s to attend university and continue his Arabic studies. After graduating he stayed on in Beijing teaching Arabic for over a decade. While based there he developed contacts with several embassies and was able to persuade them to offer scholarships to promising Chinese Muslim students to pursue advanced Islamic studies overseas. A system was put in place to recruit students from across China to come to Beijing to sit for placement exams held in the embassies.

In 2001, he moved to Kuwait where he worked as a translator for an Islamic organization and started to build a network among Chinese Muslims who had continued their studies overseas. A few years later, he was recruited to Dubai by the Kalemah Islamic Center. Soon after arriving in Dubai he used his contacts with the networks of Chinese Muslims who had studied at different international centers of Islamic learning around the world to recruit those fluent in Arabic to expand the course offerings available to the growing Chinese Muslim community in Dubai, as well as those interested in learning more about Islam. Working closely with the Kalemah Islamic Center allowed Imam Han to get to know more about local Islamic charitable organizations, and well as religious leaders. With the mosque now complete, Imam Han is able to provide weekly *khutbahs* (sermons) in Arabic, English, and Chinese during Friday prayers. The English version is primarily for the South Asians living in the neighborhood who may not understand Arabic.

11 Role of Chinese Embassy Officials

Over the past ten years the Chinese Consulate in Dubai has had three Consul Generals who have played an active role in directly and indirectly supporting the Chinese Muslim community there. Not surprisingly, all were seasoned Chinese diplomats fluent in Arabic. The first, Gao Youzhen, served in Dubai from 2005 and 2011. He was instrumental in supporting the Dragon Mart project and facilitating many Chinese businesspeople moving to Dubai and setting up small and large companies in Dubai. His work on Dragon Mart was especially influential in facilitating the arrival of many Hui and Uyghur to Dubai. He left Dubai in 2011 to take up the ambassador position in neighboring Qatar. The second influential Consul General was Zhan Jingbao, who served there from 2011–2015. In addition to continuing Gao's focus on trade and business relations, Zhan also initiated China's new soft-power cultural activities and exchanges. It was under his leadership that the Dubai Consulate began organizing regular *iftar* dinners during Ramadan. Zhan also worked together with Ma Xuezhong, a Dubai-based Hui scholar from Ningxia, to establish the first Confucius Institute in the region, at the University of Dubai in 2011 (the following year another one was opened at Zayed University in Abu Dhabi).

The third, and most influential Consul General was Li Lingbing. A Han Chinese who was born in Xinjiang and grew up in Ningxia, Li had an in depth understanding of Hui and Uyghur culture and society. She had earlier served in the embassy in Abu Dhabi, so was also familiar with the UAE and Emirati culture, and like her predecessors was fluent in Arabic. She arranged for several well-known music and dance troupes from Xinjiang to perform in Dubai, and was known to spontaneously join in the traditional singing and dancing. Her deep respect and sincere affection for Xinjiang meant a great deal to the Chinese Muslim community in general, and the Uyghur community in particular. Moreover, her commitment to China-UAE friendship, as well as the Chinese Muslim community in the UAE, was very much appreciated by local Emirati officials. In 2018, as she prepared to depart for her next posting as ambassador to Oman, there were a series of gatherings to thank her for her service in Dubai.

12 Creating a New Society? – Changing Attitudes towards Transnational Identities, Mixed Marriages and Hunxuar Children

Historically, Chinese have referred to those who are mixed-race as *hunxur* 混血儿 (mixed-blood), a term that might generously be translated as "half-breed." In the past, this term had very negative connotations, with the implication being the "pure" Han Chinese blood was being somehow polluted or contaminated by foreign "barbarian" blood. Recently though, when used to refer to the children of Chinese and white westerners it can have a more positive connotation.

Dubai has developed into one of the most comfortable cities in the world for transnational couples. Included among these mixed couples are growing numbers of Chinese Muslims, both Hui and Han Chinese who converted when they married either local and foreign-born Muslims living in Dubai. Many of the wives in these marriages are especially active in organizing events for the Chinese Muslim community, in part because of their broader networks and understanding of local or one of the large immigrant communities. What's interesting about these cases is the extent to which they are accepted, without any signs of stigmatization, as natural developments, given the multi-cultural and transnational culture of Dubai. In some respects, these mixed families in Dubai embody the imagined ideal expressed by several of the converts back in

China. According to Ma Qiang, converts saw Chinese Muslims as being more globalized; first because Muslims in China had a connection with the global Islamic *ummah* or community, and second because those who converted after marrying Muslims in China, or foreign Muslims, were also exposed to new cultures. In his interviews with converts in Qinghai, Stewart concludes that for many of them, Islam represents a "transnational identity and a universally applicable moral system" (Stewart 2016:219).

Although not exactly promoting transnational marriages, at this moment in time the Chinese government realizes the importance of having more and more of its citizens gain a deeper understanding of foreign cultures and societies. It has become clear that for the various BRI related projects to succeed having local buy-in from the communities affected is crucial. China has developed a range of different undergraduate and graduate programs (with corresponding scholarship programs) to meet the needs of neighboring BRI countries. In addition, they have established three branch campuses of Chinese universities in Southeast Asia, with several more in the works. These branch campuses (so far in Laos, Malaysia, and Thailand), are not just for local students, but also opportunities for students from China to learn foreign languages and become immersed in different societies and cultures. For China to effectively manage projects across the countries involved in BRI projects, it needs to have people experienced in dealing with foreigners and foreign cultures.

13   Conclusion

Over the past twenty years, as China-UAE trade and political relations have increased dramatically and become increasingly important, the Chinese Muslim community has facilitated these ties in a myriad of ways. Initially, it was Hui who had graduated from Islamic colleges and universities and were fluent in Arabic, who acted as translators and interpreters. As more Chinese businesspeople moved to Dubai, they sought out Hui to assistant them in setting up their companies. In the early years, it was the Hui who had studied overseas who took the lead in offering Chinese and Arabic classes to the growing community of Chinese, thus providing crucial assistance to newcomers wanting to adapt to a foreign culture. More recently, Han Chinese converts have also actively taken part in organizing and teaching these courses.

At the same time, the networks created by Chinese Muslims who have continued their religious studies overseas will also lead to more and more

Chinese Muslims to settle, at least for a few years, in Dubai where they can enjoy a degree of religious freedom unknown back in China, and cultural acceptance not found in much of the rest of the Arab world. As the center of international finance shifts toward China, and China invests in the ever expanding Belt and Road Initiative, infrastructure projects and investment ties with the Gulf region and neighboring Southeast Asian countries, are increasing dramatically. Chinese Muslims fluent in Arabic and with extensive experience living overseas have the potential to facilitate these economic linkages.

One of the most important, and least discussed dimensions of China's BRI projects, is the long-term education and research commitments that are presently being developed. There are currently in China thousands of students from neighboring countries studying to become Chinese language teachers in primary and secondary schools on their return home. In 2019, the UAE announced plans to incorporate Chinese language classes in 60 primary and secondary schools across the country. Over 150 teachers were recruited from China to develop the curriculum and teach the courses. The theme of the textbooks is "Across the Silk Route" and in addition to emphasizing historic links between the Gulf and China, the textbooks will also introduce Chinese culture and society. Several of the schools are located in more remote desert regions of the country, and not surprisingly the challenges faced by the newly arrived teachers are daunting, especially given the fact that in these regions there would be few, if any local people who spoke English, let alone Chinese. There is also the challenge of understanding a new and very different culture and society. Sensing a need, one of the Hui teachers who had already lived in the UAE for several years volunteered to meet regularly with the teachers to give them a crash-course in daily Arabic, as well as an introduction to Emirati society and Islamic culture. It is these efforts to foster intercultural competence that will facilitate and inculcate growing understanding, and hopefully respect, between these two societies with ambitious plans to work together over the next few decades.

At this moment in time Chinese Muslims, such as those living and working in Dubai, can play increasingly important roles in China's BRI projects across Asia, providing essential cultural understanding and inter-cultural communication skills. However, at present, the government is also developing policies within China that restrict the religious activities of Chinese Muslims. It is difficult to know where current policy trends are heading and their long-term impact on both the Chinese Muslims in China, as well as Chinese Muslim communities overseas. In discussions with Chinese Muslims in Dubai in early 2020, although there was concern with recent policy initiatives in China directed at the Hui in particular (Shih 2019), there was also hope that the worst was over, and that *Insha'Allah* the campaign to restrict religion in China would gradually end.[6]

References

Armijo, Jacqueline. 2008. "Islam in China." Pp. 197–228 in *Asian Islam in the 21st Century*, edited by J. Esposito, J. Voll, and O. Bakar. Oxford: Oxford University Press.

Armijo, Jacqueline. 2009. "Muslim Education in China: Chinese *Madrasa*s and Linkages to Islamic Schools Abroad." Pp. 169–87 in *The Madrasa in Asia: Political Activism and Transnational Linkages*, edited by F. Noor, Y. Sikand, and M. van Bruinessen. Amsterdam: Amsterdam University Press.

Armijo, Jacqueline. 2013. "China and the Gulf: The Social and Cultural Implications of their Rapidly Developing Economic Ties." Pp. 225–39 in *Asia-Gulf Economic Relations in the 21st Century: The Local to Global Transformation*, edited by T. Niblock and M. Malik. Berlin & London: Gerlach Press.

Atwill, David. 2005. *The Chinese Sultanate: Islam, Ethnicity, and the Panthay Rebellion in Southwest China, 1856–1873*. Stanford: Stanford University Press.

Ben-Dor Benite, Zvi. 2005. *The Dao of Muhammad: A Cultural History of Muslims in Late Imperial China*. Cambridge and London: Harvard University Press.

Broomhall, Marshall. 1910. *Islam in China: A Neglected Problem*. London: Morgan and Scott.

Cieciura, Wlodzimierz. 2018. "Chinese Muslims in Transregional Spaces of Mainland China, Taiwan, and Beyond in the Twentieth Century." *Review of Religion and Chinese Society* 5(2):135–55.

Forbes, Andrew D.W. 1987. "The 'Čīn-Họ̄' (Yunnanese Chinese) Caravan Trade with North Thailand During the Late Nineteenth and Early Twentieth Centuries." *Journal of Asian History* 21(1):1–47.

Frankel, James. 2008. "'Apoliticization': One Facet of Chinese Islam." *Journal of Muslim Minority Affairs*, 28(3): 421–34.

Frankel, James. 2011. *Rectifying God's Name: Liu Zhi's Confucian Translation of Monotheism and Islamic Law*. Honolulu: University of Hawai'i Press.

---

6 The authors would like to thank James Frankel and Mohammed Al Sudairi for their feedback on an earlier draft of this chapter, as well as those who attended a talk where preliminary research on this project was presented at the Annual Meeting of the Association of Asian Studies for the panel "The Role of Past and Present Networks among Chinese Muslim (Hui) Diaspora Communities", held in Chicago, March 2015.

Frankel, James. 2017. "Islamisation and Sincisation: Inversions, Reversions and Alternate Versions of Islam in China." Pp. 495–514 in *Islamisation: Comparative Perspectives from History*, edited by ACS Peacock. Edinburgh University Press, 2017.

Gladney, Dru. 1996. *Muslim Chinese: Ethnic Nationalism in the People's Republic*. Cambridge: Harvard University Asia Center.

Hew Wai Weng. 2018. *Chinese Ways of Being Muslim: Negotiating Ethnicity and Religiosity in Indonesia*. Copenhagen: NIAS Press.

Jeong, Hyeju. 2016. "A Song of the Red Sea: Communities and Networks of Chinese Muslims in the Hijaz." *Dirasat*, 13:1–28.

Krahl, Regina, J. Guy, J.K. Wilson, and J. Raby (editors). 2010. *Shipwrecked: Tang Treasures and Monsoon Winds*. Singapore: Smithsonian Books.

Lipman, Jonathan. 1997. *Familiar Strangers: A History of Muslims in Northwest China*. Seattle: University of Washington Press.

Ma Qiang. 2013."中国的归信穆斯林：一份来自田野调查的初步报告"(*Zhongguo de gui xin Musilin: Yi fen laizi tianye diaocha de chu baogao*),《伊斯兰文化》*Islamic Culture* 1:171–181.

Mao Yufeng. 2016. "Selective learning from the Middle East: The case of Sino-Muslim students at al-Azhar University." Pp. 147–70 in *Islamic Thought in China: Sino-Muslim intellectual evolution from the 17th to the 21st century* edited by J. Lipman. Edinburgh: Edinburgh University Press.

Masudi, Faisal. 2020. "UAE Golden Visa Gives Expats Security, Says Top Official," *Gulf News* [UAE], February 5.

People's Daily [English edition]. 2003. "Islam's Lasting Connection with China: Feature," May 20.

Rossabi, Morris. 1981. "The Muslims in the Early Yüan Dynasty." Pp. 257–95 in *China under Mongol Rule*, edited J. Langlois. Princeton: Princeton University Press.

Shih, Gerry. 2019. " 'Boiling us Like Frogs': China's Clampdown on Muslims Creeps into the Heartland, Finds New Targets," *Washington Post*, September 20.

Stewart, Alexander. 2016. "Individual Agency through Imagining Transnational Community: Converting to Islam in Modern China." *Contemporary Islam* 10:201–221.

United Nations, Department of Economic and Social Affairs, Population Division. 2019. *International Migrant Stock 2019: Country Profile – United Arab Emirates*.

Vora, Neha. 2013. *Impossible Citizens: Dubai's Indian Diaspora*. Durham: Duke University Press.

Wang Yuting. 2018. "The Construction of Chinese Muslim Identities in Transnational Spaces." *Review of Religion and Chinese Society* 5(2):156–82.

Index

activity 67
ancestral hometown 116, 119, 125, 133–134
ancestral village 120, 125, 128, 132
Anglican Church 87, 158
Arabic 244–245, 255, 258, 260, 263, 267–276
Austria 175, 179–182, 181n, 183–185, 187, 189

belief 8, 42, 80, 82, 86, 89, 91, 97, 99, 140, 151–152, 157, 160, 164, 166, 188, 212, 216–218, 231, 236, 238, 241, 244, 246, 249, 270
believer 15, 22, 42, 48, 53, 97–99, 101, 104, 111, 140, 188, 222, 239, 249
Bible study group 28, 82, 88, 99, 103, 107, 110–111, 239, 241, 243
Bologna 3, 6, 6–7, 68
Britain 77–81, 84–85, 87–89, 92
Buddhism 41–43, 46–47, 51–53, 66, 127, 166, 170, 223, 239, 246–248
business 1–2, 4–5, 9–11, 14–15, 23–24, 27–28, 37, 78, 120, 178, 186, 244, 251, 263, 265

Canada 100, 103, 142, 144, 150, 152–153, 203
children 4–5, 7, 15, 44n, 49–50, 53, 67, 165, 181, 266–267, 274
Chinese Anti–Cult Association 194, 207
Chinese Catholic Church 70–71
Chinese Catholicism 58–60n, 63, 72
Chinese Christianity 21–23, 25, 28, 30, 32, 34
Chinese communities 23, 60, 64, 67, 77, 115, 118–119, 121, 131, 185, 228, 239, 245, 252
Chinese Coordination Center for World Evangelism 133
Chinese diaspora 2–3, 20, 23, 34, 60, 65, 77, 79, 82n, 97, 101, 174, 224, 247, 252, 263
Chinese expatriates 238–239, 243–245, 249, 252
Chinese government 32, 60, 104–105, 194, 197, 199, 203–204, 206–207, 237, 252, 275
Chinese immigrant church 1, 6–7, 22, 25–28, 30, 34
Chinese immigrant family 1, 5, 27–28
Chinese immigrants 2–10, 15–17, 20, 23, 26, 29, 31–32, 34, 37–40, 43–44, 49, 54, 59, 62, 68–69, 101, 106, 133, 163

Chinese migrants 2–10, 16–17, 30, 39–40, 60, 64, 78–82, 84–85, 88–89, 92, 104, 180, 185, 215, 241, 251
Chinese migration 31, 40, 43, 59–60, 101, 185
Chinese Muslim communities 244, 252, 276
Chinese Muslim 214, 244–246, 252, 255–256, 258–261, 263–265, 267–269, 271–275
Chinese Protestantism viii, 66
Chinese religions vii, xi, 33, 213, 219–220, 238
Chinese students 79, 82, 85, 101–106, 109–112, 130–131
Chinese–ness 78, 82n, 143, 145, 152
Christian commitment 91–92
Christian conversion 28, 80–82, 84–85, 88, 92
Christian fellowships 82, 85, 103, 107, 110, 120
Christian mission 30–32, 34, 85–86
Christian network ix, 100, 102–103, 242–243
Christianity 2, 6, 8, 15, 17, 21, 30, 58, 72, 77, 79–80, 82, 84–86, 89–90, 92, 102, 110, 115, 117, 125, 127–128, 133–134, 151–152, 159, 210, 212, 218, 238, 241–242, 246
church construction 124–125, 127–128, 130, 132–133
city 3, 6, 104–105, 112, 180, 206, 239, 241, 261–262, 268
civil society 70
Confucianism 41, 166, 219, 229–230, 238
congregation vii, 15, 22, 66, 78, 82, 111, 115, 123, 128, 139, 181, 187, 213, 241, 247
conversion 21–22, 65, 72, 80–82, 84–85, 88–89, 91–92, 111, 164, 179, 213, 242, 268–269
convert to Christianity 81, 85, 87
convert to Islam 269
cultural reproduction 157–159, 159n
cultural translation 157–159, 167

Dao 158–159, 162, 188, 200, 223
donation 116, 122–123, 125, 127–128, 148, 247, 260

economic activity 60, 72, 77, 99
economic development 2, 72, 119, 129, 240

ethnic Chinese   ix, 29, 32, 100, 103, 107–110
Europe   21–24, 26–27, 29–32, 32–34
Evangelicalism   22, 152n, 152
"evil cults"   194, 197, 199

faith   21, 32, 34, 59, 66, 70, 90, 98, 149
faithful   59, 62–63, 65–68, 71–73
Falun Gong   43, 194–197, 199–200, 203–204
family ethics   2, 15–16
family-style church   28
France   22–25, 30, 34
Fuji, see South Fuji
funding   116, 122, 126, 129, 186

Germany   97–105, 107, 110–112, 207
global Christianity   31
global migration   vii, 21
globalization   21, 25, 35, 171, 175, 177, 184, 220, 236
God   10, 23, 33–34, 91, 124, 138, 148–150, 152, 221, 241–242, 258
Guanyin   164–166

Han Chinese   255–256, 258, 263–264, 268, 274
homeland   28, 58, 64, 66, 69, 71, 100, 105, 108, 115, 142, 203, 256
hometown   117, 122, 132, 182, 204
Hong Kong   24, 87, 98, 100, 108–110, 112, 122, 130, 169, 176–177, 180, 185, 214, 238, 243, 257
Huaqiao   115–119, 122–125, 127, 129–130, 132–133, 245
Hui diaspora   260–261

identity   x, 31, 81, 212–220, 223–224, 228–231
immigrant communities   69, 79, 274
indigenous Chinese Christianity   22–23
industrial district   38–40
interaction ritual chain   138, 140, 152
Islam   42, 54, 158, 223, 237–238, 241, 244, 246, 252, 256, 259–260, 265–266, 268, 271, 274
Islamic education   xi, 244, 256, 259, 263
Islamic values   267, 270
Italy   3–5, 7–8, 15–16, 22–23, 25–27, 29–30, 32, 38, 46–47, 49–50, 58–62, 64, 66–67, 69–73

JinBodhi   201, 203–204

Letian Dashi   202, 205–206
liturgical activity   65
liturgy   67, 141
local church   23, 28, 122, 146
London   158, 160, 162, 168

mainland China   31, 79, 98, 100, 102, 106, 120, 157, 167, 214, 241
Malaysian Chinese   162–163, 167, 169
Manchester   167–168
meditation   46, 64, 182–183, 188, 204
migrant church leadership (leaders)   23–24, 27
migrant entrepreneurship   4–5, 17
migrant workers   1, 4, 9, 122, 262
ministry   110
modernity   vii, 149, 152, 157, 171
moral ambivalence   2, 11, 16
Mosque   40, 41, 228, 241, 245–246, 255, 262, 271–272
motherland   vii, 64, 67, 148
Muslim communities   215, 244, 256, 259–260, 267, 276

new Chinese migrant   78–79, 81, 84–85, 88–90, 92
non–Chinese   2, 34, 45–46, 54, 87, 182, 188, 214, 237
North America   vii, viii, ix, 22, 35, 41, 58, 79, 99–100, 102, 112, 119, 139, 176, 185, 188, 202, 210, 231

overseas Chinese   105, 115, 127, 167, 239

pastoral activity   63
pastoral system   26–27
persecution   41, 177, 260
Philippines   120, 122–123, 130–131, 176
political views   109
Pope Benedict   XVI, 67, 70
Prato (Italy)   25, 37–39, 43, 46, 50, 52–54, 64, 68
prayer   52, 89, 111, 161, 247, 270
province   4, 37, 40, 62, 124, 150, 175, 185, 199, 201, 204
Puhuasi   38, 40, 45–46, 50–51, 53

INDEX 281

qigong association   195, 199–200
qigong group   x, 194–195, 199, 202, 206, 237

religion and globalization   21, 25, 31, 35
religious activity   59, 129
religious agents   25
religious capital   25
religious diversity   236
religious ethics   1–2, 9, 12–14, 16–17
religious experience   2, 50, 71, 139, 149, 213, 216–217, 230, 238–239, 251
religious freedom   42, 71, 219–220, 236, 276
religious language   34, 89–90
religious morality   2, 9, 13, 15–17
religious networks   x, 2, 99–100, 186
religious teacher   90, 259
ritual activities   226–227

sacred   53, 71, 141, 150, 152, 162, 165–166, 217, 226–227, 238, 249
second generation   xi, 4, 32, 34, 79, 111, 139, 160, 167
secular   xi, 28, 34, 162, 203, 213, 217
secularism   30, 139, 148–149, 212
Singapore   106, 108, 120, 125, 157, 168, 196, 198, 236n

South Fuji   ix, 115, 119, 122, 125–126, 128–131, 133–134
Southeast Asia   ix, x, 99–100, 102, 107, 115–120, 122, 130–134, 176–178, 180, 185–230, 266, 275

Taiwan   x, 98, 100, 102, 107, 130
theological training   ix, 102, 116, 130–131
tolerance   228, 237, 239–240, 242
traditional belief   169
transnational networks   129, 186–187, 252
transnationalism   69, 71–72, 100

United Arab Emirates   237, 239

Vietnamese Chinese Enclave   x, 164, 171
volunteer workers   7, 14

worship   14, 42, 50, 104, 134, 165, 213, 225, 241–242

Yiguandao template   157–158, 162–164, 166, 169–170, 186

Zhongguo   106, 108–109, 195, 199, 204

Printed in the United States
By Bookmasters